HANDBOOK

OF

RAILROAD CONSTRUCTION;

FOR THE USE OF

AMERICAN ENGINEERS.

CONTAINING THE

NECESSARY RULES, TABLES, AND FORMULÆ

FOR THE

LOCATION, CONSTRUCTION, EQUIPMENT, AND MANAGEMENT OF RAILROADS, AS BUILT IN THE UNITED STATES.

With 158 Illustrations

BY

GEORGE L. VOSE,
CIVIL ENGINEER.

"RULES THEMSELVES OBLIGE US TO REFLECT, THAT WE MAY SEE WHETHER WE HAVE NOT DEPARTED FROM THEM." — NAPOLEON.

BOSTON AND CAMBRIDGE:
JAMES MUNROE AND COMPANY.
1857.

CAMBRIDGE:
ALLEN AND FARNHAM, PRINTERS.

PREFACE.

THE object of this work is to give in the plainest possible manner all instructions, rules, and tables necessary for the location, construction, equipment, and management of railroads.

As a general thing, American engineers are not educated for their business; and when they do possess a knowledge of pure science, they are at a loss how to apply it.

The reader is presumed acquainted with the elements of arithmetic, geometry, algebra, and mechanics; being thus provided, he will, by a perusal of what follows, be enabled to correctly proportion bridges, of wood, stone, and iron; abutments, piers, retaining walls, superstructure, and locomotive engines; and to plan and lay out, execute, and estimate any description of work occurring upon railroads.

As the object has been more to be useful than original, the best engineering writers and experimenters have been consulted; among whom are,— Gauthey, Navier, Vicat,

Tredgold, Barlow, Totten, Fairbairn, Hodgkinson, Clark, and Lardner. Also a great number of reports by American civil engineers upon railroad matters.

If assumptions take the place of demonstration, it will be on good authority. Readers will bear in mind that the work is a "handbook," and not a "treatise." It is intended more as an office companion than as a text-book for students. It will give in all cases the actual numerical result needed, whether it be the scantling of a bridge chord, the thickness of a wall, or the dimensions of a locomotive boiler.

In connection, it will be found convenient to use the works of Trautwine and Henck, on Field Work; of Lieutenant Smith, on Topography; Davies, on Surveying; and Gurley, on the Use of Instruments.

Any one wishing a complete treatise on the principles of bridge construction is referred to the excellent work of Hermann Haupt.

I take this opportunity of heartily thanking the engineers who in many ways have aided in making the work, as it is believed, of some worth.

G. L. V.

GENERAL TABLE OF CONTENTS.

	PAGE
INTRODUCTION,	1
CHAPTER I.—RECONNOISANCE	12
II.—SURVEY	24
III.—LOCATION	41
IV.—PRELIMINARY OPERATIONS	55
V.—LAYING OUT WORK	89
VI.—EARTHWORK	97
VII.—ROCKWORK	115
VIII.—WOODEN BRIDGING	122
IX.—IRON BRIDGING	192
X.—STONE BRIDGING	233
XI.—MASONRY	248
XII.—FOUNDATIONS	261
XIII.—SUPERSTRUCTURE	272
XIV.—EQUIPMENT	302
XV.—STATIONS	403
XVI.—MANAGEMENT	413
APPENDIX	459

ANALYTICAL INDEX.

INTRODUCTION.

	PAGE
Rise and progress of railroads	1
Influence of railroads	3
Safety of railroad travelling	5
Preliminary operations	5
Mechanical principles of locomotion	6
Determination of character of road	7
Gauge	8
General establishment of route	10

CHAPTER I.

RECONNOISSANCE.

General topography	12
Barometrical levelling	18

CHAPTER II.

SURVEY.

Topographical sketching	24
General establishment of grades	32
Equating for grades	34
Comparison of surveyed lines	39

CHAPTER III.

LOCATION.

Alignment 41
Final adjustment of grades 46
Comparison of located lines 47

CHAPTER IV.

PRELIMINARY OPERATIONS.

Specification 55
Contract 82
Solicit 84
Bid 86
Comparison of bids 87

CHAPTER V.

LAYING OUT WORK.

Slopes 89
Culverts 90
Masonry 91
Tunnels 95

CHAPTER VI.

EARTHWORK.

Form of railroad sections 98
Excavation and embankment 104
Transport of material 106
Average haul 106
Drainage 109
Method of conducting construction operations 111

CHAPTER VII.

ROCKWORK.

Rock excavation 115
Blasting and quarrying 115–117
Tunnelling 118

CHAPTER VIII.

WOODEN BRIDGING.

Of the forces at work in bridges 122
Extension 123
Compression 123
Cross strain 124
Detrusion 126
Strength of materials 126
Rules for practice 131
Of the truss 139
Of the arch 169
Of the road-way 174
Lateral bracing 175
Pile bridging 178
Trestling 180
Draw bridges 181
Centres 182

CHAPTER IX.

IRON BRIDGES.

Nature and strength of iron 192
Classification of iron bridges 194
Iron truss frames 202
Suspension bridges 203
Boiler plate bridges 223

CHAPTER X.

STONE BRIDGING.

Of the water-way 233
Form of the arch 236
Thickness of voussoirs 238
Form and thickness of abutments 239
Form and dimensions of piers 245

CHAPTER XI.

MASONRY.

Stone 248
Cements, mortars, and concretes 249
Construction of arches, wings, and parapet . . 253
Culverts and drains 255
Retaining walls 256

CHAPTER XII.

FOUNDATIONS.

Pile driving, common system 262
Mitchell's screw pile 266
Potts's atmospheric system 266
Coffer-dam 267
Caisson 269

CHAPTER XIII.

SUPERSTRUCTURE.

Timber work 273
Rail section 276

Chairs and joints 282
Frogs 290
Switches 294
Sidings and crossings 298
Tracklaying 298
Elevation of exterior rail 298

CHAPTER XIV.

EQUIPMENT.

PART I. LOCOMOTIVES.

Introduction 302
Birth and growth of the locomotive 302
The English locomotive of 1850 304
The American locomotive of 1855 305
General description 306
Mechanical and physical principles 312
Resistance to the motion of trains 312
Traction and adhesion 316
Fuel 317
Generation of steam 330
Application of steam 336
Boiler proportions and dimensions 340
Rules and tables for practice 354
Adaptation of locomotives to the movement of trains . . 360
Classification of engines 371

PART SECOND.

CARS.

Wheels and axles 396
Classification of cars 400
Retarding of trains 401

CHAPTER XV.

STATIONS.

Classification of buildings 403
Location of buildings 403
Terminal passenger house 403
Terminal freight house 405
Way passenger and freight house 407
Engine house and appurtenances 405
Wood shed and tank 405

CHAPTER XVI.

MANAGEMENT.

Organization of employees 413
Duties of employees 415
Number of trains to be used 418
Amount of service of engines 418
Expenses, receipts, profits 420
Express trains 428
Comparative cost of working heavy and light trains . . 434
Branch roads 436
Reproduction of road and of stock 437
Working railroads by contract 439
Classification of freight 439
Time tables 443
Locomotive registers 444
Electric telegraph 454
New York and Erie Railroad 456

APPENDIX.

A.—Decimal Arithmetic 459
B.—Algebraic formulæ 461
C.—Weights and measures 464
D.—Value of the Birmingham gauges 465
E.—Locomotive boilers 466
F.—Effect of grades on the cost of working 468
G.—Form for a locomotive specification 471
H.—Relative cost of transport by railroad and by stage . . . 476
I. — Form for experimental trips with locomotives 478
K.—Proper weight for locomotives 479

ADDITIONS, ALTERATIONS, AND CORRECTIONS.

The reader is particularly requested to apply the following errata before perusing the work. They are partly mistakes in printing, and partly errors in the original MS. The only excuse the writer can offer for the number is, that, being engaged in Missouri, while his publishers were in Boston, he has been prevented from seeing a single proof-sheet in time for its correction.

Page 5, line 7, for "499.999," read "499,999."
— 5, l. 9, for "49.999," read "49,999."
— 10, l. 1, for "can be," read "can never be."
— 12 to 23, headings, for "reconnoitre," read "reconnoissance."
— 18, l. 24, for "36.9," read "36.8."
— 19, l. 6, for "table B," read "table D."
— 24, l. 1, for "any thing," read "every thing."
— 25, l. 17, for "horizontal line m m m," read "line 1, 2, 3," etc.
— 26, l. 2, for "land," read "level."
— 27, l. 1, for "at the place," read "at the right place."
— 28, l. 29, "for "reconnoitre," read "reconnoissance."
— 30, l. 3, for "A *c d* B," read "A C D B."
— 32, l. 2, the point *m* in the cut, is one whole division above C; it should be only three fourths of a division.
— 38, l. 10 from bottom, for "276," read "268."
— 39, l. 10 from bottom, for "142.13," read "143.13"; and last line, for "58.46," read "48.46."
— 40, l. 7, for "10,310,667," read "10,277,333."
— 42, l. 9, for "Thus," read "These."
— 43, l. 8 from bottom, for "2°.81 or 2° 48′.6" read "2°.86 or 2°.51.6."
— " l. 27, for "Hencke," read "Henck."
— 47, 48, 49, for "McCullum," read "McCallum."

Page 47, l. 18, for "distance," read "resistance."

— 48, l. 6, for "infringing," read "impinging"; line 9, for "slacking," read "shackling"; l. 8 from bottom, for "increased," read "increases."

— 50, l. 17, for "110 + 15.60," read "110 + 15.62."

— 52, l. 15, for "45.59," read "45.49"; also l. 17, for "1132," read "11.32."

— 58, l. 10, for "of size," read "and size."

— " l. 5 from bottom, for "one cent," read "$\frac{}{100}$ of a cent."

— 61, l. 3, for "are necessary," read "are not necessary."

— 63, l. 28, for "stretches," read "stretchers."

— 65, l. 15, for "spanded," read "spandrel."

— 71, l. 6 from bottom, for "left," read "let."

— 73, l. 19, for "chains," read "chairs."

— 74, l. 5, for "across ties," read "on cross-ties."

— " l. 12, for "28 inches," read "27 inches."

— 75, l. 18, for "land," read "haul."

— 76, l. 8, for "top," read "bottom," and for "charred when," read "charred where."

— " l. 11, for "twopenny," read "tenpenny."

— 78, l. 1 and 2, for "base," read "basis."

— 84, l. 13, for "as," read "or."

— 89, l. 6, for "whenever," read "wherever"; l. 12, for "Letting," read "Setting."

— 90, l. 4, for "cost," read "cut."

— 93, l. 6, for "37 and 38," read "36 and 37."

— 95, l. 1, for "beach," read "bench"; l. 3, for "to so," read "so to"; l. 13, for "b being 10 ft. back of 2 is . . . . 100.00," read "b being 10 ft. back of 2 is 0.1 ft. higher than 2, or . . . . 100.10."

— 102, l. 1, head of middle col., for "slopes 1¼," read "slopes 1½."

— 103, l. 4 from bottom, for "and ten feet," read "and one end ten feet."

— 104, l. 9, for "any," read "very."

— 108, l. 9, for "Elwood," read "Ellwood."

— 115, l. 5, for "a loam," read "a berm"; l. 16, for "a rent," read "a vent."

— 117, l. 7, for "volcanic," read "voltaic."

— " l. 9, for "Round Drum," read "Round Down."

— " l. 18, for "Col. Puseling," read "Col. Pasley."

— 118, l. 2, for "Muillefaut," read "Maillefert."

— " l. 16, for "insert," read "invert."

— " l. 25, for "quointed," read "grouted."

— 119, l. 30, for "furnished," read "finished."

— 120, Table, for "Nochistingo," read "Nochistongo"; for "Supperton," read "Sapperton"; and for "Black Rock W. S." read "Black Rock U. S."

— 121, l. 19, for "Belchingly," read "Blechingly."

— 125, in table at bottom, for "$\frac{90}{69}$," read "$\frac{90}{66}$," and for "140, $\frac{20}{140}$, $\frac{20}{160}$, or 0.13," read "111, $\frac{20}{111}$, $\frac{20}{131}$, or 0.15."

— 126, l. 1, for "extensive," read "extensile."

— 127, l. 10, for "67,200," read "65,251."

Page 127, l. 26, for "Hodgekinson," read "Hodgkinson."
— 128, l. 4, for "12000," read "11000."
— " l. 15 and 22, for "Hodgekinson," read "Hodgkinson."
— 129, l. 5, for "12000," read "11000."
— 129, l. 2 from bottom, for "Sunwood," read "Ironwood."
— 130, l. 7, for "$WL^2 = 4\,S\,b\,d^2$," read "$WL = 4\,S\,b\,d^2$."
— 131, l. 9, for "wood 143," read "wood 133."
— 134, in art. 164, for "700," read "952."
— 136, for example there given, place the following: —

Span . . . 30 feet,
Length . . . 34 "
Load . . . 10 tons at centre.

$$a = \frac{6 \times 10 \times 12 \times 30}{26 \times \frac{34 \times 12}{16}} = 32.58.$$

and $\frac{32.58}{6.1} = 5.34$.

Whence —
Length . . . . 34 feet,
Span . . . . . 30 "
Depth . . . . $25\frac{1}{2}$ inches,
Lower flange . . 32.58 square inches,
Upper flange . . 5.34 " "

— 141, last line, Fig. 63 A was omitted; it is the same as fig. 102, page 200, inverted.
— 142, last line, for "span," read "spans."
— 146, head of col. 7, for "top washer," read "thickness of washer."
— 150, after line 9, figs. 67 D and 67 E (page 153) should be inserted.
— 151, l. 3, for "W = 2249," etc., read "W = 2240," etc.
— " l. 18, for "opposite to 31,416, is the diam. $1\frac{5}{8}$," read "opposite to 41,415, is the diam. $1\frac{7}{8}$."
— " l. 19, for "$1\frac{5}{8}$," read "$1\frac{7}{8}$."
— 154, last line, for "tubular," read "tabular."
— 156, l. 1 from bottom, for "washer band," read "washer used."
— 164, l. 10 to 14, inclusive. The first number of ratios should be 20 instead of 15.
— 166, l. 11, for "69 B," read "69 A."
— 171, head of col. 5 of table, for "rod of arch," read "rad. of arch."
— 173, l. 25, for "ability," read "stability."
— " l. 32, for "Whence," read "where."
— 175, l. 8, for "triangular," read "diagonal."
— 178, l. 3, for "article," read "outside."
— 184, l. 4 from bottom, for "barriers," read "voussoirs."
— 187, fig. 96 is upside down; also, fig. 97, page 188, and fig. 98, page 189.
— 193, l. 4, col. 3 of table, for ".00000675," read ".00000685"; also, l. 16, col. 5, for "straining," read "shearing"; l. 7 from bottom, for "15,000," read "18,000;" and l. 6 from bottom, for "75,000," read "105,000."
— 199, l. 7 from bottom, for "20,132," read "20,312."
— 200, l. 4, for "A C," read "A G"; and l. 6, for "that on A R," read "that on A K."
— 202, l. 7, for "on page 193," read "on page 138."
— 204, l. 5 from bottom, for "varied line," read "versed sine."

Page 207, l. 5 and 6, for "F G, G E, in place of E F, E C," read "G L, G E, in place of F L, F C."

— 210, in place of "$f' = \frac{\pi F}{4 p h}$," put "$D = \sqrt{\frac{3}{4}[l'^2 - d^2]} - \sqrt{\frac{3}{4}[l^2 - d^2]}$,

where D = depression,
l = half length of curve before elongation,
l' = half length of curve after elongation,
d = half distance between points of suspension." Omit the remainder of the paragraph.

— 211, omit the 6th and 7th lines, and in place of formula there given, use that on page 210, (as corrected,) l' being the length of semi-curve as elongated by heat instead of by tension; the elongations, both by heat and tension, being found by table on page 193.

— 212, l. 2, for "510.69," read "510.80," which result, of course, runs through the whole example.

— 213 and 214. The remarks under "Anchoring Masonry," are evidently wrong throughout: 1st, the whole tension should be divided by *two*, instead of *four*, as half of the whole tension acts at each point of suspension; 2d, no reduction should be made for the direction of the pulling force. One half of the tension is 3,321,250 lbs.; which is resisted by a column of masonry of $\frac{3,321,250}{160}$ = 20,758 cubic feet, or 20 × 20 × 52 feet, or by a mass 15 × 15 × 91 feet.

— 214, l. 6, for "561,527," read "562,542."

— 215, l. 14 from bottom, for "stiffening towers," read "stiffening trusses."

— 225, l. 14, for "194," read "193."

— 226, l. 3, for "see p. 128," read "see p. 193."

— 227, l. 4, for "detensional," read "detrusional."

— 228, in place of equations at l. 16, put "$R \times a = R' \times (2\,d \times t)$,

whence $d = \frac{R \times a}{2\,R' \times t}$;

where a = area of rivet,
d = distance,
t = plate thickness.

— 229, in art. 242, the strengths of "wrought iron," have been taken for those of "boiler plate"; that is, 11,000 for 7,500, and 15,000 for 12,740, which is wrong.

— 231, l. 21, for "chopped," read "dropped."

— 234, l. 4, for "joint," read "just."

— 235, l. 14, for "0.016 feet," read "0.047 feet."

— 236, l. 9, for "care," read "ease."

— 237, l. 3 from bottom, for "representing," read "separating."

— 241, l. 2, for "localities," read "locality."

— 242, l. 7, omit "and *c e*, the parapets."

— 243, l. 9, for "embankment," read "abutment."

— 244, l. 9, for "is thus," read "is found thus."

— 245, l. 17, for "latter," read "batter."

Page 249, l. 23, for " common hydraulic," read " common mortar, hydraulic."
— " l. 27, for " argyle magnesia," read " argil, magnesia."
— 251, l. 16, for " $7\frac{1}{2}$ to 2," read " $1\frac{1}{2}$ to 2."
— 254, last l., for " corners," read " courses."
— 256, l. 13, for " formed," read " found."
— 258, art. 276, in place of " $\frac{20}{2} \times 15 \times 1 \times 100 \times \frac{20}{3}$," put " $20 \times 15 \times 1 \times 100 \times 2 \times \frac{20}{3}$," where 2 represents the ratio between Ca 6, and 6-2; thus, $20 \times 15 \times 1 \times 100 \times \frac{6 \cdot 6}{12} \times \frac{20}{3} = 111,111$, for the overthrowing force in place of 100,000. The overthrowing force is thus large, because the maximum weight of earth has been assumed to press against the wall with its whole force, no allowance being made for friction. In practice, $\frac{4}{10}$ of the height has been found amply thick for walls retaining ordinary earth.
— 262, last l. but one, for " superstratum," read " substratum."
— 264, in example, l. 5, for " 26,667," read " 48,000."
— 266, l. 25, for " Godwin," read " Goodwin."
— " l. 26, for " There, sands," read " These sands."
— 267, l. 22, for " bottom," read " proper level."
— 281, l. 4 from bottom, for " curve," read " cone."
— 282, l. 20, for " Daniel," read " David."
— " l. 4 from bottom, for " cup," read " cap."
— 284, l. 10, and 285, l. 8, for " compressed rails," read " compound rails."
— 285, l. 5, for " extension," read " extensile."
— 289, invert col. 1 of table, so that it shall read —

At 100° place the rails in contact.
" 90° at a distance of .00136 feet, or 0.016 inches.
" 80° " " .00272 " 0.032 " Etc.

— 289, last l., for " levelled," read " bevelled."
— 291, last l., for " *a c*, 4.8," read "*a c*, L 8."
— 292, l. 9, for " *e h* and *d k*," read " *e* L and *d k* "; same p. l. 6 from bottom, for " *a*, 9 is three, etc." read " *a b* is three," etc.
— 293, l. 6 and 7, for " *i g*, *e h*, *b b*, 8, 9, *A s* 79," read " *i g*, *e h*, *a c*, *b c*."
— 296, l. 14, for " $R^2 - \overline{R - 8}^2$," read " $R^2 - \overline{R - g}^2$."
— 303, art. 299, for " M. Leguire," read " M. Seguin."
— 306, l. 2, for " R. R. and G.," read " R. K. and G."
— 314, l. 2, for " D. R. Clark," read " D. K. Clark."
— 320, l. 1, for " Railroad, three pounds (Pennsylvania)," read " Railroad (Pennsylvania), three pounds."
— " l. 7, for " coal," read " coke."
— 331, near bottom, for " The area is, therefore,

Sides, twice length, etc.,	read " Sides, twice length by height, etc.,
Back, twice height, etc.,	Back, height by width, etc.,
Front, twice height, etc.,	Front, height by width, etc.,
Top, twice length, etc.,"	Top, length by width, etc."

Page 334, l. 15, for "44.7 lbs.," read "14.7 lbs."
— 335, l. 7, for "Railway Mechanics," read "Railway Machinery."
— " l. 10, for "two velocities," read "low velocities."
— 336, last l., for "entering part," read "entering port."
— 341, l. 11, for "properties," read "proportions."
— " last l., for "Nollan," read "Nollau."
— 346, l. 17, for "part," read "port," and for "construction," read "contraction."
— 355, l. 7, for "6300," read "5170"; and l. 9, for "16,905," read "15,775."
— 363, l. 17, for "$44 \times 2 = 80$," read "$44 \times 2 = 88$."
— " l. 18, for "$54\frac{1}{2} \times 3 = 103\frac{1}{2}$," read "$54\frac{1}{2} \times 3 = 163\frac{1}{2}$."
— 367, l. 16, for "$\frac{150}{10}$," read "$\frac{150}{16}$."
— 368, l. 15, for "$u = 135$," read "$n = 135$," etc.
— 370, l. 7, for "feet," read "per cent."
— 376, for "19090," read "19050."
— 384, in last part of example, for "$\frac{5280}{4\frac{1}{2} \times 3.1416} \times 4 = 37300$,"

$$\text{read "} 25 \times \frac{5280}{4 \times 3 \cdot 1416} \times 4 = 37348.\text{"}$$

— 421, bottom line, for "decision," read "division."
— 423 and 424, in table, for "count," read "cost."
— 427, l. 32, for "which," read "we."
— 428, l. 4, transpose "Dr. Lardner, (1850,)" to the end of line 3.
— 443, l. 28, for "valuation," read "solution."
— 446, l. 11, for "attained," read "obtained."
— 459, l. 20, for "Hectametre," read "Hectometre."
— " l. 21, for "Ridometre," read "Kilometre."
— 461, l. 7, for "less than a, or o," read "less a, or 0."
— 468, l. 30, for "fractions," read "functions."
— 474, l. 18, for "Balbett," read "Babbitt."
— 479, l. 10, for "one sixth, with much less," read "one sixth; with sand, much less."

HANDBOOK

OF

RAILROAD CONSTRUCTION.

INTRODUCTION.

"They build not merely roads of earth and stone, as of old, but they build iron roads: and not content with horses of flesh, they are building horses of iron, such as never faint nor lose their breath." — DR. BUSHNELL.

RISE AND PROGRESS OF RAILROADS.

1. IN 1825, the Stockton and Darlington Railroad (England), was opened.

In 1827, the Quincy (of Massachusetts), and Mauch-Chunk (Pennsylvania), were completed.

In 1829, the Liverpool and Manchester road, (England), was finished.

In 1833, a road was opened from Charleston, (South Carolina), to Augusta (Georgia).

In 1840, Belgium opened 190 miles of railroad.

In 1843, the railroad from Paris to Rouen (France), was completed.

In 1844, Belgium finished her system of 347 miles.

In 1846, Russia opened a railroad from the Wolga to the Don.

In 1847, Germany had in operation 2,828 miles.

In 1852, the Moscow and St. Petersburg road was finished.

2. In 1856, the United States of America had in operation 23,000 miles, and in progress 17,000 miles; employing 6,000 locomotive engines, 10,000 passenger and 70,000 freight cars; costing in all about 750,000,000 of dollars; running annually 114,000,000 miles, and transporting 123½ millions of passengers, and 30 millions of tons of freight per annum; performing a passenger mileage of 4,750,000,000, and a freight mileage of 3,000,000,000.

3. By mileage is meant the product of miles run, by tons or by passengers carried. Thus, 500 persons carried 100 miles, and 750 persons carried 75 miles, give a passenger mileage of

$$500 \times 100 + 750 \times 75 = 106{,}250.$$

4. The rate of progress in the United States has been as follows:—

In 1828, there were	3 miles.
In 1830,	41 miles.
In 1840,	2,167 miles.
In 1850,	7,355 miles.
In 1856,	23,242 miles.

At the present time, January 1, 1857, there is probably, in round numbers, 25,000 miles of completed road, or enough to extend entirely around the world. As regards the ratio of completed road to population, and as regards the actual length of railroad in operation, the United States stand before any other country.

INFLUENCE OF RAILROADS.

5. The effect of a judicious system of railroads upon any community is to increase consumption and to stimulate the production of agricultural products; to distribute more generally the population, to cause a balance between supply and demand, and to increase both the amount and safety of travelling. It is stated that within two years after the opening of the New York and Erie Railroad, it was carrying more agricultural produce than the entire quantity which had been raised throughout the tributary country before the road was built.

6. The following table, cut from a Chicago paper, shows the effect of railroad transport upon the cost of grain in that market:—

	Wheat.		Corn.	
	By R. R.	By Wagon.	By R. R.	By Wagon.
At market,	$49.50	$49.50	$25.60	$25.60
10 miles,	49.25	48.00	24.25	23.26
50 miles,	48.75	42.00	24.00	17.25
100 miles,	48.00	34.50	23.25	9.75
150 miles,	47.25	27.00	22.50	2.25
200 miles,	46.50	19.50	21.75	0.00
250 miles,	45.75	12.00	21.00	0.00
300 miles,	45.00	4.50	20.25	0.00
330 miles,	44.55	0.00	19.80	0.00

Thus a ton of corn carried two hundred miles, costs, per wagon transport, more than it brings at market; while moved by railroad, it is worth $21.75 per ton. Also wheat will not bear wagon transport of three hundred and thirty miles; while moved that distance by railroad it is worth $44.55 per ton.

7. By railroads, large cities are supplied with fresh meats and vegetables, butter, eggs, and milk. An un-

healthy increase of density of population is prevented, by enabling business men to live five, ten, or fifteen miles away from the city and yet do business therein. The amount of this diffusion is as the square of the speed of transport. If a person walks four miles per hour, and supposing one hour allowed for passing from the house to the place of business, he cannot live at a greater distance than four miles from his work. The area, therefore, which may be lived in, is the circle of which the radius is four, the diameter eight, and the area fifty and one quarter square miles. If by horse one can go eight miles per hour, the diameter becomes sixteen miles, and area two hundred and one square miles; and, if by railroad he moves thirty miles per hour, the diameter becomes sixty miles, and the area 2,827 miles. The effect of such diffusion is plainly seen about Boston, (Massachusetts). People who in 1830 were mostly confined to the city, now live in Dorchester, Milton, Dedham, Roxbury, Brookline, Brighton, Cambridge, Charlestown, Somerville, Chelsea, Lynn, and Salem; places distant from two to thirteen miles.

8. In railroads, as in other labor saving (and labor producing) machines, the innovation has been loudly decried. But though it does render some classes of labor useless, and throw out of employment some persons, it creates new labor far more than the old, and gives much more than it takes away. Twenty years of experience shows that the diminished cost of transport by railroad invariably augments the amount of commerce transacted, and in a much larger ratio than the reduction of cost. It is estimated by Dr. Lardner, that 300,000 horses working daily in stages would be required to perform the passenger traffic alone, which took place in England during the year 1848. It is concluded, also, from reliable returns, that could the whole number of passengers carried by railroad, have been trans-

ported by stage, the excess of cost by that method above that by railroad would have been $40,000,000.

SAFETY OF RAILROAD TRAVELLING.

9. If we know that in a given time the whole distance travelled by passengers was 500,000 miles, and that in such time there occurred one fatal accident, it follows that when a person travels one mile, the chances are 499.999 against one of losing life. If he travel ten miles, the chances are 49.999 against one, or ten times as many of meeting with loss of life; and generally the chances of accident are as the distance travelled. In 1855, the whole number of miles run by passengers in the United States was, in round numbers, 4,750,000,000, while there were killed one hundred and sixteen; or one in every 41,000,000, very nearly. (The ratio in England is one in every 65,000,000.) Now if for each 400,000 miles travelled by stage passengers, (a distance equal to sixteen times round the world,) one passenger was killed, and if the whole railroad mileage could be worked by stages, there would be annually 11,875 lives lost; or one hundred times the number annually lost by railroad. Thus it would be one hundred times safer to travel by railroad than by stage. The danger of steamboat travelling is far greater than by stage.

PRELIMINARY OPERATIONS.

10. The first step to be taken in starting a railroad enterprise, is the choice of a board of directors (provisional), whose duty is to find all that can be known of the commercial, financial, and agricultural nature of the country to be traversed. To determine as near as possible its ability to

build and support a road; and to obtain the necessary legislative enactments.

11. The determination of the increase of traffic which the road may be expected to excite, is a difficult matter. There can be few rules given for proceeding in such an inquiry. It seems very easy to prove by what roads have done, that any project will be profitable.

An abstract of a report lately published, tries to prove that a road will pay forty-five and one half per cent. net; the working expenses being assumed at only thirteen and one half per cent. of the gross receipts. The error here lies in assuming the working expenses too low, as few roads in the country have been worked for less than forty per cent.; a more common ratio being fifty one-hundredths of the gross receipts.

Not one half of railroads are built for the original estimate. In few cases has sufficient allowance been made for the sacrifice undergone in negotiating the companies' securities. All general instructions that can be given relating to the determination of prospective profits, are, to keep the estimate of constructing and working expenses high, and that of the assumed traffic low; not so low, however, as to require a too lightly built road.

MECHANICAL PRINCIPLES OF LOCOMOTION.

12. The superiority which the modern railroad possesses over the common, McAdam, plank, or turnpike-road, consists, first, in the reduction of the resistance to motion, and second, in the application of the locomotive steam-engine.

13. The effect of grades of a given incline upon a railroad is *relatively* more than upon common roads; for as the *absolute* resistance on a level decreases, the *relative* resistance of grades augments: whence to obtain the full benefit of the system, we must reduce much more the

grades and curvature upon a railroad, than on a common road. For example, if the resistance to moving one ton upon a level upon a railroad was ten pounds, and upon a common road forty pounds, where a twenty-three feet grade would be admissible upon the former, we might use an incline of ninety-three feet per mile upon the latter.

14. The resistance to the motion of railroad trains increases rapidly with the speed;* whence the grades of a passenger road where a high average speed is used, may be steeper than those of a road doing a freight business chiefly.

DETERMINATION OF CHARACTER OF ROAD.

15. Upon a correct idea of what the road ought to be, depends in a great degree its success. The amount of capital expended upon the reduction of the natural surface, depends upon the expected amount of traffic. The traffic remaining the same, the greater the capital expended in reducing grades and curvature, the less will be the working expense; and the less the construction capital, the greater that for maintenance. The limit of expenditure must be such as to render the sum of construction and maintaining capital a minimum.

The bad effect of grades upon the cost of maintaining and of working railroads, is not so great as many suppose. Of the whole cost of working, only about forty per cent. can be charged to locomotive power; and of this, not more than sixty-two per cent. is effected by grades.†

16. The degree of curvature to be admitted upon any road depends somewhat upon the speeds at which trains are to be run. The larger the radius of curvature, the

* See chapter XIV. † See appendix F.

greater may be the speed; at the same time the elevation of the exterior rail upon curves may be less, and therefore more adapted to freight trains. High rates of speed are considered upon some competing roads necessary; but are, even in such cases, necessary evils. The wear of cars and of engines, of permanent way and of bridges, increase in a rapid ratio with the velocity. The maximum speed for freight trains should never exceed fifteen miles per hour, or for passenger trains from twenty to twenty-five miles per hour.*

17. The agricultural nature of the country and its commercial position, will determine the nature of the traffic, whether passenger or freight, and also the amount. The amount and nature of the traffic will limit the curvature, and will partially determine the arrangement of grades.

GAUGE.

18. The question of broad and narrow gauge has led to much discussion, and both plans claim among their advocates some of the best engineers. The narrow gauge (American and English,) is four feet eight and one half inches (from inside to inside of rail). The maximum adopted, is (the Great Western of England) seven feet. The American maximum (New York and Erie, and Ohio and Mississippi) is six feet. There is also in America four feet ten inches, five feet, and five feet six inches. The advantage of the broad gauge for a road doing an extensive business, is the increased stowage room in freight cars, thus rendering admissible shorter trains; by which the locomotive power is more directly applied on curves. More

---

* See chapter XVI.

comfortable passenger cars, (the same length of car of course accommodates the same number of passengers). The disadvantages of a wide gauge are, increased expense of cutting, embanking, bridging, and masonry; increased expense of engines, cars, rails, sleepers, and all machinery; more wear and tear upon curves, by reason of greater difference between the lengths of inner and outer rails, and increased atmospheric resistance to fast trains, from increased bulk.

19. The general conclusion arrived at by a commission appointed by the Great Western Railway Company, (England,) consisting of Messrs. Nicholas Wood, J. K. Brunel, and John Hawkshaw, was, that four feet, eight and one half inches was rather narrow, but still enough for a certain class of roads; that two or three inches made no material difference; that seven feet was too wide for any road; that the weight of the broad gauge engine, compared with the small increase of power, was a serious evil; that engines could be run with perfect safety upon the narrow gauge at any speed from thirty to sixty miles per hour, and that no more had been attained upon the broad; that rolling friction was less upon the broad, owing to the increased diameter of wheels, but that friction from curves and atmospheric resistance was greater.

20. D. K. Clark, in "Railway Machinery," p. 300, 301, makes the resistance as deduced from experiments made upon both the four feet, eight and one half inches, and the seven feet gauge, considerably greater upon the former than on the latter; but as the narrow gauge trials were made upon a curved road, with rails in a bad state, in average weather, while those upon the broad were made in good weather, upon a good and straight line, he leaves the gauge question open, and uses the same formula for all widths.

21. Want of increased power, can be an apology for increased gauge, until the capacity of the narrow gauge has been filled. The strongest engines in the world are upon the four feet, eight and one half inch gauge. No engines in America surpass or compare for absolute strength, with those upon the Baltimore and Ohio Railroad. The most powerful passenger engine ever built for high speeds, is Crampton's engine "Liverpool," (London and North-western Railroad, England,) gauge four feet, eight and one half inches.

GENERAL ESTABLISHMENT OF ROUTE.

22. The straight and level line connecting any two points, is of course the best for the completed road; but this is seldom practicable. Way towns must be accommodated to a certain extent; but the main line should not be lengthened on that account, unless the traffic and capital furnished by such town is not only sufficient to pay for the construction and maintenance of the extra length, but also to carry the entire through traffic over such increased distance. If the town is unable to support such a burden, it may be able to build and maintain a branch.

23. Routes placed upon the immediate bank of a large stream, are generally crossed by a great number of deep gorges, which serve to drain the side lands.

24. Routes placed upon sloping land, when the axis of the road and the natural descent are at right angles to each other, are more subject to slides than when placed upon plateaus or "bottoms."

25. Lines crossing the dividing ridges of separate waters, rise and fall a great deal; thus rendering necessary a strong motive power to work the road. Such roads are the West-

ern of Massachusetts, passing from the valley of the Connecticut at Springfield, to the Hudson River valley at Greenbush. Also those roads crossing the Alleghanies. And such will be the Pacific road, crossing first the Rocky Mountains to the Great Basin, and second, the Sierra Nevada into the Sacramento valley.

CHAPTER I.

RECONNOITRE.

---

26. THE object of the reconnoitre is to find approximately the place for the road, (i. e. within half of a mile,) to find the general form of the country, and to choose that part which with reference to the expected traffic, shall give the best gradients; to determine the elevations of summits upon competing routes; and, in fine, to prepare the way for the survey.

27. The general topography of a country may be ascertained by reference to State maps, where such exist, and when not, by riding over the district. The direction and size of watercourses, will show at once the position of summits.

Fig. 1.

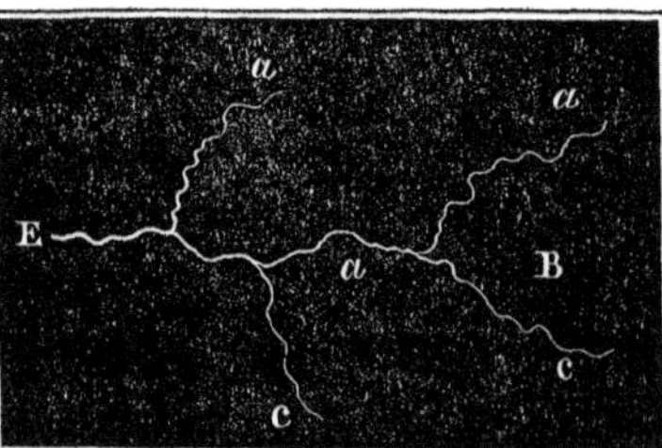

28. Water flowing as in fig. 1, indicates a fall from B to E; and also transverse slopes from *a a* and *c c* to *d d*.

29. Fig. 2 shows a broken ridge *a a a* from which the water flows in both directions; and in general, the sources of streams point towards the higher lands.

Fig. 2.

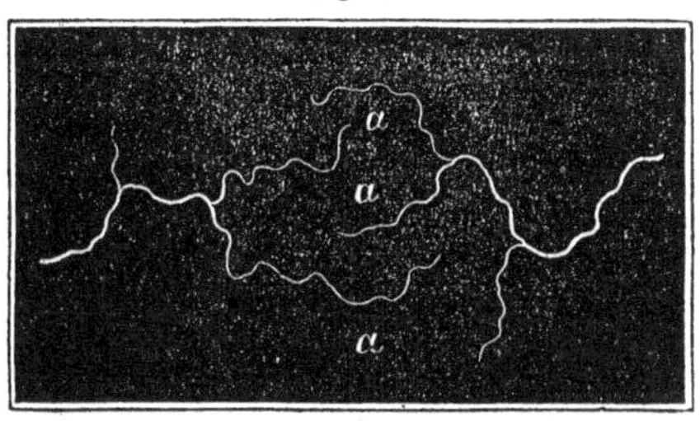

30. If it be required to join the points A and D by railroad, (fig. 3,) it may be better to pass at once from A through B and C, than to go by the

Fig. 3.

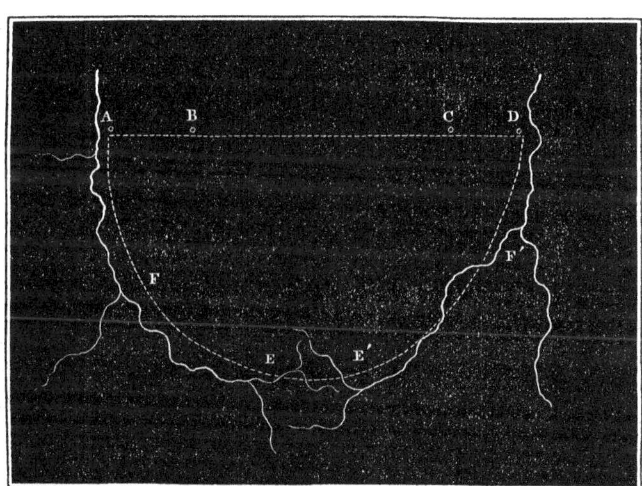

streams F E, F′ E′. By the latter route the road would *ascend* all of the way from A to E; and descend from E′ to D. By the first if it requires steep gradients to rise from A to B, and to fall from C to D, still if the section B C is a plateau, and if the rise between A and B and A and E is the same, by grouping the grades at B and C we may so adapt the motive power, as to take the same train from A to D without breaking. The general arrangement of grades by the line A B C D is then as fig. 4; and by A F E E′ F′ D, as in fig. 5. The saving in this case is by length, as

Fig. 4.

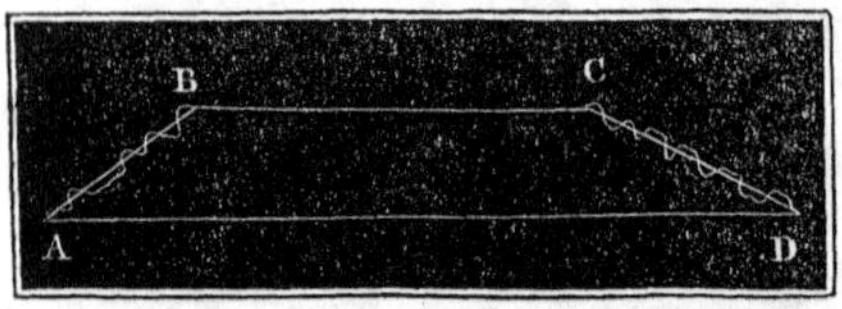

Fig. 5.

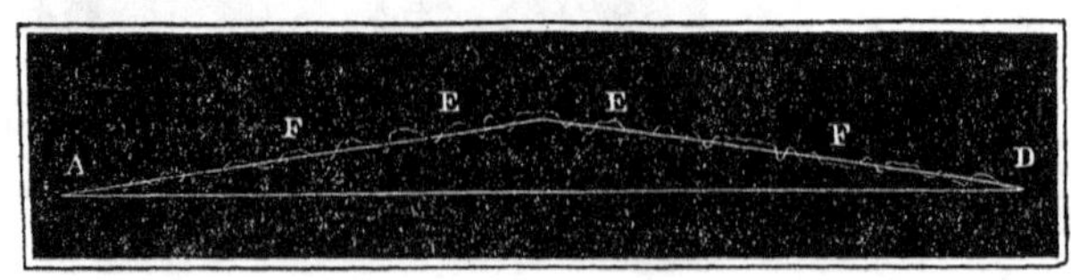

the same amount of power is required to overcome a given ascent.

31. Valleys generally rise much faster near their source, than at any point lower down; also the width increases as we approach the debouch. Fig. 6 shows the cross sections of a valley from its source to the mouth.

Fig. 6.

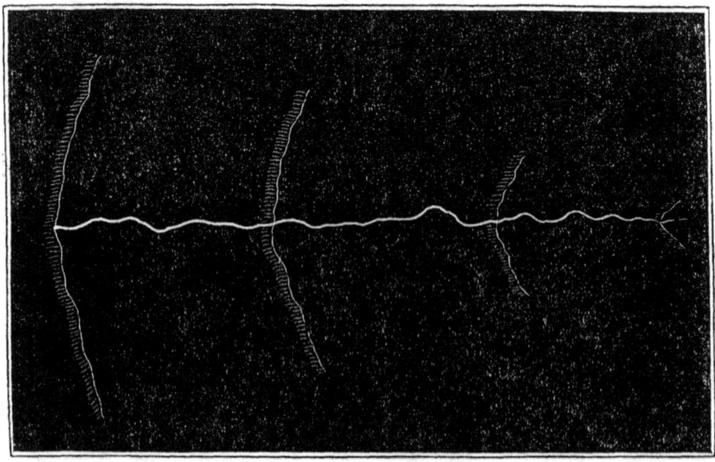

32. In the case of parallel valleys running in the same

direction, the form will be as in fig 7. Let 1 2, 1 2, etc., represent a datum level, or a horizontal plane passing through the lowest point. The line *a b*, shows the height of the bottom at B; *c d* that at D, *e f* that at E, and *g h* that at C. The broken lines *i*, *k*, *l*, *m*, *n*, show the general form of the land. Now by the route *m m m m*, from A to F, we have the profile *m m m m*, fig. 8, by *n n n n*, the profile *n n n n*, and by *o o o*, the profile *o o o*.

Fig. 7.

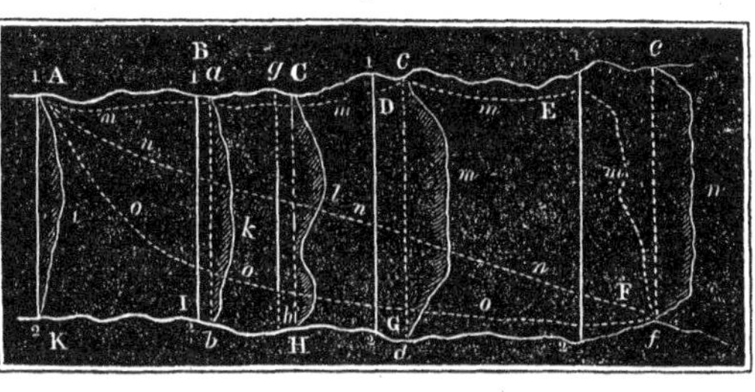

Fig. 8.

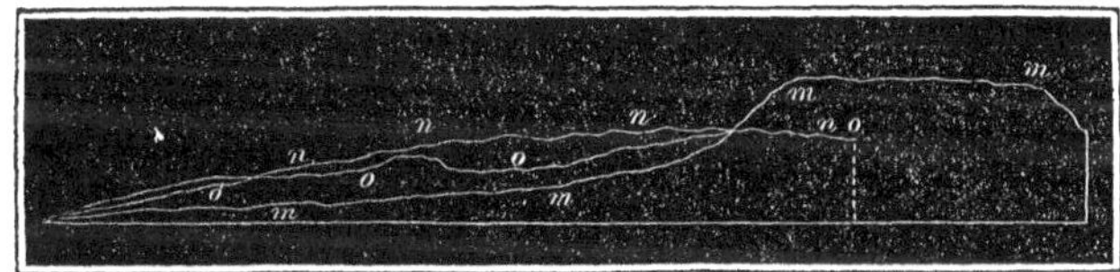

33. In the case of parallel valleys running in opposite directions, as in fig. 9, we have the form there shown; and the profiles corresponding to the several lines are shown in

Fig. 9.

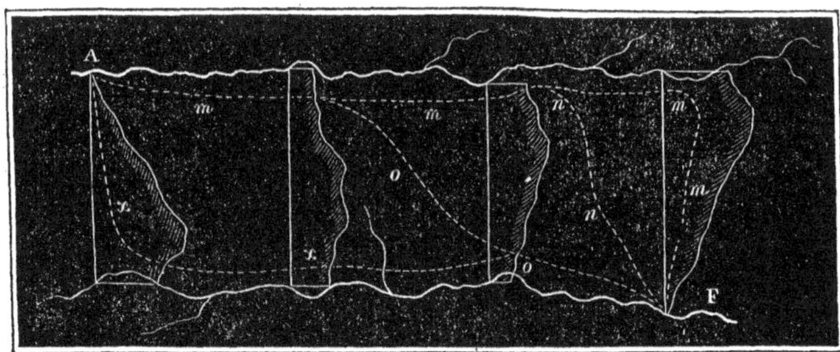

fig. 10. As we should always adopt the line giving the least rise and fall, other things being equal, it is plain which line on the plan we must follow.

Fig. 10.

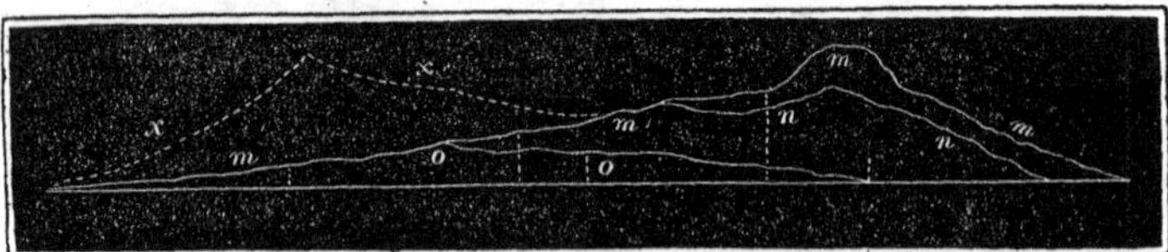

34. In passing from A to B, figs. 11 and 12, by the several lines *c*, *d*, *e*, *f*, we have the profiles shown at *c*, *d*, *e*, *f*, from which it appears, that the nearer we cross to the heads of streams, the less is the difference of heights.

Fig. 11.

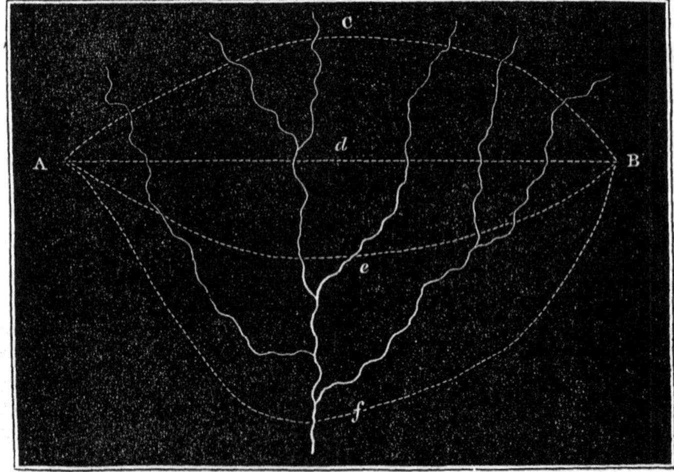

Fig. 12.

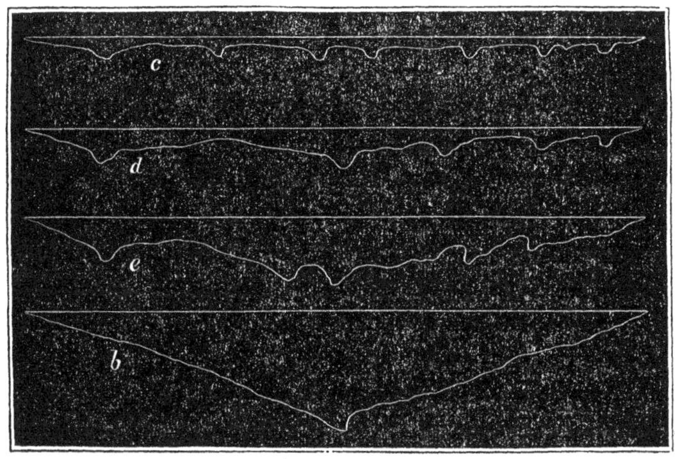

35. If we wish to go from A to B, fig. 12 (*a*), we should of course take first the straight line; but being obliged to avoid the hill C, on arriving at *d*, we should not try to recover that line at *e*, but proceed at once to B. Also as we are obliged to pass through *d*, we ought to go *directly* to *d* and not by the way of *c*; and the same idea is repeated between A and *d*; the last line being A *b* *d* B. Few rules can be given in the choice of routes. Practice only will enable the engineer to find the best location for a railroad.

Fig. 12 (*a*).

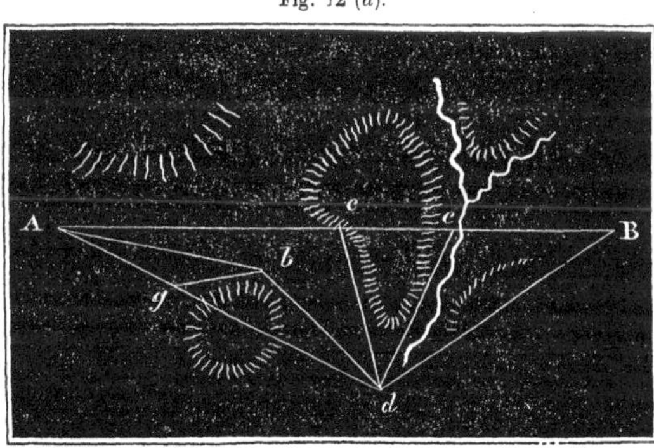

BAROMETRICAL LEVELLING.

36. The relative height of summits, the rate of fall of streams, and absolute elevation, within a few feet, may be easily, rapidly, and cheaply found by the barometer. This also affords an excellent check upon subsequent levelling operations. The results thus obtained depend upon the physical property, that the density of the air decreases as the square of the height.

37. The barometer is a glass tube, partly filled with mercury, having a vacuum in the upper part. By it the exact density of the air at any point is determined. Accompanying are two thermometers; one *attached*, showing the temperature of the *barometer;* the other *detached*, showing the *atmospheric* temperature.

38. Knowing now the manner of finding the density of the air at any two points, and also the relation between density and height, the operation of levelling by the barometer is very simple.

The *modus operandi* is as follows, (see tables A, B, C, and D):—

Let us have the notes.

	Barom.	Attached Therm.	Detached Therm.
Upper Station,	29.75	28.5	27.9
Lower Station,	26.80	36.9	36.3

Latitude 46° N.

We have by table A, against the bar. point, 29.75,	6108.6
also " " " " " " 26.80,	5276.6
The difference	832.0
Diff. of attached therm. 36.8° — 28.5° = 8.3° (table B)	—12.2
	819.8

Double the sum of detached thermometers multiplied by $\frac{1}{1000}$ of 819.8 is

$2\,(27.9 + 36.3) \times .8198 =$	$+\,105.3$
	925.1
Correction (see table C) for lat. 46° N. and approximate height 925.1	$+\,3.1$
	928.2

Final correction by table B. The barometer at the lower station being 26.80, and the tabular number against 27.56 being 0.22, that for 26.80 will be 0.31, and we have

1000 to .31 as 928.2 to 0.287, or 0.3,

which add to 928.2 and we have as the final height

928.5 metres, or $928.5 \times 3.28 = 3045.48$ feet.

The tables above referred to, are those of Mr. Oltman, and are considered as the most convenient and reliable of any published.

TABLE A.

English Inches.	Metres.	English Inches.	Metres.	English Inches.	Metres.	English Inches.	Metres.
14.56	418.5	16.30	1313.3	18.03	2117.6	19.76	2848.1
14.61	440.0	16.34	1332.5	18.07	2135.0	19.80	2864.0
14.65	461.5	16.38	1351.7	18.11	2152.3	19.84	2879.8
14.68	482.9	16.42	1370.8	18.15	2169.6	19.88	2895.6
14.72	504.2	16.46	1389.9	18.19	2186.9	19.92	2911.3
14.76	525.4	16.50	1408.9	18.23	2204.1	19.96	2927.0
14.80	546.6	16.54	1427.9	18.27	2221.3	20.00	2942.7
14.84	567.8	16.57	1446.8	18.31	2238.4	20.04	2958.4
14.88	588.9	16.61	1465.7	18.35	2255.5	20.08	2974.0
14.92	609.9	16.65	1484.7	18.39	2272.6	20.12	2989.6
14.96	630.9	16.69	1503.4	18.42	2289.6	20.16	3005.2
15.00	651.8	16.73	1522.2	18.46	2306.6	20.20	3020.7
15.04	672.7	16.77	1540.8	18.50	2323.6	20.24	3036.2
15.08	693.5	16.81	1559.5	18.54	2340.5	20.28	3051.7
15.12	714.3	16.85	1578.2	18.58	2357.4	20.31	3067.2
15.16	735.0	16.89	1596.8	18.62	2374.2	20.35	3082.6
15.20	755.6	16.93	1615.3	18.66	2391.1	20.39	3097.9
15.24	776.2	16.97	1633.8	18.70	2407.9	20.43	3113.3
15.28	796.8	17.01	1652.2	18.74	2424.6	20.47	3128.6
15.31	817.3	17.05	1670.6	18.78	2441.3	20.51	3143.9
15.35	837.8	17.09	1689.0	18.82	2458.0	20.55	3159.2
15.39	858.2	17.13	1707.3	18.86	2474.6	20.59	3174.4
15.43	878.5	17.17	1725.6	18.90	2491.3	20.63	3189.7
15.47	898.8	17.20	1743.8	18.94	2507.9	20.67	3204.9
15.51	919.0	17.24	1762.1	18.98	2524.3	20.71	3220.0
15.55	939.2	17.28	1780.3	19.02	2540.8	20.75	3235.1
15.59	959.3	17.32	1798.4	19.05	2557.3	20.79	3250.2
15.63	979.4	17.36	1816.5	19.09	2573.7	20.83	3265.3
15.67	999.5	17.40	1834.5	19.13	2590.2	20.87	3280.3
15.71	1019.5	17.44	1852.5	19.17	2506.6	20.90	3295.3
15.75	1039.4	17.48	1870.4	19.21	2622.9	20.94	3310.3
15.79	1059.3	17.52	1888.3	19.25	2639.2	20.98	3325.3
15.83	1079.1	17.56	1906.2	19.29	2655.4	21.02	3340.2
15.87	1098.9	17.60	1924.0	19.33	2671.6	21.06	3355.1
15.91	1118.6	17.64	1941.8	19.37	2687.9	21.10	3370.0
15.95	1138.3	17.68	1959.6	19.41	2704.1	21.14	3384.8
15.98	1157.9	17.72	1977.3	19.45	2720.2	21.18	3399.6
16.02	1177.5	17.76	1994.9	19.49	2736.3	21.22	3414.4
16.06	1197.1	17.79	2012.6	19.53	2752.3	21.26	3429.2
16.10	1216.6	17.83	2030.2	19.57	2768.3	21.30	3443.9
16.14	1236.0	17.87	2047.8	19.61	2784.4	21.34	3458.6
16.18	1255.4	17.91	2065.3	19.65	2800.4	21.38	3473.3
16.22	1274.8	17.95	2082.8	19.68	2816.3	21.42	3487.9
16.26	1294.1	17.99	2100.2	19.72	2832.2	21.46	3502.5

TABLE A, Continued.

English Inches.	Metres.	English Inches.	Metres.	English Inches.	Metres.	English Inches.	Metres.
21.50	3517.2	23.23	4134.3	24.96	4707.1	26.69	5241.4
21.54	3531.8	23.27	4147.8	25.00	4719.7	26.73	5253.2
21.57	3546.3	23.31	4161.3	25.04	4732.2	26.77	5264.9
21.61	3560.8	23.35	4174.7	25.08	4744.7	26.81	5276.6
21.65	3575.3	23.39	4188.1	25.12	4757.2	26.85	5288.3
21.69	3589.8	23.43	4201.5	25.16	4769.7	26.89	5300.0
21.73	3604.2	23.46	4214.9	25.20	4782.1	26.93	5311.6
21.77	3618.6	23.50	4228.2	25.24	4794.6	26.97	5323.2
21.81	3633.0	23.54	4241.6	25.28	4807.0	27.01	5334.8
21.85	3647.4	23.58	4254.9	25.31	4819.4	27.05	5346.4
21.89	3661.7	23.62	4268.2	25.35	4831.7	27.09	5358.0
21.93	3676.0	23.66	4281.4	25.39	4844.1	27.13	5369.6
21.97	3690.3	23.70	4294.7	25.43	4856.4	27.17	5381.1
22.01	3704.6	23.74	4307.9	25.47	4868.7	27.21	5392.7
22.05	3718.8	23.78	4321.1	25.51	4881.0	27.25	5404.2
22.09	3733.0	23.82	4334.3	25.55	4893.3	27.28	5415.6
22.13	3747.2	23.86	4347.4	25.59	4905.6	27.32	5427.2
22.17	3761.3	23.90	4360.5	25.63	4917.8	27.36	5438.7
22.20	3775.4	23.94	4373.7	25.67	4930.0	27.40	5450.1
22.24	3789.5	23.98	4386.7	25.71	4942.2	27.44	5461.5
22.28	3803.6	24.02	4399.8	25.75	4954.4	27.48	5472.9
22.32	3817.7	24.06	4412.8	25.79	4966.6	27.52	5484.3
22.36	3831.7	24.09	4425.9	25.83	4978.7	27.56	5495.7
22.40	3845.7	24.13	4438.9	25.87	4990.9	27.60	5507.1
22.44	3859.7	24.17	4451.9	25.91	5003.0	27.64	5518.4
22.48	3873.7	24.21	4464.8	25.94	5015.1	27.68	5529.8
22.52	3887.6	24.25	4477.7	25.98	5027.2	27.72	5541.1
22.56	3901.5	24.29	4490.7	26.02	5039.3	27.76	5552.4
22.60	3915.4	24.33	4503.6	26.06	5051.2	27.80	5563.7
22.64	3929.3	24.37	4516.4	26.10	5063.2	27.84	5575.0
22.68	3943.1	24.41	4529.3	26.14	5075.3	27.87	5586.2
22.72	3956.9	24.45	4542.1	26.18	5087.2	27.91	5597.5
22.76	3970.7	24.49	4554.9	26.22	5099.2	27.95	5608.7
22.80	3984.5	24.53	4567.7	26.26	5111.2	27.99	5619.6
22.83	3998.2	24.57	4580.5	26.30	5123.1	28.03	5631.1
22.87	4011.9	24.61	4593.2	26.34	5135.0	28.07	5642.2
22.91	4025.6	24.65	4606.0	26.38	5146.9	28.11	5653.4
22.95	4039.3	24.68	4618.7	26.42	5158.8	28.15	5664.6
22.99	4052.9	24.72	4631.4	26.46	5170.6	28.19	5675.7
23.03	4066.6	24.76	4644.0	26.50	5182.5	28.23	5686.8
23.07	4080.2	24.80	4656.7	26.54	5194.3	28.27	5697.9
23.11	4093.8	24.84	4669.3	26.57	5206.1	28.31	5709.0
23.15	4107.3	24.88	4682.0	26.61	5217.9	28.35	5720.1
23.19	4120.8	24.92	4694.5	26.65	5229.7	28.39	5731.1

TABLE A, Continued.

English Inches.	Metres.	English Inches.	Metres.	English Inches.	Metres.	English Inches.	Metres.
28.43	5742.1	29.09	5927.5	29.76	6108.6	30.43	6285.7
28.46	5753.1	29.13	5938.2	29.80	6119.1	30.47	6296.0
28.50	5764.2	29.17	5949.0	29.84	6129.6	30.51	6306.2
28.54	5775.1	29.21	5959.7	29.88	6140.1	30.55	6316.5
28.58	5786.1	29.25	5970.4	29.92	6150.6	30.59	6326.7
28.62	5797.1	29.29	5981.2	29.96	6161.1	30.63	6337.0
28.66	5808.0	29.33	5991.9	30.00	6171.5	30.67	6347.2
28.70	5819.0	29.37	6002.5	30.04	6182.0	30.71	6357.4
28.74	5829.9	29.41	6013.2	30.08	6192.4	30.75	6367.6
28.78	5840.8	29.45	6023.8	30.12	6202.8	30.79	6377.8
28.82	5851.7	29.49	6034.4	30.16	6213.2	30.83	6388.0
28.86	5862.5	29.53	6045.1	30.20	6223.6	30.87	6398.2
28.90	5873.4	29.57	6055.7	30.24	6234.0	30.91	6408.3
28.94	5884.2	29.61	6066.3	30.28	6244.4	30.94	6418.5
28.98	5894.9	29.65	6076.9	30.32	6254.7	30.98	6428.6
29.02	5905.8	29.69	6087.5	30.35	6265.0	31.02	6438.7
29.06	5916.7	29.72	6098.0	30.39	6275.4	31.06	6448.8

TABLE B.

Deg.	Met.	Deg.	Met.	Deg.	Met.	Deg.	Met.	Deg.	Met.
0.2	0.3	4.2	6.2	8.2	12.1	12.2	17.9	16.2	23.8
0.4	0.6	4.4	6.5	8.4	12.4	12.4	18.2	16.4	24.1
0.6	0.9	4.6	6.8	8.6	12.6	12.6	18.5	16.6	24.4
0.8	1.2	4.8	7.1	8.8	12.9	12.8	18.8	16.8	24.7
1.0	1.5	5.0	7.4	9.0	13.2	13.0	19.1	17.0	25.0
1.2	1.8	5.2	7.6	9.2	13.5	13.2	19.4	17.2	25.3
1.4	2.1	5.4	7.9	9.4	13.8	13.4	19.7	17.4	25.6
1.6	2.3	5.6	8.2	9.6	14.1	13.6	20.0	17.6	25.9
1.8	2.6	5.8	8.5	9.8	14.4	13.8	20.3	17.8	26.2
2.0	2.9	6.0	8.8	10.0	14.7	14.0	20.6	18.0	26.5
2.2	3.2	6.2	9.1	10.2	15.0	14.2	20.9	18.2	26.8
2.4	3.5	6.4	9.4	10.4	15.3	14.4	21.2	18.4	27.1
2.6	3.8	6.6	9.7	10.6	15.6	14.6	21.5	18.6	27.4
2.8	4.1	6.8	10.0	10.8	15.9	14.8	21.8	18.8	27.7
3.0	4.4	7.0	10.3	11.0	16.2	15.0	22.1	19.0	28.0
3.2	4.7	7.2	10.6	11.2	16.5	15.2	22.4	19.2	28.2
3.4	5.0	7.4	10.9	11.4	16.8	15.4	22.7	19.4	28.5
3.6	5.3	7.6	11.2	11.6	17.1	15.6	22.9	19.6	28.8
3.8	5.6	7.8	11.5	11.8	17.4	15.8	23.2	19.8	29.1
4.0	5.9	8.0	11.8	12.0	17.6	16.0	23.5	20.0	29.4

The degrees refer to the centigrade thermometer.

TABLE C.

Approximate Height.	0°	15°	40°	55°	Approximate Height.	0°	15°	40°	55°
200	1.2	1.0	0.6	0.4	3200	19.1	18.0	11.5	7.0
400	2.4	2.2	1.4	0.8	3400	20.5	19.3	12.4	7.7
600	3.4	3.2	2.0	1.2	3600	21.8	20.4	13.4	8.2
800	4.5	4.3	2.8	1.7	3800	23.1	21.6	14.3	8.7
1000	5.7	5.3	3.4	2.2	4000	24.6	22.9	15.1	9.4
1200	7.0	6.4	4.2	2.6	4200	25.9	24.3	15.9	10.1
1400	8.2	7.6	4.8	3.0	4400	27.5	25.8	16.9	10.8
1600	9.2	8.8	5.6	3.4	4600	28.9	27.1	18.0	11.5
1800	10.4	9.8	6.3	3.8	4800	30.4	28.4	19.0	12.1
2000	11.6	11.0	7.0	4.2	5000	31.8	29.8	19.9	12.7
2200	12.8	12.1	7.6	4.6	5200	33.0	31.0	20.8	13.3
2400	14.0	13.3	8.4	5.1	5400	34.3	32.4	21.7	13.9
2600	15.2	14.4	9.2	5.6	5600	35.7	33.7	22.6	14.5
2800	16.5	15.6	10.0	6.2	5800	37.1	35.0	23.6	15.1
3000	17.7	16.8	10.8	6.6	6000	38.5	36.3	24.6	15.7

TABLE D.

Barometrical Height.	Metres.	Barometrical Height.	Metres.
15.75	1.71	23.62	0.63
17.72	1.39	25.59	0.42
19.68	1.11	27.56	0.22
21.65	0.86	29.53	0.03

CHAPTER II.

SURVEY.

TOPOGRAPHICAL SKETCHING.

39. TOPOGRAPHICAL drawing includes any thing relating to an accurate representation upon paper, of any piece of ground. The state of cultivation, roads, town, county, and state boundaries, and all else that occurs in nature. The sketching necessary in railroad surveying, however, does not embrace all of this, but only the delineation of streams and the undulations of ground within that limit which affects the road, perhaps 500 feet on each side of the line. The making of such sketches consists in tracing the irregular lines formed by the intersection of the natural surface, by a system of horizontal planes, at a vertical distance of five, ten, fifteen, or twenty feet, according to the accuracy required.

Fig. 13.

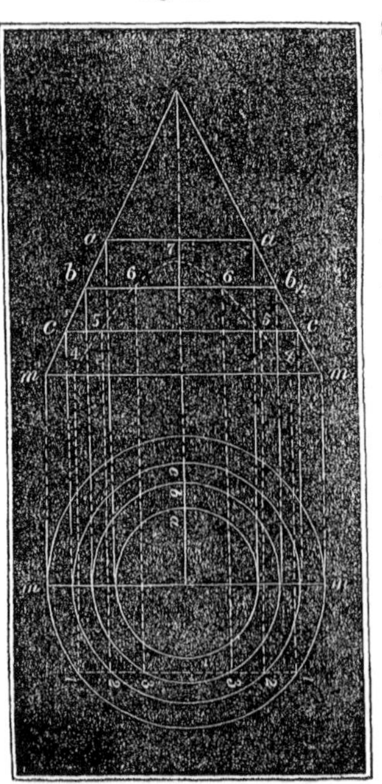

40. Suppose that we wish to represent upon a horizontal surface a right cone. The base *m m*, fig. 13, is shown by the circle

of which the diameter is *m*, *m*. If the elevation is cut by the horizontal planes *a a*, *b b*, *c c*, the intersection of these planes with the conical surface is shown by the circles *a*, *b*, *c*, in plan. The less we make the horizontal distances, on plan, between the circles, the less also will be the vertical distance between the planes.

Wishing to find the elevation of any line which exists on plan, as 1, 2, 3, 3, 2, 1, we have only to find the intersection of the verticals drawn through the points 1, 2, 3, 3, 2, 1, and the elevation lines *a a*, *b b*, *c c*; this gives us the curve 4, 5, 6, 7, 6, 5, 4.

Fig. 14.

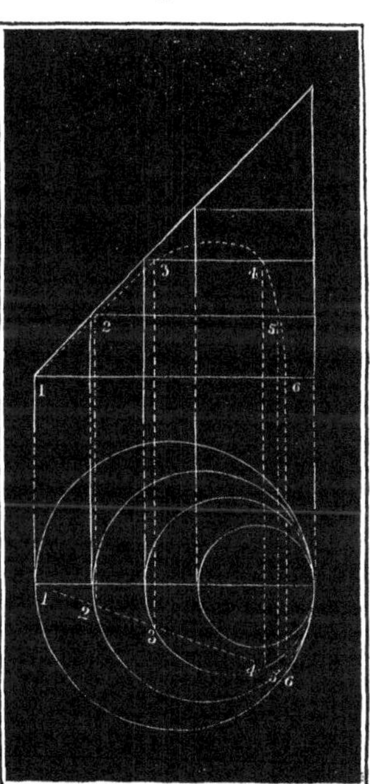

41. Again, in fig. 14, the cone is oblique, which causes the circles on plan to become eccentric and elliptic. Having given the horizontal line *m m m*, as before, we find it upon the elevation in the same manner.

42. In the section of regular and full lined figures, the horizontal and vertical projections are also regular and full lined; but in a broken surface like the ground, the lines become quite irregular.

Suppose we wish to show on plan the hill of which we

have the plan, fig. 15, and the sections figs. 16, 17, and 18.

Fig. 15.

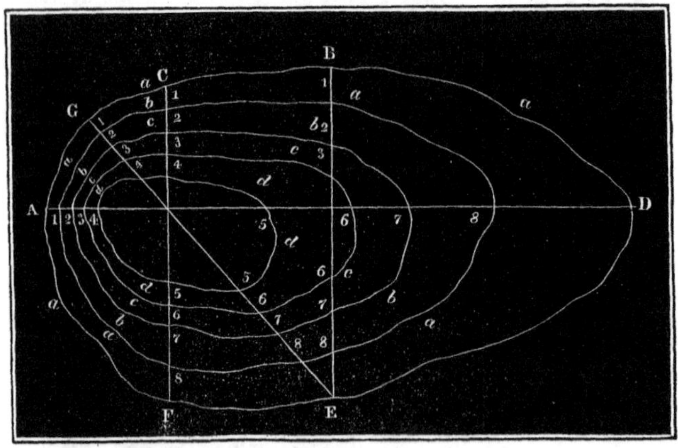

Let A D be the profile (made with the land) of the line A D on plan, fig. 15. B E that of B E, and C F that of C F.

Fig. 16.

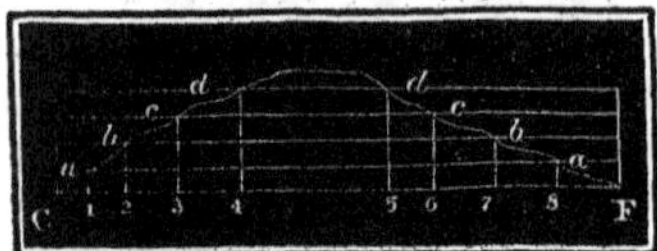

Fig. 17.

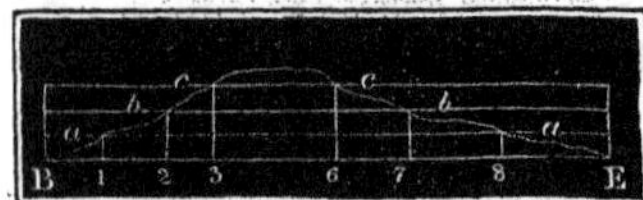

To form the plan from the profiles proceed as follows:—

Intersect each of the profiles by the horizontal planes *a a*, *b b*, *c c*, *d d*, equidistant vertically. In the profile A D, fig. 18, drop a vertical on to

Fig. 18.

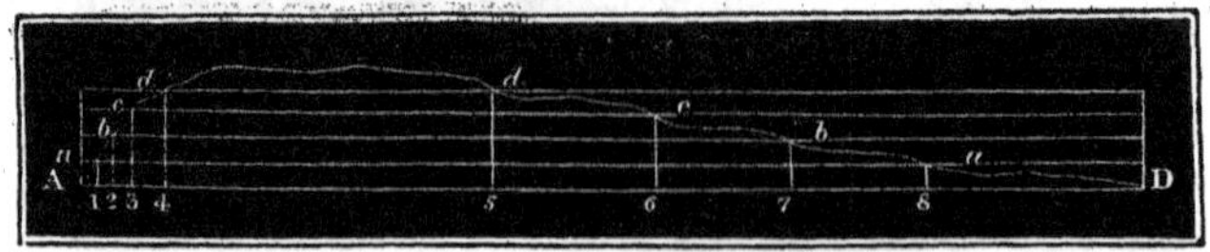

the base line from each of the intersections *a*, *b*, *c*, *d*, *d*, *c*, *b*, *a*. Make now A 1, 1 2, 2 3, 3 4, etc., on the plan equal to the same on the profile. Next draw, on the plan, the line B E, at the place and at the proper angle with A D; and having found the distances B 1, 1 2, 2 3, etc., as before, transfer them to the line B E on plan. Proceed in the same manner with the line C F.

The points *a a a*, *b b b*, *c c c*, are evidently at the same height above the base upon the profiles, whence the intersections of these lines with the surface line or 1 1 1, 2 2 2, 3 3 3, etc., on the plan, are also at the same height above the base; and an irregular line traced through the points 1 1 1, or 2 2 2, will show the intersection of a horizontal plane, with the natural surface.

When as at A we observe the contour lines near to each other, we conclude that the ground is steep.. And when the distances are large, as at 6, 7, 8, we know that the ground falls gently. This is plainly seen both on plan and profile.

Having now the topographical sketch, fig. 15, we may

Fig. 15.

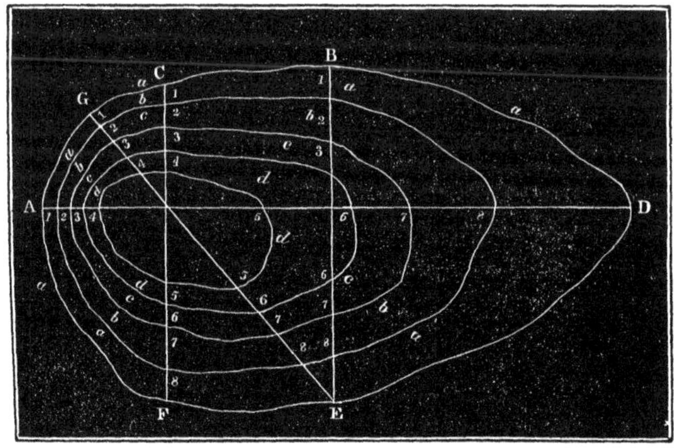

easily deduce therefrom at any point a profile. If we would have a profile of G E, on plan, upon an indefinite line G E, fig. 19, we set off G 1, 1 2, 2 3, 3 4, etc., equal to the same distances on the plan. From these points draw verticals intersecting the horizontals *a a*, *b b*, *c c*; and lastly, through the intersections draw the broken line (surface line or profile) *a*, *b*, *c*, *d*, *d*, *c*, *b*, *a*. Thus we see how complete a knowledge of the ground a correct topographical sketch gives.

Fig. 19

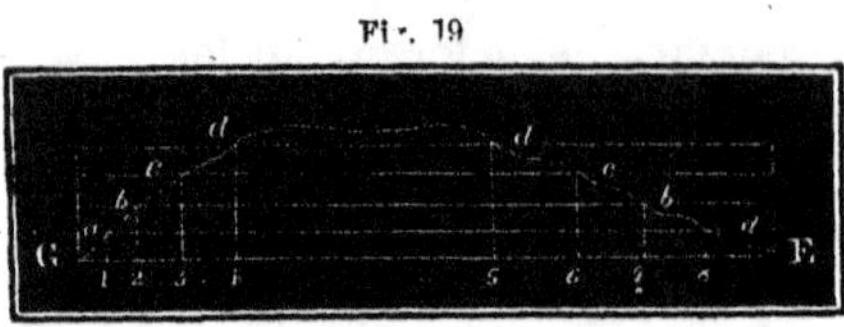

43. Field sketches for railroad work are generally made by the eye. The field book being ruled in squares representing one hundred feet each. When we need a more accurate sketch than this method gives, we may cross section the ground either by rods or with the level.

By making a very detailed map of a survey, and filling in with sketches of this kind, the location may be made upon paper and afterwards transferred to the ground.

So far we have dealt with but one summit; but the mode of proceeding is precisely the same when applied to a group or range of hills, or indeed to any piece of ground.

44. As a general thing, the intersection of the horizontal planes with the natural surface (contour lines) are concave to the lower land in depressions, and convex to the lower land on spurs and elevations. Thus at B B B *b b*, fig. 20, upon the spurs, we have the lines convex to the stream; and in the hollows *c c c*, the lines are concave to the bottom.

45. Having by reconnoitre found approximately the place for the road, we proceed to run a trial line by compass. In doing this we choose the apparent best place, stake out the centre line, make a profile of it, and sketch in the topography right and left.

Fig. 20.

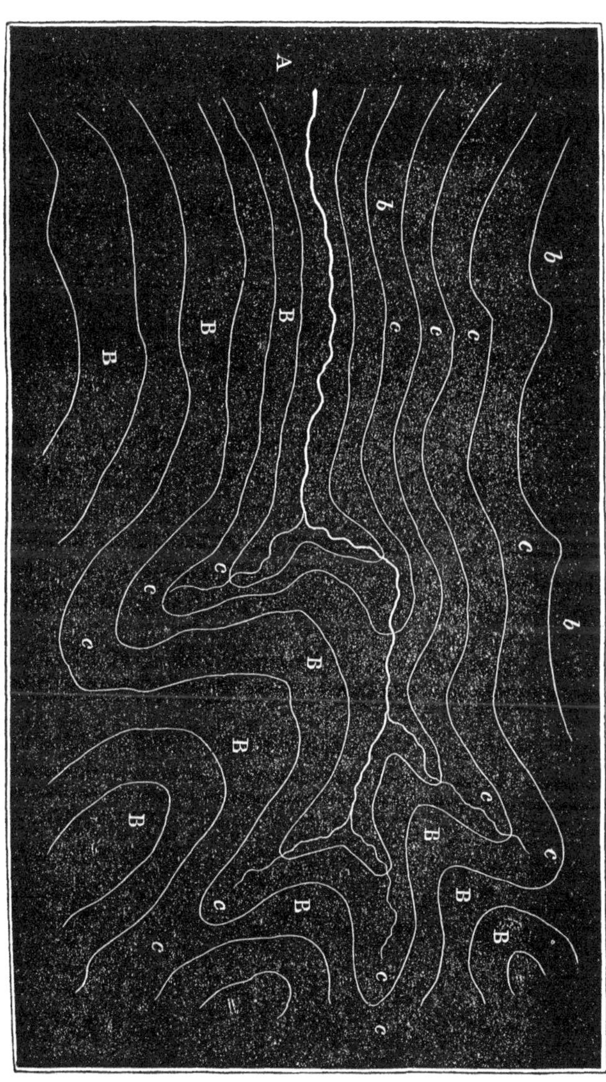

Suppose that by doing so we have obtained the plan and profile shown in figs. 21 and 22, where A *a a* B is the profile of A *c d* B, on the plan. The lowest line of the valley though

Fig. 21.

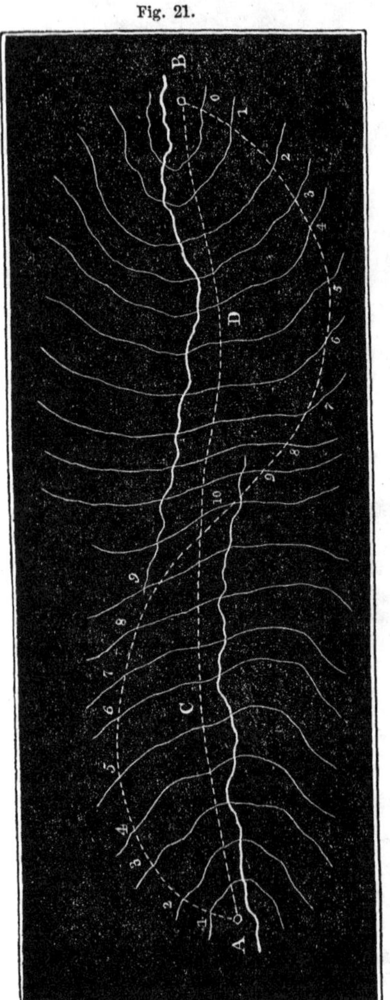

Fig. 22.

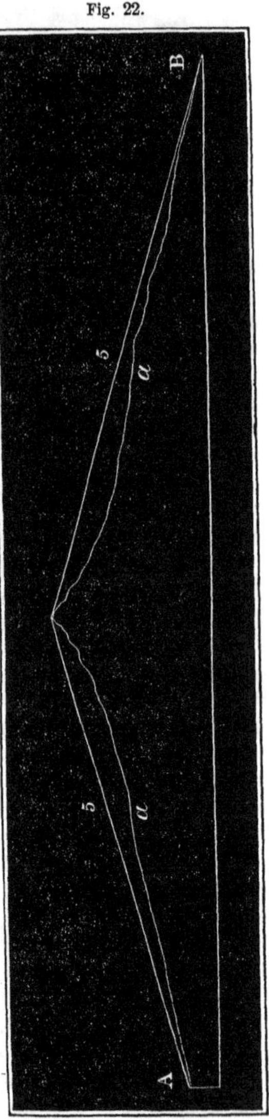

quite moderately inclined at first, from A to C, rises quite fast from C to the summit; and as the inclination becomes greater, the contour lines become nearer to each other.

Now that the line may ascend uniformly from A to the summit, the horizontal distances between the contour lines must be equal; this equality is effected by causing the surveyed line to cut the contours *square* at 1, 2, 3, 4, and *obliquely* at 5, 8, 10. Thus we obtain the profile A 5 5 B.

46. Having given the plan and profile, figs. 23 and 24, where A C D B represents the bed of the stream, in profile,

Figs. 23 and 24.

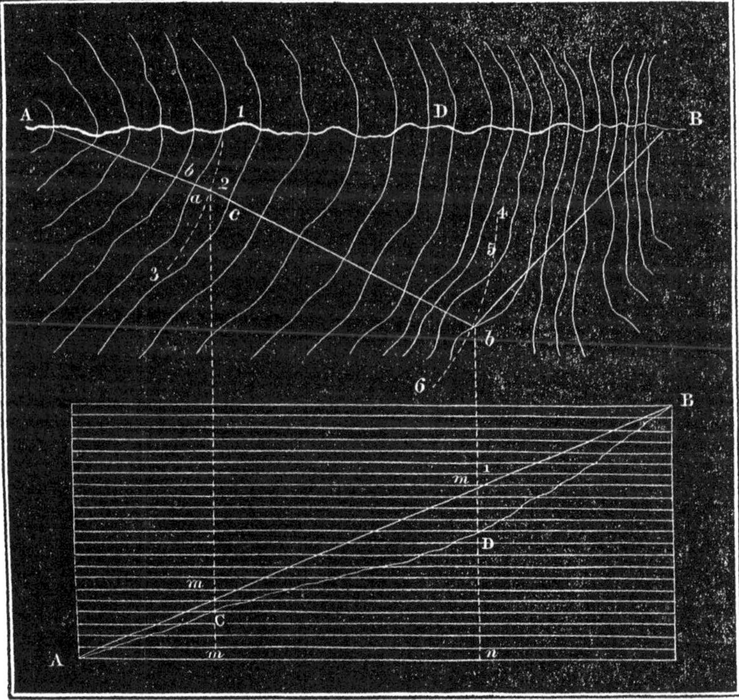

if it were required to put the uniformly inclined line A *m m* B, upon the plan, we should proceed as follows. Take the horizontal distance A *m* from the profile, and with

A (on plan) as a centre, describe the arc 1, 3. The point *m* on the profile is evidently three fourths of a division above the bed of the stream. So on the plan we must trace the arc 1, 3, until we come to *a*, which is three fourths of *b c*, from *b*. Again, m^1 is nine and one half divisions above *m*. From *a*, with a radius *m n* on profile, describe the arc 4, 5, 6. Now, as on the profile, in going from *m* to m^1, we cross nine contour lines, and come upon the tenth at m^1, so on the plan we must cross nine contour lines and come upon the tenth, and at the same time upon the arc 4, 5, 6.

Proceeding in this way, we find A, *a*, *b*, B, on the plan, as corresponding to A *m* m^1 B on the profile.

To establish in this manner any particular grade, we have first to place it upon the profile, and next to transfer it to the plan.

47. It may be remembered as a general thing, that the steepest line is that which cuts the contour line at right angles; the contour line itself is level, and as we vary between these limits we vary the incline.

GENERAL ESTABLISHMENT OF GRADES.

48. Considerable has been written upon the relation which ought to exist between the maximum grade, and the direction of the traffic. Some have given formulæ for obtaining the rate and direction of inclines as depending upon the capacity of power. This seems going quite too far, as the nature of the ground and of the traffic generally fix these in advance.

49. Between two places which are at the same absolute elevation, there should be as little rise and fall as possible.

50. Between points at different elevations, we should if possible have no rise while descending, and consequently no fall while on the ascent.

51. Some engineers express themselves very much in favor of long levels and short but steep inclines. There are cases where the momentum acquired upon one grade, or upon a level, assists the train up the next incline. The distance on the rise during which momentum lasts, is not very great. A train in descending a plane does not receive a constant increase of *available* momentum, but arrives at a certain speed, where by increased resistance and by added effect of gravity, the motion becomes nearly regular. Up to this point the momentum acquired is useful, but not beyond.

Any road being divided into *locomotive sections*, the section given to any one engine should be such as to require a constant expenditure of power as nearly as possible; i. e., one section, or the run of one engine, should not embrace long levels and steep grades. If an engine can carry a load over a sixty feet grade, it will be too heavy to work the same load upon a level economically. It is best to group all of the necessarily steep grades in one place, and also the easy portions of the road; then by properly adapting the locomotives the cost of power may be reduced to a minimum.

As to long levels and short inclines the same power is required to overcome a given rise, but quite a difference may be made in the means used to surmount that ascent.

52. Suppose we have the profiles A E D and A B D, fig. 25. The resistance from A to D by the continuous twenty feet grade is the same as the whole resistance from A to B and from B to D. The reason for

Fig. 25.

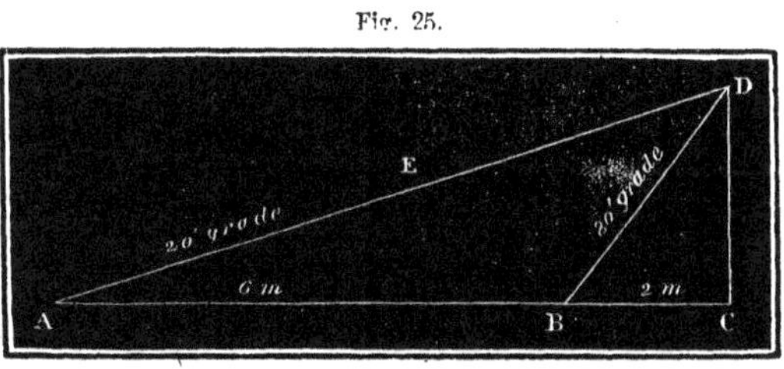

preferring A E D is, that an engine to take a given load from B to D would be unnecessarily heavy for the section A B; while the same power must be exerted at each point, of A E D. Also the return by A E D is made by a small and constant expenditure of power, being all of the way aided by gravity; while in descending by B, we have more aid from gravity than we require from D to B, after which we have none.

When the distances A B, B C, are sixty and twenty miles in place of six and two, we may consider the grades grouped at B D, and use a heavier engine at that point, as we should hardly find eighty miles admitting of a continuous and uniform grade.

EQUATING FOR GRADES.

53. In comparing the relative advantages of several lines having different systems of grades, it is customary to reduce them all to the level line involving an equal expenditure of power.

The question is to find the vertical rise, consuming an amount of power equal to that expended upon the horizontal unit of length. This has been estimated by engineers all the way from twenty to seventy feet. For simple comparison it does not matter much what number is used if it is the same in all cases; but to find the equivalent horizontal length to any location, regard must be had to the nature of the expected traffic.

The elements of the problem are, the length, the inclination or the total rise and fall, and the resistance to the motion of the train upon a level, which latter depends upon the speed and the state of the rails and machinery.

From chapter XIV. we have the following resistances to the motion of trains upon a level:—

Velocity, in miles, per hour.	Resistance, in lbs. per ton.
10	8.6
15	9.3
20	10.3
25	11.6
30	13.3
40	17.3
50	22.6
60	27.1
100	66.5

The power expended upon any road is of course the product of the resistance per unit of length, by the number of units. Calling R the resistance per unit upon a level, and R' the resistance per unit on any grade, and designating the lengths by L and L', that there shall be in both cases an equal expenditure of power, we must have

$$R\,L = R'\,L',$$

whence the level length must be

$$L = \frac{L'\,R'}{R}.$$

Thus assuming the resistance on a level as twenty lbs. per ton, that on a fifty feet grade is

$$20 + \tfrac{50}{5280} \text{ of } 2240, \text{ or } 20 + 21.2 \text{ or } 41.2,$$

and if the length of the inclined line is ten miles, the equivalent level length is

$$L = \frac{41.2 \times 52800}{20} = 108768 \text{ feet, or } 20.6 \text{ miles.}$$

Also 10 miles $\times$ 41.2 lbs. $= 412$,

and 20.6 " $\times$ 20 " $= 412$.

54. The above may be somewhat abridged as follows: Let R be the resistance on a level. The resistance due to any grade is expressed by

$$W \times \frac{1}{a},$$

where $\frac{1}{a}$ is the fraction showing the grade, and W the weight of the load.

The vertical height in feet, to overcome which we must expend an amount of power sufficient to move the train one mile on a level, must be such that

$$W \times \frac{1}{a} = R,$$

or

$$\frac{1}{a} = \frac{R}{W};$$

and to find the number by which to equate, we have only to place the values of R and W in the formula. For example, let the speed be twenty miles per hour, the corresponding resistance is 10.3 lbs. per ton. W being one ton, or 2240 lbs., we have

$$\frac{1}{a} = \frac{R}{W} = \frac{10.3}{2240} = \frac{1}{218} \text{ of } 5280, \text{ (the number of feet in one mile,)}$$

$$\frac{1}{218} \text{ of } 5280 = 24 \text{ feet.}$$

In the same manner we have

Speed, in miles, per hour.	Equating number.
15	22
20	24
30	32
40	41
50	53
60	67
100	155

Thus when we take the speed as thirty miles per hour, for each thirty-two feet rise we shall consume an amount of power sufficient to move the train one mile on a level. In descending, the grade instead of being an obstacle, becomes an aid; indeed the incline may be such as to move the trains independently of the steam power. Thus if on account of ascending grades we increase the equated length, so also in descending we must reduce the length. The amount of reduction is not, however, the reverse of the increase in ascending, as after thirty or forty feet any additional fall per mile instead of being an advantage is an evil; as too much gravity obliges us to run down grades with brakes on. Twenty-five feet per mile is sufficient to allow the train to roll down, and any more than this is of very little use. Therefore for every mile of grade descending at the rate of twenty-five feet per mile we may deduct one mile in equating, and for every mile of grade descending twelve and one half feet per mile deduct a proportional amount; but for any *more* fall per mile than twenty-five feet, no allowance should be made; i. e., if we descend at the rate of forty feet per mile, we may deduct one mile in equating for the twenty-five feet of fall, and throw aside the remaining fifteen feet.

55. This is a common method of equating for grades, and represents a length which is proportional to the power expended, but not proportional to the cost of working, as the ratios of power expended and cost of working under different conditions are very different, double power requiring only twenty per cent. more working capital. The above rules, therefore, require a correction.

The cost of working a power represented by unity being expressed by 100;

That of working a power 2 is expressed by 125;

That of working a power 3 is expressed by		150;
" " " 4 " "		175;
" " " 5 " "		200.

(See Appendix F.)

Now the resistance on a level being at a velocity of twenty miles per hour, 10.3 lbs. per ton by the formula

$$\frac{1}{a}=\frac{R}{W},$$

the vertical height in feet causing a double expenditure of power is twenty-four; but as above, the whole expense of a double power is increased by only twenty-five per cent.; we should not add one mile for twenty-four feet rise, but one fourth of a mile only, or one mile for each ninety-six feet; and by correcting our former table in this manner, we have the following table:—

Speed, in miles, per hour.	Equating number.
15	88
20	96
25	110
30	128
40	164
50	212
60	276
100	620

So much for equating for the ascents. In descending, we have allowed one mile reduction for each mile of twenty-five feet of descending grade; but as in ascending we correct the first made table, so in descending we must also correct as follows. If we needed no steam power either while descending or afterwards, we should only save wood and water; as a general thing the fire must be kept up while descending, and the only gain is a small part of the expense of fuel; so small, in fine, that with the exception of roads which incline for the whole or a great part of their length, no reduction should be made.

COMPARISON OF SURVEYED LINES.

56. The requisite data for an approximate comparison of lines are, the measured length, total rise, total fall.

Let the length of line A be	100 miles,
" " " B "	90 "
Whole rise on A	2000 feet,
" " B	5100 "
Whole fall on A	1200 "
" " B	4300 "

Assume the number by which to equate, as ninety-six, and we shall have

Line A.

Ascending, $100 + \frac{2000}{96} =$		120.83
Descending, $100 + \frac{1200}{96} =$		112.50
	Sum	233.33
	Mean	116.66

Line B.

Ascending, $90 + \frac{5100}{96} =$		142.13
Descending, $90 + \frac{4300}{96} =$		134.80
	Sum	276.93
	Mean	138.46

The mean equated length of A is		116.66
The measured length of A is		100.00
	The difference	16.66
The mean equated length of B is		138.46
The measured length of B is		90.00
	The difference	58.46.

The cost of construction being assumed as the actual length, and that of working as the equated length, we have the final approximate comparison thus:—

Assume the construction cost as $25,000 per mile, and the cost of maintenance $4,000 per mile, and we have

The line A to the line B as

$$100 \times 25000 + \overline{116.66 \times 4000} \times \tfrac{100}{6} = 10310.667, \text{ is to}$$

$$90 \times 25000 + \overline{138.46 \times 4000} \times \tfrac{100}{6} = 11480.667;$$

or A is to B as 10.3 to 11.5 nearly, although the line A is ten miles longer than B.

CHAPTER III.

LOCATION.

ALIGNMENT.

57. The broken line furnished by the survey is of course unfit for the centre line of a railroad. The angles require to be rounded off to render the passage from one straight portion to the other easy.

58. Let A X B, fig. 26, represent the angle formed by

Fig. 26.

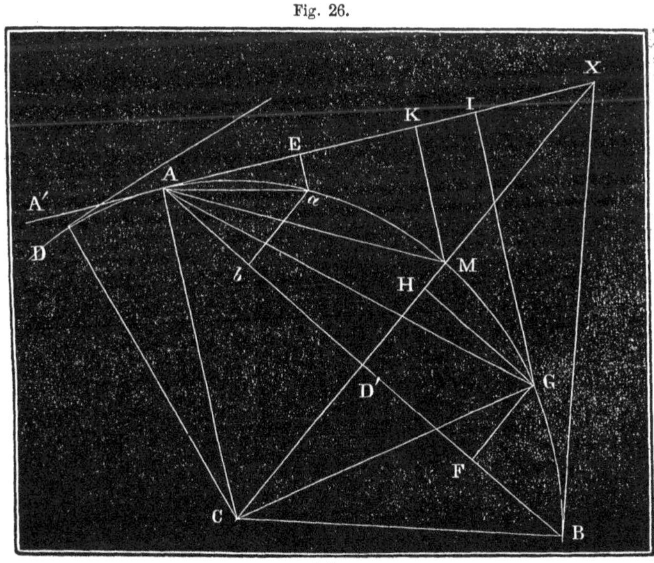

any two tangents which it is required to connect by a circular curve. It is plain that knowing the angle of deflection of the lines A X, B X, we obtain also the angles A C X, X C B. The manner of laying these curves upon the ground is by placing an angular instrument at any point of the curve, as at A, and laying off the partial angles E A *a*, E A M, E A G, etc., which combined with the corresponding distances A *a*, *a* M, M G, fix points in the curve.

Thus small chords are generally assumed at one hundred feet, except in curves of small radius (five hundred feet) when they are taken less.

The only calculation necessary in laying out curves, is, knowing the partial deflection to find the corresponding chord, or knowing the chord, to get the partial angle.

As the radius of that curve of which the angle of deflection is 1° is 5730 feet, the degree of curvature for any other radius is easily found. Thus the radius 2865 has a degree of curvature per one hundred feet of

$$\tfrac{5730}{2865} = 2^\circ;$$

again,

$$\tfrac{5730}{2000} = 2^\circ.81, \text{ or } 2^\circ\ 48'.6.$$

The radius corresponding to any angle is found by reversing the operation. If the angle is 3° 30′, or 210′, we have

$$\frac{5730 \times 60}{210} = 1637 \text{ feet radius.}$$

The following figures show the angle of deflection for chords one hundred feet long, corresponding to different radii:—

Angle of deflection.	Radius, in feet.
$\frac{1}{4}°$ or 15′	22920.0
$\frac{1}{2}°$ or 30′	11460.0
$\frac{3}{4}°$ or 45′	7640.0
1° or 60′	5730.0
$1\frac{1}{4}°$	4585.0
$1\frac{1}{2}°$	3820.0
$1\frac{3}{4}°$	3274.0
2°	2865.0
$2\frac{1}{2}°$	2292.0
3°	1910.0
$3\frac{1}{2}°$	1637.0
4°	1433.0
$4\frac{1}{2}°$	1274.0
5°	1146.0
$5\frac{1}{2}°$	1042.0
6°	955.4
$6\frac{1}{2}°$	822.0
7°	819.0
$7\frac{1}{2}°$	7.64.5
8°	716.8
10°	573.7

Points in any curve may also be fixed by ordinates, as *a b*, M D′, G F, or by E *a*, K M, etc.

For the details of locating, of running simple and compound curves, and of the calculations therefor, the reader is referred to the works of Trautwine, and of Hencke.

Fig. 27.

59. Suppose now that we have the surveyed lines *m m*, and *n n*, fig. 27, one of which is to be finally adjusted to the ground. The shortest line is the straight one, which is generally impracticable. The most level line is the contour line, which is also impracticable. Between these two lies the right line, which is to be found by an instrumental location. The line A *n n n n* B, on the plan, gives the profile A *n n n n* B. The line A *m m m m* B gives the profile A *m m m m* B, while the finally adjusted line A 1 2 3 4 5 6 gives the profile A 1 2 3 4 5 6 B.

60. Again, in fig. 28, the straight line A *n n n* B gives the profile A *n n n* B, requiring either steep grades or a great deal of work. By fitting the line to the ground, as by the line A *a b c d* . . . *m n o* B, we obtain the profile A *a b c* . . . *m n o* B.

Fig. 28.

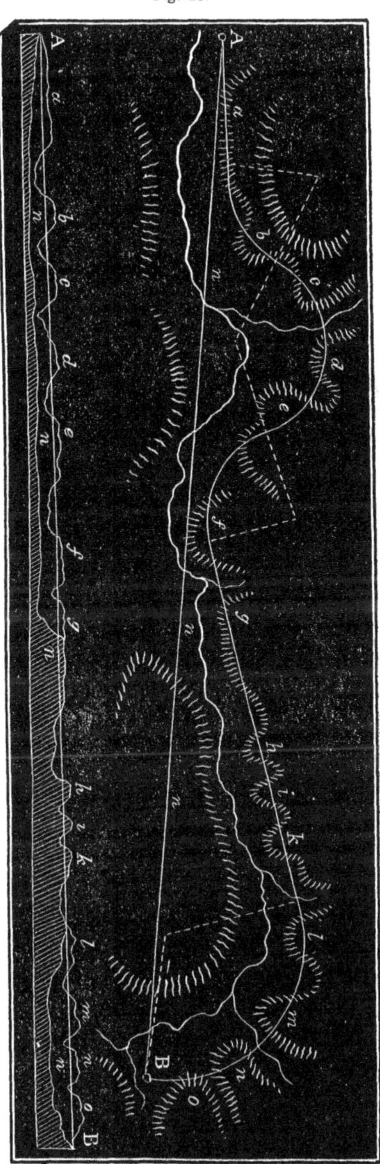

FINAL ADJUSTING OF GRADES.

Fig. 29.

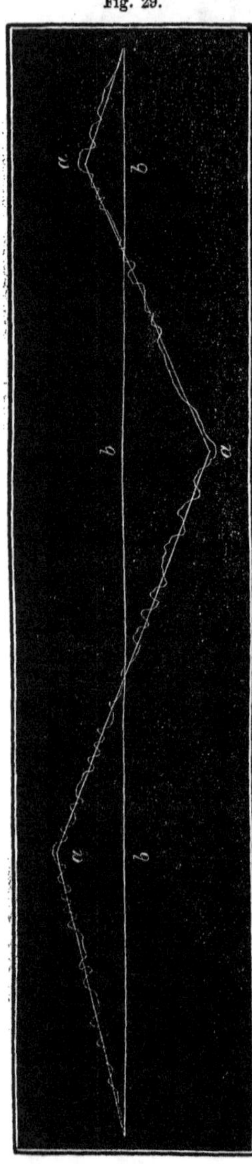

61. The general arrangement of inclines must not be interfered with to save work, but a large part of the excavation and embankment may be saved by breaking up long grades so as not to affect materially the character of the road. Upon some lines the grades must necessarily undulate, as in fig. 29. The difference in the amount of work is plainly seen. The steepest grades thus applied must not be greater than the ruling grade upon the travel of one engine.

62. In long and shallow cuts and fills, the best plan is to place the grade line quite high, avoiding much cutting, and to make the embankments from side cuttings, (ditching). Banks must at least be placed two or three feet above the natural surface, first to prevent the snow from lodging too much upon the rails, second, to insure draining.

63. Snow fences are much used in the northern parts of the United States. These are high pieces of lattice-work, made roughly, but well braced; from eight to twelve feet high, and standing from sixty to one hundred feet from the road. The object of the fence is to break the current of

the wind, and cause it to precipitate its snow. Close fences effect the object no better than the open ones, are more liable to blow down, and cost more.

64. In locating a road which is to have a double track eventually, regard must be paid to this fact in side-hill work. The first track should, if possible, be so placed as not to require moving when the double line is put on.

COMPARISON OF LOCATED LINES.

65. In this comparison there is an element which does not enter the approximate comparison of surveyed lines, curvature. The resistance arising from this cause has never been accurately determined. Mr. McCullum estimates the resistance at one half pound per degree of curvature per one hundred feet; i. e., the resistance due to curvature on a 4° curve, would be two lbs. per ton, (see report of September 30, 1855). Mr. Clark estimates the resistance due to curves of one mile radius and under, as 6.3 lbs. per ton, or twenty per cent. of the whole distance. The average radius encountered, therefore, by Mr. Clark, would be, at Mr. McCullum's estimate,

$$\frac{6.3}{0.5} = 12° \text{ nearly, or } 477.5 \text{ feet.}$$

So small a radius is by no means allowable upon English roads; thus the estimate of Mr. Clark and of Mr. McCullum differ considerably. Experiments might easily be made with the dynamometer upon different curves, by which we might find very nearly the correct resistance caused by curves.

The curvature on any road cannot be adjusted to trains moving at different speeds.

66. The tractive power acts always tangent to the curve

at the point where the engine is, and thus tends to pull the cars against the *inner* rail. The tangential force, generated by the motion of the cars, tends to keep the flanges of the wheels against the *outer* rail; and only when a just balance is made between the tractive and tangential forces, the wheel will run without infringing on either rail, (the wheel being properly coned). For these forces to balance, there must be a fixed ratio between the weight of a *car* and the speed, (not the weight of a *train*, as the slacking allows the cars to act nearly independently, some indeed rubbing hard for a moment against the rail, while the next car is working at ease). Whenever the right proportion is departed from, as it nearly always is, (and perhaps necessarily in some cases,) upon railroads, the wheels will rub against one rail or the other. Thus on any road where the speed on the same curve, or the radii of curvature under the same speed, differ, there must be loss of power, and dragging or pushing against the rails.

67. We are obliged to elevate the outer rail (see chapter XIII.), for the fastest trains, and the slower trains on such roads will therefore always drag against the inner rails. Thus in practice we generally find the inside of the outer rail most worn on passenger roads, and the inside of the inner rail upon chiefly freight roads.

68. It has been the practice of some engineers in equating for curvature, to add one fourth of a mile to the measured length for each 360° of curvature, disregarding the radius, as the length of circumference increased inversely as the degree of curvature.

69. Now in equating for grades, in doubling the power we do not double the expense of working. We however increase it more by curvature than we do by grades, because besides requiring double power, the wear and tear of cars and rails and all machinery is increased upon curves, which is not the case upon grades.

70. The analysis of expense (in Appendix F.) upon the New York system of roads, gives the following: —

Locomotives,	40 per cent.
Cars,	20 " "
Way and works,	15 " "
or in all,	75 per cent.

Now each 360° will be equal to $\frac{75}{100}$ of one quarter of a mile, or $\frac{75}{400}$ of a mile; whence the number of degrees which shall cause an expense equal to one straight and level mile, will be 1920°.

71. The number of degrees by Mr. McCullum's estimate would be thus: —

The resistance upon a level being ten lbs. per ton, and that due to curves one half pound per ton, per degree per one hundred feet; the length of a 2° curve to equal one mile will be

$$\frac{10 \text{ lbs.}}{1 \text{ lb.}},$$

or ten miles. Also ten miles, or 530 hundred feet by 2° is 1060°.

72. Again, by Mr. Clark's resistance of twenty per cent. of the level resistance, upon curves averaging 2°, we have as the length of 2° curve

$$\frac{10}{2} = 5 \text{ miles},$$

or 265 hundred feet, which by 2° gives 530°.

73. Averaging the first and last, we have as the number of degrees which should be considered as causing an amount of expense equal to one straight and level mile, 1225°, which averaging with the estimated resistance by Mr. McCullum, gives finally 1142½° as causing an expense

equal to one straight and level mile, or, in round numbers, 1140°.

74. Suppose now that we would know which of the lines below to choose.

Line A.	Line B.	Description.
100 miles,	110 miles,	Actual length,
5000 feet,	3000 feet,	Rise,
3500 "	1500 "	Fall,
3600°	9000°	Degrees of curvature.

Assuming the speed as twenty miles per hour, the number by which to equate for grades, see chapter II., is ninety-six, also the number of degrees for curvature 1140, whence,

$$\left.\begin{array}{l}\text{Line A ascending } 100 + 52.1 + 3.16 = 155.26 \\ \text{Line A descending } 100 + 36.5 + 3.16 = 139.66\end{array}\right\} 147.46$$

$$\left.\begin{array}{l}\text{Line B ascending } 110 + 31.25 + 7.89 = 149.14 \\ \text{Line B descending } 110 + 15.60 + 7.89 = 133.49\end{array}\right\} 141.31,$$

and if the cost of construction is as the actual, and the cost of maintaining and working as the mean equated length, we have, as a final comparison,

A to B as $100 + 147.46$ to $110 + 141.31$,

or as

247.46 to 251.31.

Here the extra grades on the one hand nearly equal the curvature and the extra length on the other hand.

75. As a further example in the comparison of competing lines, let us take the actual case of the location of the eastern part of the New York and Erie Railroad.

It was questioned which of the two lines between Binghampton and Deposit should be adopted, and also between the mouth of Callicoon Creek and Port Jervis.

Fig. 30.

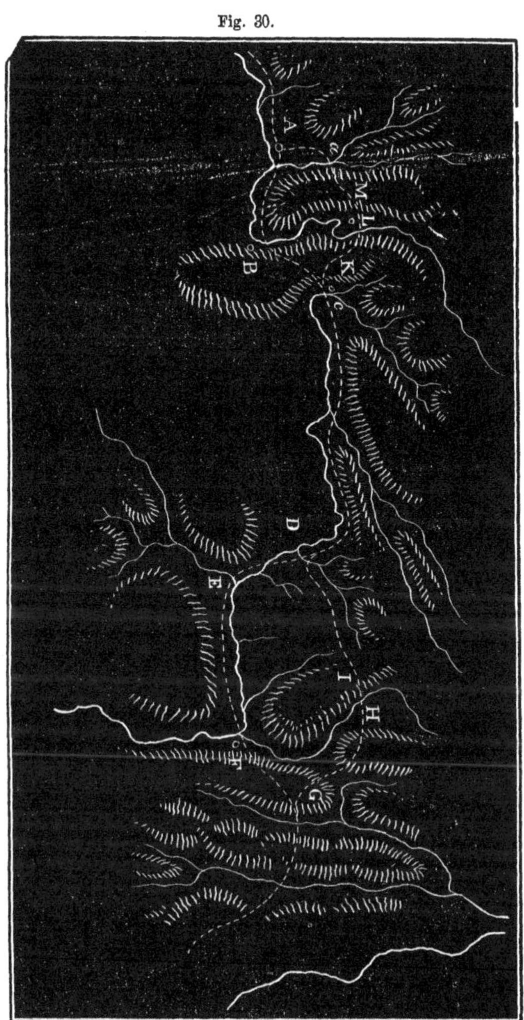

Between A and *c*, fig. 30, were located the lines shown in the sketch, one following the Susquehanna river from A to B, thence crossing the dividing ridge between that river and the Delaware to Deposit (*c*). The other passing up the Chenango river to *a*, thence crossing first the summit M to the Susquehanna at L, and second the summit K, to Deposit (*c*). The elements of the two lines are as follows:—

	A route, A B *c*.	B route, A M K *c*.
Length,	39.29	43.58
Rise A to *c*,	540.00	1087.00
Rise *c* to A,	395.00	936.00
Whole rise and fall,	935.00	2023.00
Degrees of curvature,	2371°.00	3253°.00
Estimated cost,	$746,900.00	$628,600.00.

Assuming the number by which to equate for grades, as 96, and the equating number of degrees of curvature as 1140°; equating for grades and curvature in both directions, we have,

Route A. A to *c*.

$$39.29+\frac{540}{96}+\frac{2371}{1140}=39.29+5.63+2.08=47.00$$

Route A. *c* to A.

$$39.29+\frac{395}{96}+\frac{2371}{1140}=39.29+4.12+2.08=45.59$$

Mean, 46.25.

Route B. A to *c*.

$$43.58+\frac{1087}{96}+\frac{3253}{1140}=43.58+1132+2.85=57.75$$

Route B. *c* to A.

$$43.58+\frac{936}{96}+\frac{3253}{1140}=43.58+9.75+2.85=56.18$$

Mean, 56.96.

Assuming the cost of working and of maintaining as $4,000 per mile, we have

The cost of building A to B as $746,900 to $628,600

The cost of operating A to B as $(46.25 \times 4000) \times \frac{100}{6}$ to $(56.96 \times 4000) \times \frac{100}{6}$,

or as	$3,083,334 to	$3,797,334
and the sum as	$3,830,234	$4,425,934

giving the preference of $595,700 to the route A B *c*, notwithstanding that the estimate thereon exceeds that on B by $118,300. The route A B *c* was adopted.

Again, it was doubtful whether to adopt the route E F, in going from D to G, or the line I H. The following are the elements of the two lines: —

	I H.	E F.
Measured length,	61.14	58.53
Rise D to G,	1187	454
Rise G to D,	1049	316
Degrees curve,	7609°	4588°
Estimated cost,	$1,094,950	$1,496,430.

The mean equated lengths are as follows: —

Line I H. D to G.

$$61.14 + \frac{1187}{96} + \frac{7609}{1140} = 61.14 + 12.36 + 6.68 = 80.18$$

Line I H. G to D.

$$61.14 + \frac{1049}{96} + \frac{7609}{1140} = 61.14 + 10.93 + 6.68 = 78.75$$

Mean, 79.46,

Line E F. D to G.

$$58.53 + \frac{454}{96} + \frac{4588}{1140} = 58.53 + 4.73 + 4.02 = 67.28$$

Line E F. G to D.

$$58.53 + \frac{316}{96} + \frac{4588}{1140} = 58.53 + 3.29 + 4.02 = 65.84$$

Mean, 66.56.

The comparison as to cost is

I H to E F as $1,094,950 to $1,496,430,

and as to working,

I H to E F as $(79.46 \times 4000) \times \frac{100}{6}$ to $(66.56 \times 4000) \times \frac{100}{6}$, and the sum as

	1,094,950	to	1,496,430
	+5,297.334		+4,437.334
or	\$6,392,284	to	\$5,933,764.

Although the cost of E F is \$401,480 more than that of I H, the line E F was adopted.

CHAPTER IV.

PRELIMINARY OPERATIONS.

SPECIFICATION.

76. The object of this paper is to define exactly the terms of the contract as regards execution of work. Every thing therein should be expressed in a manner so plain as to leave no room for misunderstanding.

The following has the approval of the best engineers: —

A AND B RAILROAD.

77. *Specification for Graduation.*

LINE.

The centre of the road-bed to conform correctly to the centre line of the railroad, as staked out or otherwise indicated on the ground, and to its appropriate curvatures and grades as defined and described by the engineer; and the contractor shall make such deviations from these lines or grades at any time, as the said engineer may require. The road-bed to conform to the cross section which shall be given or described, or to such other instructions as may be given as hereinafter limited; and the same of the ditches and slopes of the work, and of all operations pertinent to the satisfactory performance of the graduation or masonry on the part or parts of the line contracted for.

CLEARING.

The ground forming the base of all embankments, and five feet beyond the foot of the slopes of all embankments, to be cleared as close to the surface as practicable, of all timber, saplings, brush, logs, stumps, or other perishable material. The valuable timber to be laid aside, beyond the clearing as directed by the engineer, the rest to be burned, if this can be done safely, otherwise to be moved beyond the limits of the cleared ground. The ground for ten feet beyond the top lines of all slopes of cuttings shall be cleared in like manner, of all timber and saplings. Wherever additional ground has to be taken in widening excavations to obtain materials, or in widening embankments to dispose of surplus material, or in grading for turnouts or depot grounds, an additional amount of ground shall be cleared in like manner; and when directed by the engineer, wherever additional space is required for outside ditching, or for alterations of roads or watercourses, or otherwise.

GRUBBING.

All stumps and large roots within ten feet of the grade line shall be grubbed out to the entire width of the work, and moved at least ten feet beyond the slopes. The cost of all clearing and grubbing is included in the price for earth work, which price is also understood to include all clearing and grubbing necessary in borrowing pits, spoil banks, road crossings, alterations of roads and watercourses, the formation of ditches or otherwise. The necessary clearing and grubbing in all cases to be kept completed five hundred feet in advance of any work in progress.

MUCKING.

Wherever mud, muck, or similar soft material occurs in excavations or embankments, within two feet of subgrade, it shall be removed and replaced by compact earth or gravel.

GRADE.

The grade lines on the profiles show the true grade, and correspond with a line two inches below the bottom of the iron rail of the superstructure. What is called subgrade corresponds with a line placed eighteen inches below the grade.*

WIDTH OF ROAD, AND SLOPES.

The width of road-way, unless otherwise directed, shall be twenty-two feet wide at grade in earth excavations, and eighteen feet wide in rock excavations. Both rock and earth shall be taken out eighteen inches below grade for the entire width of road-way. The bottoming to be replaced by gravel, broken stone, or spawls, in such manner as shall be directed by the engineer, leaving the necessary ditches of the width and depth directed on either side. The contractor will not be paid for any rock excavated beyond the slope lines of one to eight from the required width, or for any earth excavated beyond slope lines of one and

* The distance between grade and subgrade depends somewhat upon the climate, but is generally between one and two feet. See chap. XIII.

one half horizontal to one vertical, unless directed by the engineer to move additional rock or earth.

BLASTING.

All blasting shall be done at the risk of the first party, who shall be liable to the second parties, or to the railroad company, for any damages incurred in consequence, to dwelling-houses, individuals, or otherwise.

DITCHES.

Whenever required, ditches shall be cut along the tops of the slopes, of the form of size and in the position directed.

SURPLUS MATERIAL.

Whenever the earth or rock required for the adjoining embankments exceeds the amount in the neighboring excavations, the contractor, when required, shall increase the width of said excavations, as directed by the engineer, to a sufficient width for a double track, provided that this additional width shall not be extended so as to produce an average haul of more than eight hundred lineal feet, on said borrowed stuff. And whenever the earth or rock to be moved from any cut exceeds in amount the adjoining embankments, (unless elsewhere wanted,) it shall be applied to widening the embankment to a width for a double track, within the same limits of haul; but for a greater haul than eight hundred feet, the contractor shall be paid one cent per yard per hundred feet of excess.

BORROW PITS.

Where the excavation does not furnish sufficient material to make the adjoining embankments, borrow pits may be opened. But no earth shall be deposited in spoil banks nor borrow pits opened without the knowledge and consent of the superintending engineer, who shall take care that such operations are arranged so as not to damage the road or its slopes, nor interfere with the widening of the road-bed at a future time for additional tracks.

MATERIAL TO BE SAVED.

If materials be found in the excavations applicable to useful purposes, such as building stone, limestone, gravel, minerals, etc., they shall be laid aside in such place as the engineer may direct, for use, to be applied then or subsequently to the construction of the road under the conditions of these specifications and of the contract.

CLASSIFICATION OF MATERIALS.

Earth — every thing except solid and loose rock. *Loose rock* — all boulders and detached masses of rock measuring over one cubic foot in bulk and less than five cubic yards. *Solid rock*, includes all work in ledge, which requires drilling and splitting, and all *loose rocks* containing more than five cubic yards.

The prices for excavation include all earth or rock excavated in ditching, bottoming, borrowing, road crossings, alterations of road crossings and water channels, and the construction of temporary roads, provided the average distance hauled on each section, be the same as stated on the schedule here annexed; but if the actual average haul on any section is found, on completion, to have been greater or less than the distance stated, a corresponding addition or deduction shall be made, of one cent per cubic yard per hundred feet which the actual haul exceeds or falls short of that stated.

EMBANKMENTS.

The embankments to be formed fifteen feet wide on the surface, unless otherwise directed, with slopes of one and one half horizontal to one vertical. Wherever the embankment is formed from ditching on either side, such ditching, and the crest of the slopes thereof shall in no case approach within six feet, nor within double the depth of ditch, of the foot of the proper embankment slope, allowing always on one side for a double track; and no soft mud or muck shall be allowed to enter the bank. Wherever watercourses or new channels for rivers require to be formed, they shall not approach within once and one half of the depth of such stream, plus twenty-five feet. Care shall be taken in forming embankments to exclude all perishable material.

SUBSIDENCE.

To allow for the after settlement of materials on embankments, they shall, when delivered to and accepted by the second parties, be finished to the full width to the following heights above subgrades, namely: all banks below five feet in height to be finished three inches above subgrade; at ten feet in depth, five inches; at twenty feet, six inches; and twenty-eight feet, seven inches; at thirty-five feet, eight inches; and at forty feet in depth, nine inches above grade; and intermediate heights in proportion; the engineer having the power to change these proportions at his discretion.

EXTRA EXCAVATION AND EMBANKMENT.

Whenever it is considered necessary to increase the width of the road-way for turnouts, water stations, or depot grounds, whether in excavation or embankment, such work shall be done at the contract prices, as may be directed. The opening of foundation pits in simple excavation, where coffer-dams or such like expedients are necessary, and in places where such expedients are necessary, all excavation above the water line shall also be done at such increase or decrease of the contract price as shall be deemed proper by the engineer.

EMBANKING AT BRIDGES AND CULVERTS.

The contractor for earthwork shall not carry forward in the usual way any embankments within fifty feet of any piece of masonry, finished or in progress, (counting from the bottom of the slopes,) but shall in every such case have the earth wheeled to the walls or abutments, and carefully rammed to such width and depth, and in such manner as may be directed, when the embankment may be carried on as usual. The expense attendant upon any damage or re-building of mason work, consequent on neglect of these directions, shall be charged to the account of the first party. In case the mason work shall not be finished when the embankment approaches it, the contractor shall erect a temporary structure to carry over the earth, and proceed with the embankment on the opposite side; and the expense of said structure shall be paid by, and charged to, the contractor for masonry, in case such contractor shall have delayed beyond the proper or required time, the construction of the mason work; but if the mason work could not have been ready in season for the bank, then shall the expense belong to the contractor for the earthwork, whose price for graduation is understood to comprehend all such contingencies. For the above work of wheeling and ramming efficiently the earth around any piece of masonry, the contractor shall be paid —— cents per cubic yard, by the engineer's measurement.

ROADS AND WATERCOURSES.

The first party is to make good and convenient road crossings wherever directed, and shall also make such alterations of existing roads, or watercourses, or river channels, or such new pieces of these pertinent the section undertaken by him, as may be required, and shall be paid for such work, whether earth, rock, or masonry, the prices, and no more, applicable to this contract. And such road crossings or other alterations referred to, he shall make at and within such times and in such form and manner as the engineer shall direct; and whenever the operations of the first party interfere with a travelled road, public or private, either by crossing or by making required alterations on it, the first party shall so operate as to afford at all times a safe and free passage to the public travel; and the first party shall be liable for any damage to which the second parties or the railroad company may become lawfully liable by reason of his neglect to maintain a safe and properly protected passage for the current travel.

BALLASTING.

Where gravel is used for the ballasting of the road-bed, it shall be of a quality satisfactory to the engineer, and shall be spread upon the road-bed to the width and depth required. When broken stone is used, it shall be of durable quality, and shall be broken so as to pass through a ring of three inches in diameter. The quantity will be measured in the road-bed as finished, and the contractor will be required to keep the ditches trimmed and clear.

RIP-RAP, OR RUBBLE SLOPES.

The first party shall distribute rubble stone over the slopes of earth embankments, whenever required to do so, to protect said slopes from the action of water. Such stone to be arranged by competent hands, and laid to such thickness, and with stones of such size, as shall be directed. Where the contractor has rock in the neighboring cuttings which is available, it shall be reserved and applied to this purpose; and when not, good rock shall be obtained where the contractor can conveniently get it.

MEASUREMENTS.

All earth or rock necessarily moved to complete the grading of this contract according to direction, will be measured in excavation only; and if the contractor (with the consent of the engineer,) should find it convenient to waste earth from an excavation, instead of carrying it to its proper embankment, and to borrow at some nearer point earth for said embankment to replace that which was wasted, he shall be paid for the earth from the original excavation in the order of its most economical arrangement for the second parties. All earth moved from borrowing pits shall also be measured in excavation only.

78. *Specification for Masonry.*

FIRST CLASS MASONRY.

First class masonry will apply to bridge abutments exceeding twenty-five feet in height, to the ring stones of arches, and to the piers of bridges in running water. The stone shall be laid at the rate of one header to two stretches, disposed so as to make efficient bond. No header to be less than forty incles long, and no stretcher to be less than eighteen inches in width. No stone less than twelve inches in thickness, no stone to have a greater height than width, all stones to be placed upon the natural bed. The masonry throughout to have hammer dressed beds and joints. Vertical joints to be continued back at least ten inches from the face of the wall. The mortar joints on the face not to exceed one fourth of an inch in thickness. The stone to be laid with regard to breaking joints in the adjoining courses. The stone must be dressed complete before laying, and not be moved after being placed in the mortar. The face will not be tooled, but only roughly hewed, except for one half inch from the beds and joints, where it will be hammered. The ring stones of arches shall have beds to conform to the radius of the arch, with the end joints vertical, and be made to set smoothly on the centering, with the beds with the proper inclination. Each stone must extend through the whole thickness of the arch, and not be less than eight inches thick on the intrados. No spawls or pinners will be admitted. The ring stone shall be dimension work, according to the plans furnished, the beds and joints being truly dressed, but the faces left rough.

All first class work shall be carefully laid in good cement mortar, (see Art. Cement). Each stone before being laid shall be carefully cleaned and moistened; and masonry built in hot weather shall be protected from the sun as fast as laid, by covering with boards. Copings shall be built of stone of equal thickness, neatly dressed and laid.

All first class masonry shall be well pointed with cement pointing.

SECOND CLASS MASONRY.

To be applied to abutments less than twenty-five feet high, ring and face walls of bridges and culverts, and to piers not in running water, shall consist of stones cut in bed and build to a uniform thickness throughout, before being laid, but not hammered; they shall be laid on a level bed, and have vertical joints continued back at right angles at least eight inches from the face of the wall. The work need not be carried up in regular courses, but shall be well bonded, having one header for every three stretchers, and not more than one third of the stones shall contain less than two cubic feet, or be less than nine inches thick; and none of that third shall contain less than one and one half cubic feet, or be less than six inches thick. No more small stones shall be used than necessary to make even beds, the whole to be laid in cement mortar and pointed.

THIRD CLASS MASONRY.

Applicable to culverts, and to the spanded backing of arches, shall consist of strong and well built rubble masonry, laid dry for culverts, but wet for backing. The culverts to be of such form and dimensions as the engineer may direct. The foundation courses of the side walls to consist of large flat stones, from eight to ten inches in thickness, laid so as to give a solid and regular basis for the side walls. The side walls to be laid with sound stone, and of sufficient size, and with beds having a fair bearing surface and good bond. The covering stone for culverts being not less than ten inches thick for two feet culverts, twelve inches for three feet culverts, and fifteen inches for four feet culverts; to be free from flaw or defect, and to have a well bedded rest upon each side wall, of not less than twelve inches for two and three feet culverts; and not less than fifteen inches for larger ones. In case such stone cannot be obtained, a dry rubble arch may be thrown instead, well pinned and backed; but the price for the arch shall not be more than the general price for third class masonry, with an allowance for the centering.

FOURTH CLASS MASONRY.

Applicable to cattle-guards, pavement of culverts, and slope and protection walls, shall consist of stones of not less than one cubic foot in contents, so laid and bonded as to give the greatest degree of strength in preference to appearance; being laid when directed with beds perpendicular to the inclined face. Pavements under culverts shall be made by excavating one foot in depth of that part to be paved, which space shall be filled with flat stones one foot wide, set on edge, close together, and made to present an even upper face.

TIMBER AND PLANK FOUNDATIONS.

Timber and plank foundations require the beds to be perfectly well levelled, and timber of such dimensions, and so laid, as shown by the plans; to be well bedded and brought to an even and level top surface. The spaces between them to be filled and well rammed with such material as the engineer may direct. On these timbers planks shall be laid, and trenailed or spiked if required. The materials shall be of quality and shape approved by the engineer, and the price shall be in full for material and labor in laying the whole in a thorough and workmanlike manner.

PILING.

Piling may be used either as bearing piles for foundations, or for piled bridges. In the former case they will be bid for by the running foot driven, and in the latter by the stick of twenty-five feet in length. The piles in either case must be straight round timber, of a quality approved by the engineer, not less than ten inches in diameter at the small end, barked, and properly banded and pointed for driving. They shall be driven in such places, and to such depths as required, and the heads cut off square, or finished with a tenon to receive caps, as may be required. Bearing piles will be cut off so far below the lowest water that any timber foundation laid thereon shall be at all times entirely immersed.

CEMENT.

Cement when used shall be of the best quality, hydraulic, newly manufactured, well housed and packed, and so preserved until required for use. And none shall be used in the work until tested and approved by the engineer.

CEMENT MORTAR.

The proportion of sand and cement for construction shall be one of cement, to two of clean, sharp sand, unless in special cases the engineer direct otherwise, for which due allowance shall be made. It shall be used directly after mixing, and none remaining on hand over night shall be remixed.

LIME MORTAR.

Lime mortar (which in all cases shall contain cement), will consist, unless otherwise directed, of two parts of best quick lime, one of cement, and five of sand; the ordinary mortar of lime and sand being first properly made, and the cement thrown in and thoroughly mixed immediately before using.

CONCRETE.

Whenever concrete is required to be used, it shall be formed of clean broken stone, cement, and sharp, clean sand. The stone, which shall be of satisfactory quality, shall be broken so as to pass through a ring three inches in diameter. The cement and sand shall be thoroughly mixed in the proportions already described for cement mortar. Thus prepared, it shall be carefully mixed with the broken stone in the proportion of one of mortar to two or two and one half of broken stone, as the engineer upon experiment shall determine, and shall be immediately laid carefully in its place, and well rammed. The concrete shall be protected on the sides by boards, and be allowed to remain undisturbed after laying until it is properly set; and in special cases the engineer shall direct the mode of application. For the proper preparation and laying of such concrete, there shall be paid the price applicable to second class masonry. The contractor shall furnish all tools and plank necessary to the operation.

POINTING.

All masonry in cement or lime will be finished with a good pointing of cement, without extra charge.

BRICKWORK.

When bricks are required, or allowed to be used, they shall consist of sound, hard-burned brick, laid in cement, or common mortar, as directed, and no soft or salmon brick will be admitted; and none but regular bricklayers must be employed.

CENTERING AND BACKING.

The whole top of all arches, whether brick or stone, shall be finished by plastering with a good coat of cement, so as to prevent the percolation of water, and turn it away from the arch. The centering shall be such as the engineer approves of in every respect, and shall not be removed until he directs. The cost of backing to be included in the price bid. For arches of more than twenty-five feet span, compensation shall be made, at the engineer's estimate, for the extra value and cost of the centering proper for large arches.

GENERAL PROVISION.

79. The engineer reserves the right to require the whole or any part of the above described work of masonry to be laid in cement, lime, mortar, or dry, at his discretion. First and second class masonry, and brickwork, will be bid for at prices for laying in cement, from which will be deducted fifty cents per yard if laid in lime mortar, and one dollar if laid dry. Third and fourth class masonry at prices for laying dry, to which will be added fifty cents per yard if laid in lime mortar, and one dollar if laid in cement.

SCAFFOLDING.

80. Nothing shall be allowed for workmanship or timber of any scaffolding used in the construction of timber bridges, or in carrying up abutments, piers, coffer-dams, or otherwise. Should the timber used in any coffer-dam be carried away by floods, the renewal of it shall fall upon the first party.

FOUNDATIONS.

81. The foundations for all structures shall be executed by the contractor for masonry in such manner and to such depth as to secure a safe and secure foundation, of which the engineer will judge. If a natural foundation cannot be procured at a reasonable depth, then the contractor shall prepare such artificial foundation as the engineer may direct. The stuff moved from the foundations, if of the proper quality, shall be deposited in the adjoining embankment, provided the site for said embankment has been cleared of all perishable material. So much of the stuff as shall not be fit for the embankment, and all roots, stumps, etc., shall be deposited beyond the limits of the clearing, so as not to obstruct roads, watercourses, or ditches.

For the earth moved from such foundations, and for all earth used according to direction, in the construction of coffer-dams, there shall be paid —— cents per cubic yard.

Whenever it may be necessary to pump or bale water in the foundations, the contractor shall furnish the pumps or buckets, and all scaffolding and apparatus necessary to work them. He shall be allowed the net cost of all labor employed in the operations of pumping or baling water, and shall make a monthly return to the engineer of the value of such labor, provided that these operations are conducted in an economical manner, with efficient men, pumps, and tools, under the direction and to the satisfaction of the engineer. He shall also be allowed such compensation for the use of the pumps and apparatus, and for superintendence, as the engineer shall judge to be fair and reasonable.

TRESTLE WORK.

82. Includes all wooden structures commonly used as substitutes for abutments and piers, and for farm passes, etc., etc. These shall be built according to the plans furnished, and directions given by the engineer, of sound, durable material, to be approved by him. The price bid shall be by the thousand feet board measure, and will be considered as in full for all material except iron, and for the labor of building and erecting complete. The iron used will be of the best American, and the workmanship of approved quality. The bids will be by the pound, and will cover all cost of material and the labor incident to its use. Spikes and nails when used will be furnished by the contractor at cost.

BRIDGING.

83. Contractors may submit plans for bridging in connection with, or separate from their bids; but the engineer of the company may reject such plans if he choose, and substitute others, which if the contractor decline building at the approved prices, may be left to other parties. In every case, the exact manner of building, erecting, adjusting, and finishing bridges, and the determination of the nature and amount of material, will be specified by the engineer. The price bid must be by the running foot of the whole *length* of bridge, as erected and finished complete.

84. *Specifications for Superstructure.*

SUBSILLS.

To maintain the track in good adjustment until embankments are settled, subsills will be laid on certain banks, and likewise in cuts where the imperfect nature of the bottoming may, in the opinion of the engineer, render them expedient. These subsills to be fairly bedded in the earth or ballasting, and carefully adjusted and rammed so as to correspond with the grade lines given by the engineer. An additional piece of sill, four feet long, shall be laid at each joint of the subsill, either under the sill, or alongside, as may be directed. The sills will be of 3 × 9 plank, in length of twelve, fifteen, eighteen, and twenty-one feet; of which one fourth may be below fifteen, one fourth below eighteen, and one fourth below twenty-one feet. The plank must be square at the ends, and of sound, durable material, and not have more than two inches waine on one end only. There will be about 25,000 feet, board measure, laid per mile where it may be required, and 660 joint sills, 3 × 9 inches, and four feet long. When the depth of stuff to be moved to admit the subsills exceeds six inches, an allowance shall be made for extra labor, the amount of which shall be noted by the assistants on their receiving notice of such extra labor from the contractor or his agent.

CROSS TIES.

The cross ties shall be of white, black, or yellow oak, burr oak, chestnut, red elm, black walnut, or other sound timber of suitable character in the opinion of the engineer. Eight feet long, and not more than three inches out of straight, hewn to a smooth surface on two parallel plane faces six inches apart, the faces being not less than seven inches wide for at least half of the number, and the remainder not less than six inches wide. The ties shall be carefully and solidly laid on the subsills, or ballasting, or earth previously properly prepared, so as to give the true planes required by the rails, whether on straight or curved lines. They shall be laid at the rate of eight ties to each eighteen feet rail. All imperfect ties shall be excluded by the track-laying party. The surface of the ties to be faithfully adjusted to the grades given, and to the web of the rail; and the rail to be truly laid and firmly spiked so as to correspond neatly to the alignment of the road. There will be about 2,500 ties required per mile of road.

CHAIRS AND JOINTS.

When chairs are used, they shall be such as directed by the engineer, and furnished by the company, and shall be well and accurately placed and spiked in such manner and position as required. When chains are used, the largest ties shall be selected for the joints. When the joint is made by fishing, there will be no tie directly under the joint.

RAILS.

The rails will weigh about sixty pounds per lineal yard. No rail shall be laid on the tangents which is in any way twisted or bent. It shall be the duty of the first party to correct and make true any crooked rails received by him, also to bend to the proper curve, and in such a manner as not to affect the strength of the bar, all rails laid in curves. Punching of rails, and cutting, will also be done by the contractor.

TRACK LAYING.

The materials composing the track will be furnished by the company, and it will be laid in the best manner according to the conditions following. The track will be laid across ties, and the ties at the proper places on subsills. Where the sills are used, they will be laid with four feet blocks at the joints, and with six feet blocks at the rail joints, the whole being set to their places by stakes, and by the engineer's directions, and mauled down to a perfect bearing, being settled at least half an inch by mauling. The cross ties will be placed uniformly distant, (twenty-eight inches from centre to centre). The iron must be so cut or selected that the joints of the parallel rails shall be within two inches of being opposite to each other; no joint tie being allowed a greater amount of askew than this, whether on tangents or curves. A slip of metal shall be inserted at the rail joints while laying, to keep the rails apart sufficiently to allow for expansion, which thickness, (depending upon the temperature,) shall be fixed by the engineer. Notches to be cut at the centre of each bar, to correspond with half a spike, to prevent longitudinal motion of the rails. Each joint chair to be fastened with four spikes. Two spikes at each end of each tie upon straight lines and upon curves of less than 1,500 feet radius at the outer end of the tie two spikes outside and one inside, and at the inner end two spikes outside and one inside of the rail. Upon curves the outer rail to be raised by such an amount, depending on the radius of curvature, as the engineer may direct.

TURNOUTS.

The contractor to put in such turnouts and sidings, with the necessary frogs and switches, as may be required; the frogs and switches to be firmly and truly placed in position so as to work easily.

FILLING AND DITCHING.

The stuff moved in bedding the sills and ties, to be placed between the latter. The ditches to be properly cleaned out after the track is laid; the filling never to rise higher than the top of the cross tie. Any surplus stuff to be moved out of the cuts, or if on embankment, to be thrown over the bank, leaving the track and road-bed in a neat and workmanlike shape.

DELIVERY OF MATERIALS.

The ties and sills to be delivered at some point on the road as near as possible to the places where they are to be used, in no case requiring more than one thousand feet of land; to be so piled as easily to be counted and inspected. The bids for ties will be by the piece; the proposal stating the number and conditions; the sills to be bid for by the thousand, board measure. All material furnished in connection with track laying to be delivered in such manner and time as to comply in good season with the contract for laying the rails.

MEASUREMENT OF TRACK.

The measurement of track laid shall include the turnouts, measuring from heel to heel of switch. No extra allowance being made for putting in frogs or switch machinery.

85. *Specification for Fencing.*

Bids for fencing will be by the running foot, or mile, including both sides of the road. Where required, it will consist of posts placed eight feet apart from centre to centre, set three feet into the ground, either by digging or boring, and not by mauling. The posts shall be of oak, elm, chestnut, or other durable wood, not less than eight inches in diameter at the top, barked and charred when put into the ground. The boards to be 6 × 1 inches, and to square sixteen feet long, to be placed six inches apart vertically, and fastened to the posts with twopenny nails at each bearing, and breaking joint with each other. There will be five bars in depth, the top of the uppermost being five feet from the ground. In side hill and in ground liable to slide, particular care shall be taken to place the posts firmly in the ground. At cattle guards, the fence will be turned in to the proper distance, and such arrangement made as to prevent the passage of animals.

86. *General Provisions.*

CLASSIFICATION.

The classification of material excavated will be referred to the engineer, in all cases where the nature of the material is questioned, and his judgment taken thereon. Also all material used in structures will be submitted to the inspection of the engineer or his assistants.

QUANTITIES AND QUALITIES APPROXIMATE.

The quantities and qualities of work presented in the schedule are merely approximate, and the information given on the maps and profiles in relation thereto is according to the best present knowledge. The company retains the right to change at any time during the progress of the work, the alignment, grades, and width of the road, or any part thereof; and also the limits of the sections, or to alter the character, vary the dimensions, or change the location of structures, or substitute one kind of work or material for another, or to omit entirely, when found necessary, or to require to be built where not now contemplated; and the contractor shall carry into effect all such alterations when required, without the contract prices being thereby affected, unless the aggregate value of all work contemplated by the contract be changed full twenty per cent., in which case a fair allowance, either for the company or the contractor, shall be made by the engineer. In case, however, the aggregate value of the work be changed by over twenty per cent. of the original amount, and the contractor be not satisfied with the altered compensation, then said contractor may throw up said contract, on condition, that within ten days after receiving notice from the engineer of such alteration, he give written notice to the engineer or the company of his desire to do so. In which case, as in other cases of throwing up the contract, he shall as soon as desired, give peaceable possession to the company or their agents; leaving also in their possession any tools or machinery upon which they have advanced any thing; and the company may then settle with the contractor on the measure of damages which either shall suffer.

BASE FOR ESTIMATING EFFECT OF CHANGES.

The base for estimating any changes as above mentioned is understood to be the schedule exhibited at the letting.

NO LIQUOR, AND GOOD ORDER.

The contractor shall not sell, or allow to be sold or brought within the limits of his work any spirituous liquors, and will in every way discountenance their use by persons in his employ. He will do all in his power by his own act, or by assisting the officers of the county, or of the corporation, in maintaining the laws and such regulations as conduce to good order and peaceable progress, and prevent encroachment on the rights of persons or property; and he shall discharge from his service, when required by the engineer, any disorderly, dangerous, insubordinate, or incompetent person, and refuse to receive into his employ any who may have been discharged for such cause from other parts of the work.

MONTHLY ESTIMATES.

Measurements and estimates shall be made by the engineer once in each month, by means of which may be known approximately the amount of work done, and the contractor shall be entitled to payment therefor at such rates below his contract prices as the engineer or president of the company deems expedient; it being understood that the contractor has no claim on account of any material not laid in its place in the roadway, or for labor bestowed thereon; and the quantities shall be estimated from the dimensions when so laid, though on the advice of the engineer, advances may be made on such material when delivered for use, in which case it becomes the property of the company, in the contractor's care and keeping, and he becomes liable for its loss or injury.

EXTRA WORK.

No claim for extra work or for work not provided for in the contract shall be allowed, unless a written order to perform such work shall have been given by the engineer; or that the work be subsequently certified by him, and the certificate produced at the time of demanding the payment of the monthly estimate next after such work shall have been performed.

SUB-CONTRACTS.

The contractor will be required to perform the work himself, and no sub-contracts relieving him from the responsibility of a proper performance of his contract will be permitted, unless by the written consent of the president of the company. And no moneys shall be paid to any such sub-contractor for work or materials, without sufficient authority from the principal contractor.

WHEN WORK TO BE COMMENCED.

On the acceptance of a proposal, the chief engineer will give notice thereof to the person proposing, by letter directed to his stated address; and in twenty days from the date of such notice, provided there be no impediment on the part of the company, or in twenty days after such impediment is removed if there be, the work shall be begun with an adequate force, and from that time be prosecuted vigorously until its completion.

HOW TO PROGRESS.

It shall be understood that proper progress is not made, if the amount of work done in each month is not in due proportion to the total amount to be done up to the time fixed for completion by the contract; in which case the engineer shall call the attention of the contractor (or whoever may be in charge of the work if the contractor be absent,) to the fact, and state to him what additional exertion is necessary to be made, and what further force is required, in such reasonable time as may be prescribed.

PUTTING ON MORE FORCE.

In default of the contractor's making such additional exertion, and supplying such force, the chief engineer, or president of the company may have such force sent to the work, and the necessary buildings may be erected to receive them at the contractor's charge and expense, who shall receive the said force in his employ, and work it at whatever price it may have been found necessary to employ it, without diminishing the previous force of the work, and regarding always such extra force as if employed by himself.

CAUSES FOR DETENTION.

There shall be no claim for detention on account of work not being laid out, unless a written notice three days in advance, that it is required, shall have been given to the engineer; and the damage for such detention shall be estimated by the engineer. The right of way shall be furnished by the company, but if it fail to do so for any particular place, damages for detention shall not be claimed unless the contractor be detained full twenty days after he shall have given written notice to the engineer of his wish to commence work at such place. Then the engineer may either estimate to him the amount of damage which he shall take as satisfactory, or he may extend the time of the completion of such work by as many days beyond the contract time, as the contractor is detained beyond the twenty days following his notice to the engineer.

THE ENGINEER.

In all cases where the word "engineer" is used, the engineer in charge of construction is meant; but the directions of any subordinate engineer shall be obeyed when given in regard to any of the ordinary operations, or where they are evidently in accordance with the specifications, or when transmitting the orders of his superiors. In other cases they may be referred to the resident engineer, and finally to the chief engineer, he being the authorized officer, at the time acting in that capacity.

CONTRACTOR.

The word "contractor" applies to and includes all persons contracting jointly, any one of whom shall be considered the authorized agent for and in behalf of his associates, and empowered to receipt payment of moneys, receive and act upon orders.

THE CONTRACT.

87. This is the mutually binding legal article of agreement between the contractor and the company, specifying the times of completing, manner of payment, and describing the work which is to be done. Thus: —

A AND B RAILROAD COMPANY.

Contract.

Graduation on sections A C D,
Masonry on sections A C D,
Ballasting on sections A C D,
Bridging on sections A X T,
Fencing on sections O O O,
Sills and ties on sections O O O,
Track laying on sections O O O.

Articles of agreement made and concluded this first day of January, A. D. 1857, between ——— of the first part, and the A and B Railroad Company of the second part, being a company duly incorporated by the State of ——— of the second part, whereby it is mutually agreed as follows, namely: The said $\substack{\text{party}\\\text{parties}}$ of the first part hereby agree to and with the said party of the second part that $\substack{\text{he}\\\text{they}}$ will perform in a substantial and workmanlike manner the following work, namely: —

[*The work here described.*]

The said work to be performed and completed agreeably to the directions and to the approval of the chief engineer of said company for the time being, and subject to all the general provisions of the specification attached to and forming a part of this agreement, and also subject to such of the special provisions of said specifications as are applicable to the work hereby contracted for.

And in consideration of the full and faithful performance by the said $\substack{\text{party}\\\text{parties}}$ of the first part of this agreement on $\substack{\text{his}\\\text{their}}$

part, the said party of the second part hereby agrees to pay for the same in the time and in the manner hereinafter mentioned, at the rates as follows, namely:—

[*Here insert the items and corresponding prices.*]

It is mutually agreed that this contract applies only to those items to which prices are attached, and that where it embraces both labor and materials introduced in the work, such prices are in full compensation therefor when introduced in the manner required. When it embraces materials only, such prices are in full compensation for the materials and the labor necessary to deliver the same to the company, and when it embraces labor only, such prices are in full compensation for such labor, and every incident to its complete and proper performance. In every case the estimate for ascertaining the amount of compensation shall be made by the engineer from the actual work, from the material furnished, or from that on which the labor contracted for is bestowed.

It is also agreed that partial payments shall be made from time to time during the progress of the work as follows:—

[*Times and manner of payment.*]

And that in thirty days after the contract is fully completed to the satisfaction of the chief engineer of the company for the time being, and the work is surrendered to and accepted by the company, a final measurement and estimate thereof shall be made under the direction of the chief engineer, and be duly certified by him, on the return of which to the president of the company the whole amount then found to be due to the said party parties of the first part shall be paid to him them on demand as follows:—

[*Insert mode of payment.*]

And it is also hereby further agreed, that bank-bills current in the State of ——— shall be accepted for cash in payment for all claims under this contract.

And the said party/parties of the first part further agree/agrees that in twenty days after he/they shall be notified to do so, as provided for in said specifications, he/they will begin the work hereby contracted to be performed, with a force of all kinds sufficient for its completion in the time herein prescribed, and that he/they will finish and deliver the same to the company fully completed in all its parts as follows:—

And the said specifications hereunto annexed are hereby made a component part of this contract and (except so far as any provision therein may not be pertinent to the subject-matter of the contract as may be specially modified herein,) shall be looked to in ascertaining the meaning, extent, and purport of this agreement, and in determining the rights, powers, duties, privileges, and obligations of the contracting parties as to any particular embraced therein.

In virtue whereof the said party/parties of the first part has/have hereunto set his/their hand and seal, and the said party of the second part have caused their president to subscribe his name and affix the corporate seal of the company hereto, all done in triplicate the day and year first above written.

Contractor's name, [SEAL.]
President's name, [SEAL.]

SOLICIT FOR BIDS.

88. The approximate estimates, plans, and profiles being made, and other preliminaries settled, proposals for executing work are solicited by the public papers. Thus:—

NEW YORK, January 1, 1857.
Office of the A and B Railroad Company.

Proposals for executing the graduation, bridging, masonry, and track laying, and for the supply of materials upon the A and B railroad will be received at this office until the 31st day of January, 1857.

Plans, profiles, and schedules of amounts of work may be seen, and blank bids obtained by application at this office.

All proposals must be directed to the chief engineer of the A and B Railroad Company.

No bids will be received after January 31st, at 12, M.

Per order,

C. D., *Secretary A and B R. R. Co.*

FORM FOR A BID.

89. That proposers may make their bids in a convenient form for comparison, a blank, somewhat like the following, is given them to fill out.

Number of Section.		Sec. 1.	Sec. 2.	Sec. 3.	Sec. 4.
Length in miles.		1½	1¼	1¾	1½
Graduation.	Clearing and grubbing, Price per acre, Cost on the section, Earth excavation, Price per yard, Cost on the section, Loose rock excavation, Price per yard, Cost on the section, Solid rock excavation, Price per yard, Cost on the section, Average haul on section, Ballasting, Price per yard, Cost on the section, Whole cost of graduation,				
Masonry.	First class masonry, Price per yard, Cost on the section, Second class masonry, Price per yard, Cost on the section, Third class masonry, Price per yard, Cost on the section, Foundation timber, Cost per M., b'd measure, Cost on the section, Excavation for foundation, Price per yard, Cost on section, Rip rap, Price per yard, Cost on the section, Whole cost of masonry,				
Bridging.	Detailed as above,				
Track laying.					
Fencing.					

This form being filled out, evidently gives the cost of each or all of the items upon any one or all of the sections, the cost of all the items upon any one section being at the foot of that section, and the whole cost of any one item at the extreme right and on the line of that item.

On the bottom of the form is printed, "The undersigned having read the specifications, and made due examination, hereby proposes to the A and B Railroad Company, to perform the work in the above schedule, to which he/they has/have set figures, at those prices and under the conditions described, and upon acceptance of this proposal by the company, binds/bind himself/themselves to enter into a written contract to that effect, and to furnish the required security.

Name,

Address,

Name of Surety,

Address of Surety."

COMPARISON OF BIDS.

90. The bids being received, are compared as follows:—

Name of bidder.	Graduation.					Masonry.				
	Sec. 1.	Sec. 2.	Sec. 3.	Sec. 4.	Total.	Sec. 1.	Sec. 2.	Sec. 3.	Sec. 4.	Total.
A										
B										
C										

Name of bidder.	Bridging.					Superstructure.				
	Sec. 1.	Sec. 2.	Sec. 3.	Sec. 4.	Total.	Sec. 1.	Sec. 2.	Sec. 3.	Sec. 4.	Total.
A B C										

Name of bidder.	Fencing.					Grand Total.
	Sec. 1.	Sec. 2.	Sec. 3.	Sec. 4.	Total.	
A B C						

From which the names may be easily selected either for one or more sections, for any or all of the items, that shall give the least cost.

CHAPTER V.

LAYING OUT WORK.

---

91. The running of the line consists in placing a stake at every one hundred feet upon tangents, and at every fifty feet distance upon sharp curves; also a permanent post at each tangent point, and at points of compound and reversed curvature. This is the centre line, the axis of the road, and the base of all field operations. Whenever the work is going on, the centre pins should be referred to fixed points outside of the ground occupied by the road.

92. The first operation in preparing for excavation is to place side stakes at one half the width of road-bed plus the ditch, on each side of the centre line.

93. Letting out slopes is a term applied to laying off upon the ground, on each side of the centre, the distance to which the slope, commencing at the outer edge of the ditch, will extend, depending upon the angle of slope, width of road-bed and ditch, and depth of cutting. There are here five distinct cases which may occur: —

In embankment when the natural surface is horizontal. In embankment when the natural surface is inclined. In excavation when the natural surface is horizontal. In excavation when the natural surface is inclined.

In mixed work (side hill,) when the road-bed is partly in cut and partly in fill. In both excavation and embankment, when the natural surface is horizontal, we have only to add the cost, in feet and decimals, multiplied by the slope, to one half the width of road-bed plus ditch.

Thus suppose the cut is . . .	20.55 feet,
half the road-bed, ...	10.25 "
ditch, ...	3.00 "
slope $1\frac{1}{2}$ horizontal to 1 vertical,	

and we have

$$(20.55 \times 1\tfrac{1}{2}) + 10.25 + 3.0 = 44.075 \text{ feet.}$$

When the ground is inclined transversely to the axis of the road, first assume a point upon the ground, (apparently right,) find its height above grade with the level, multiply this by the slope and add one half the distance between the outer edge of ditches, and see how near it comes to the measured distance from the centre to the assumed point; if within a foot, it will answer; if not, a second trial will fix the place.

CULVERTS.

94. The length of any structure passing under a railroad embankment is $L - 2\,R\,h$, where L is the distance between slope stakes, R inclination of slopes, h the height of structure from the natural surface. Thus, suppose the distance between slope stakes to be 100 feet, slope $1\frac{1}{2}$ to 1, and h 10 feet, we have

$$L = 100 - (10 \times 1\tfrac{1}{2} \times 2) = 100 - 30 = 70 \text{ feet.}$$

The length of an oblique structure will of course be greater than that of one at right angles to the road; the length depending upon the obliquity.

MASONRY.

95. There are eight general cases which may occur in laying out such structures as bridge abutments with wings.

1. A right bridge on a level tangent.
2. A right bridge on a level curve.
3. A skew bridge on a level tangent.
4. A skew bridge on a level curve.
5. A right bridge on an inclined tangent.
6. A right bridge on an inclined curve.
7. A skew bridge on an inclined tangent.
8. A skew bridge on an inclined curve.

And these eight cases will vary again according to the natural surface of the ground, whether horizontal, or inclined transversely.

96. The general position of wing walls and general form of the line inclosing the base of the bridge, is shown from fig. 31 to fig. 38. Fig. 31 represents case one. The points

Fig. 31.

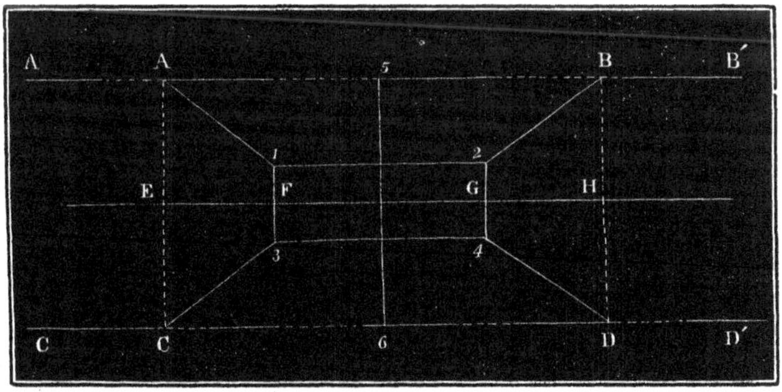

A, B, C, D, are fixed by squares from the centre line at E F, G H.

Fig. 32 represents case two. The wings 3 *c*, 4 *d*, must

Fig. 32.

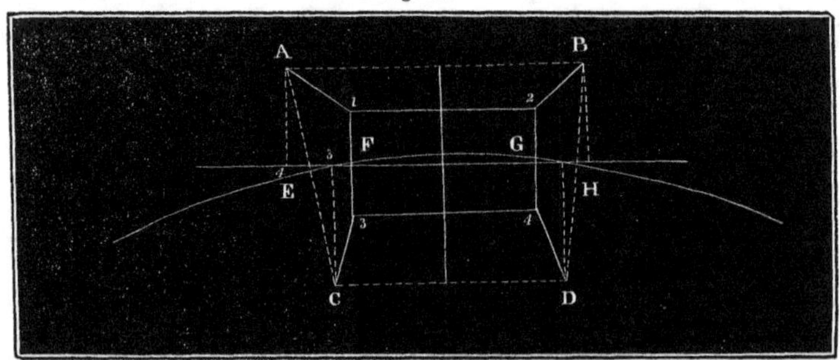

evidently have a different inclination from A 1, B 2. The points A, B, *c*, *d*, 1, 2, 3, 4, as before, are laid off by squares from a tangent to the curve.

Fig. 33 explains itself.

Fig. 33.

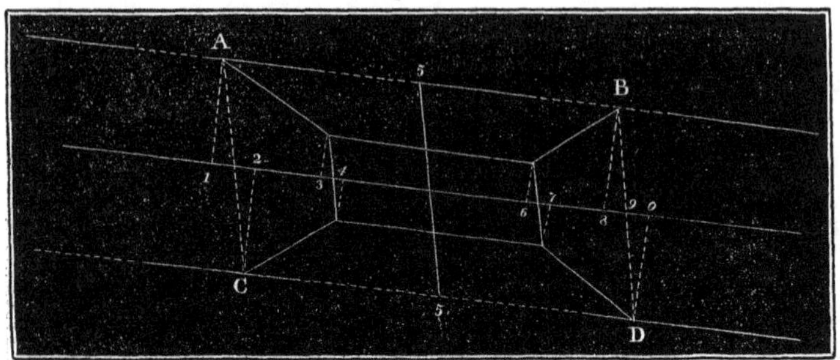

Fig. 34, case five. Here the wings A 1, C 4, are the

Fig. 34.

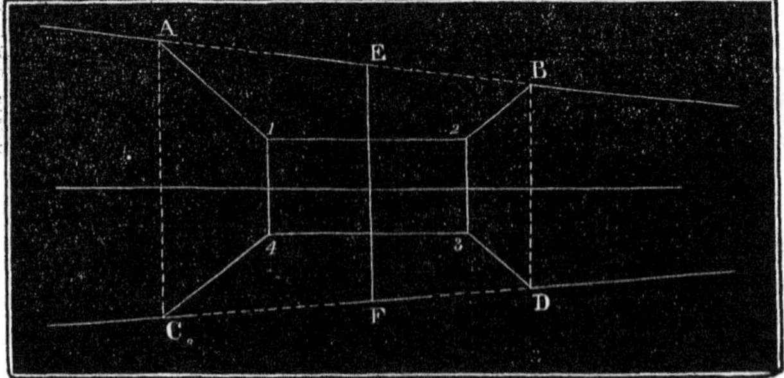

same, as also B 2, D 3, the former being longer, on account of the greater depth of the fill.

Fig. 35, case seven. Here each wing is peculiar; the

Fig. 35.

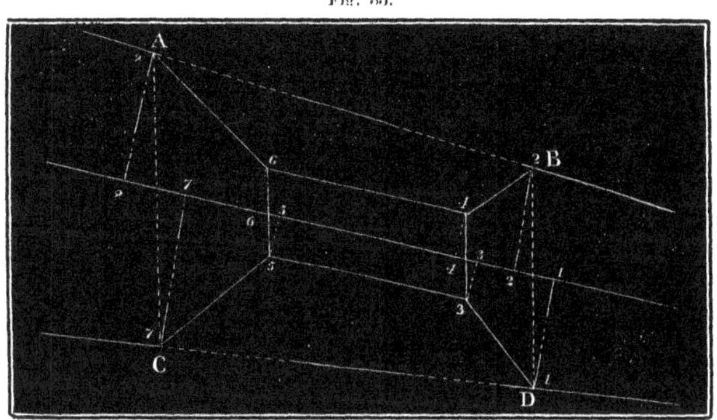

figure being a compound of figs. 33 and 34.

Figs. 36 and 37, case 8. This is the most difficult of all.

Figs. 37 and 38.

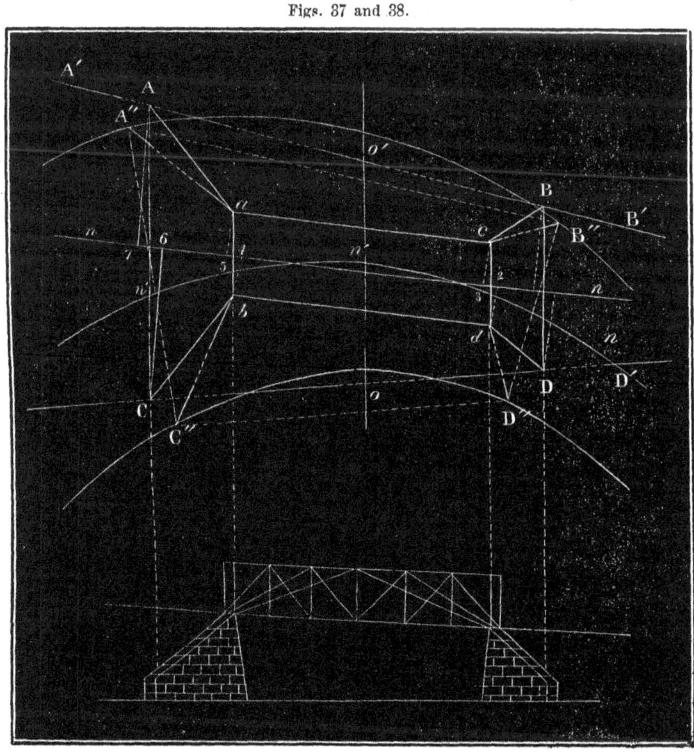

No two wings have the same length or inclination on plan. The natural surface being horizontal, the line inclosing the bridge is A″ B″ C″ D″. If the natural surface descended from C″ to A, the position taken would be A, B, C, D. Fig. 37 is the elevation of the position A B C D. The several points are laid off from the line n, n.

The general manner of fixing the lines of figures 31 to 38, is to assume the angle of some one wing, as A 1, in fig. 34, to draw A C parallel to E F; and from C, the intersection of A C with the base of the embankment, C 4 gives the other wing. Local circumstances will of course often fix at once the length and angle of the wings. Upon simple curves, as in fig. 32, the lines A c and B d are made radial.

97. In curving a viaduct, the axes of the piers are made radial to the centre of the located curve, and the planes of the springing lines are made parallel to the axes of the arches. The pier thus becomes a wedge, and should be strengthened by a starling, upon the outside of the curve, to resist the resultant of the thrusts of two adjoining arches.

98. We should never try to stake out the exact horizontal projection of a complicated piece of work upon rough ground, but only the trenches, which being cut, give a horizontal surface to work upon. In placing the stakes, we must be careful to have them so far outside of the work that they will remain undisturbed while operations are going on. The pegs for cutting pits and trenches may be placed at the angles of the latter, but the working pegs must be so placed that the lines stretched from one to the other will define the masonry. All measurements made in laying out work should be made by graduated rods, and carefully checked.

99. In founding piers, and in aquatic operations generally, two stakes upon the shore, or a fixed transit, will define any line in the water. Two transits will define points.

100. A permanent beach mark should be carefully fixed at each structure, from which its levels may be obtained.

101. In adjusting oblique bridges, care must be taken to so place the bridge seats that the floor beams shall lie in a correct plane, and not be at all warped or winding.

102. As an example of laying out work with regard to heights, take the case of fig. 38. Let the grade of the cen-

Fig. 38.

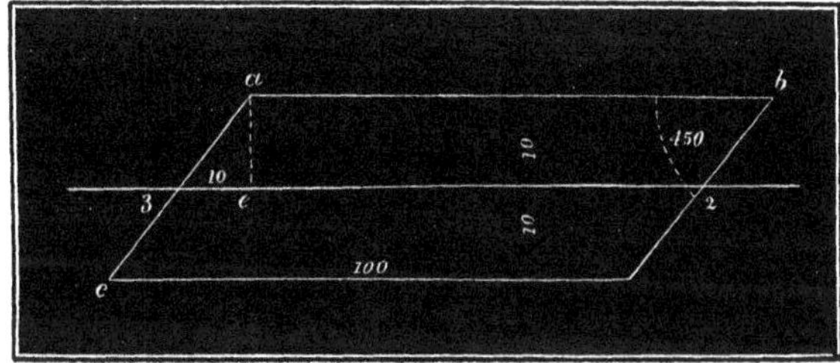

tre line be one in 100, the angle of obliquity 45°, the width of bridge twenty feet, and span on the skew one hundred feet. Required the elevations of the points A, B, C, D.

Assume the height of (2) as	100.00
That of (3) will be	99.00
b, being 10 feet back of 2, is	100.00
and d 0.1 feet less than (2) or	99.90
also $a = 99.00 + 0.10$, or	99.10
and $c = 99.00 - 0.10$, or	98.90.

TUNNELS.

103. The maintaining a correct centre line through tunnels is generally considered difficult. The fixing of the line in deep shafts requires great care, owing to the short distance between the only two fixed points, that can be transferred from the surface to the bottom of the pit. This is a matter of manual skill and of instrumental manipulation.

There is no difficulty in aligning the upper ends of two plumb-lines; and the lower ones will certainly be governed by their position. The following method has been found to answer every purpose.

Let the opening of the shaft be ten feet in diameter. Place two horizontal bars at right angles to the road across the opening, upon which slide blocks holding the upper end of the plumb-lines. Adjust these lines, at the surface, with a transit; and when fixed, place iron pins at the point marked by the plumbs at the bottom of the shaft. Upon these pins fix the exact centres. For keeping the line in the shaft headings, a straight rod, with steel points at each end, should be used, which being placed upon the iron centre pins, fixes the centre line of the tunnel. When the tunnel is curved, the line should be laid off by offsets from the tangent to the curve at the shaft.

By this method points at ten feet distance may be fixed within $\frac{1}{100}$ of an inch, a difference of which would cause an error of $\frac{1}{10}$ of an inch per one hundred, or an inch per thousand feet.

CHAPTER VI.

EARTHWORK.

---

104. The reader is presumed to be acquainted with the manner of finding the areas and cubes of simple geometric figures and bodies. The following fifteen figures show the forms which may be taken by the cross section of a railroad in cutting; for embankment invert the same. They are easily separable into simple figures.

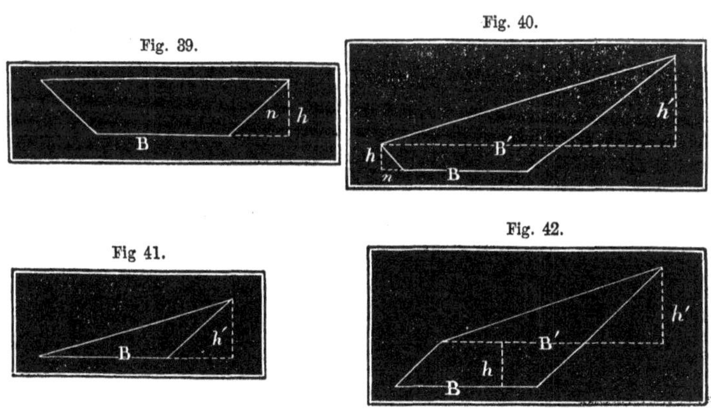

Fig. 39.

Fig. 40.

Fig 41.

Fig. 42.

Fig. 43.

Fig. 44.

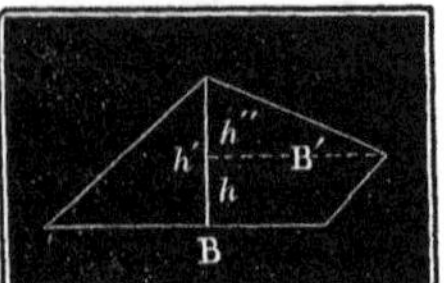

Fig. 45.

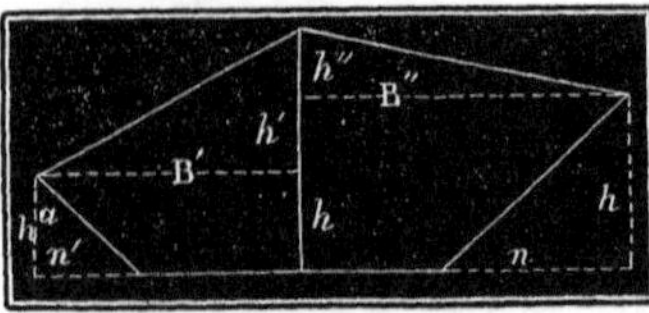

Fig. 46.

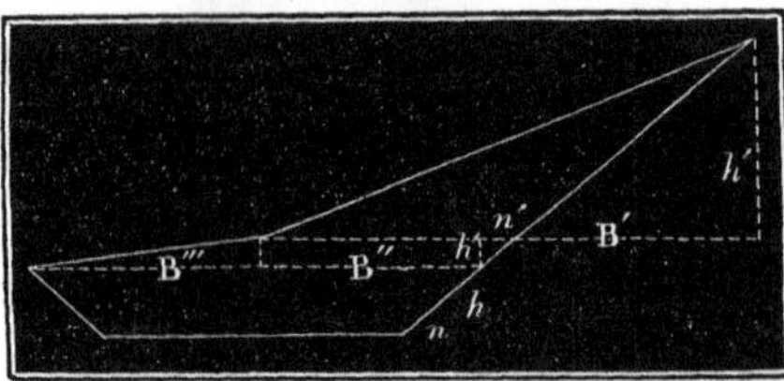

Fig. 47.

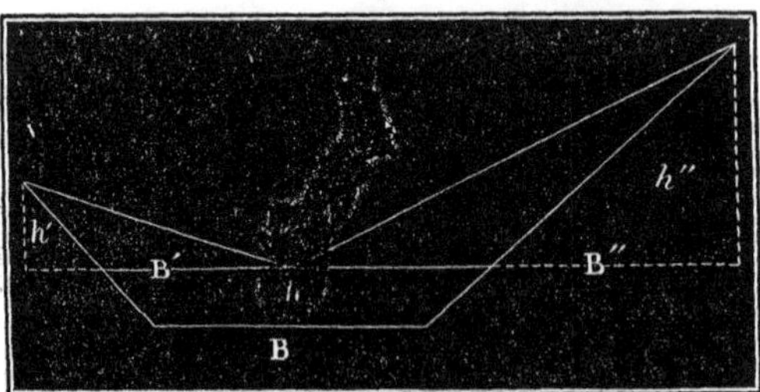

Fig. 48.

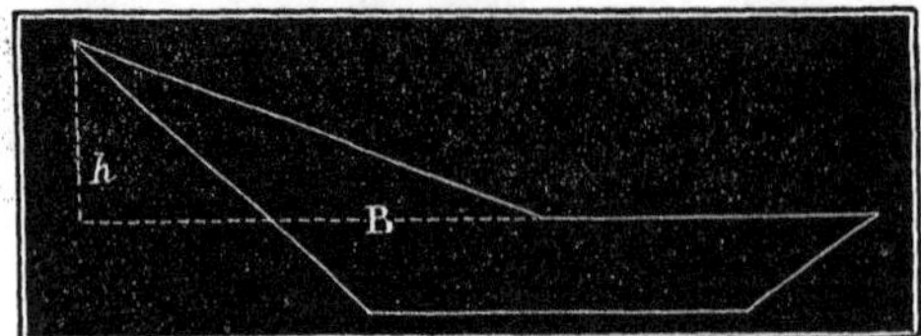

Fig. 49.

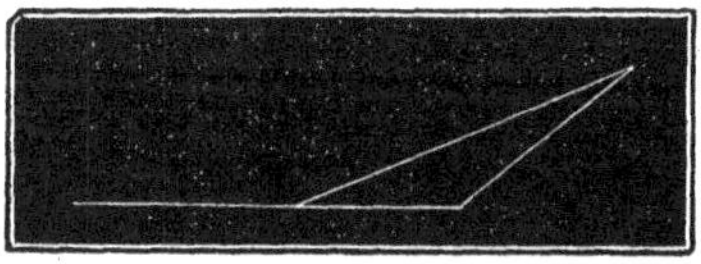

Fig. 50.

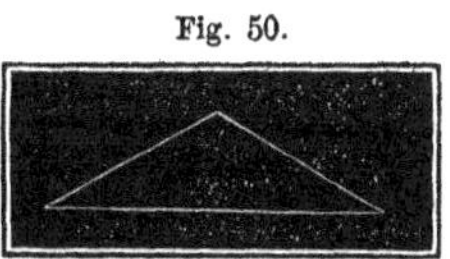

Fig. 51.

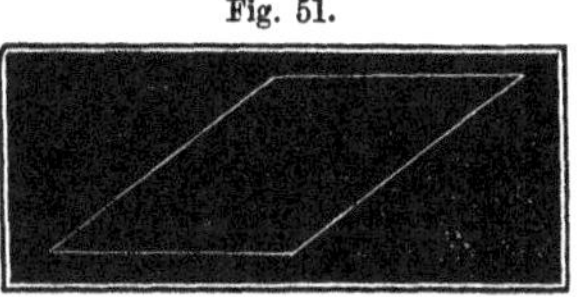

Fig. 52.

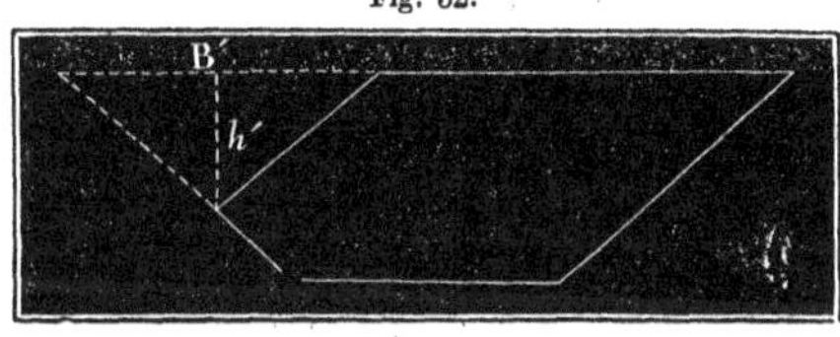

Fig. 53.

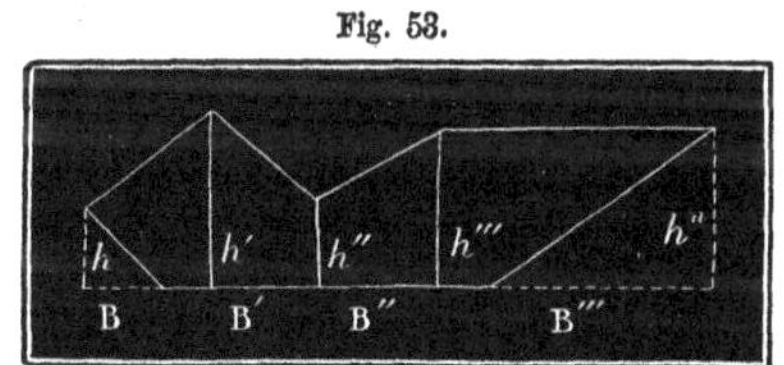

105. The formation of tables for the amount of earth in level cutting is very simple. The area of the following section, where B is the base, and R the horizontal dimension of the slope, is

Fig. 54.

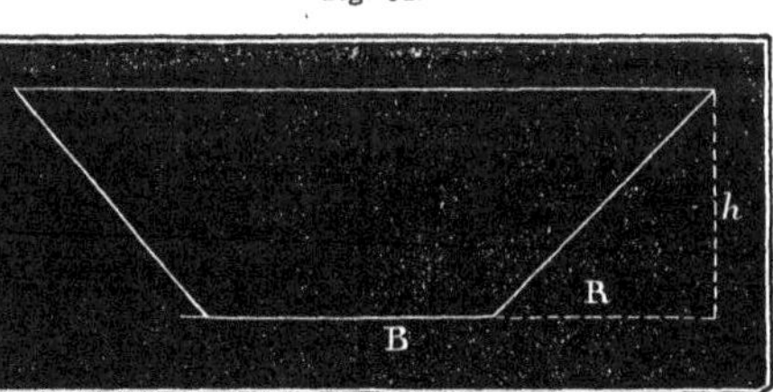

$$\frac{B+B+2\,r}{2} \times h, \text{ or } \frac{2\,B+2\,r}{2} \times h,$$

or finally

$$\underline{B+r} \times h,$$

i. e., the base of a rectangle by its height. Multiply this by 100 and divide the product by 27; or divide by $\frac{27}{100}$, and we have the cubic amount in a prism one hundred feet long. The road-bed being nineteen feet wide, and slopes one and a half to one, the formula for the amount of a prism one hundred feet long is

$$\frac{(19 + 1\frac{1}{2}h)\,h}{0.27},$$

and assuming the base of rock cutting as eighteen feet, and slope one quarter to one, and embankment eighteen feet at subgrade, we have, rock,

$$\frac{(72 + h)\,h}{1.08},$$

and embankment,

$$\frac{(18 + 1\frac{1}{2}h)\,h}{0.27},$$

the figure being inverted for embankment. For a prism of ten or of one thousand feet in length, we have only to move the decimal point. In forming a table, proceed as follows: —

h	$B + 1\frac{1}{2}h$	$\underline{B + 1\frac{1}{2}h} \times h$	$\frac{\overline{B + 1\frac{1}{2}h} \times h}{0.27}$
a	b	c	d
a'	b'	c'	d'
a^n	b^n	c^n	d^n.

It is evident from inspection of fig. 55, that c exceeds c°

Fig. 55.

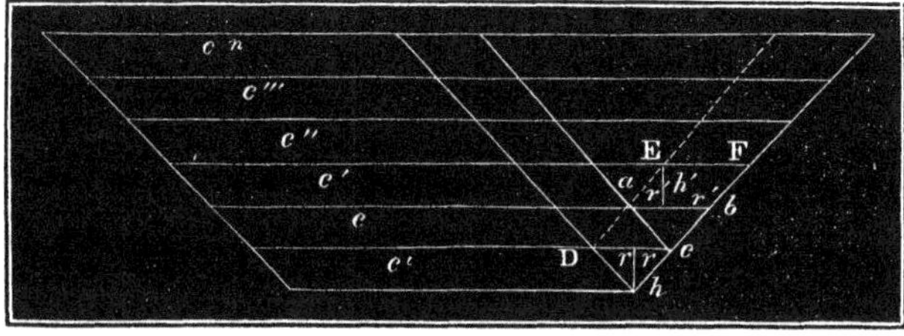

by $h \times 2r$; and that c'' exceeds c' prime by $h' \times 2r'$; and so on as far as we go; this increase being constant, we have then to find the area of c, and for the area $c + c'$ double c, and add the increment; whence the rule:—

Having found the increase (which varies with the angle of the slope) for the *second* section, add the increase to twice the first. For the *third*, add twice the increase to three times the first; and for the nth, add $n - 1$ times the increment to n times the first area, or algebraically calling a the first area, a' the second, a'' the third, a^n the nth area, and we have

The first area	a	$= a$;
The second area	$2a + i$	$= a'$;
The third area	$3a + 2i$	$= a''$;
The nth area	$na + (n - 1)i$	$= a^n$.

We might operate at once upon the cubic contents, but for the length to which some decimals run; some indeed circulating.

106. The table thus made may be of the following form:—

Cut (or fill), in feet.	Cubic yards Earth. Slopes 1½ to 1.	Cubic yards Rock. Slopes ¼ to 1.
1	76	68
2	163	137
3	261	208
4	371	282
5	491	356
6	622	433
7	802	512
8	919	593
9	1083	675
10	1260	759

i. e., cut being eight feet, each one hundred feet length gives nine hundred and nineteen cubic yards; one thousand feet, 9190 yards, and ten feet of length 91.9 cubic yards.

107. The preceding system is intended only for approximate estimates. Let one person read off the cuts or fills from the profile, a second give the corresponding number of yards by the table made as above, while a third sets the figures down; being careful to separate the cuts from the fills.

For final measurements, none but the prismoidal formula should be used; the length of the prismoids being taken at each one hundred feet, and nearer when the ground is rough.

108. As an example of the comparative amounts given by the above formula, and by the common method of averaging end areas, take the following, the slopes being 1½ to 1.

Base.	Distance.	Cut.	End Area.	Mean Area.	Middle Area.
20	0	0	000	000	000
20	50	5	137	069	059
20	50	10	350	244	236
20	50	15	637	493	483
20	50	00	000	318	236

By averaging end areas we have

$$
\begin{aligned}
50 \times 69 &= 3{,}450 \\
50 \times 244 &= 12{,}200 \\
50 \times 493 &= 24{,}650 \\
50 \times 318 &= 15{,}900 \qquad \text{Sum, } 56{,}200.
\end{aligned}
$$

And by the prismoidal formula,

$$
\begin{aligned}
&50 \times 305 \\
&50 \times 1{,}257 \\
&50 \times 2{,}669 \\
&50 \times 1{,}755 \qquad \text{Sum } 299{,}300 \div 6 = 49{,}000,
\end{aligned}
$$

$$\text{and } 56{,}200 - 49{,}000 = 7{,}200$$

cubic feet in favor of the method of end areas.

109. The prismoidal formula is algebraically

$$\frac{a + a' + 4\,a''}{6} L = c,$$

$$
\begin{aligned}
\text{when } L &= \text{length}, \\
c &= \text{cubic contents}, \\
a &= \text{area of one end}, \\
a' &= \text{area of other end}, \\
a'' &= \text{middle area};
\end{aligned}
$$

or, verbally, *to the sum of the end areas add four times the middle area, and multiply the result by one sixth of the length;* the *middle* area being the area made upon the mean height of the two ends. Thus if the length is one hundred feet, and ten feet high, the other twenty feet high, and slopes one and a half to one, the cubic amount is, (the base being twenty-two feet,)

$$\frac{\left[\left(\frac{22+22+30}{2} \times 10\right) + \left(\frac{22+22+60}{2} \times 20\right) + \left(\frac{22+22+45}{2} \times 15 \times 4\right)\right]}{6} \times 100.$$

EXCAVATION AND EMBANKMENT.

110. Some writers have considered that the grades of a road should be so adjusted as to equalize the cutting and the filling. The total rise and fall might not be much affected by this, but the mechanical effect of grades might. A perfect balance between the cuts and fills is not to be desired. The whole cost of earthwork must be a minimum, and it is often cheaper to waste and borrow, than to make any long hauls, and to form the grade line by interchange of material on the profile only.

111. The transverse slopes depend upon the nature of the soil in which the cut is made. Gravel will stand at a slope of one and a half horizontal to one vertical, and in some cases one and a quarter, or even one to one. Clay stands nearly vertical for some time, but finally assumes a very flat slope, in some cases two, three, and even four horizontal to one vertical. In places where a stratum of clay underlies more reliable earth, to avoid a very long slope, it may be economical to support the clay by a wall, and to slope the earth only.

112. Care should be taken in every case to secure good drainage and to protect the slopes by surface drains at the top. The drains in long cuts should be slightly inclined to insure the running off of the water. A fall of ten feet per mile is enough; five will answer in many cases. On side hill cuts a surface drain along the top of the upper slope will do good service. On many high embankments, catchwater drains, commencing at the road-bed and gradually sloping to the base, will prevent, in a great degree, cutting of the bank.

113. Embankments, when made rapidly, should be finished to the full width, somewhat above true grade, to allow for the after settlement. (See specification.)

114. The following allowances have been made for the shrinkage of material in some parts of America.

Light, sandy earth	0.12
Clayey earth	0.10
Gravelly earth	0.08
Gravel and sand	0.09
Loam	0.12
Clay	0.10
Clay puddled	0.25
Wet surface earth	0.15

The bulk of quarried rock on the contrary increases from twenty-five to fifty per cent.

115. When embankments are carried up slowly, in layers of three or four feet at a time, the after settling is very little; when carried up all at once it will be more. The full width must be kept, even above the required height. Fig. 56 shows the forms of a bank both before and after settlement.

Fig. 56.

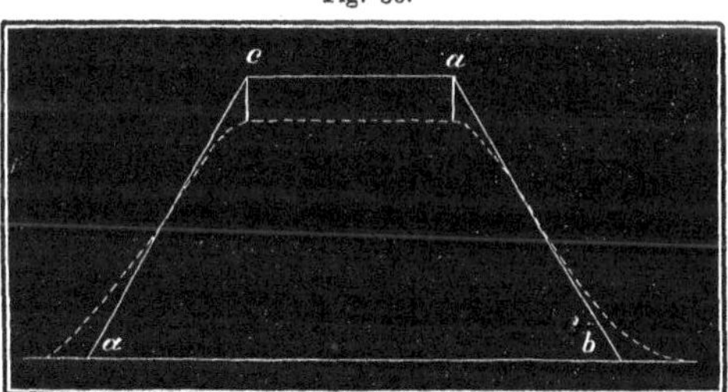

The best method of forming a bank of bad material is to ram the layers as in fig. 57; thus the tendency is to consolidate by settling, and not to destroy the work by sliding.

Fig. 57.

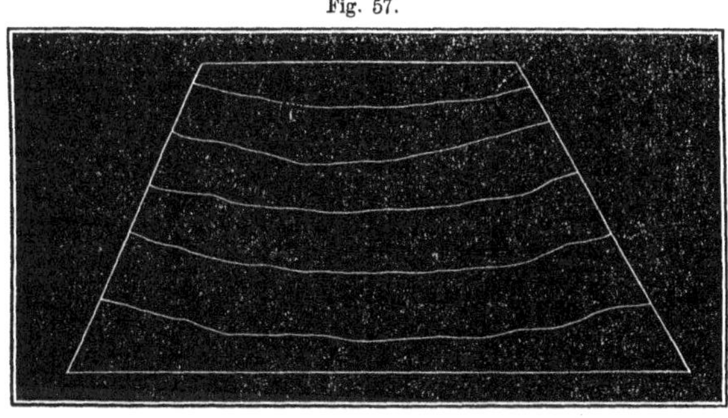

TRANSPORT OF MATERIAL.

116. In the formation of embankments it is not always advisable to make the whole bank from an adjoining cut or cuts. The length of haul may be too long. In this case it is customary to waste a part of the cut and to borrow earth from some nearer point for the bank. That the transport shall be effected in the most economical manner, the product of the cube of earth, by the mean distance, (the distance between the centres of gravity, of excavation and embankment) must be a minimum. To determine the theoretical minimum expense, the problem becomes very complicated on account of the great number of variable elements entering therein; and the result obtained is applicable only to a particular case. Local circumstances more than any other thing, determine the position of a borrow pit, and the path over which the material is to be transported.

OF THE AVERAGE HAUL.

117. To find the cost of the movement of earth on any section, we must have, the total amount of earth to be moved, and the *average haul;* the latter being the distance through which, if the whole amount were moved, the cost would be the same as the sum of the costs of moving the partial amounts their respective distances. To find the average haul proceed as follows: *First,* find the distance between the centres of gravity of each mass both before and after moving, which may be done with sufficient accuracy for practice by inspection of the profile. *Next,*

118. *Divide the sum of the products of the partial amounts by their respective hauls, by the total amount;* the result is the average haul in feet. Or algebraically, representing the partial amounts by m, m', m'', m''', the respective hauls by

d, d', d'', d''', the total amount by S, and the average haul by D, we have

$$\frac{m\,d + m'\,d' + m''\,d'' + m'''\,d'''}{S} = D.$$

Example. — Let column 1 show the partial amounts in cubic yards. Column 2 the corresponding hauls.

$$\begin{array}{rcr} 1{,}000 \times 200 & = & 200{,}000 \\ 2{,}000 \times 300 & = & 600{,}000 \\ 5{,}000 \times 400 & = & 2{,}000{,}000 \\ 8{,}000 \times 600 & = & 4{,}800{,}000 \\ \hline 16{,}000 & & 7{,}600{,}000 \end{array}$$

and $\frac{7{,}600{,}000}{16{,}000} = 475$ feet *average haul.*

Proof. — Assume the cost of moving 1,000 yards one foot as ten cents, the costs of the separate masses are

1,000 yards	200 feet is		$20.00
2,000 "	300 "		60.00
5,000 "	400 "		200.00
8,000 "	600 "		480.00
		Sum,	$760.00

also the cost of moving 16,000 yards 475 feet is

$$16 \times 475 \times 10 = \$760.00.$$

119. The movement of earth is effected by shovels, barrows, horses and carts, or by cars. In round numbers we can move earth

By shovels alone	10 to 20 feet,
By barrows alone	20 to 100 "
By carts	100 to 500 "
By cars	500 to 5,000 "

As the haul increases, the number of vehicles of transport remaining the same, the number of excavators must decrease. Earths easily removed do not admit of so large a haul, with a given number of excavators, as hard earths. The nature of the ground, form of carts, kind of horses, season of the year, and price of labor are some of the elements entering the problem of transport. The best illustration of the matter will be found among the very able writings of Elwood Morris, Esq., C. E., in the Journal of the Franklin Institute. Knowing the value of wages, the nature of the earth and length of haul, it is easy to see what mode of transport must have the preference.

CONTRACTOR'S MEASUREMENTS.

120. The price of executing any piece of work is paid to the contractor at stated intervals, generally once each month. The amount of work done at these partial payments is obtained by instrumental reference to the ground. Towards the completion of operations the most correct and easiest method of finding the rate of progress is to deduct the amount already done from the total as given by primary measurement. The full price is not paid to the contractor, but a percentage is kept back, which insures a faithful performance of work. It is impossible to establish a *pro rata* price at first, owing to the uncertain nature of the work; what appears to be earth may be rock. By deducting a maximum price estimate for all but one of the items, an approximate *pro rata* value for that one may be determined. An analysis of cost will define the minimum limit for advantage to the contractor; and the *pro rata* value less the percentage, the maximum for the company's benefit.

DRAINING.

121. When a level is to be drained, or the water carried off from the surface of a swamp, the first point to be ascertained is the location of the lowest outfall. The direction in which aquatic plants lie show the natural fall of the water, these always pointing down stream. When the most available outlet has been decided upon, a main drain should be set out, from which oblique branches are to be cut, pointing in the direction of the current; into these all minor cuts are to be collected so that the whole district may be equally drained. The fall should be greatest at the most remote points, decreasing as the amount of water increases. Large and deep rivers run sufficiently fast when the fall is one foot per mile. For small rivers, double that is necessary. Ditches and ordinary drains require eight feet per mile. When the water is made to pass away from the surface, it should flow very gradually, that the sides and bottom of the ditches may not be worn away by friction; it should be in constant motion that the channel may be kept clean and increase in velocity as it proceeds. When the surface is a perfect level, the drains should of course be made straight.

After the quantity of water has been determined by careful observation, the section of the main and branches must be fixed, so that regarding both their areas and velocities, the main drain will not be overcharged.

To facilitate the current, the sides should be inclined about one and a quarter to one; and the breadth of base should be two thirds of the depth of water. These results are obtained from the practice of English engineers, who have given a great deal of attention to the subject.

Drains cut through bogs, may have sides nearly, if not quite vertical, as the fibres of plants forming the soil resist the action of the water.

SUBSOIL DRAINING.

Geology has assisted this operation very materially by rendering us acquainted with the quality and nature, as well as of the succession of strata. The soils which are impervious are usually the heaviest, and the porous are those of lighter quality. Clays, when they receive water, will only part with it by evaporation, when left in a natural state; and therefore to make such a surface fit for a useful end requires considerable ingenuity, and often great expense. Such a soil is not rendered unstable by underground springs, and may be effectually drained by boring through, and letting the water off into an under stratum, when this is of a porous nature.

When land abounds with springs, or is subject to the oozing out of subterraneous water, draining is effected in a different manner. Springs have their origin in the accumulation of rain water, which falling upon the earth, after passing the porous strata, lodges upon the impervious, and glides along the sloping surface until it crops out, generally in some valley where it forms a watercourse.

Descending streams are easily taken care of by collecting them into a body before they reach the low lands.

When a morass is to be drained, the strata upon which it reposes should be examined, and if, as is often the case, a layer of clay intervenes between the substratum and the mossy covering, which holds the water, by tapping this in well chosen places, the whole will sink away.

A fine example of embankment upon a bad bottom was

performed by Mr. Stephenson, on the Great Western Railroad, England, at the crossing of Chatmoss. This moss was so soft that cattle could not walk upon it, and an iron bar sank into it by its own weight. The moss was first thoroughly drained by a system of longitudinal and cross drains, and the embankment made of the lightest material possible — the dried moss itself. Without this treatment, the moss would have sank beneath the bank alone; it now supports the passage of the heaviest railroad trains.

METHOD OF CONDUCTING OPERATIONS.

122. The organization of the engineer corps upon a railroad is as follows, differing somewhat in different parts of the country.

The Chief Engineer has entire charge of all the work, of all assistants, appointing and dismissing members of the corps, designing of all structures, making of specifications, and of all mechanical operations incident to the thorough, correct, and timely construction of the road; and should be able also to specify, generally, the amount and character of the equipment needed.

The Resident Engineer has charge of the detailed construction of from twenty-five to fifty miles of road, according to the nature of the work, being responsible to the chief engineer for the proper execution of the orders from headquarters; he returns to the chief engineer a monthly account of the exact condition of his work, both as to the amount executed, and also that remaining to be done.

The assistants of the resident engineer are a leveller and transit man; to whom, under his supervision, is the duty of laying out, measuring, and estimating the work. The leveller has with him one or more rodmen. The transit man, two chainmen, and one or more axemen.

In some cases, added to the above are inspectors of masonry, bridging, and superstructure. These are necessary only when the road embraces a great number of mechanical structures; too many to leave the proper time to the resident engineer for his other duties. Once each month the exact amount of graduation, bridging, and masonry *executed* is obtained by the resident and his assistants. The chief engineer applies the prices to these amounts, and the percentage deduction being made, the estimate is ready for the treasurer.

123. The abstract prepared from the monthly estimate should show clearly, without unnecessary figures, the amount of work completed, and also that remaining to be done.

For convenience, the various blanks used on railroads should fold to the same form and size. The blanks are,

The Contract,
The Specification,
The Resident Engineer's Monthly Return,
The Assistant's Weekly and Monthly Returns,
The Force Return,
The Pay Roll,
Vouchers.

The contract and specification are given in chapter IV. The resident's monthly return to the chief engineer is somewhat as follows: —

Monthly return of work done on the *first* division of the A and B Railroad, for the month ending ——, showing also the whole amount of work up to ——; also the present estimate for completion.

Section.	Contractor.	GRADUATION.											
		Clearing and Grubbing.						Excavation.					
		In July.			Total to date.			In July.			Total to date.		
		Acres.	Price.	Am't.	Acres.	Pr.	Am't.	Yards.	Pr.	Am't.	Yards.	Pr.	Am't.
1		15	100	1500	300	100	30000	44000	10	4400	100000	10	10000

MASONRY.														
First Class.						Second Class.		Third Class.		Foundation in Excavation.		Foundation Timber.		
In July.			Total to date.			In July.	Tot. to date.	In July.	Tot. to date.	In July.	Tot. to date.	In July.	Tot. to date.	
Yds.	Pr.	Am't.	Yds.	Pr.	Am't.									

BRIDGING AND TIMBERWORK.								
Truss Bridges.								
In July.			Total to date.			Pile Bridges.	Stringer Bridges.	Trestling.
Feet.	C.	Am't.	Feet.	C.	A m't.			

SUPERSTRUCTURE AND FENCING.							
Superstructure.						Fencing.	
In July.			Total to date.			In July.	Total to date.
Miles.	Price.	Am't.	Miles.	Price.	Am't.		

VALUE OF WORK AND PAYMENTS MADE.				
Value of Work In July.	Amount paid in July.	Whole value to date.	Whole amount paid.	Amount left due.

VALUE OF LABOR.				
Foreman and Mechanics.	Laborers.	Carts with Horses.	Carts with Oxen.	Whole value.

RECAPITULATION.		
Value of work done in July.	Value of work up to date.	Remaining Value.

The resident engineer's assistants return to him weekly a statement of the amount and value of the force employed upon the several sections, and monthly the exact amount of work done on the same, for each of which there should be a blank. The above forms may be printed and folded in 8vo., or may be the continuous headings of a large sheet.

CHAPTER VII.

ROCKWORK.

---

125. The sides of rock excavation are sometimes cut to a small slope, as one fourth or one fifth horizontal to one vertical, and sometimes cut quite perpendicularly. The earth, when it occurs, which covers the rock, is first taken out at the proper slope; a loam of one or two feet being left between the foot of the earth and the crest of the rock.

126. Rock is taken out one or two feet below grade, as well as earth, to allow the introduction of the necessary ballast.

127. The most common mode of removing rock is by blasting; for this holes are drilled by steel-edged jumpers, worked either by hand or by steam. The first object in cutting a passage through rock, is to open a working face, so as to get the necessary lines of least resistance, (this line is that by which the powder finds the least opposition to a rent at right angles to the length of the drill); these lines should, if possible, be at right angles to the beds of stratification; the holes should be drilled parallel to the seams of the rock, as the powder will then lift off the strata. In working a vertical face, it may be best to blast out the lower part first, and so undermine the overhanging mass.

128. The amount of powder in different charges to produce proportional results should be as the cube of the line of least resistance; for example:—

$$2^3 \text{ is to } 4\text{oz. as } 3^3 \text{ is } 13\tfrac{1}{2}\text{oz.},$$

or

$$8 \text{ to } 4 \text{ as } 27 \text{ to } 13\tfrac{1}{2};$$

and generally,

$$L^3 : w :: L'^3 : w';$$

whence

$$w' = \frac{w\ L'^3}{L^3}.$$

129. The following charges corresponding to lines of least resistance are from the works of Sir John Burgoyne.

Line of least resistance.	Charge of powder.
2 feet,	0 lbs. 4 oz.
4 "	2 " 0 "
6 "	6 " 12 "
8 "	16 " 0 "

130. After the powdered stone is removed, the powder is placed in the lower part of the hole; after which a wad of turf, or some other light material, follows; next the tamping of powdered brick, dried clay, or something similar, and finally a stopper of wet clay, or some other firm substance. A hole is left through all, communicating with the powder by ramming the tamping around a wire; through this hole a fuse is inserted by which to light the charge. The most perfect tamping would offer a resistance as great as that by the natural rock. A great improvement upon the above method is the sand blast; the powder is put in, and the hole filled with loose, dry sand, simply poured in and settled by a gentle stirring, but not at all rammed; the explosion of the powder spreads the sand as a wedge, and causes

the power of the blast to be exerted sideways. In some cases a small cone of wood has been placed (base down) in the hole with the sand, which aids very much in stopping the exit of the blast through the drill.

131. Of late years an admirable method of lighting large charges simultaneously has been employed, namely, volcanic electricity.

132. A gigantic example of the application of this method has been furnished by the English engineers in overthrowing a portion of Round Drum Cliff, about two miles from Dover, (England). Two chambers, 13 × 5½ × 4½, and one 10 × 5½ × 4 feet were cut in the rock. Within these were placed fifty bags of powder, amounting in all to eight and one half tons. The charges were lighted by the voltaic system, by which operation a mass of rock (chalk) 380 × 360 × 80 feet, amounting to 400,000 cubic yards, was thrown into the sea, and by which there was estimated to have been saved nearly $40,000.

133. The following table from Colonel Puseling's memoranda on mining, shows the capacity of different drills for powder, by weight, and also the depth of holes of different diameters, to contain one pound of powder.

Diameter of hole in inches.	Ounces of powder in one inch depth.	Powder in one foot deep.		Depth of hole in inches to contain one pound.
		lbs.	oz.	
1	0.4	0	5.0	38.2
1½	0.9	0	11.3	16.9
2	1.7	1	4.1	9.5
2½	2.6	1	15.4	6.1
3	3.7	2	13.2	4.2
3½	5.1	3	13.5	3.1
4	6.7	5	0.4	2.4
4½	8.4	6	5.7	1.9
5	10.5	7	13.6	1.5
5½	12.7	9	8.0	1.3
6	15.1	11	4.9	1.0

134. Blasting under water has been practised to some extent, and with great success by Messrs. Maillefaut and Raasloff, both in New York harbor and in the St. Lawrence River. The method is merely to explode bodies of powder *upon the surface of the rock*, the water itself being a sufficient source of reaction to the blast.

TUNNELLING.

135. Tunnels are driven through hills to avoid very deep cutting. When in rock of a solid nature, the roof supports itself; but when in earth or in loose rock, an artificial arched lining becomes necessary. Figs. 58 and 59 show sections in both rock and earth; the insert *b b* is placed in a bed of concrete. In excavating earth, a temporary roof is made use of while the work is in progress, which is afterwards replaced by an arch of brick or stone. The back of the arch must be closely wedged, quointed, and the earth well rammed in.

Fig. 58.

Fig. 59.

The great disadvantages attending the construction of tunnels are want of air, light, room, and drainage. To facilitate the latter requirement, a very light grade may be introduced; this may easily be done, as they generally occur on summits, or on the approach to summits; $\frac{1}{1000}$ or five feet per mile is sufficient.

In working a tunnel which is upon a grade, one end naturally drains itself if the approach is taken out; the other drains the wrong way, to meet which obstacle we must resort to pumps which follow the work, keeping always in the lowest place, or by sinking a well at the shaft through which the water is raised to the surface.

The ventilation of tunnels is effected by drawing off the bad air when a fresh supply must enter.

136. In taking out the rock, the expense will depend much upon the nature and stratification of the rock encountered.

SHAFTS.

137. In tunnels of considerable length, a long time would be consumed in working from the ends only. In such cases it is customary to sink shafts at the most convenient places (the shallowest when at the proper distance,) and to commence at the bottom of these to work both ways. This operation involves considerable expense, as all draining, ventilating, and removal of excavated materials must be effected through the shaft.

In leaving openings for the exit of smoke and for admission of light in artificial arches, regard must be had to their position. They should be at the springing rather than at the crown of the arch, as they will thus less affect the strength of the masonry.

The approaches of tunnels in cities and in other places where appearance is of importance, are furnished with face coping and wings.

138. Tunnels, when conducted in the most expeditious

manner, require for their completion a long time. The following table shows the rate of progress upon some of the most important tunnels of America.

Name of Tunnel.	Length in feet.	Time in days.	Average daily advance, in feet.
*Penn Railroad,	3,612	697	5.18
*Kingwood B. & O. R. R.	4,100	750	5.47
Board Tree B. & O. R. R.	2,250	675	3.32
*Welling, B. & O. R. R.	1,240	524	2.37
Pacific Railroad,	700	210	3.33
Pittsburgh and Connelsville, (estimated)	4,500	810	5.56
General average daily advance, in feet,			4.205

Those marked * being for a double track.

The following table also gives the time and cost of other tunnels in different parts of the world.

Name and location of tunnel.	Material.	Length in feet.	Time in days.	Daily average in feet.	Section.	Cost per foot.
						$
Nerthe, France,	Hard limestone	15,153	——		$29\frac{1}{2} \times 26\frac{1}{4}$	
Riqueral "	Chalk	18,623	2,139	8.7	$26\frac{1}{4} \times 26\frac{1}{4}$	39.89
Pouilly, "	Chalk & clay	10,928	2,504	4.4	$20\frac{1}{3} \times 20\frac{1}{3}$	113.96
Arscherville, France,	——	7,348	1,878	3.9	$26\frac{1}{4} \times 26\frac{1}{4}$	68.38
Maurage, "	——	15,752	2,085	7.5	$25\frac{1}{2} \times 25\frac{1}{2}$	94.43
Rolleboise "	Chalk	8,670	626	13.9	25×25	62.98
Roule, "	——	5,645	522	10.8	25×25	62.98
Lioran, "	——	4,548	2,087	2.2	$21\frac{1}{3} \times 21\frac{1}{3}$	56.98
Kilsby, England,	Clay and sand	7,233	1,252	5.8	$27 \times 23\frac{1}{2}$	194.31
Belchingly, "	Blue clay	3,972	626	6.3	24×25	102.86
Thames & Medway, Eng'd,	Chalk	11,880	939	12.6	$30 \times 38\frac{2}{3}$	45.59
Box, England,	Marble, freestone and marl	9,680	1,252	7.7	35×39	148.15
Harecastle, England,	Rock and sand	8,778	939	9.3	14×16	57.05
Nochistingo, Mexico,	Clay and marl	21,659	287	75.4	$13\frac{3}{4} \times 11\frac{1}{2}$	——
Blisworth, England,	Rock and clay	9,240	2,191	4.2	$16\frac{1}{2} \times 18$	23.18
Supperton, "	Rock	12,900	1,878	6.9	15×15	12.44
Black Rock, W. S.	Greywacke slate	1,932	——	——	$19 \times 17\frac{1}{4}$	77.18
Blaisy, France,	Chalk and clay	13,455	1,043	12.9	$26\frac{1}{4} \times 26\frac{1}{4}$	136.06
Edge Hill, England,	Clay & freestone	6,600	——	——	22×16	30.15
Littlebourg, "	——	8,607	590	14.6	$27\frac{1}{2} \times 24$	129.61
Woodhead, "	Millstone	15,840	1,800	8.8	——	——

The cost per cubic yard for excavating tunnels in some places has been as follows: —

Name.	Material.	Cost per cubic yard.
Blackrock, U. S.	hard greywache slate,	$6.60
Lehigh, U. S.	very hard granite,	4.36
Schuylkill, U. S.	slate,	2.00
Union, U. S.	slate,	2.08½
Blue Ridge, U. S.	———,	4.00

The Blue Ridge tunnel on the Virginia Central Railroad is 4,280 feet long, made for a single track, 21×15 feet. Lining about four feet thick. Excavation where lining is used is 26×23.

The Hoosac tunnel (Massachusetts) is proposed to be four and one half miles long, 23×22 feet section. To have two shafts eight hundred and fifty and seven hundred and fifty feet deep, and ten feet in diameter.

Artificial ventilation becomes necessary in headings over four hundred and fifty or five hundred feet in length.

The cost of the shafts of the Belchingly tunnel, (England,) ninety-seven feet deep, and ten and one half feet in diameter, cut through blue clay, and lined, was $68.44 per yard down.

The shafts of the Blaisy tunnel average five hundred feet deep, through clay and chalk and loose earth, (being lined,) cost $139.11 per yard down.

The shafts of the Black Rock tunnel, one hundred and thirty-nine feet deep, in hard slate, cost $18.72 per cubic yard.

CHAPTER VIII.

WOODEN BRIDGES.

---

139. WOODEN bridging, owing to its cheapness and fitness for universal application, has been and is being adopted in all parts of the country. Almost any variety of form may be seen upon our railroads, and though less durable than stone or iron, it may with proper precaution be made to last a long time.

OF THE FORCES AT WORK IN BRIDGES.

140. There are four distinct strains to which a piece of timber or a bar of metal may be exposed, each of which tends to destroy the piece in a different manner. The amount and character of these strains, depend upon the position of the bar or beam, and upon the direction of the force.

A beam may be pulled apart by stretching,— *Tension.*
It may be destroyed by crushing,— *Compression.*
It may be broken transversely,— *Cross strain.*
It may be crushed across the grain,— *Detrusion.*

TENSION.

141. If one thousand pounds were hung from the end of a suspended timber, so that the direction of the weight coincides with the axis of the timber, then will the tension upon the beam be one thousand pounds.

If the direction of the force is vertical, and the beam is inclined, then the strain is increased by as much as the diagonal of inclination exceeds the vertical; for example, let one thousand pounds be suspended from the lower end of a beam ten feet long, inclined at an angle of 45°. The diagonal being ten, the vertical will be 7.07 feet, and the strain is increased as follows: —

7.07 to 10 as 1,000 to 1,414 lbs.

As the angle of inclination, from the horizontal, increases, the strain from a given load decreases, until the beam is vertical, when a weight acts with its least power.

COMPRESSION.

142. If a vertical post is loaded with one thousand pounds, the compressive strain upon that post will also be one thousand pounds. If a post is inclined, the amount of strain is increased, as noticed in the case of tension, and to the same amount, that is, depending upon the inclination.

A piece of wood or metal acting as a post, or pillar, must not only be able to resist crushing, but also bending or bulging laterally.

143. A cylinder of which the length is only seven or eight times the diameter, will not bulge by any force that can be applied to it longitudinally, but will split. When the length exceeds this, it will be destroyed by a similar movement to that produced by a cross strain. When the

length of a cast-iron pillar is thirty diameters, the fracture is produced by bending alone; when less, partly by bending and partly by fracture. When the column is cast hollow, and enlarged towards the middle, the strength is increased in a very great ratio.

144. The formula for finding the weight which any beam acting as a post, will support before bending, is, according to Barlow, who considers the weight as varying inversely as the length, as follows:—

$$\frac{W L^2}{80 E} = b d^3,$$

and the value of W is

$$\frac{b d^3 \times 80 E}{L^2},$$

and the weight being given, and the sectional dimensions assumed, we have

$$d = \sqrt[3]{\frac{W L^2}{80 E b}},$$

and

$$b = \frac{W L^2}{80 E d^3},$$

Where W represents the weight in pounds,
L " " length in feet,
E " a constant,
d " the depth in inches,
b " " breadth in inches.

CROSS STRAIN.

145. The amount of strain caused by any weight applied in a transverse direction, to a beam supported at both ends, is as the breadth, as the length inversely, and as the

square of the depth. Whatever depression takes place, tends to shorten the upper, and to extend the under-side; whence the fibres of the top part suffer compression, and those of the bottom extension. The amounts of compression and extension must of course be equal, and therefore if any material resists these two strains in a different degree, the number of fibres opposing each will also be different.

The top being compressed, while the bottom is extended, of course at some point within the beam there exists a line which suffers neither compression nor extension. The position of this line (the neutral axis) depends upon the relative power of the material to oppose the strains, upon its form and upon its position. Thus if wood resists two thousand pounds per square inch of extension, and one thousand pounds of compression, the axis will be twice as far from the top as from the bottom.

In some materials the neutral axis changes its place while the bar is at work; thus wrought iron, after being a little compressed, will bear a great deal more compression than when in its original state; also the lower fibres, after being extended, will resist less than at first; the effect of which two actions is to move the neutral axis up.

146. The following table shows the relative resisting powers of wood, wrought and cast-iron; with the corresponding positions of the axis, with sufficient accuracy for practice.

Material.	Resistance to extension.	Resistance to compression.	Ratio.	Distance of axis from top, in fractions of the depth.
Wrought iron,	90	66	$\frac{90}{69}$	$\frac{90}{156}$ or 0.58
Cast-iron,	20	140	$\frac{20}{140}$	$\frac{20}{160}$ or 0.13
Wood,	2	1	$\frac{2}{1}$	$\frac{2}{3}$ or 0.66

Thus in beams subjected to a cross strain, as well as to a

direct extensive or compressive one, the resistance is effected by the incompressibility and inextensibility of the material.

147. The formula for dimensioning any beam to support a given weight transversely is

$$S = \frac{4\,b\,d^2}{e},$$

Where S represents the ultimate strength in lbs.
b " " breadth in inches,
d " " depth "
e " " length "

DETRUSION.

148. Detrusion, or crushing across a fixed point, is such as occurs wherever a brace abuts against a chord, or where a bridge bears upon a bolster or wall plate; also the shearing of bolts, pins, and rivets.

GENERAL RESISTANCE OF MATERIALS.

149. The resistance to extension, to compression, (as regards simple crushing,) and to detrusion, is as the area of cross section; i. e., if we double the area, we double the strength. The resistance to a cross strain is *as the breadth, as the length inversely*, and *as the square of the depth;* i. e. if we double the breadth we double the strength; if we double the length, we divide the strength by two; and if we double the depth, we multiply the strength by four.

ACTUAL STRENGTH OF MATERIALS.

150. Any material will bear a much larger load for a short time than for a long one. The weight that does not so injure materials as to render them unsafe, is from one

third to one fourth only of the ultimate strength. Throughout the present work one fourth will be the most that will in any case be used.

WROUGHT IRON.

151. *Extension.*

	lbs. per square inch.
Mean of 17 experiments by Barlow (p. 270)	62,720
Weisbach's Mechanics (Vol. ii., p. 71)	60,500
Overman's Mechanics, (p. 408, 409)	61,333
Brown, Rennie, and Telford, (mean)	67,200
The mean	62,451
Reducing by 4 for safety	15,613

Or in round numbers 15,000 lbs. per square inch, is the resistance of wrought iron to extension, to be used in practice.

152. *Compression.*— Great discrepancies appear among writers on the strength of materials, as to the compressive strength of wrought iron. Though all estimate the resistance to compression, as great as to extension, yet no one in summing up the general result of experiment, places the former at more than from 50 to 75 per cent. of the latter. William Fairbairn gives, as the relative resistances to extension and compression in bars applied as girders, 2 to 1.

We have by Weisbach	56,000
" " Rondelet	70,000
" " Hodgekinson	65,000
The mean	63,667
Reducing by 4	15,917
In round numbers	16,000 lbs. per square inch.

As far as practice is any guide, from 8,000 to 12,000

pounds per inch is the most to be used. The ratio of 90 to 66, seems to express very nearly the action as in the most reliable structures; which will, therefore, be adopted, or 12,000 pounds per square inch nearly. The resistance to compression is very much greater after wrought iron has been somewhat compressed.

CAST-IRON.

153. *Extension.*— This material is seldom used to resist a tensile force. That the tables may be complete, however, the following is given:—

By Weisbach	20,000	pounds.
By Barlow	18,233	"
By Overman	20,000	"
By Rennie	18,000	"
By Hodgekinson	16,577	"
By the British Iron Commission	15,711	"
The mean	18,087	"
Reducing by 4	4,522	"
In round numbers	4,500	"

154. *Compression.*

By Weisbach	109,800	pounds.
By Hodgekinson	107,520	"
By Iron Commission	100,000	"
Stirling's toughened	130,000	"
Mean of Common	105,773	"
Mean of Stirling's	130,000	"
Reducing by 4 for safety (Common)	26,443	"
Reducing by 4 for safety (Stirling's)	32,500	"
In round numbers (Common)	25,000	"
In round numbers (Stirling's)	30,000	"

155. Following are given the condensed results of the

preceding figures, which may be relied upon as giving perfectly safe dimensions in practice.

Wrought Iron.	Cast-Iron.	
15,000	4,500	Tensile strength,
12,000	25,000	Compressive strength.

For additional remarks on iron, see chap. IX.

156. *Nature and Strength of American Woods.*

Name of the wood.	Weight per cubic foot.	Resistance to Extension.	Resistance to Compression.	Value of *S*.	Elasticity.
White Pine	26	12,000	6,000	1,229	——
Yellow Pine	31	12,000	6,000	1,185	——
Pitch Pine	46	12,000	6,000	1,727	4,900
Red Pine	35	12,000	6,000	1,527	7,359
Virginia Pine	37	12,000	6,000	1,456	——
Spruce	48	12,000	6,000	1,036	——
Larch	33	12,000	6,000	907	2,465
Tamarack	26	12,000	6,000	907	——
White Cedar	22	8,000	4,000	766	——
Canada Balsam	34	12,000	6,000	1,123	——
White Oak	48	15,000	7,500	1,743	8,595
Red Oak	41	15,000	7,600	1,687	——
Live Oak	72	15,000	7,200	1,862	——
White Beech	44	18,000	9,100	1,380	5,417
Red Beech	48	18,000	9,000	1,739	——
Birch	44	15,000	7,000	1,928	——
Black Birch	41	15,000	7,200	2,061	——
Yellow Birch	36	15,000	7,200	1,335	——
Ash	38	16,000	8,100	1,795	6,581
Black Ash	35	16,000	8,000	861	——
Swamp Ash	57	16,000	8,000	1,165	——
Hickory	51	15,000	7,200	2,129	——
Butternut	54	15,000	7,600	1,465	——
Sun Wood	54	16,000	8,100	1,800	——
Rock Elm	45	16,000	8,011	1,970	2,799

The mean tensile strength of wood is	14,080 lbs.
Reducing by 4 for safety	3,520 "
Reducing for want of seasoning	2,000 "
The reduced mean compressive strength	1,000 "
Reduced resistance to detrusion	150 "
Ratio of tensile to compressive strength	2 to 1.
Mean value of S in formula ($WL^2 = 4\,Sbd^2$) for the woods most used in practice	1,250.

157. The lateral adhesion of fir was found, by Barlow, to be six hundred pounds per square inch. (Lateral adhesion is the resistance which the fibres offer to sliding past each other in the direction of the grain; as, in pulling off the top of a post where it is halved on to the chord.)

158. As regards the nature of timber, seasoning, time of cutting, etc., although these are important items, still, generally, commercial considerations outbalance all else. The most complete treatise on the nature of woods, is "Du Hamel, *L'exploitation des bois;*" from which it appears that the best oaks, elms, and other large trees, are the product of good lands, rather dry than moist. They have a fine, clear bark, the sap is thinner in proportion to the diameter of the trunk, the layers are less thick, but more adherent the one to another; and more uniform than those of trees growing on moist places. The grain of the latter may look very fine and compact, but microscopic examination shows the pores to be full of gluten.

The density of the same species of timber, in the same climate, but on different soils, will vary as 7 to 5; and the strength, both before and after seasoning, as 5 to 4.

In trees not beyond their prime, the density of the butt is to that of the top, as 4 to 3; and of centre to circumference, as 7 to 5. After maturity, the reverse occurs in both cases.

Oak, in seasoning, loses from $\frac{1}{4}$ to $\frac{1}{3}$ of its weight; but its strength is increased from 30 to 40 per cent.

GENERAL TABLE OF THE NATURE OF MATERIALS.

159. *The tensile strength of wrought iron assumed as* 1,000.

Material.	Tension.	Compression.	Cross Strain.	Sum.	Weight per cubic ft.	Sum divided by weight per cub. ft.
Cast-Iron	300	1,666	31.68	1,997.68	450	4.4
Wrought Iron	1,000	733	55.40	1,788.40	480	3.7
Wood	143	66	5.60	204.60	30	6.8

The advantage possessed by iron over wood, is in durability only. The above figures show how much more of the strength of the material is consumed by its own weight in iron than in wood. In actual practice, however, the method of making joints and other details often render iron the lightest material.

RULES FOR PRACTICE.

TENSION.

160. The tensile strength of any material, is expressed by the formula

$$T = S a,$$

Where T represents the whole strength,
S " " strength per square inch,
a " " area of section in inches.

whence the necessary area of section of any material to resist a tensile strain, is found by the following rules: —

Wrought Iron

$$a = \frac{W}{15,000},$$

Cast-Iron

$$a = \frac{W}{4,500},$$

Wood

$$a = \frac{W}{2,000}.$$

COMPRESSION.

161. Wrought Iron

$$a = \frac{W}{12,000},$$

Cast-Iron

$$a = \frac{W}{25,000},$$

Wood

$$a = \frac{W}{1,000}.$$

CROSS STRAIN.

162. The power of any material to resist a cross strain, is shown by the formula

$$W = \frac{4\,s\,b\,d^2}{L},$$

Where W represents the breaking weight in pounds,
s " " constant in the table of woods,
b " " breadth in inches,
d " " depth in inches,
and L " " length in inches,

and to reduce the load to one fourth of the breaking weight

$$W = \frac{4\,s\,b\,d^2}{4\,L},$$

and finally, by substituting for 4 s, 4 × 1,250, (1,250 of the table of woods,) we have

$$W = \frac{5000\,b\,d^2}{4\,L}.$$

Also, knowing the weight to be supported, and requiring the dimensions, we take out the values of d and b, and have

$$d = \sqrt{\frac{W \times 4\,L}{5000\,b}} = \text{the depth},$$

$$b = \frac{W \times 4\,L}{5000\,d^2} = \text{the breadth}.$$

As an example of the use of the formula, take the following: —

Let the span, or length, be 20 feet,
The breadth 12 inches, and depth 18,

required the load.

The formula

$$W = \frac{5000\,b\,d^2}{4\,L}.$$

becomes

$$W = \frac{5000 \times 12 \times 18^2}{4 \times 240} = 20,250 \text{ lbs.}$$

Again, the weight to be supported being 15,000 lbs., length 30 feet, breadth 16 inches, the formula for the depth becomes

$$d = \sqrt{\frac{15000 \times 1440}{5000 \times 16}} = \sqrt{270} = 16 \text{ inches},$$

also,

$$b = \frac{15000 \times 1440}{5000 \times 256} = \frac{21600000}{1280000} = 16 \text{ inches}.$$

CAST-IRON.

163. The formula, expressive of the strength of a cast-iron beam, is

$$850\,b d^2 = W L,$$

from which we have

$$b = \frac{L\,W}{850\,d^2} = \text{the breadth},$$

$$\text{and } d = \sqrt{\frac{L \times W}{850\,b}} = \text{the depth}.$$

WROUGHT IRON.

164. $$700\,b d^2 = W L,$$

whence

$$b = \frac{W L}{700\,d^2} = \text{the breadth},$$

$$\text{and } d = \sqrt{\frac{L\,W}{700\,b}} \text{ the depth}.$$

Fig. 60.

165. Mr. Hodgekinson found, that by arranging the material in a cast-iron beam, as in fig. 60, that the resistance per unit of section was increased over that of a simple rectangular beam, in the ratio of 40 to 23. He makes the general proportion of such girders as follows:—

Length	16
Height	1
Area of top flánge	1.0
Area of lower flange	6.1

In this consummate disposition of material, the areas of top and bottom flanges are made inversely proportional to the power of cast-iron to resist compression and extension.

166. Mr. Fairbairn found, that in wrought iron flanged girders, (under which come the various rails, chap. XIII.,) the top web should contain double the area of the lower one. This agrees with the conclusion adopted on page 129, as wrought iron resists more extension than compression.

167. In cast-iron girders, on no account should there be introduced webs, or openings of any kind, either from economic or ornamental motives; as the uniformity of cooling is thereby very much opposed.

168. Mr. Hodgekinson gives, as the result of his experiments, the following formula for dimensioning the cast-iron girder above referred to.

$$W = \frac{26ad}{L},$$

Where W is the breaking weight in tons,
a the area of the bottom flange,
d the depth of the girder in inches,
L the length in inches.

As it is not considered safe to load a cast-iron beam with more than one sixth of the breaking load, the formula may be expressed as follows: —

$$W = \frac{26ad}{6L},$$

for the weight in tons which may be safely borne, and transforming

$$a = \frac{6WL}{26d}$$

for the area of the lower flange.

Example. — Required the dimensions of a cast-iron beam, of Mr. Hodgekinson's form, for a span of thirty feet, to support a load of ten tons at the centre.

$$a = \frac{6 \times 10 \times 30 \times 12}{26 \times \frac{30 \times 12}{16}} = \frac{21,600}{598} = 36,$$

and the area of the top flange will be

$$\frac{36}{6} = 6,$$

whence the following dimensions: —

Length	30 feet,
Depth	23 inches,
Lower flange	36 square inches,
Upper flange	6 " "

OF POSTS.

169. A post may be very well able to resist the compressive strain thrown upon it by any load, but may bulge, or bend, laterally.

The formula by which beams are dimensioned for this requirement, changes with the material, and with the form of section. For rectangular posts of wood, we have the formula below.

$$W = \frac{2240\, b\, d^3}{L 2},$$

Where W represents the weight in lbs., which may be safely borne,
b " " breadth in inches,
d " " depth in inches,
and L " " length in feet.

170. The value of the formula for the strength of cast-iron posts, seems to depend more upon the authority con-

sulted than upon the nature of iron. For example, assume the length of a post as twenty feet, and the diameter as ten inches; the load which may be safely borne is, according to six different authorities, as follows: —

A	4,000,000
B	181,100
C	370,000
D	940,000
E	307,242
F	300,000

and assuming the length as ten feet, and diameter as ten inches, we have

A	8,007,500
B	204,500
C	1,442,500
D	3,640,000
E	1,170,000
F	600,000

showing not only a great difference in the unit resistance taken, but also in the effect of the ratio between the length and diameter.

Such being the discrepancy, there will be given no formula; but in place of such, the table following, which is calculated from the rules least opposed to experimental evidence.

TABLE SHOWING THE LOAD IN POUNDS SAFELY BORNE BY CAST-IRON COLUMNS.

HOLLOW CYLINDERS.

Diameter in inches.	Length or height in feet. 6	8	10	12	15	18	20	22	24
2	6000	5000	4000	3000	2500	1800	1500	1300	1100
3	16000	14000	13000	11000	9000	7000	6000	5000	5000
4	30000	29000	26000	24000	22000	18000	16000	14000	13000
5	50000	37000	45000	42000	39000	37000	31000	28000	26000
6	59000	57000	55000	52000	49000	44000	41000	38000	36000
7	101000	99000	96000	92000	88000	81000	76000	72000	68000
8	131000	129000	126000	122000	118000	109000	105000	100000	96000
9	169000	167000	164000	160000	156000	146000	141000	136000	131000
10	210000	200000	200000	200000	190000	180000	180000	170000	170000
11	250000	250000	240000	240000	240000	230000	220000	220000	210000
12	300000	300000	290000	290000	290000	270000	270000	260000	260000
14	450000	430000	410000	380000	370000	350000	330000	320000	300000
16	520000	500000	480000	460000	440000	420000	400000	370000	350000
18	650000	630000	610000	590000	560000	520000	470000	430000	400000
20	800000	760000	740000	690000	650000	590000	540000	490000	450000
Diameter in inches.	6	8	10	12	15	18	20	22	24
	Length or height in feet.								

H AND + SECTIONS.

Metal thickness.	Length or height in feet. 6	8	10	12	15	18	20	22	24
1/4	4000	3000	2400	1800	1400	1100	1000	900	800
3/8	12000	11000	10000	9000	8000	7000	5000	4000	3000
1/2	25000	23000	21000	18000	16000	13000	12000	9000	6000
5/8	36000	34000	31000	28000	25000	23000	21000	20000	18000
3/4	40000	38000	37000	36000	35000	34000	32000	30000	28000
13/16	60000	59000	58000	57000	56000	54000	53000	51000	49000
7/8	100000	98000	96000	94000	91000	88000	83000	78000	70000
1	140000	130000	126000	120000	114000	110000	106000	100000	90000
1 1/8	190000	180000	170000	160000	150000	140000	130000	125000	120000
1 1/4	230000	220000	210000	200000	190000	180000	170000	160000	150000
1 1/2	280000	260000	250000	240000	230000	220000	200000	190000	180000
1 3/4	360000	320000	310000	300000	290000	280000	270000	260000	240000
2	460000	430000	400000	370000	350000	330000	310000	300000	280000
2 1/2	560000	530000	510000	480000	440000	410000	380000	350000	330000
3	600000	580000	550000	520000	500000	460000	430000	400000	380000
Metal thickness.	6	8	10	12	15	18	20	22	24
	Length or height in feet.								

OF THE TRUSS.

171. The most simple bridge that could be built, consists of a single piece of timber placed across the opening to be spanned. This form is applicable to spans under twenty feet. The proper dimensions are found by the formula —

$$d = \sqrt{\frac{4\,w\,L}{5000\,b}} = \text{the depth.}$$

Example. — The depth of a beam of twenty feet span, and twelve inches wide, to support a load of twenty thousand two hundred and fifty lbs. is

$$d = \sqrt{\frac{4 \times 20\,250 \times 20 \times 12}{5000 \times 12}} = 18 \text{ inches.}$$

A beam 12 × 18, and of 20 feet span, will therefore bear safely a load of 20,250 lbs., applied at the centre.

In this manner is formed the following table, giving the scantling of sticks for railroad stringer bridges, of twenty feet span and under.

Span.	Breadth.	Depth.
5	12	12
10	12	13
12	12	15
15	12	18
18	12	20
20	12	21 inches.

The first scantlings exceed the requirement of the rule, but are none too large to resist the shocks to which such sticks are exposed.

Cross-ties of plank, 2 or 3 by 6 or 8 inches, and plank braces underneath, (as shown in the fig. at the end of chapter VIII.,) should be bolted to the main timbers; the same bolt passing through the tie beam and plank. The longitudinal pieces should be firmly notched and bolted to the wall-plates, and these latter either built in or scribed on to the masonry.

172. For a span of from 20 to 50 feet, we may use the combination shown in fig. 61. The piece A B, must be so strong as not to yield between A and D, or D and B. The pieces C E, must be stiff enough to resist the load coming upon them which is as follows. A locomotive engine of the heaviest class will not exceed fifty tons weight, each pair of driving wheels will support ten tons, and on each side five tons, 2240 × 5, 11,200 lbs.; or to allow for shocks and extra strains, 15,000 lbs. Each brace, then, must support seven thousand five hundred pounds, which for compression simply would require only seven and one half square inches of sectional area; but the brace being inclined, the strain is increased as follows:—

Fig. 61.

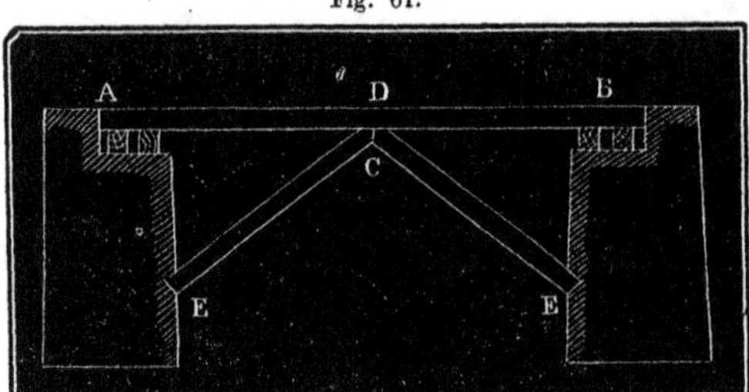

A E to E C as 7,500 to X.

And A E being ten feet, and A D fifteen feet, E C becomes eighteen feet, whence

10 to 18 as 7,500 to 13,500 lbs.;

which would require only thirteen and one half inches for compression, or a piece 4 × 3½. But is this enough for flexure?

On page 124 the load which may be safely borne, by a rectangular post of wood, is shown by the formula

$$W = \frac{2240\,b\,d^3}{L^2}.$$

Substituting for b and d, the dimensions 4×4, we have

$$W = \frac{2240 \times 4 \times 4^3}{18^2}, \text{ or } \frac{573{,}440}{324}, = 1{,}770,$$

which is evidently too small.

Placing 6×7, for $b \times d$, we have

$$W = \frac{2240 \times 6 \times 7^3}{18^2} = 14{,}227;$$

exceeding by a small amount the requirement.

173. It is evidently immaterial whether we *support* the the point D *upon* C, or *suspend* it as in fig. 62, provided we prevent any motion in the feet of the inclines A c B c. Abutting them against A B, throws a tension against A B, found as follows: —

Fig. 62.

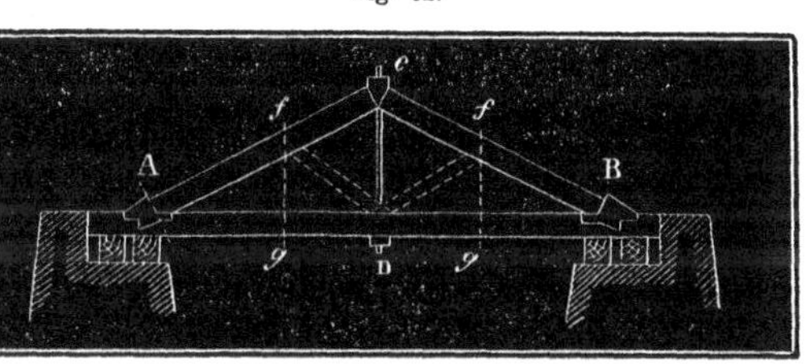

Representing by c D, the applied weight, draw D E parallel to c B; also Ef parallel to A B; Ef is the tension. The graphic construction gives results near enough for practice. Rigorously we have

Fig. 63.

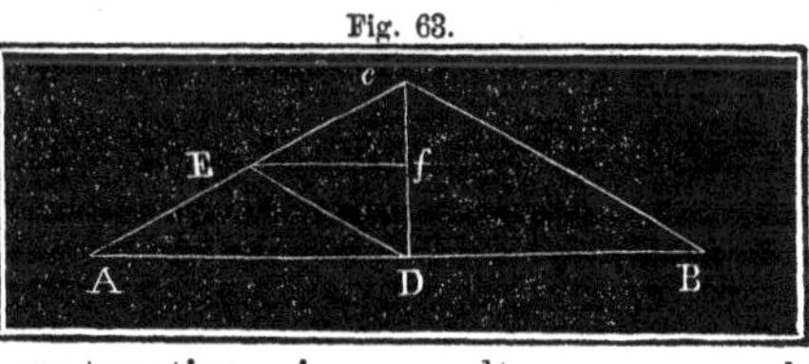

A c D, similar to E $c f$;

also,

A c, to E c, as A D, to Ef;

and

$$Ef = \frac{E\,c \times A\,D}{A\,c}.$$

When $a\,d$ and $c\,d$ are differently inclined, proceed as follows. See fig. 102, p. 200.

Let $d\,b$ represent the weight; $e\,h$ shows the tension. The triangles $a\,c\,d$, and $a\,b\,e$, are similar; as also $e\,b\,h$ and $d\,b\,c$; whence

$$b\,e = \frac{a\,b,\,c\,d}{a\,c},\ \text{and}\ e\,h = \frac{c\,b,\,b\,e}{d\,c} = \text{tension.}$$

In practice place w for $b\,d$; i. e. the actual weight.

In this plan, if the chord is able to resist the cross strain between A and D, it will also resist the tension. This cross strain is found by the formula already given and illustrated.

174. From what precedes, we have the following dimensions for bridges such as are shown in figs. 61 and 62. The details of 62, at f and c, and at E, 61, are shown in figs. 62 A, 62 B, and 61 C.

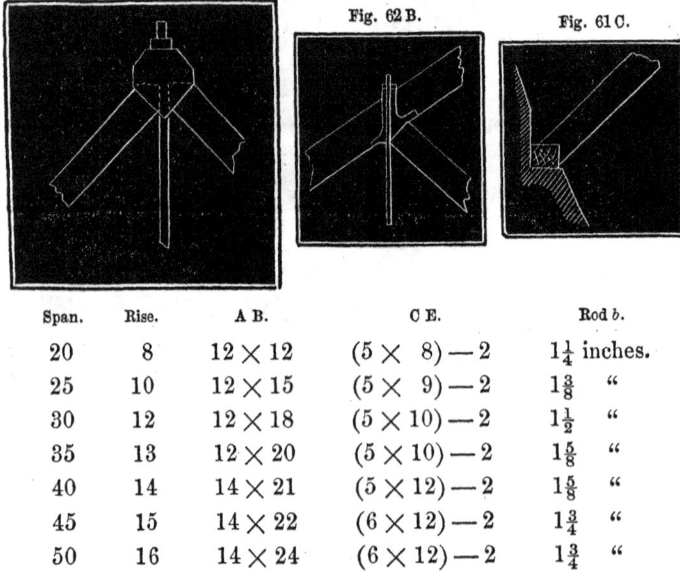

Fig. 62 A. Fig. 62 B. Fig. 61 C.

Span.	Rise.	A B.	C E.	Rod b.
20	8	12 × 12	(5 × 8) — 2	$1\frac{1}{4}$ inches.
25	10	12 × 15	(5 × 9) — 2	$1\frac{3}{8}$ "
30	12	12 × 18	(5 × 10) — 2	$1\frac{1}{2}$ "
35	13	12 × 20	(5 × 10) — 2	$1\frac{5}{8}$ "
40	14	14 × 21	(5 × 12) — 2	$1\frac{5}{8}$ "
45	15	14 × 22	(6 × 12) — 2	$1\frac{3}{4}$ "
50	16	14 × 24	(6 × 12) — 2	$1\frac{3}{4}$ "

The braces, (column 4,) being in pairs and blocked together. In span exceeding twenty-five feet, the braces $d\,f$, and the rods *fg*, should never be omitted. The size of the rod *gf*, is found by considering A, *d*, *f*, as a small bridge.

175. In all light bridges, like the one under consideration, all parts should be *fastened* by bolts, to prevent springing by reaction. A bridge with but little inertia, or dead weight, tends to jump up when the engine has passed over it. *Fastening* takes the place of *weight* in a large span.

As soon as the rise admits, the points C, on each side of the bridge, should be connected to resist lateral motion. When the height is not enough for this, the same points may be joined to a floor beam extended out beyond the truss.

Though the dimensions are given for this plan up to fifty feet span, it is very seldom advisable to go beyond twenty-five or thirty feet; as frames consisting of a few long timbers are not so rigid, and free from vibration, as those made of a greater number of short pieces.

176. In extending this system one hundred or two hundred feet, we see at once that the pieces A *c*, B *c*, would become very long and would need to be made large and heavy. We should always so proportion any beam in a bridge that it is at once able to resist all of the several strains to which it may be exposed, without being unnecessarily large.

As to compression, the above system might be extended to almost any amount; but the braces would yield by flexure.

Instead of producing the braces A *c*, A′ *c*′, fig. 64, to their intersection, we stop at *c* and *c*′, insert *c c*′; to prevent the approach of these points, suspend the points B and B′ from *c* and *c*′, and commence again with the braces B D, B′ D; and so on as far as necessary.

To prevent the backward motion of the points B, and B′,

either the chord A A′, or the counter-braces *m*, *m*, are necessary.

Fig. 64.

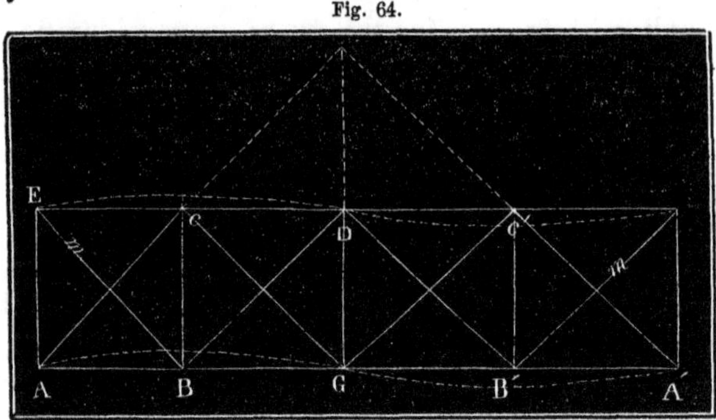

The pieces A *c* A′ *c*′ must support all of the load, including the weight of the bridge, lying within the rectangle B *c* B′ *c*′. The next set of braces must sustain that part of the load only which comes over the centre of the bridge. Thus the braces should decrease in size as the centre is approached. The rods *c* B, *c*′ B′, must resist a tension equal in amount to the pressure on the braces, only being vertical they do not need the increase given to the braces on account of their inclination.

177. There is another method of stiffening a beam, as shown in figs. 65 and 66, by trussing rods, and a post. The dimensions being the same, the forces in both cases will be equal. The second, fig. 66, leaves the passage beneath the bridge clear.

Fig. 65.

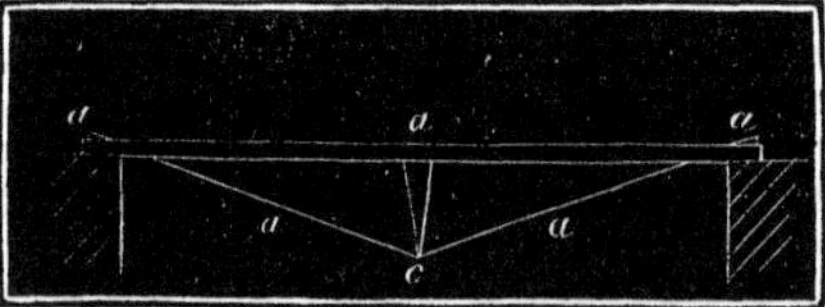

The tension on the rods A *c*, B *c*, fig. 66, tends to draw the points A and B together, an effort which is resisted by the top chord A B.

In extending this system, as in art. 176, the rods become

Fig. 66.

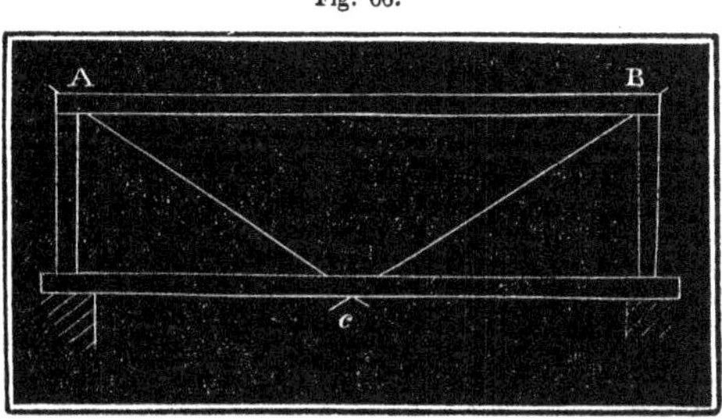

either very long, or very large, from the small angle of inclination; evils which are remedied as before, by supporting the post c B, fig. 64, from the foot of the first rod, fig. 64, and commencing again from c.

To prevent the motion of the triangle c B G, fig. 64, about the angle B, we must introduce either the upper chord $c\,c'$, or the counter rod c A. If the lower chord is omitted the rod D B must be of the same size as E B. In this truss, either the top or the lower chord simply may theoretically be omitted, due allowance being made in the size of the rods. In practice it is never advisable to omit either, as both are required for lateral bracing, and for support of the road-way.

Having said thus much of the general ideas that apply to all bridges, let us now look at some of the plans most in use; and to become familiar with the subject, work out the dimensions of an example of each kind.

178. As rods, nuts, and washers are used in all bridges, the following table may not be out of place:—

Column 1 gives the diameter of rod.
" 2 strength at 15,000 lbs. per square inch.
" 3 the weight per lineal foot.
" 4 side of the square nut.
" 5 the thickness of the same.
" 6 the dimensions of washers.
" 7 the thickness of washers.
" 8 breadth (side to side) six-sided nut.
" 9 breadth (across angles) six-sided nut.

Column 10 thickness of six-sided nut.
" 11 number of screw threads per inch.
" 12 gives the diameter of rod.

1 Diameter.	2 Strength of Rod.	3 Weight per Foot.	4 Square Nut.	5 Thickness.	6 Square of Washer.	7 Top Washer.	8 Six-Sided Nut.	9 Six-Sided Nut.	10 Six-Sided Nut.	11 Screw.	12 Diameter.
$\frac{1}{2}$	2,940	0.66	$1\frac{1}{4}$	$\frac{3}{4}$	$2\frac{1}{2}$	$\frac{1}{4}$	$1\frac{3}{8}$	$1\frac{1}{2}$	$\frac{9}{16}$	12	$\frac{1}{2}$
$\frac{3}{4}$	6,630	1.49	$1\frac{1}{2}$	$\frac{7}{8}$	3	$\frac{1}{4}$	$1\frac{3}{4}$	2	$\frac{7}{8}$	10	$\frac{3}{4}$
1	11,775	2.65	2	1	4	$\frac{3}{8}$	$1\frac{7}{8}$	$2\frac{1}{4}$	$1\frac{1}{8}$	8	1
$1\frac{1}{8}$	14,910	3.36	2	$1\frac{1}{8}$	$4\frac{1}{2}$	$\frac{3}{8}$	$2\frac{1}{8}$	$2\frac{7}{16}$	$1\frac{1}{4}$	7	$1\frac{1}{8}$
$1\frac{1}{4}$	18,405	4.17	$2\frac{1}{4}$	$1\frac{1}{4}$	5	$\frac{1}{2}$	$2\frac{1}{4}$	$2\frac{11}{16}$	$1\frac{7}{12}$	7	$1\frac{1}{4}$
$1\frac{3}{8}$	22,260	5.02	$2\frac{1}{2}$	$1\frac{3}{8}$	$5\frac{1}{2}$	$\frac{1}{2}$	$2\frac{1}{2}$	$2\frac{7}{8}$	$1\frac{7}{16}$	6	$1\frac{3}{8}$
$1\frac{1}{2}$	26,505	5.97	$2\frac{3}{4}$	$1\frac{1}{2}$	6	$\frac{1}{2}$	$2\frac{5}{8}$	$3\frac{1}{8}$	$1\frac{11}{16}$	6	$1\frac{1}{2}$
$1\frac{5}{8}$	31,095	7.01	$2\frac{7}{8}$	$1\frac{5}{8}$	$6\frac{1}{2}$	$\frac{5}{8}$	$2\frac{7}{8}$	$3\frac{5}{16}$	$1\frac{13}{16}$	5	$1\frac{5}{8}$
$1\frac{3}{4}$	36,075	8.13	3	$1\frac{3}{4}$	7	$\frac{5}{8}$	3	$3\frac{1}{2}$	2	5	$1\frac{3}{4}$
$1\frac{7}{8}$	41,415	9.33	$3\frac{1}{4}$	$1\frac{7}{8}$	$7\frac{1}{2}$	$\frac{5}{8}$	$3\frac{1}{4}$	$3\frac{3}{4}$	$2\frac{1}{8}$	$4\frac{1}{2}$	$1\frac{7}{8}$
2	47,130	10.62	$3\frac{1}{2}$	$1\frac{7}{8}$	8	$\frac{5}{8}$	$3\frac{1}{2}$	4	$2\frac{1}{4}$	$4\frac{1}{2}$	2
$2\frac{1}{8}$	53,190	12.00	$3\frac{3}{4}$	2	$8\frac{1}{2}$	$\frac{3}{4}$	$3\frac{5}{8}$	$4\frac{3}{16}$	$2\frac{3}{8}$	4	$2\frac{1}{8}$
$2\frac{1}{4}$	59,640	13.40	4	$2\frac{1}{8}$	9	$\frac{3}{4}$	$3\frac{3}{4}$	$4\frac{6}{16}$	$2\frac{1}{2}$	4	$2\frac{1}{4}$
$2\frac{3}{8}$	66,450	15.00	$4\frac{1}{8}$	$2\frac{1}{4}$	$9\frac{1}{2}$	$\frac{3}{4}$	4	$4\frac{5}{8}$	$2\frac{5}{8}$	4	$2\frac{3}{8}$
$2\frac{1}{2}$	73,620	16.70	$4\frac{1}{4}$	$2\frac{1}{2}$	10	$\frac{3}{4}$	$4\frac{1}{4}$	$4\frac{7}{8}$	$2\frac{3}{4}$	$3\frac{1}{2}$	$2\frac{1}{2}$
1	2	3	4	5	6	7	8	9	10	11	12

179. Let us now assume the following data:—

Span	200 feet,
Rise (centre to centre of chords) .	25 "
Width	20 "
Length of panel	15 "
Weight (bridge and load) per lineal ft.	4,000 lbs.

Fig. 67.

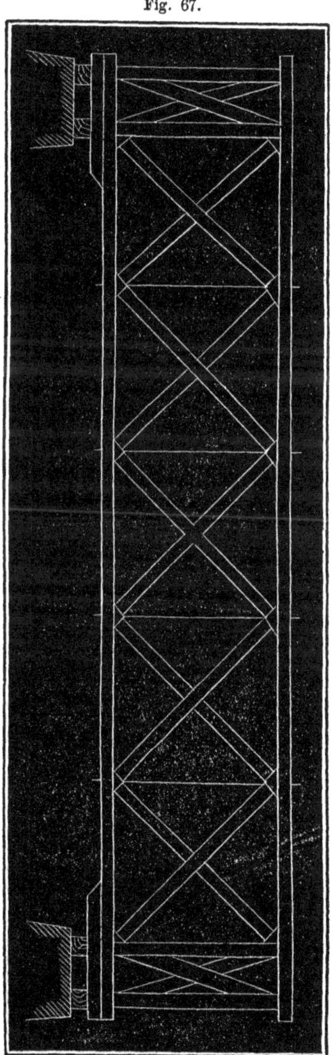

HOWE'S BRIDGE.

Fig. 67.

Lower Chords. — The *tension*, at the centre of the lower chord, is found *by dividing the product of the weight of the whole bridge and load by the span*, by eight times the height, or

$$T = \frac{W \times S}{8h},$$

which becomes, with the above data,

$$T = \frac{800000 \times 200}{200}, = 800{,}000 \text{ lbs.}$$

Here the tension and the total weight are equal, a result which can occur only when the rise is one eighth of the span. This is the best ratio between these dimensions, as then the horizontal and vertical forces are equal.

As to the proportion of the *panel*, (or the rectangle inclosed by the chords and any two adjacent posts,) the ratio of base to height should be such as to make the inclination of diagonal about 50° from the horizontal; if much less, the timbers become large and heavy; and if more, the number of pieces is unnecessarily increased.

The braces at the end of a long span, may be nearer to the vertical than those near the centre, as they have more work to do. If the end panel be made twice as high as long, and the centre panel square, the intermediates varying as their distance from the end, a good architectural effect is produced.

To determine the size of the lower chords, to resist the above 800,000 pounds of tension, proceed as follows: Each side truss will support one half of the whole load, or 400,000 pounds; which, at 2,000 pounds per inch, will require 200 square inches of section. Four sticks of 8×12 inches, give an area of 384 square inches, which must be reduced as follows: Deduct 72 square inches for the area cut out by the splicing blocks, 40 inches for the bolts connecting the pieces, 28 inches for inserting the foot blocks, and 10 inches for inserting the washer, and we have remaining 234 square inches; which exceeds by a little the exact demand. This excess (about one seventh) is a necessary allowance for accidental strain, to which all bridges are subjected.

The splices used in bridge framing are shown in fig. 67 A

Fig. 67 A.

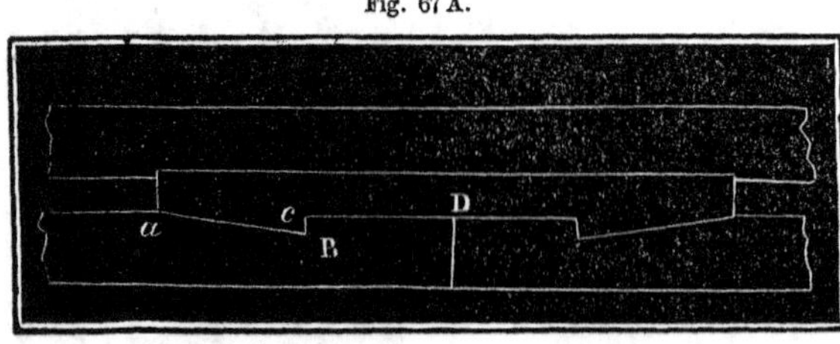

and fig. 67 B. For the first, the depth of insertion and length of the block depend upon the tension upon the chord. The following dimensions have been much used and are perfectly reliable: —

Fig. 67 B.

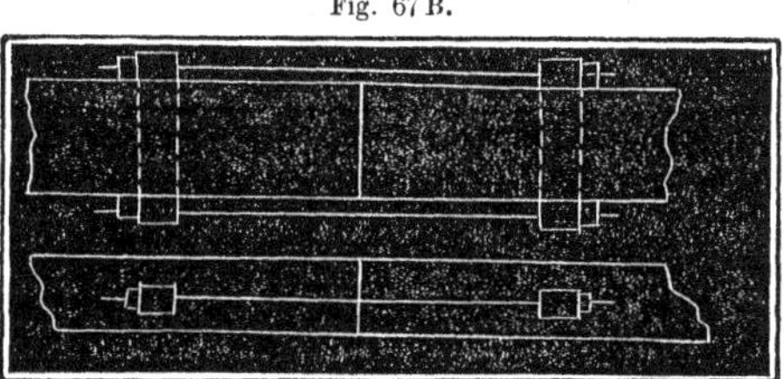

Span of Bridge. Feet.	A C Feet.	B C Inches	C D Feet.
50	1.00	$1\frac{1}{2}$	1.50
100	1.25	2	2.00
150	1.75	$2\frac{1}{2}$	2.25
200	2.00	3	2.75

There is no need of cutting more than one notch, as in the figure; the resistance of the triangles is thereby lessened, and the work increased.

In fig. 67 B, the rods must of course be able to resist the tension upon the one piece which is cut.

Upper Chord. — The upper chords of a bridge suffer compression, to the same amount numerically, as the tension on the lower chord; as whatever tension is thrown by any brace upon the lower chord, reacts as just so much compression upon the upper. In the case at hand, 800,000 lbs. in all, or 400,000 on each chord.

The resistance to compression being one thousand pounds per inch, renders necessary four hundred inches of section to each chord; four pieces 8×12 give in all three hundred and eighty-four inches of section, which requires no reduction, as the whole chord pressing together and being properly framed is not weakened by splicing. The splicing blocks in the upper are merely plain pieces, inserted one half inch, the only duty being to keep the sticks at the proper horizontal distance.

The spaces between the pieces should be large enough to

allow the rods to pass without cutting the chords; (two inches answers every purpose). The bolts for splicing, have no very great strain to bear. In small spans from ½ to ⅝, and in large bridges from ⅝ to an inch is enough.

The object in framing a built beam for a bridge chord, is to make a stick which shall be uniformly strong. This is done by cutting the pieces in the centre of the panel, and by having no two joints in either chord in one panel; though in long spans this cannot always be done.

BRACES.

The whole load being	800,000	pounds,
Each truss supports	400,000	"
Each set of braces	200,000	"
Each brace (there being 4)	50,000	"

which must be increased for inclination as follows: The length of diagonal is twenty-nine feet, (the height being twenty-five and length 15,) whence

25 to 29 as 50,000 to 58,000 lbs.;

which would need fifty-eight square inches, or 7×8 for compression; which, however, is quite too small for flexure. 12×12 placed in the formula gives

$$W = \frac{2240 \times bd^3}{L^2},$$

or

$$W = \frac{2240 \times 12 \times 1728}{841} = 55{,}296 \text{ lbs.}$$

In practice, smaller braces than 12×12 would answer, because the four braces in a set may be fastened together, making a post of four pieces 8×12, or in all a built post of 44×12 inches; twelve being the depth, whence

$$W = \frac{2249 \times 44 \times 1728}{841} = 202{,}511 \text{ lbs.};$$

the forty-four inches being made by blocking the braces four inches apart. The second set of braces are to be treated in the same manner, the weight to be supported being only the rectangle included by those braces; i. e. the whole bridge and load less the two end panels.

As the centre of the span is approached, the pressure on the braces becomes very small; and the scantling of the braces will be reduced to about 6×7 inches.

RODS.

The weight upon the first set of rods is the same as that upon the end sets of braces; in the present case $800000 \div 2 = 400000$ on each side truss, and $400000 \div 2 = 200000$ on each end; and if there are five rods in each set, each rod bears 40,000 lbs. Referring to the table on p. 146, opposite to 31,416 lbs., is the diameter $1\frac{5}{8}$ inches; whence the first set must contain five rods, of $1\frac{5}{8}$ inches diameter. The second set decrease in size as the weight is lessened by the two end panels. The nut and washer for the rod are also found in the same table.

COUNTERBRACING.

180. When a load is placed on the point C′, fig. 64, the truss tends to sink at that point, and a corresponding rise takes place at C. This motion changes the figure A B C E, from a rectangle to an oblique angled figure; the diagonal E B being shortened, and A C lengthened. This motion is

Fig. 64.

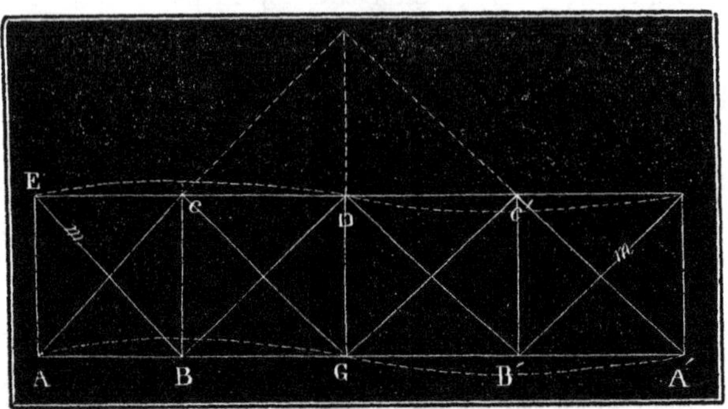

easily checked by the introduction of the counter brace E B.

The action which this timber is called upon to resist, being caused by the moving or variable load on one panel, the brace must resist the load coming thereon, (say fifteen feet,) and is thus the same size as the brace at the centre of the span.

The counter braces may be so confined between the braces, at the intersection, as not to move laterally or vertically, but must not be fastened to the braces; because the action of the separate timbers is thus trammelled.

The manner of adjusting the braces and counter braces to the chord is shown in fig. 67 C. It was formerly the custom to abut the braces against a block on one side of the chord, and to screw the rod against a block on the opposite side; the whole strain acting to crush the chord crosswise. This has been remedied by the arrangement shown in the figure, the

Fig. 67 C.

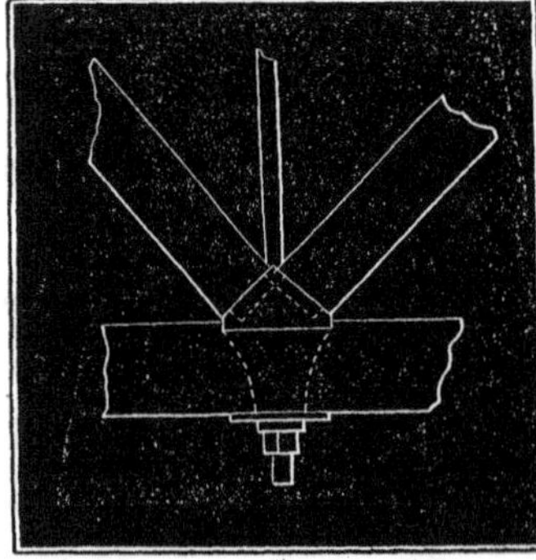

two blocks being cast in one piece and connected by a small hollow cylinder passing between the chord sticks.

This system is known as Howe's bridge, and may be seen in almost any section of the country; and though in many cases badly proportioned, and of bad material, if properly made answers a very good end.

The following table has been formed for the use of engineers and builders, giving, together with the table of nuts and washers, all dimensions required.

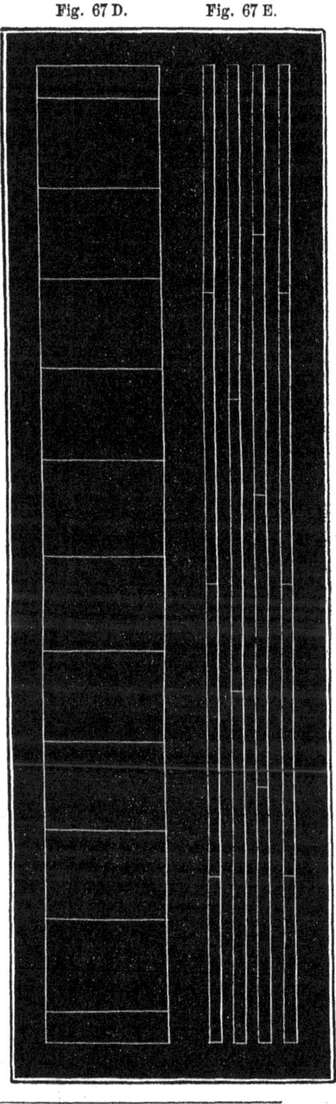

Fig. 67 D. Fig. 67 E.

Span.	Rise.	Panel.	Chords.	End braces.	Centre braces.	End rod.	Centre rod.
50	10	7	2 — 8 × 10	7^2	5 × 5	2 — 1⅛	2 — 1
75	12	9	2 — 8 × 10	8^2	5 × 5	2 — 1½	2 — 1
100	15	11	3 — 8 × 10	9^2	6 × 6	2 — 1¾	2 — 1
150	20	13	4 — 8 × 12	10^2	6 × 7	3 — 2	3 — 1
200	25	15	4 — 8 × 16	12^2	7 × 7	5 — 2	5 — 1

PRATT'S BRIDGE.

Fig. 68.

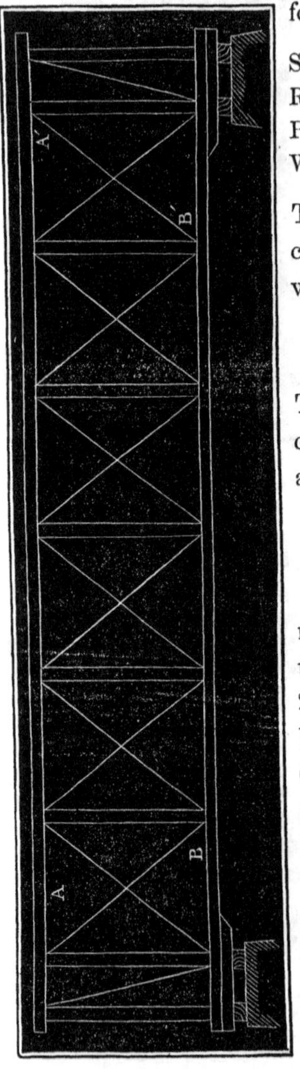

181. Assume the following data for an example: —

Span	100 feet,
Rise	12 "
Panel	10 "
Weight per lineal ft. .	2,500 lbs.

The tension on the lower, or the compression on the upper chord, will be

$$\frac{250000 \times 100}{96} = 260,417 \text{ lbs.}$$

The manner of dimensioning the chord, and of splicing, is the same as already described for Howe's.

SUSPENSION RODS.

The first sets of rods, A B, A′ B′, must sustain the whole weight of the bridge and load; which is 250,000 lbs. Each side 125,000 lbs.; and each end set of rods 62,500 lbs.; and if each set has four rods, each rod must support 15,625 lbs.

The rod being inclined, this amount is increased by the following proportion: —

12 (height) to 15.8 (diagonal) as 15,625 to 20,573 lbs.

This is half-way between the tubular numbers for rods

of 1¼ and 1⅜ inches in diameter; 1⅜ will therefore answer. The next set of rods must be considered as supporting the whole load, less the two end panels, and so on as already explained for Howe's bridge. The manner of applying the rods to the chords is shown in fig. 68 A. The bevel block should be connected with the block at the foot of the post, so as to prevent crushing the chord.

Fig. 68 A.

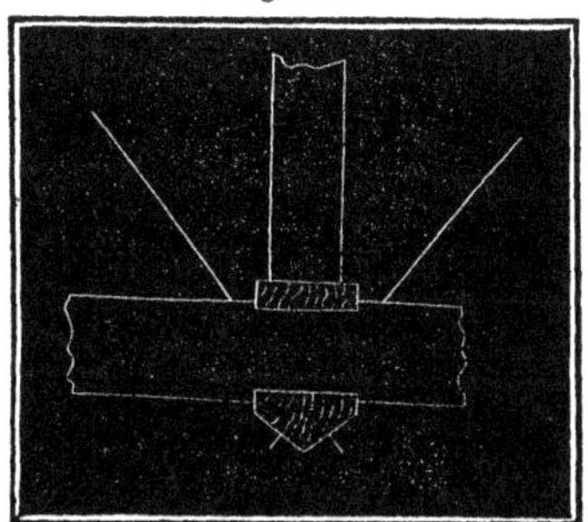

COUNTER RODS.

As both top and bottom chords are always used in this bridge, the counter rods have only the variable load on one panel to resist. The action is, in amount, the same as that on the counter braces in Howe's bridge; but acts in a different direction, and in the other diagonal.

The weight of a passing load cannot be more than two thousand pounds per lineal foot. The panel being ten feet long, the whole weight coming on two sets of counter rods, (one set in each side truss,) is twenty thousand pounds; or ten thousand pounds on each set; and if there are put three rods in each set, we have 3,333 pounds per rod, which increase for inclination as follows:—

12 : 15.8 : : 3333 : 4389 lbs.,

requiring a rod of three fourths inch diameter.

The posts in this structure, correspond to the braces in the Howe bridge; only being vertical, they need not be so large.

182. The following table gives all the dimensions necessary for proportioning this truss.

Span.	Rise.	Chords.	End post.	C post.	End rod.	C rod.	Counter rod.
50	10	2 — 8 × 10	5 × 5	4^2	2 — $1\frac{3}{8}$	2 — 1	1 — $1\frac{1}{2}$
75	12	2 — 8 × 10	6 × 6	5^2	2 — $1\frac{5}{8}$	2 — 1	1 — $1\frac{1}{2}$
100	15	3 — 8 × 10	7 × 7	6^2	2 — $1\frac{3}{4}$	2 — 1	2 — $1\frac{1}{8}$
125	18	3 — 8 × 10	8 × 8	6^2	3 — $1\frac{7}{8}$	3 — 1	2 — $1\frac{3}{8}$
150	21	4 — 8 × 12	9 × 9	6^2	3 — $2\frac{1}{8}$	3 — 1	3 — $1\frac{1}{8}$
200	24	4 — 8 × 16	10 × 10	6^2	5 — $1\frac{7}{8}$	5 — 1	3 — $1\frac{1}{8}$

And the following, the sizes of counter rods, for different panels.

Length of panel.	Height of panel.	Approximate diagonal of panel.	Diameter of the rod. One in a set.	Two per set.	Three per set.
10	12	16	$1\frac{5}{8}$	$1\frac{1}{8}$	$\frac{7}{8}$
11	13	17	$1\frac{5}{8}$	$1\frac{1}{4}$	$1\frac{1}{8}$
12	14	18	$1\frac{3}{4}$	$1\frac{1}{4}$	$1\frac{1}{8}$
13	15	20	$1\frac{3}{4}$	$1\frac{1}{4}$	$1\frac{1}{8}$
14	16	21	$1\frac{7}{8}$	$1\frac{3}{8}$	$1\frac{1}{8}$
15	18	23	$1\frac{7}{8}$	$1\frac{3}{8}$	$1\frac{1}{8}$
16	21	26	2	$1\frac{3}{8}$	$1\frac{1}{8}$
18	25	27	2	$1\frac{3}{8}$	$1\frac{1}{8}$

The advantage possessed by this bridge, over Howe's plan, is that the panel diagonals may be adjusted by the screws; by which control is had over the form of the truss, and of the duty done by the several parts. Change of form cannot be had by working upon verticals. Howe's bridge must be adjusted by wedging the braces and the counter braces.

183. The manner of drawing the bevel block in this bridge, is shown in fig. 68 b. The proportions of the block depend upon the proportions of the panel; and the dimensions, upon the size of washer band.

Let C C be the centre line of the post, and A B the chord. Let *o m*, and *o n*, be the panel diagonals, and H and *y*, the length of the washers.

Fig. 68 B.

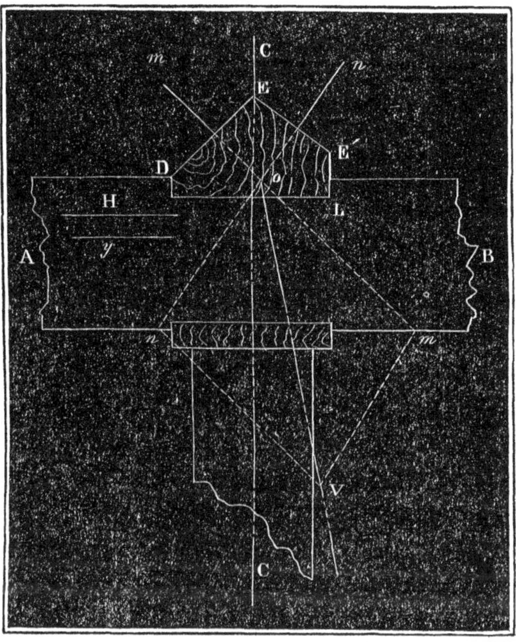

The depth of insertion of the block into the chord, depends upon the horizontal strain upon it. In a span of one hundred and fifty feet, with the rods at an angle of 50°, two inches have been found ample at the end of the truss, and one half inch at centre.

From D, perpendicular to *m m*, lay off D E; equal to H, also from E, at right angles to *n n*, make E E′ = *y*. From E′ draw the vertical E′ L.

The strain upon the rod *o m*, being represented by *o m*; and that upon *o n*, by *o n*, the resultant is shown, both in direction and amount, by *o* V. It is not necessary that this should pass through the centre of the post, as the excess of tension on *o m*, over that on *o n*, is absorbed by the lower chord.

NOTE.—Screwing up truss bridges, is a more scientific operation than is generally supposed. Many builders commence at each end, and lift the bridge from the scaffolding. By this method the greater part of the load is often borne by a few of the end sets of rods. The better method is to begin at the centre and work both ways towards the ends, being sure that each set of rods does its duty before the next is touched. The lift to be made by each set of rods, should first be calculated, and tested while screwing up, with the level.

LATTICE BRIDGES.

184. *Town's lattice*, consists of a simple lattice-work of plank, 3 × 12 inches, treenailed together at an angle of forty, forty-five, or fifty degrees. It possesses great stiffness, without by any means having the material disposed in the best manner. Such bridges might well be made by the mile, and cut off to order according to the span.

The improved lattice, by Hermann Haupt, Esq., C. E., avoids all of the evils attendant upon the common lattice, and gives a very cheap, strong, and rigid bridge. In this plan the braces are placed in pairs, with vertical tie planks between them; by which the twisting seen in the common lattice, is removed. The braces are also brought to the vertical, as the point of support is reached, by which a good bearing is given to the end sets of timbers.

To vary the size of the braces, as the strain upon them decreases, would be both inconvenient and expensive; but the same effect may be produced by varying the distance between them, making it greater as the centre is approached.

S. W. HALL'S WOODEN TRUSS AND ARCH BRIDGE.

Inverting Mr. Haupt's design for a lattice of improved construction, (which consists of vertical ties and inclined braces,) we have the base of the above-named bridge; where the inclined timbers are used to resist tension, as below.

This being a very good plan, and the arrangement for

building being such as to secure the thorough execution of the work in its most minute detail; it is thought best to extract at some length from a letter from the inventor, dated July 31st, 1856, not however being confined to the matter therein.

The first claim, is for a *new form of truss*, formed of posts vertical, or nearly so, and *tension* pieces, inclining downwards toward the centre; thus differing from nearly all other plans. Timber resists double as much extension as compression; and when large enough to resist the simple tension, does not have to be increased as in resisting compression for flexure; but requires a larger allowance for joints, as tension tends to pull the joints apart, while compression forces them together.

The following result was obtained, showing the superior strength of timber work in resisting by *tension*. Two models, containing the same amount of timber, were tested. The one built with vertical ties and *braces*, broke by crippling the brace, under 2,400 lbs.; while that constructed with verticals and *suspenders*, inclining towards the centre, sustained 4,200 lbs. with no visible change of form.

The second claim is for more efficient bearings and connections than common, and this with less cutting away of timber. The arch and arch braces have a full, fair bearing at top and bottom. The first sets of tension braces, (those extending from the top of the arch braces towards the centre,) are sustained by two pins at each joint; which gives six pin bearings, or twelve for one set of braces, of six inches each, (the pin being two inches in diameter, and plank three inches thick,) equal in all, to seventy-two inches of bearing surface at least, for each five feet lineal of bridge, or one hundred and forty-four inches for ten feet.

The third claim, is that the bearings, at joints, are *central*, and that the shrinkage of the timber is *towards* and not *from* them as in many plans.

The pin holes are bored by machinery smooth and true; the treenails when of wood are of seasoned oak or locust, turned to a perfect fit, and when of iron are made hollow.

These bridges, after three years, stand within an inch of their shape as framed without exception. One indeed supporting an aqueduct, which throws upon the truss a constant load of 2¾ tons per foot, not including the weight of the bridge, without any apparent settling.

The connections being fast, prevent reaction and vibration from variable loads, the strains in this case are reversed, the bridge tending to spring up instead of settling.

The fourth claim, is for the small brace connecting the lower with the intermediate chord; by which additional connections are obtained, and smaller timbers rendered available.

The fifth claim, is the formation of a stronger chord than by the plan of using a few large sticks. The chord being made of a great number of small pieces, the strength is of course less affected at any one point, by a joint, than when only a few pieces are used.

In the bridges built by the above engineer, are to be seen some of the most perfect built beams in the country. The following conditions being observed, the most uniform, and highest average strength possible is obtained.

First. To cut but one stick in any one panel.
Second. To cut no stick at the centre of the bridge.
Third. To place every joint in the middle of the collateral piece.

The chords are cut by two rows of pins, two inches each; and if the chord be fifteen inches, the cutting at centre, where there is no joint, is but four fifteenths of the whole section. To resist the parting of any two sticks, there is the resistance to shearing of ninety-six pins; and the section of each being three square inches, the whole resistance is two hundred and eighty-eight inches of area. If the intermediate chord has the same number, the whole area to resist shearing, in the lower chord, is five hundred and seventy-six square inches. The bearing surface of each pin in the chord stick is 2×3 inches, or six inches; and $96 \times 6 = 576$: and in both chords 1152 inches.

	Sq. in.
The whole chord timber, (both chords,) is $(6 \times 3 \times 14)$,	252
In the intermediate chord, $(6 \times 3 \times 12)$,	216
Whole timber section,	468
Deduct 4 pins for both chords, $468 - (4 \times 2 \times 3 \times 6)$ or $468 - 144 =$	324
Deduct for joints $3 \times 10 + 3 \times 8$ or $324 - 54$,	270
Square inches of available area.	

Comparing the amount thus cut away with that cut away in other plans, we have the following figures: —

A.	Hall's Bridge, (actual bridge,)	$\frac{30}{100}$
B.	Howe's bridge, (actual bridge,)	$\frac{35}{100}$
C.	Page 163, (Handbook R. R. Construction,)	$\frac{39\frac{1}{2}}{100}$
D.	McCallum's, (Susquehanna bridge,)	$\frac{58}{100}$

The sixth claim, is the peculiarly convenient form for applying an arch, — the superiority consisting in convenience for attachment; in the connections being less affected by shrinkage than when posts are locked into arches; in the timbers not being weakened by cutting. The arch is loaded with the tension timbers, inwardly, and acts as a general arch brace, transferring at once all of the several tensions to the abutment, thus really combining the arch with the truss.

The liability of this plan to decay, certainly appears to be less than that of most plans of wooden bridges now in use; as will be plainly seen by observing the position of the joints; falling rain finds a much easier access to almost any other joint than the pin hole. The timber work being made of plank, all the timbers are small, and are thus much more likely to be sound.

Fig. 69.

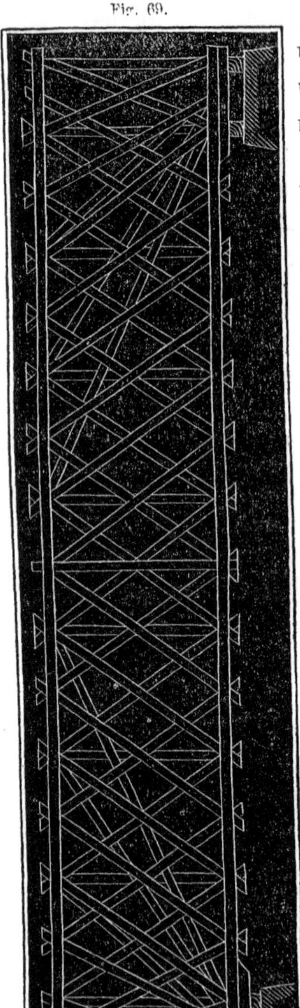

The bridges built upon this plan upon the Alleghany Valley, and upon the Williamsport and Elmira roads, illustrate plainly the design.

185. Applying arch braces to lattice bridges, has suggested *The Arch-brace truss bridge*, in which the whole strength lies in a series of differently inclined braces, extending from the abutment to the head of each post; a very light lattice being used to prevent reaction, or as a counter-brace or stiffener. See fig. 69.

In trusses consisting of a series of triangles, when the span is large, (150 to 200 feet,) the immense weight coming at the feet of the second and third sets of braces, causes a settling or depressing at twenty or thirty feet off from the abutment, which can hardly be removed. The remedy for such settling, is to transfer the load at once to the abutment; which is completely done in the above-named bridge. Each brace does its duty directly and well. Before the lattice-work is fastened, the bridge should be loaded with a maximum load. Then by fastening the diagonals, the recoil is prevented; and the effect of a passing load is to ease the counterbracing lattice, without otherwise affecting the truss.

NOTE. — A model of this bridge, made by the writer, of the following dimensions: —

Length,	7 feet.
Height,	1 foot.
Width,	1 "
Chords,	$\frac{1}{4} \times \frac{1}{2}$ inch.
Braces,	$\frac{1}{4} \times \frac{1}{3}$ "
Lattice,	$\frac{1}{4} \times \frac{1}{16}$ "

Supported 2,500 lbs. at centre, besides a variable load of 150 lbs. applied as a rolling weight in the most disadvantageous manner. It represented a span of one hundred and fifty feet, and according to Weisbach's formula for testing a model, proved the actual structure, (as far as can be proved by a model,) both strong and rigid to any desired amount. The longest bridge ever built upon this principle, was that of Schaffhausen, over the Rhine, which had a single span of three hundred and ninety feet. This bridge was not stiff, having no lattice, but was very strong. B. H. Latrobe, Esq. has adopted this form upon the Baltimore and Ohio Railroad.

The calculations for the parts of this bridge are as follows: —

The Span being	150 feet,
The Rise	20 "
The Panel	15 "
Weight per foot of bridge and load	3,000 lbs.

The half number of panels is five; the diagonals of which, neglecting fractions, are

$$\sqrt{20^2+15^2}=25 \text{ feet,}$$

$$\sqrt{20^2+30^2}=37 \text{ feet,}$$

$$\sqrt{20^2+45^2}=49 \text{ feet,}$$

$$\sqrt{20^2+60^2}=64 \text{ feet},$$

$$\sqrt{20^2+75^2}=78 \text{ feet}.$$

The weight upon each of these sets of braces, is the weight of the length of one panel; which, in the present case, is 3,000 × 15 = 45,000 lbs. As there is a brace under each chord stick, and assuming four sticks in each chord, we divide by eight, and have, in round numbers, 6,000 lbs. per brace; and correcting for inclination, as follows, we have the numbers below.

15 : 25 : : 6000 : 10000
15 : 37 : : 6000 : 15000
15 : 49 : : 6000 : 20000
15 : 64 : : 6000 : 25000
15 : 78 : : 6000 : 30000.

The last column has the several weights coming upon the different braces at their several inclinations; to resist which, the scantling might be very small, for compression, but flexure requires larger dimensions.

These braces should be confined laterally and vertically, as they pass each post, but not connected therewith; as this would not permit a free action of the brace, without straining transversely the post.

The length of beam, therefore, in which flexure is to be checked, is the distance between posts in any panel.

In panel No. 1, it will be 25 feet.
" " 2, " " 18 "
" " 3, " " 17 "
" " 4, " " 16 "
" " 5, " " 16 "

and applying the formula

$$\frac{2240\, b\, d^3}{L^2}=W$$

we get, in round numbers, the following dimensions, the braces being bolted and blocked together:—

For the 1st panel,	25 feet long,	8 × 10
" 2d "	37 " "	8 × 10
" 3d "	49 " "	8 × 10
" 4th "	64 " "	8 × 10
" 5th "	78 " "	8 × 10.

For the lattice-work, a double course on each side of each truss, in long spans, (150 to 200 feet); and a single course in shorter spans, of 3 × 6 plank, treenailed at intersections, is ample.

GENERAL TABLE OF DIMENSIONS FOR ARCH BRACE TRUSS.

Span.	Rise.	Chords.	Ties.	Braces.	Lattice.
50	10	2—8 × 10	1—8 × 10	2—6 × 6	2 × 9 or 3 × 6
75	12	2—8 × 10	1—8 × 10	2—6 × 6	2 × 9 or 3 × 6
100	15	3—8 × 10	2—8 × 10	3—6 × 6	2 × 9 or 3 × 6
150	20	4—8 × 12	3—8 × 10	4—6 × 8	2 × 9 or 3 × 6
200	25	4—8 × 16	3—8 × 10	4—6 × 9	2 × 9 or 3 × 6

Fig. 69 K. Fig. 69 A.

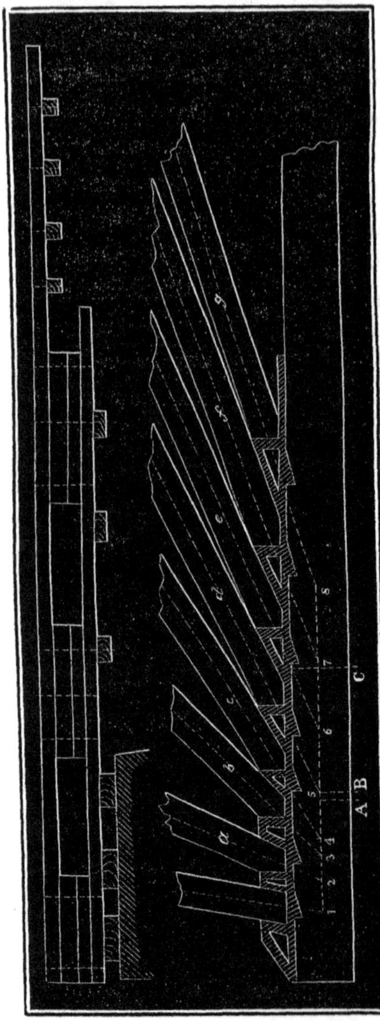

Fig. 69 A, shows the method of bringing the arch braces to the chord. To find the dimensions of the cast-iron block, make a complete drawing of all of the braces, at their proper angles, and then draw in the block around the feet, as shown in fig. 69 B.

NOTE. — The centre of pressure of the braces in fig. 69 A, is not, as might seem, at C; because the vertical components of the forces, coming down the brace, are much less in the braces at small angles than in those at the end of the span. The load applied to each brace being the same, and the inclines being found, we find the centre of pressure, or the centre of bridge seat as follows: —

The length of the brace is to the vertical height, as the applied load to the vertical pressure. In fig. 69 A, we have the following lengths of braces: *a*, 25; *b*, 37; *c*, 49; *d*, 64; *e*, 78; *f*, 92; and *g*, 106; and the weights corresponding thus,

a, 25 : 20 : : 6000 : 4800.
b, 37 : 20 : : 6000 : 3243.
c, 49 : 20 : : 6000 : 2450.
d, 64 : 20 : : 6000 : 1870.
e, 78 : 20 : : 6000 : 1540.
f, 92 : 20 : : 6000 : 1304.
g, 106 : 20 : : 6000 : 1132.

In fig. 69 A, assume the foot of the fifth brace (B) as the centre of pressure, and adding the moments, (or products of vertical components on the braces by their distance from B,) and we have the sum on the land side 18,928, and on the water side 16,930; showing that the centre is taken too far from the land side. In the same manner A will be found too far from the land side. A third trial will give the place.

Fig. 69 B.

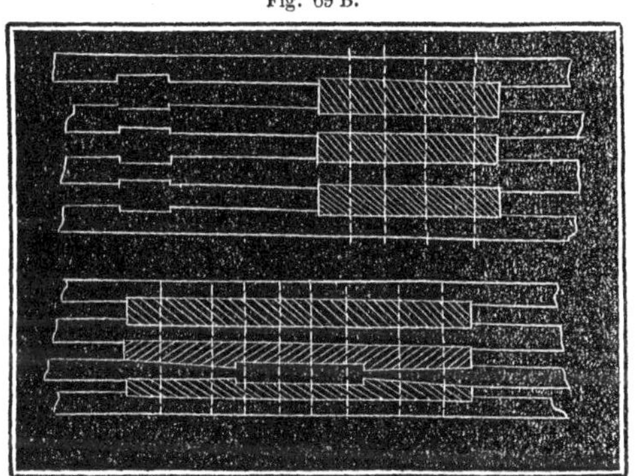

Fig. 69 C.

Fig. 69 B, shows the manner of splicing the arch braces; being subjected to compression, they are spliced in the same manner as the upper chords. Fig. C, shows the lower chord spliced. Figs. D and E, the connection of the posts, chord, and lattice. Figs. F, G, and H, the casting for applying

Fig. 69 D. Fig. 69 E. Fig. 69 F.

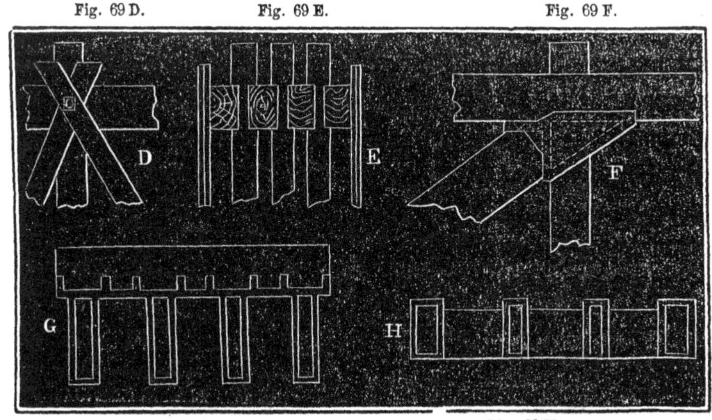

Fig. 69 G. Fig. 69 H.

the upper end of the arch brace to the chord. Fig. 69 K, the method of supporting the tracks at the end of the span, where the arch braces will not allow the floor beams to bear upon the lower chord.

McCallum's patent railroad bridge.

Fig. 70.

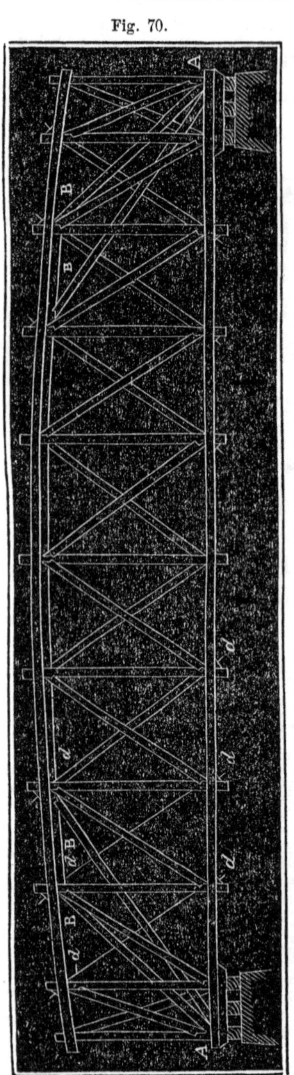

186. This bridge represents a class of structures in which the upper chord is curved upwards (7½ feet in 200 in the Susquehanna bridge, New York and Erie Railroad), which curved chord has the effect of distributing an applied load at once to all of the braces *directly*, by means of the chord, as well as *indirectly*, by means of the braces, as in the common trusses. To this bridge is applied the arch braces A B, A B, fig. 70, which serves to aid the 2d, 3d, and 4th pair of diagonal braces in bearing their load.

The great distributing power of the curved chord, is shown by the fact that a bridge of 125 feet span, actually supported a railroad train before the diagonal bracing was introduced. The whole strain was thrown through the curved chord and arch braces to the abutments. The bridge is counterbraced by the pieces *d d* and *d d*, adjustable by screws at the ends.

The following test was applied to a span of 190 feet of this plan of bridge. Placing the load as near as possible to the centre, the following deflections were produced.

Load.	Deflection.
41.40 tons,	0.013 feet,
95.35 tons,	0.038 feet,
140.70 tons,	0.061 feet,
187.20 tons,	0.061 feet.

Upon removing the load, the bridge entirely recovered its form.

187. As the span increases, the benefit derived from the curved chord also augments; and though in the latter part of the present chapter its application to small spans is shown, it may not be worth while to adopt it.

Bridges transferring the load *directly*, from each panel to the abutment, would not be aided, to an amount worth the increased expense, by adopting the curved top chord.

In case of any settling at the centre of the span, the reverse effect is seen from that produced in a truss with horizontal chords; i. e., when the ends of the upper chords in the latter *draw in*, those of the former *push out;* and when in such bridges, arch braces are not used, the top chords of adjoining spans must be *wedged apart*, in place of *tying together* as in common plans, over the centre of the piers.

THE ARCH.

188. The arch has been applied to long spans for a great while, and when care has been taken to prevent flexure, answers very well. The repair of such bridges, if any of the arch timbers decay, is difficult; but is effected, in the largest arches.

The most correct ideas on wooden arch bridge building, are to be found in Weibeking's *Traite d'une parte essential de construire les grandes pents en charpente.* This engineer,

(General Director of Roads and Bridges in Bavaria,) has built a great number of wooden arches of the best description, which show him to be master of both the science and the art.

The general plan of his bridges is shown in fig. 71. They

Fig. 71.

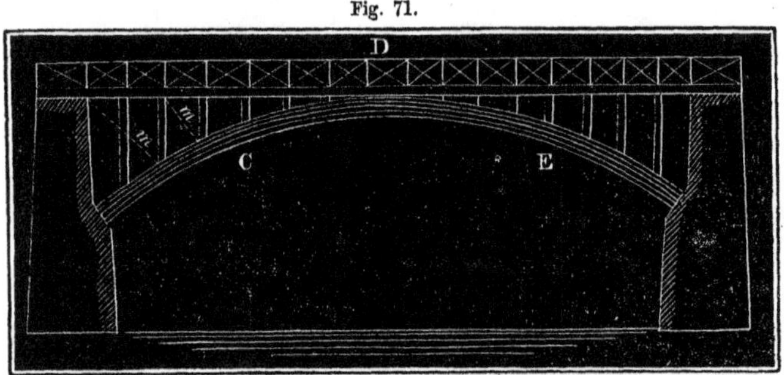

consist of curved ribs formed of long pieces scarfed and bolted together, from which the road-way is supported by posts.

The bridges of Neucettringin, Freysingin, Bamberg, Scharding, Wertach, Vilshoven, and Altenmarkt, all testify to the good judgment of this man. The spans vary from one hundred to two hundred feet; and the width from twenty-five to thirty-two feet. The proportions which he gives for the ratio of rise to span, are valuable; as they are the result of his own experience. He states, generally, that one tenth of the span is the best rise; but that for convenience, it is better to keep it lower. The following table shows the dimensions he has adopted in practice.

189.

Name.	Span.	Rise.	Width.	Rod of Arch.	Scantling of Arch.
Bamberg,	208	16.9	32	422	$13\frac{1}{2} \times 15\frac{1}{2}$
Scharding,	194	18.8	25	258	$12\frac{1}{2} \times 15\frac{1}{2}$
Vilshoven,	179	11.1	27	378	$13\frac{1}{2} \times 15\frac{1}{2}$
Freysingin,	153	11.6	25	246	$12\frac{1}{2} \times 14\frac{1}{2}$
Ettringin,	139	8.0	25	305	$12\frac{1}{2} \times 15\frac{1}{2}$
Ersingin,	126	7.0	25	285	$11\frac{1}{2} \times 14\frac{1}{2}$
Augsberg,	114	10.6	25½	158	$12\frac{1}{2} \times 14\frac{1}{2}$
Neucettringin,	103	6.8	25	200	$13\frac{1}{2} \times 15\frac{1}{2}$

The last column shows the scantling of the arch timbers; these being placed three deep, in spans of less than 150 feet; and in larger spans, 3 deep at centre, and 5 deep at ends. Mr. Weibeking's formula for determining the scantling of ribs, is as follows:—

$$\frac{W \times \left(\frac{S}{2}\right)^2}{R\,n}\ .0011 = \text{Scantling in sq. ft.}$$

Where R is the rise of the arch;
n, the number of ribs;
W, width of bridge;
and S, span of bridge.

Example.—Required the scantling of the ribs of a bridge of 300 feet span, 20 feet wide, and 30 feet high. The formula becomes,—

$$\frac{20 \times 22500}{30} \times .0011 = 16\tfrac{1}{2} \text{ sq. feet of}$$

section, of all of the arches; or two parallel arches, 2½ feet wide, by 3¼ feet deep each.

From 100 to 150 feet span, he makes the rise $\frac{1}{20}$ span,
" 150 to 200 " " $\frac{1}{18}$ "
" 200 to 300 " " $\frac{1}{15}$ "
" 300 to 400 " " $\frac{1}{14}$ "
" 400 to 500 " " $\frac{1}{13}$ "

190. The bridge built by Mr. Burr across the Delaware at Trenton, New Jersey, is a good specimen of an arch. It is composed of white pine planks, from thirty-five to fifty feet long, and of a scantling 4×12. These planks are laid close together, breaking joint, having an entire depth of three feet. The arches are stiffened by horizontal tie beams, supporting the road-way, and by diagonal bracing. The spans are 160, 180, and 200 feet, and the rise twenty-seven feet.

191. The bridge over the Susquehanna, at Columbia, built in the same manner, consists of twenty-nine arches, each two hundred feet clear span, supported on two abutments and twenty-eight stone piers. The clear water-way of this bridge is 5,800 feet; and the entire length, including piers and abutments, one and one fourth miles. There are three sets of arches, which allow of two carriage roads and one railroad, the whole width being thirty feet.

192. An arch to support a passing railroad train must be very rigid. It is customary to connect them with a light truss, which effectually counter braces the arch, and prevents that change of form which would otherwise take place; depending entirely upon the arch for strength.

Wherever the load is applied, the arch tends to sink, and a corresponding rise takes place at the opposite point. A load placed at E, fig. 71, settles the arch at that point and causes it to rise at C. A load placed at the curve of the arch depresses the centre, and elevates the haunches. To counteract these movements a light, stiffening frame may be used, its strength being able to resist the variable load passing over the bridge. The strain thrown by the arch upon the truss, advances from the opposite end to meet the train, passes it at the centre, and finally goes off from the bridge behind the load.

When the arch *is the truss*, or when a truss is made with curved chords, the counteracting effect of the truss is not completely obtained. We should not depend upon the curved chord *as an arch*, but only as a member of the truss.

193. Many combinations of arch and truss have been built in America for railroad bridges. The principle of connecting the two systems is by some thought bad, as they can hardly be made to bear equal parts of the load; whence each must have more than half the necessary strength of the whole. Others maintain that by a proper arrangement of parts a perfect adjustment may be made, by which the load may be placed more or less on either. There seems to be no very good reason why the two systems should be combined, as either may be made strong enough to bear the largest loads.

Both arches and arch braces, however, are very usefully applied to bridges which have been made too light.

194. The manner of applying arches is well shown in the bridges of the Pennsylvania Central Railroad, built by Hermann Haupt, Esq.

These bridges are on Howe's plan, to which have been added strong wooden arches. The systems are connected by adjusting the counter braces against the arch by set screws. The arrangement is simple and effectual. The name of the builder is sufficient to warrant the ability of the bridge.

195. However nicely we may form an arch, it will settle more or less when the scaffolding is removed, according to its flatness; which depression increases with time. Mr. Weibeking expresses it in inches as follows:—

$$0.806 \frac{R}{S}$$

Whence R, shows the rise,
and S, shows the span.

To allow for this settling, the curve when laid down on the platform for building the arch, should be made a little more convex than the completed arch is required to be; the amount of excess being that shown by the formula.

As a bridge composed of a curved rib when the span is large yields at D, C, and E, fig. 71, when the load is applied in the middle, the strength must of course be increased by increasing the depth of the rib; and not to make this too heavy, a framed or built beam should be used as in fig. 72.

Fig. 72.

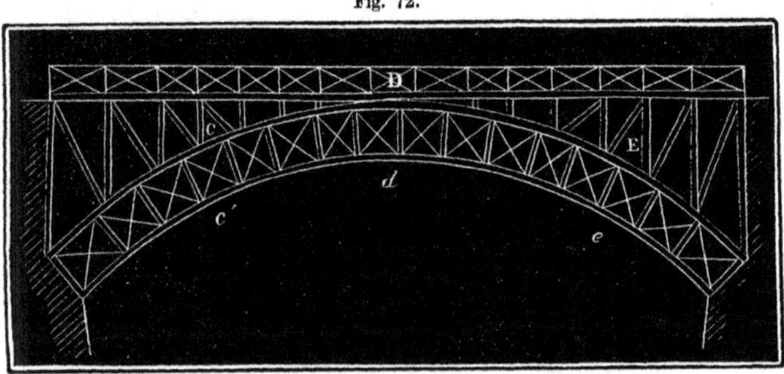

Here it must be remembered that the two ribs must be so framed as to resist both tension and compression; for when a load is placed at D, the lower rib will be extended at *d*, and compressed at *c'*, and *e*; while the upper one will be compressed at D, and extended at C and E.

OF THE ROAD-WAY.

196. The flooring of any system is about the same; consisting of transverse floor beams, placed either on the top or bottom chords, (according as the road-way is more or less elevated above the water-way,) which support longitudinal timbers, upon which are placed cross-ties. In some cases, two curves of diagonal plank have been placed across the floor beams, spiked at right angles to each other, by which the bridge is considerably stiffened laterally.

General dimensions for the floor may be thus:—

Transverse timbers, 3 feet from centre to centre,	8 × 14
Track strings, notched 2 inches to floor beams,	12 × 14
Cross-ties placed one foot apart, (clear,)	3 × 6

Fig. 73.

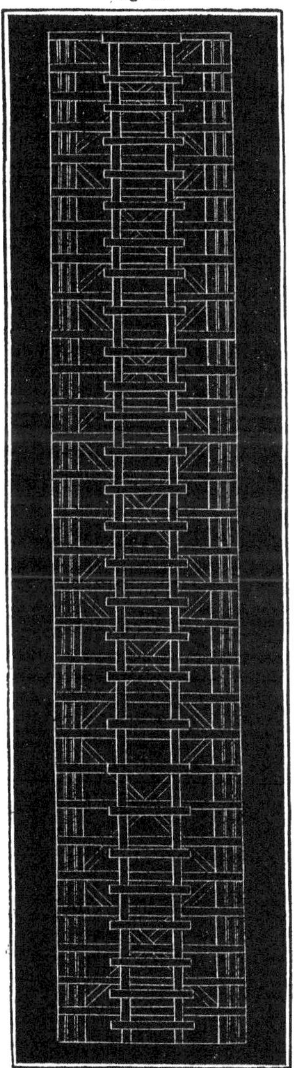

LATERAL BRACING.

197. To prevent vibration in a horizontal direction, a system of triangular bracing is necessary. The chief pressure upon these braces is caused by wind; and may be found by considering the bridge as turned over upon the side, and loaded with a weight equal to the maximum pressure of the wind, which may be taken as forty pounds per square foot.

It is unnecessary to vary the size of these braces, except in very long spans, when they should increase from the centre to the ends. For short spans, (less than one hundred feet,) a brace 5 × 5 is large enough. For larger spans 7 × 7 is sufficient.

198. Diagonal bracing, when it can be introduced, is a very desirable part of a bridge. When the road is on the lower chord this cannot have place in full, but may be applied as in fig. 74.

Fig. 74.

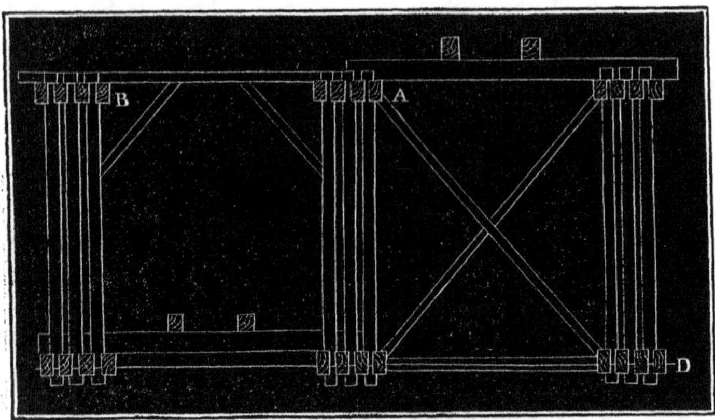

By increasing the height of truss in any bridge, the tension and compression on the chords is lessened; but the length of posts and rods is increased. As a general thing, *one eighth* of the span gives the best results.

199. In framing a large bridge, it is customary to cut the top chord sticks a little longer than to dimension; to allow for compression in settling.

200. Bridges in exposed situations have been sometimes blown off from the masonry. If a bridge *slides off* from the masonry, the whole force of the wind must be fifteen twenty-fourths of the whole weight of the bridge; but if, as is generally the case, the masonry is rough, (and not hammered,) no amount of wind will cause the bridge to *slide.*

The bridge will upset, turning about its lower edge, when the whole pressure of the wind, multiplied by half the *height* of truss, overbalances the whole weight, multiplied by the half *width.* In very exposed places the rod A D, fig. 74, answers a very good end; when the road is upon the upper chord, and a rod from B to the masonry, when upon the lower.

OBLIQUE BRIDGES.

201. The effect of running a train over a skew bridge, is to depress one side before the other; as the load comes upon the centre of one truss before it does upon the opposite one. This produces a side rocking in the engine, dangerous alike to the bridge and to itself.

The floor timbers transferring the load to the chords should not be at right angles to the axis of the road, but parallel to the abutment. Thus in fig. 75, a wheel at B, throws one third of its weight upon the abutment at E; and two thirds upon the chord at C; while in fig. 75 A, the wheel at B, throws two thirds of the load upon C, but one third also upon D.

Fig. 75. Fig. 75 A.

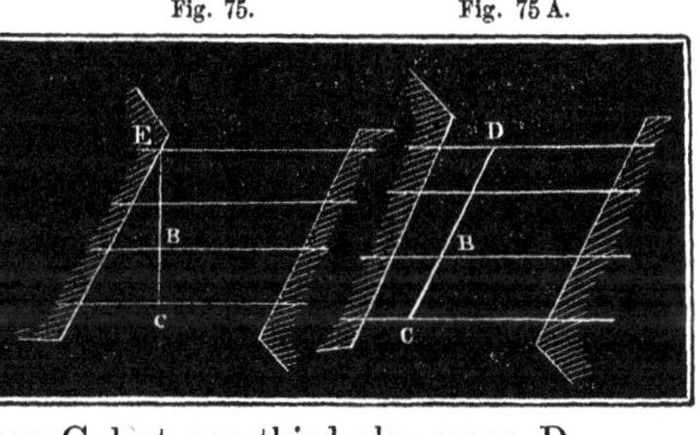

202. In a very long, oblique span, the floor timbers may be arranged as in fig. 76, that is, inclined at the entrance and exit of the bridge, but at right angles at the middle of the span.

Fig. 76.

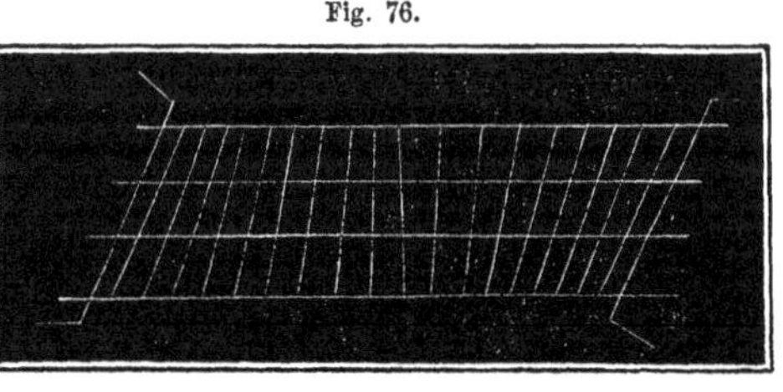

203. The preservation of timber in wooden bridges may be accomplished by covering with boards, whitewashing, painting, and by Kyanizing. Covering and whitewashing are the best, if care is taken to prevent dry rot by giving a good circulation of air about the timbers. The oil in paints prevents the escape of moisture from within as well as the entrance of that from without; and should not be

used unless the wood is well seasoned. The best plan is to thoroughly whitewash and cover the frame of the bridge, and to paint the article of the covering.

204. In framing two or more continuous spans, the chords should always be connected over the piers; as there is thus given something for the upper chords to pull against, and a counter thrust for the lower.

205. Bridges should never, when it can be avoided, be placed either upon a curve or upon a grade; particularly upon the former, as the effect of a load is thereby very much increased, in the first case causing a lateral, and in the second a vertical shock.

PILE BRIDGING.

206. In shallow water, in marshes, and in similar situations, where an embankment would be expensive, pile bridging is very useful. Indeed, whenever we are at liberty to obstruct the passage beneath the road, it is well to adopt this system, unless over twenty feet high. It is cheaper than any other, easier to repair, the parts are quite independent of each other, and such bridges last full as long as other wooden structures.

Different plans for pile bridging are given in figs. 77 to 82. Figs. 77 to 81 show plans for temporary pile work, to be used during construction. Nothing lighter than fig. 82,

Fig. 77.

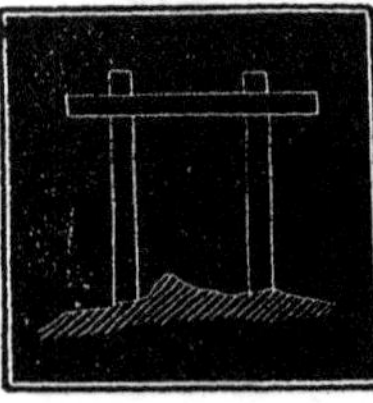

Fig. 78.

Fig. 79.

Fig. 80.

Fig. 81.

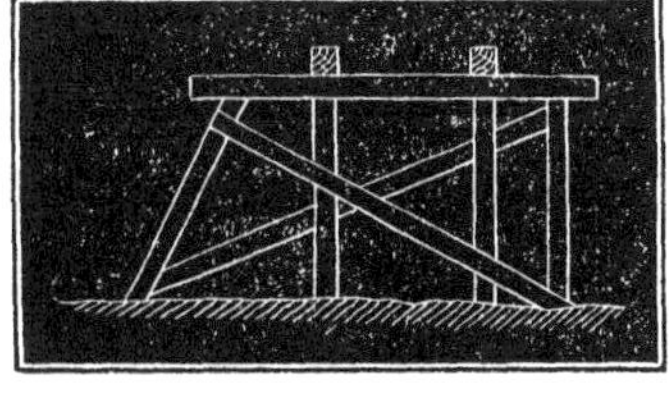

Fig. 82 A.

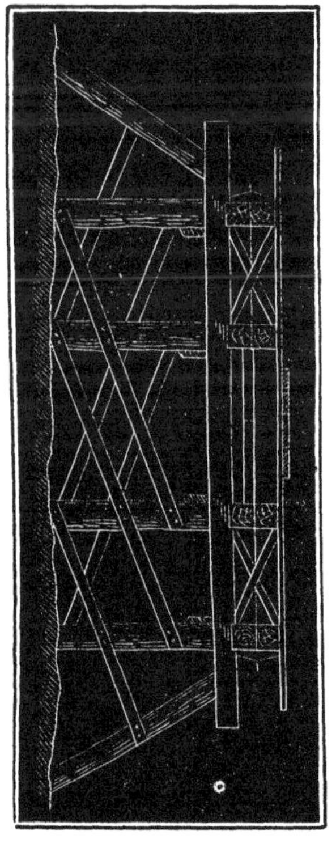

Fig. 82.

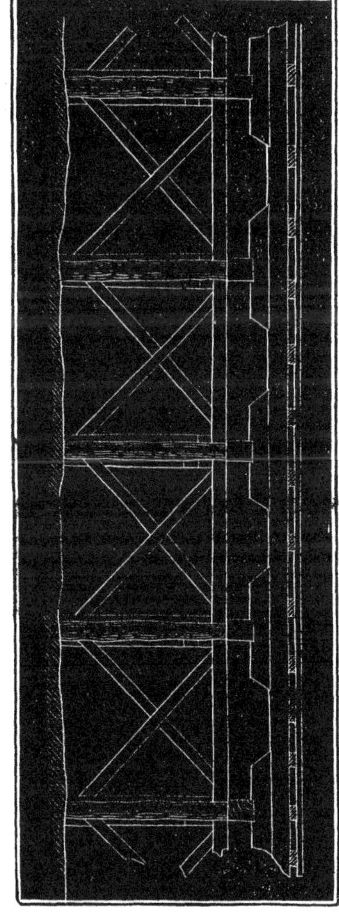

ought to be permanently used. A pile bridge upon a curve may need stronger lateral bracing upon the convex, than upon the concave side of the curve; and also in running water; in which cases, such a form as fig. 81 may do good service.

(For pile-driving, and for proper dimensions, see chap. XII.)

TRESTLING.

207. Trestling is a system of vertical posts, and of caps and braces, used both for temporary and for permanent works; temporarily to pass a road over low ground where embankments are to be made, and permanently over deep, dry gorges, where the amount of earthwork or masonry would be too great.

Fig 83.

American railroads show all sizes and arrangements of trestling, from twenty to two hundred feet high. Figs. 83 and 84 show temporary works, and fig. 85 permanent.

The main part of the design in trestles is to connect the several posts and caps by well-formed triangles; the equilateral being the best.

Fig. 84.

The finest example of this system of building is the Genesee high bridge, over Genesee River near Portageville, on the Buffalo and New York Railroad; built by H. C. Seymour.

Fig. 85.

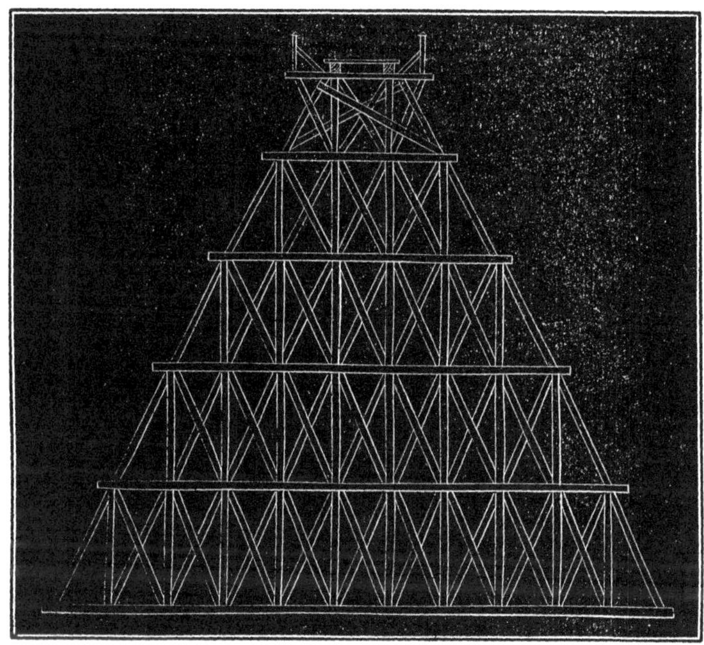

Esq. It is eight hundred feet long, and two hundred and thirty feet above the river. It has eight stone piers, thirty feet high, upon which are placed trestles one hundred and ninety feet high, seventy-five feet wide at base, and twenty-five at top. Upon the top of all is placed a bridge fourteen feet high. To build this viaduct was used 1,500,000 feet, board measure of timber, which covered, when standing, two hundred and fifty acres; also, sixty tons of bolts. The whole time occupied in building was but eighteen months, the whole cost being $140,000.

DRAWBRIDGES.

208. In crossing rivers or bays open to navigation, it is required from any companies building a bridge, to leave a

Fig. 86.

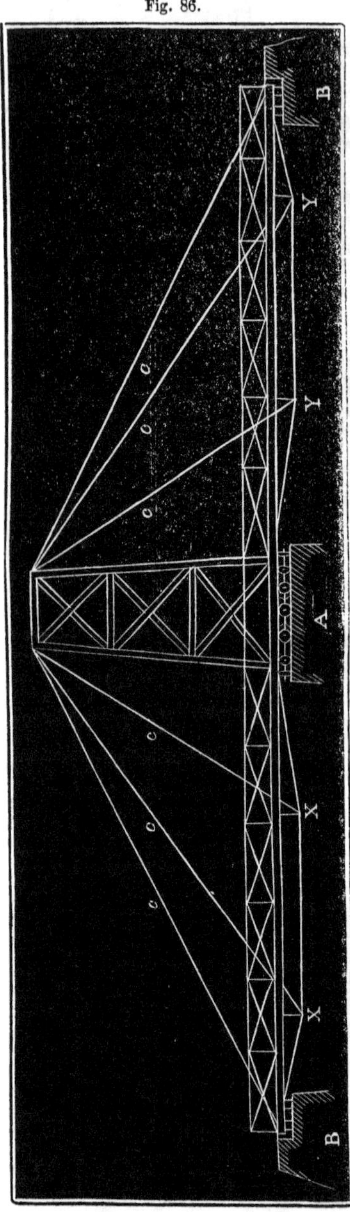

free passage for shipping. This is done by making that part of the bridge over the channel movable; (a draw).

Draws may lift up, (being counterbalanced,) may slide back upon the fixed part of the bridge, or may turn on a pivot. Fig. 86 shows a draw much used at present, and answering every purpose. Each half of the movable part must be calculated as a small bridge. The rods *c c c* support the overhanging part of the draw while open. The whole revolves upon a centre pin and a set of rollers.

CENTRES.

209. Centres are temporary wooden frames, used in the construction of stone arches. Their duty is to hold the masonry, while it is unable to support itself.

For arches from five to fifteen feet span, a centre made of boards or planks, fig. 87, is all that is necessary. For longer spans, when the ground beneath

Fig. 87.

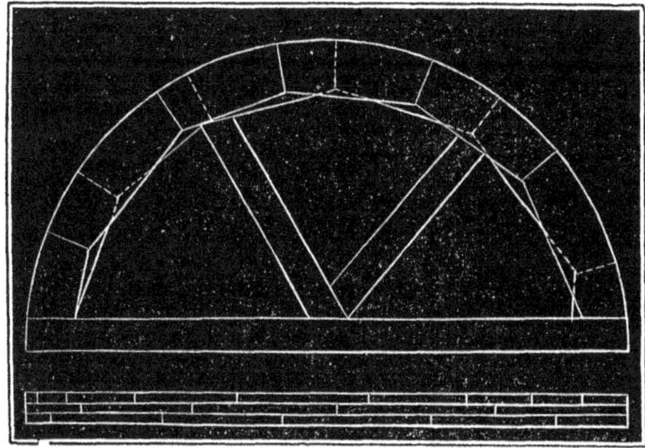

the arch can be used, the form, fig. 88, answers well. When

Fig. 88.

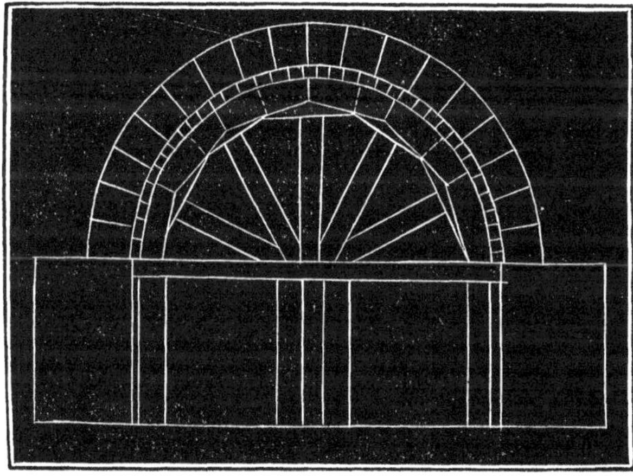

there is no support but the abutments or piers, something similar to fig. 89 must be adopted. This is the plan adopted by George Rennie, chief engineer at the Waterloo bridge over the Thames at London.

Centres are strained in a different manner as the arch progresses; first at the haunches, and last at the crown. Excess of weight at any point causes a settling at such,

Fig. 89.

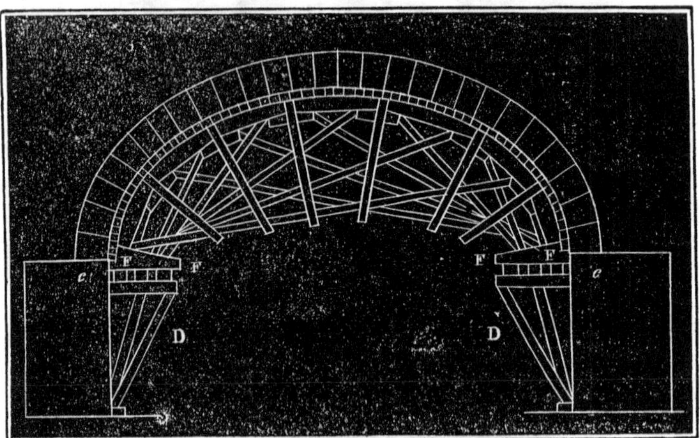

and a rise takes place at some other place. By loading the arch temporarily, such motions are checked.

These frames are placed vertically upon the pieces F F, which being connected with the braces D D by the folding wedges *c c*, admit of adjustment of the height of the centre. The distance between the ribbed frames depends upon the form of the arch, and the span, or upon the weight to be supported; varying from one to four feet. The centres are covered with a course of narrow plank, placed parallel with the axis of the arch, upon which the barriers rest.

210. The method of putting a bridge upon the masonry is shown in figs. 90, and 91; the former when the road-way is upon the upper, and the latter when upon the lower chord.

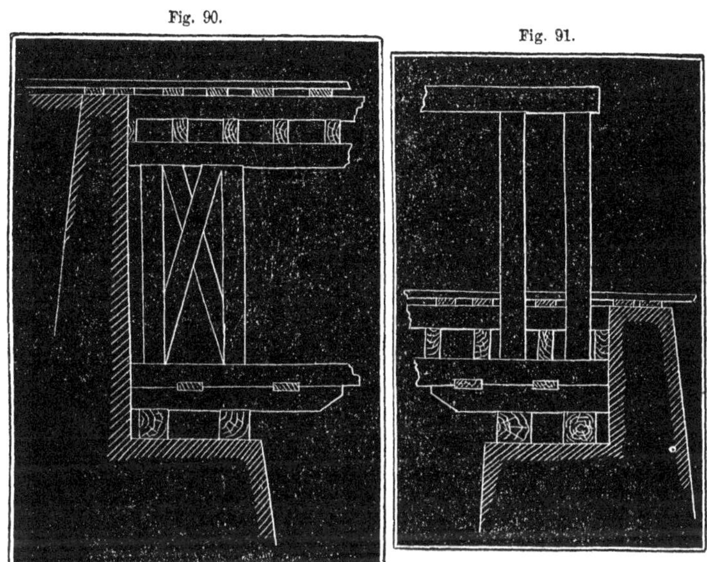
Fig. 90. Fig. 91.

211. In figs. 92 to 100, are given several plans for spans from five to seventy-five feet. Fig. 92, shows the simple beam braced beneath with diagonal plank; the bolts passing through the ties, stringers, and braces. The stringers are bolted to the wall plates, and when the bridge is upon a curve notched also, by cutting the bolster. Fig. 92 A shows the plan. This form answers for openings from five to twenty feet. From fifteen to thirty feet, we may use figs. 94, 95, 96, and 97. From twenty-five, to fifty and sixty feet, figs. 93, 97, and 98. And from fifty to seventy-five feet, figs. 99 and 100.

The following tables give reliable dimensions for bridges upon the above plans.

Fig. 92. 5 to 20 feet.

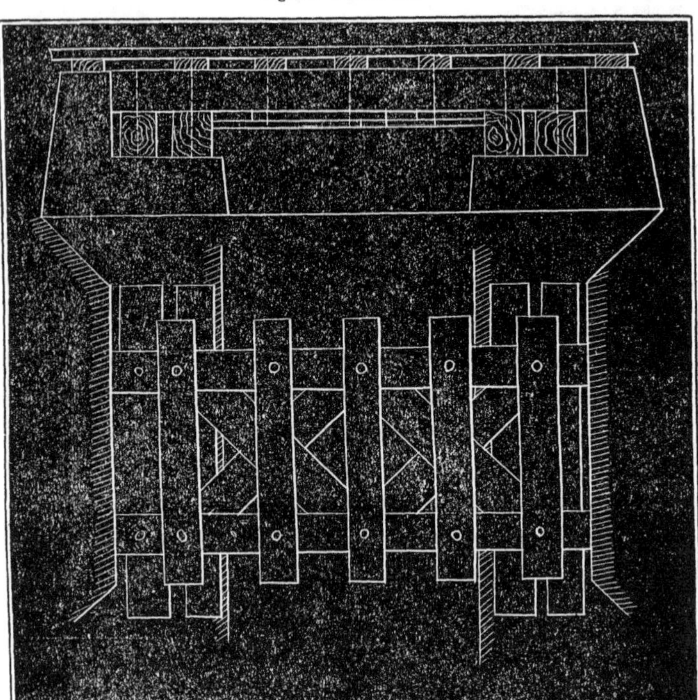

Fig. 92 A.

Span.	Bolsters.	Stringers.	Ties.	Braces.	Bolts.
5	12 × 12	12 × 12	6 × 10	2 × 10	1 inch
10	12 × 12	12 × 13	6 × 10	2 × 10	1 inch
15	14 × 14	12 × 18	6 × 10	2 × 10	1 inch
20	14 × 14	12 × 21	6 × 10	2 × 10	1 inch.

The ties being notched three inches on to the stringers, without cutting the latter.

Fig. 95. 15 to 30 feet.

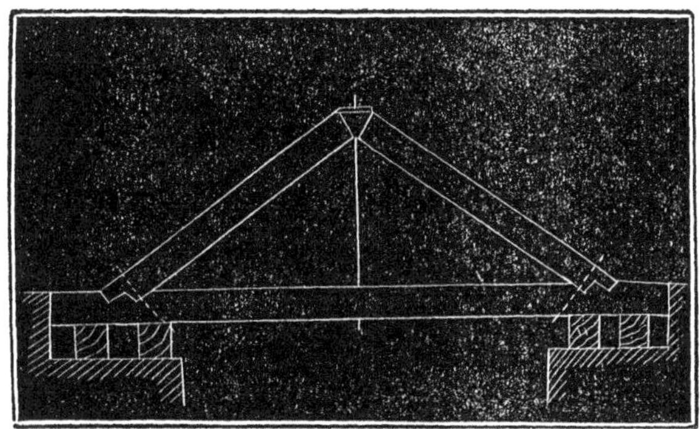

Span.	Rise.	Bolster.	Stringer.	Braces.	Rod.
15	6	12 × 12	12 × 12	2 — 5 × 6	1 inch
20	7	14 × 14	12 × 12	2 — 5 × 8	$1\frac{1}{4}$ inch
25	8	14 × 14	12 × 15	2 — 5 × 9	$1\frac{3}{8}$ inch
30	10	15 × 15	12 × 18	2 — 5 × 10	$1\frac{1}{2}$ inch.

Fig. 96. 15 to 30 feet.

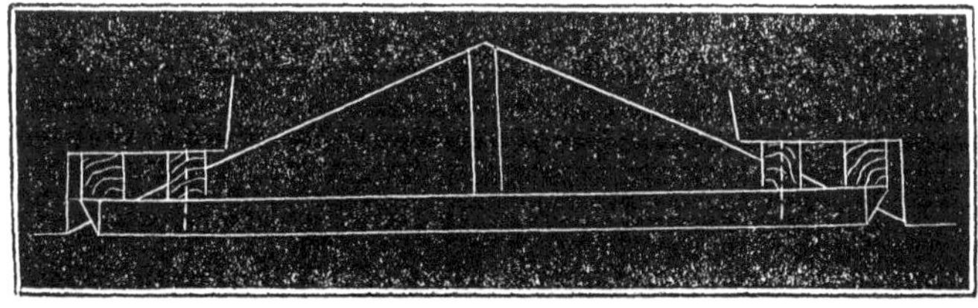

Span.	Rise.	Stringer.	Post.	Rod.
15	5	12 × 12	8 × 8	$1\frac{1}{8}$
20	6	12 × 13	9 × 9	$1\frac{1}{4}$
25	7	12 × 15	10 × 10	$1\frac{1}{2}$
30	8	12 × 18	10 × 12	$1\frac{5}{8}$

Fig. 94. 15 to 30 feet.

Span.	Rise.	Stringer.	Braces.	Rods.	Lattice.
15	5	2 — 8 × 8	2 — 5 × 5	1	2 × 6
20	6	2 — 8 × 9	2 — 5 × 6	$1\frac{1}{4}$	2 × 8
25	7	2 — 8 × 10	2 — 5 × 8	$1\frac{3}{8}$	2 × 9
30	9	2 — 8 × 12	2 — 5 × 9	$1\frac{1}{2}$	2 × 10

Fig. 97. 15 to 30 feet.

Span.	Rise.	Stringer.	Post.	Rod.	Braces.
15	5	2 — 8 × 8	8 × 8	1	4 × 5
20	6	2 — 8 × 9	9 × 9	$1\frac{1}{8}$	4 × 6
25	7	2 — 8 × 10	10 × 10	$1\frac{1}{4}$	5 × 6
30	9	2 — 8 × 12	10 × 12	$1\frac{1}{2}$	6 × 6

Fig. 93. 25 to 50 feet.

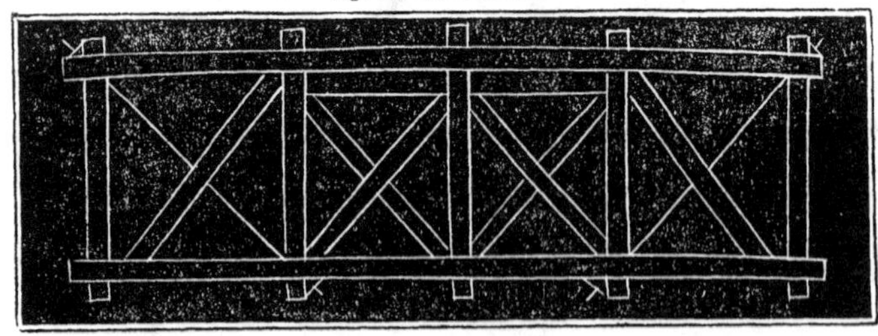

Span.	Rise.	Chords.	Braces.	Posts.	Rods.
25	8	2 — 6 × 8	6 × 6	6 × 8	1
40	10	2 — 7 × 9	6 × 7	8 × 8	$1\frac{1}{8}$
50	10	2 — 8 × 10	6 × 8	8 × 10	$1\frac{1}{4}$

Fig. 97. 25 to 50 feet.

Span.	Rise.	Chords.	Posts.	Braces.	Rods.
25	8	2 — 6 × 8	8 × 8	5 × 5	$1\frac{1}{8}$ or 2 — $\frac{7}{8}$
40	10	2 — 7 × 9	9 × 9	5 × 8	$1\frac{3}{8}$ or 2 — $1\frac{1}{8}$
50	10	2 — 8 × 10	10 × 10	6 × 8	$1\frac{3}{4}$ or 2 — $1\frac{1}{4}$

Fig. 98. 25 to 50 feet.

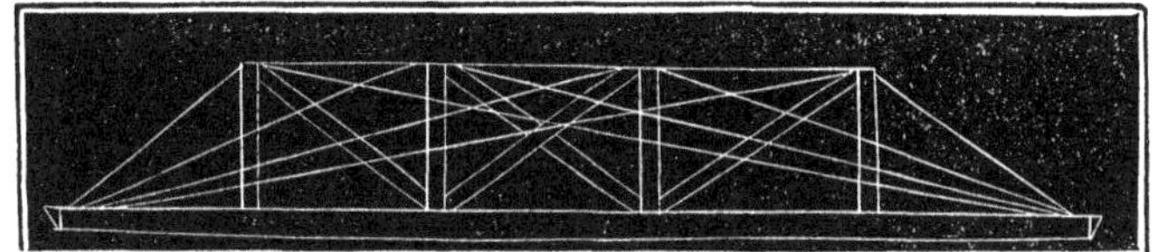

Span.	Rise.	Chords.	Posts.	Braces.	Rods.
25	8	2 — 6 × 8	6 × 8	5 × 5	2 — 1 or 1 — $1\frac{3}{8}$
40	10	2 — 7 × 9	6 × 9	5 × 8	2 — $1\frac{1}{8}$ or 1 — $1\frac{5}{8}$
50	10	2 — 8 × 10	6 × 12	5 × 10	2 — $1\frac{1}{4}$ or 1 — $1\frac{3}{4}$

Fig. 99. 50 to 75 feet.

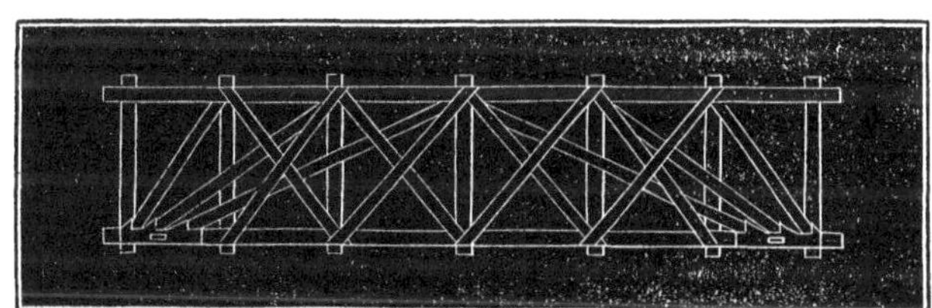

Span.	Rise.	Chord.	Posts.	Braces.	Lattice.
50	8	2. 8 × 10	1 — 8 × 10	2 — 6 × 7	2 × 6
60	9	2. 8 × 10	1 — 8 × 10	2 — 6 × 7	2 × 6
75	10	3. 8 × 10	2 — 8 × 10	3 — 6 × 8	2 × 6

Fig. 100. 50 to 75 feet.

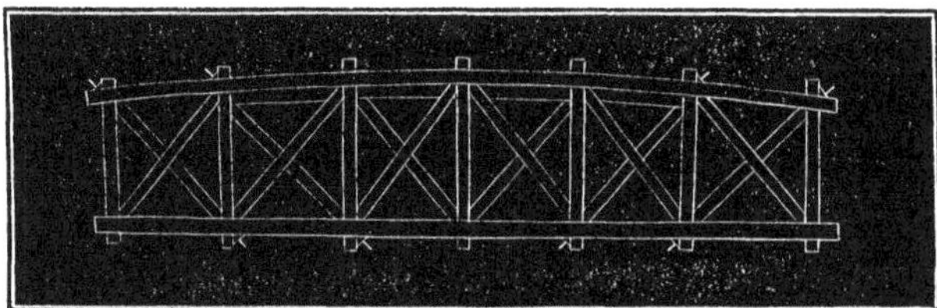

Span.	Rise.	Chords.	Posts.	Braces.	Centre braces.	Rods. No. 1.	No. 2.
50	8	2—8 × 10	1—8 × 10	2—6 × 7	5 × 5	$1\frac{1}{2}$	1
60	9	2—8 × 10	1—8 × 10	2—6 × 7	5 × 5	$1\frac{5}{8}$	$1\frac{1}{8}$
75	10	3—8 × 10	2—8 × 10	2—6 × 8	5 × 6	$1\frac{3}{4}$	$1\frac{1}{4}$

212. In dimensioning small bridges, like the above, in estimating the maximum load, more regard must be given to the weight of momentary loads than (as in large bridges) the weight per lineal foot, as the weight of the bridge itself, when under fifty or sixty feet span, is inconsiderable. The greatest load that can come upon a single post or rod, is that from the driving wheels of a locomotive. If the whole engine weighs forty tons, there will be ten tons on each pair of drivers, or five tons or 11,200 lbs. on each wheel; which, being applied over a length of ten feet only, may be considered as at a single point, and all parts must be able to bear such load. In large spans, where the weight is great, if the truss is strong enough to support the bridge and load, it will safely resist the effects of a sudden application of passing trains.

NOTE. — *On the Static and Dynamic deflection of Bridges.* Considerable variance of opinion exists as to the relative deflection of bridges, produced by stationary and by moving loads. Neither experiment nor theory has exactly settled the point.

Experiments upon the Elwell bridge, (Epsom and Croydon Railway, England).

Velocity in feet per second.	Deflection in inches.
0	0.215
25	0.215
31	0.230
32	0.225
54	0.245
75	0.235

The bridge being a cast-iron girder of forty-eight feet span, load thirty-nine tons.

Experiments on the Godstone bridge, (S. E. R. R. England).

Velocity in feet per second.	Deflection in inches.
0	0.19
22	0.23
40	0.22
73	0.25

Cast-iron girder, thirty feet span, load thirty-three tons.

Mr. W. H. Barlow, (Eng.) observed, "that in case of a timber viaduct, a freight train, at a low speed, produced a certain deflection; but an extra train, with a much lighter engine, seemed to push the bridge like a wave before it."

The Britannia tubular bridge was depressed three fourths of an inch by two locomotives and a train of two hundred and eighty tons standing still; but at seventy miles per hour, the deflection was sensibly less.

CHAPTER IX.

IRON BRIDGES.

"A little knowledge is a dangerous thing."

213. WITHIN the past ten years iron has been brought extensively into use for railroad bridging; and when employed by those who understand its chemical and mechanical nature is unequalled for strength, durability, and elegance of appearance; but when, as is too often the case in America, it is intrusted to men who neither know nor care for any thing but the price they get for it, nothing can be more unsafe. No material requires so complete a knowledge of its properties, to be safely used, as cast-iron.

NATURE AND STRENGTH OF IRON.

214. The table below shows the properties of the several descriptions of iron used in engineering.

Wrought Iron.	Cast-Iron.	Iron Wire.	Boiler Plate.	Designation of the quality.
480	450	———	480	Weight per cubic foot in lbs.
15000	4500	25000	12740	Resistance to extension in lbs. per sq. inch.
11000	25000	———	7500	Resistance to compression in lbs. per sq. in.
.0000066	.00000608	.00000675	.0000066	Expansion per degree Farenheit in lengths.
.0000000424	.000000106	.0000000446	.0000000524	Extension per lb. per square inch.
.000000149	.000000083	———	.000000189	Compression per lb. per square inch.
90 to 66	20 to 111	———	127 to 75	Ratio of extensive to compressive strength.
12500	17500	———	———	Resistance to detrusion, or straining.
55	31	———	———	Relative transverse strength.

Column four refers to boiler plate when built into tubes.

After wrought iron has become a little compressed, its power to resist a crushing force is very much increased.

215. The tenacity of wrought iron is increased by heating. Experiments upon thirty varieties gave the following mean result, the temperature ranging from 500° to 700° Fahrenheit.

Strength when

Cold.	Hot.	Cooled.
60,000	64,000	70,000

216. Stirling's process of toughening cast-iron, by the addition of malleable scrap, increases the strength in the following ratio: —

The mean tensile strength of cast-iron being	15,000 lbs.
And the compressive strength being .	75,000 "
When Stirling-toughened the tensile strength is	23,000 "
And the compressive strength . .	130,000 "

The strength of cast-iron increases rapidly up to the twelfth or fifteenth recasting, when it is nearly doubled; after the fifteenth melting the strength decreases.

217. Wrought iron exposed for some time to vibration, as in the case of railroad axles, or iron which has been wrought with light hammers, loses its toughness and becomes "short," (crystalline). The fibre may be restored in such cases by reheating and cooling slowly.

218. GENERAL RATIOS OF THE STRENGTH OF IRON.

	Tension.	Compression.	Cross Strain.
Cast,	300	1,666	31.68
Wrought,	1,000	733	55.40

OF THE STRENGTH OF BOILER PLATES.

219. The strength of rolled boiler plates is no greater in the *direction of the fibres than crosswise*, but is more regular; whence the length of the fibre must be placed as nearly as possible with the direction of the force.

A mean of twelve experiments, by Mr. Fairbairn, gives the tensile strength of wrought iron plates as 50,960 lbs. per square inch; and the compressive strength of plates, when built into tubes, as 30,464 lbs., or for safe use in practice, for extension, 12,740 lbs., and for compression, 7,500 lbs. In the remarks upon girder bridges the matter of riveting will be considered.

CLASSIFICATION OF IRON BRIDGES.

220. Iron bridges may be classified as follows: —

Those entirely of *cast-iron*, or Arch and Girder bridge.
Those of *wrought iron* alone, or Tubular and Girder.
Those of *iron wire*, or Suspension bridges.
Those of *cast and wrought iron*, or Trussed bridges.

The order in which these bridges may be placed as regards

cost of construction, and extent of application, is as follows:—

Number.	Span.	Description of bridge.
1	10 to 50 feet	Cast-iron girder.
2	50 to 200 "	Cast and wrought combinations.
3	200 to 2000 "	Suspension.
4	200 to 500 "	Cast arch.
5	25 to 100 "	Boiler plate girder.
6	100 to 500 "	Tubular.

Numbers 2, 3, and 5, are the forms which are in use upon American roads. No. 1, is very liable to failure, requires much more knowledge and care in building, and is far more expensive than a wooden truss, or trussed girder. No. 4, is very expensive, and causes a greater obstruction to the water-way than any other. The enormous expense of No. 6, should, and will prevent its adoption in the United States. Let us look at the principles of construction of numbers 2, 3, and 5.

COMBINATIONS OF CAST AND WROUGHT IRON.

221. Under this head come all of the iron trussed frames used in this country.

As before observed, skill in bridge construction consists in using always that material which with the least expense is the best able to resist the particular strain to which it may be exposed. Thus wrought iron must always be used to resist tension, and cast-iron compression. Posts, braces, and upper chords should always be cast, while ties and lower chords should be made of wrought iron.

The strength of a railroad bridge must be such as to resist all extra shocks and strains, such as are produced by derailment of engines, and breakage of axles; also incidental strains arising from change of form by expansion and contraction of the metal, and from high winds and gales.

Fig. 101.

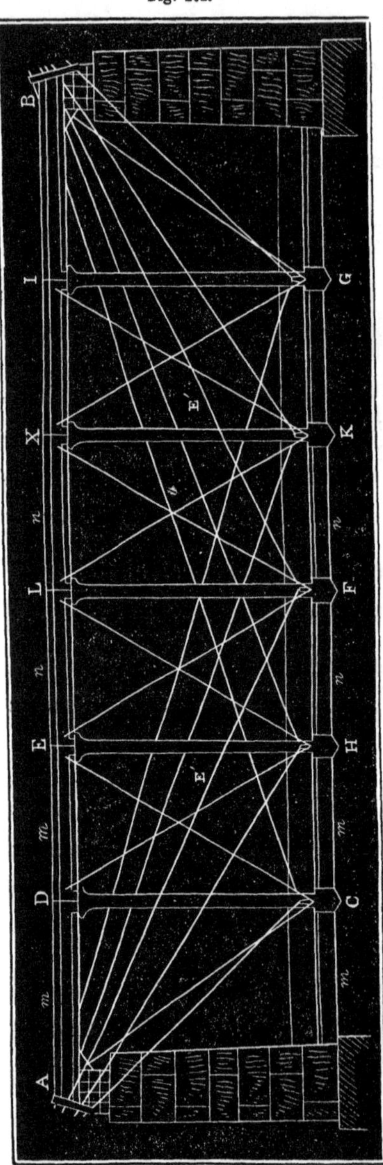

Every part of a bridge not resisting some force is worse than useless, as it adds to the weight. Lightness not only increases the economy directly, but indirectly by removing a part of the permanent load.

222. Foremost in class number two stands Wendel Bollman's Iron Suspension and trussed bridge. For simplicity of construction and directness of action, this bridge is unsurpassed. The weight at each post is transferred at once to the abutment or pier. The upper chord is of cast iron, hollow, octagonal without, and circular within. The posts consist of an H casting, the central web cast open and the flanges whole. The top is adjusted to the chord, and the bottom to the tension or suspending rods. These latter are of wrought iron, rectangular

in section, joined when the length requires it by an eye bolt. Each set after leaving the foot of the post, passes through the chair at A B, fig. 101, and is secured by a nut. The junction of the tension rod A C, and the counter rod B C, is attached indirectly to the foot of the post by a pendulum or link; which serves to equalize the effect of expansion upon the rods. Vibration and reaction are prevented by the panel diagonal ties D H, and C E. The floor is supported by flanges at the foot of each post. The lateral bracing consists of a system of hollow cast-iron posts, and of wrought diagonal tie rods. A lower chord is plainly unnecessary, its place being taken by the rods C B, F B, F A, G A.

A bridge of this description upon the Baltimore and Ohio Railroad of the following dimensions,

Clear span,	124 feet
Length of top chord,	128 "
Length of panel,	15 "
Height of truss,	17 "
Width,	16 "
Lbs. of cast-iron,	65,137
Lbs. of wrought iron,	33,527
Whole weight,	98,664
Weight per lineal foot,	796

was subjected to the following tests.

Three locomotives with tenders attached, and weighing in all one hundred and twenty-two tons, (nearly one ton per foot,) were run over the bridge at eight miles per hour, when the deflection at centre was one and three eighths inches, and at the first post nine sixteenths of an inch. The following tests were applied to a bridge of seventy-six feet span upon the Washington branch of the same road:

An engine and tender weighing forty tons, caused a de-

17 *

flection of five eighths of an inch. A fast passenger train deflected the bridge nine sixteenths of an inch.

Two engines and tenders, back to back, at rest, and weighing in all $77\frac{1}{2}$ tons, caused a deflection of	$\frac{11}{16}$	inch,
The same at ten miles per hour,	$\frac{13}{16}$	"
Engines head to head at four miles per hour,	$\frac{13}{16}$	"
at eight miles per hour,	$\frac{13}{16}$	"
at twenty miles per hour,	$\frac{14}{16}$	"

The extreme expansion of the one hundred and twenty-eight feet chord from heat, was five sixteenths of an inch at each end, or five eighths of an inch in all, or $\frac{1}{2457}$ th of the length; and that without the slightest derangement of masonry. The rod C B, being five times as long as C A, expands five times as much, but at the same time the lengths D A, D B, being so nearly proportional to C A, and C B, expand also in the ratio of one to five; and thus no bad result is experienced.

The estimate of strains upon this bridge is extremely simple; the whole consisting of as many separate systems as there are posts. Each set of rods sustain a rectangle equal to one panel, i. e., the two adjacent half panels. Thus A C, and C B, support the rectangle *m m*, *m m*, the rods A F, F B, the rectangle *n n*, *n n*. Allowance must of course be made for the inclination of the rods. The dimensions of the central pair will of course be the same; but those of the other sets will vary. The diagonals D H, and H L, prevent reaction; and must be able to resist the action produced by the variable load upon one panel (as noticed in Chapter VIII).

Any load, one at C D for example, gives to the posts a tendency to revolve on A, as a centre towards the abutment; to oppose which, there must be a force in the opposite direction. The most proper direction in which to resist such motion is the line C K, i. e., the line of the lower chord.

In this bridge there is no lower chord, but in place of such are put the rods A G, A K, B H, and B C; which prevent the change of form (by the motion of the triangle) and act against the upper chord.

As an example of the estimate of strains upon this bridge take the following.

Span, ...	90 feet.
Rise, ...	18 "
Panel, ...	15 "
Weight per lineal foot, ...	2,500 lbs.
Whole weight, ...	225,000 "
Weight on each side truss, ...	112,500 "
Weight on each post, ...	18,750 "

The weight borne by each system, i. e., one post and the two supporting rods, is 18,750 lbs. The strain to be resisted by any one rod depends upon its inclination.

The following figures show the elements of the truss in question: —

Rod.	Length.	Applied weight.			Increased strain.	Section of the bar in inches.
A B	$=90.0$					
C D	$=18.0$					
A C	$=23.4$	$18750 - 3125 = 15625$	which by	$\frac{23.4}{18}$	$=20132$	$1\frac{1}{3}$
A H	$=35.0$	$\frac{18750 \times 60}{90} = 12500$	"	$\frac{35}{18}$	$=24306$	$1\frac{2}{3}$
A F	$=48.5$	$\frac{18750 \times 45}{90} = 9375$	"	$\frac{48.5}{18}$	$=25260$	$1\frac{2}{3}$
A K	$=62.6$	$\frac{18750 \times 30}{90} = 6250$	"	$\frac{62.6}{18}$	$=21736$	$1\frac{1}{3}$
A G	$=77.6$	$\frac{18750 \times 15}{90} = 3125$	"	$\frac{77.6}{18}$	$=13472$	1

Column 1, gives the name of the rod; col. 2, the calculated diagonal length; col. 4, the applied weight, (the varying weight by reason of the varying inclination) found by multiplying the whole weight upon one panel or post by the distance of that post from the abutment, and dividing the product by the span. (Thus the load applied to A C is

$$\frac{W \times IB}{S},$$

that on A R is

$$\frac{W \times BX}{S},$$

and so on.) Col. 6, shows the increase found by col. 5 on account of inclination as noticed in Chap. VIII.; and finally, col. 4 gives the necessary sectional area of the bars or rods.

The compression on the top chord is evidently the sum of the compressions of the separate systems; the compression from any one system is as follows, fig. 102.

Fig. 102.

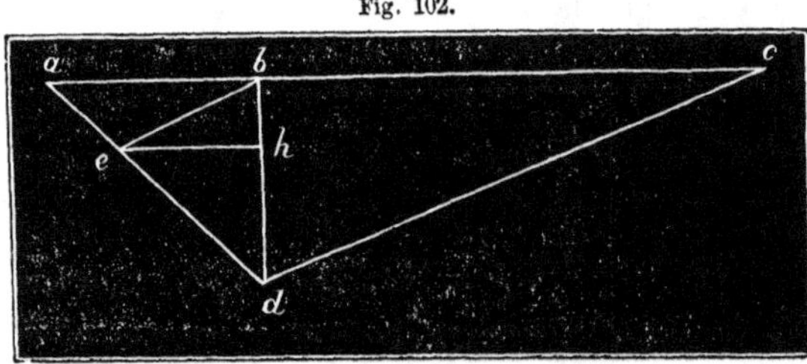

Let $a\,d$, $c\,d$ be the rods, and $a\,b\,c$ the chord; also $b\,d$, the post; now if $d\,b$ represents the weight, $e\,h$ shows the tension on a lower, or the compression on an upper chord; the triangles $a\,c\,d$ and $a\,b\,e$ are similar; as also $e\,b\,h$ and $d\,b\,c$; whence

$$b\,e = \frac{a\,b \times c\,d}{a\,c};$$

and

$$e\,h = \frac{c\,b \times b\,e}{d\,c} \text{ compression.}$$

Numerically we have the following figures:—

In the first system,

$$b\,e = \frac{15 \times 77.6}{90} = 13,$$

also

$$e\,h = \frac{75 \times 13}{77.6} = 12.$$

In the second system,

$$b\,e = \frac{30 \times 62.6}{90} = 21,$$

also

$$e\,h = \frac{60 \times 20}{62.6} = 20.$$

In the third system,

$$b\,e = \frac{45 \times 48.5}{90} = 24,$$

also

$$e\,h = \frac{45 \times 24}{48.5} = 23,$$

that is, the compression from the system A C B, is to the weight on the post, as twelve is to the length of the post; or actually

18 to 12 as 18,750 to compression;

whence

$$\text{compression} = \frac{18750 \times 12}{18} \text{ or } 12500$$

in system one, and in the second system

18 to 20 as 18750 to 20833.

In the central system,

18 to 23 as 18750 to 24000.

Doubling the sum of the first and second systems, and adding thereto the central, we have

$$2\,(12500 + 20833) + 24000 = 90666 \text{ lbs.},$$

as the whole compression upon one side of the bridge.

As to compression only, this would require a section of

about four square inches of cast-iron, which may be obtained by a tube of four and one half inches inside, and five inches outside diameter. We may however need to increase this amount to resist flexure, or transverse strains; in which case the length of tube in one panel is to be regarded as the height of a post, or the length of a beam; and the size will be found by the table on page 193.

Each post must bear 18,750 lbs., and these being of cast iron, to resist flexure, by the same table above referred to, should, if made as a hollow cylinder, be a little over four inches in diameter, and one half inch thick; and if of + or H section, should have a square of nearly five inches.

The flooring will be dimensioned by the rules given in Chapter VIII. for single beams.

There is nothing about this bridge to burn, in case of fire, except the floor; and that might easily be made of iron.

To use the words of the inventor, " The permanent principle in bridge building sustained throughout this mode of structure, and in which there is such gain in competition with any other, namely, the direct transfer of weight to the abutment, renders the calculation simple, the expense certain, and facilitates the erection of secure, economical, and durable structures."

WHIPPLE'S IRON BRIDGES.

223. The bridges built by the above-named engineer are in all respects well proportioned, rigid, safe, and durable. Cast-iron is used as a top chord, and wrought iron is employed to resist the tensile forces. The plan put up upon the New York and Erie Railroad, consists of a hollow cast-iron top chord, circular in section. Lower chords of wrought iron rods. Posts cast cruciform in section. Diagonal tension rods, as in Pratt's bridge, (Chapter VIII.) The whole

structure is in iron exactly what the above-named bridges are in wood; and the method of calculation is the same. For spans not exceeding one hundred feet, this form answers every purpose as a railroad bridge. It is open to the same objection in larger spans as are all trusses transferring the load by a series of triangles through which the weight passes successively, namely, the effect of an enormous pressure at the feet of the second and third pairs of braces, which should be taken up by arch braces, as in fig. 69; or by rods from the top of the abutment pillars to the feet of the second and third sets of posts.

A span of this plan, upon the New York and Erie Railroad, of forty feet, and which weighed only three tons, supported a load of fifteen hundred pounds per lineal foot for two days; when the bridge had settled nearly one half inch. A load of rails weighing 1318 lbs. per foot (of bridge) was then rolled over, upon a truck without springs, thus making the whole load upwards of 2,800 lbs. per foot, when the whole deflection was three fourths of an inch. Upon removing the load the bridge returned to its original position, within one fourth of an inch.

SUSPENSION BRIDGES.

224. Suspension bridges of large span have been generally considered as entirely unfit for railroad purposes; but John A. Roebling has proved the contrary by erecting a wire suspension railroad bridge of eight hundred feet clear span across Niagara River; which with heavy loads and violent gales has shown itself to be both stiff and strong to any desired amount. The construction of a bridge upon any other plan would have been hardly possible at the site of Mr. Roebling's Niagara bridge, there being no opportunity for scaffolding or for piers, pontoons or hydraulic presses.

The simple road-way supported by cables, possesses great strength with very little stiffness. It must be accompanied by stays and trusses to check vibration.

No bridge involves more simple calculations, and in none can we proceed with more absolute safety, than in the wire suspension. European suspension bridges are generally formed of cables made by linking bars of wrought iron together. This method is more expensive and more liable to failure than the American plan of forming cables of iron wire. An apparently good bar may be defective inside, while we are sure of every component fibre of the cable; indeed it is very little trouble to test each wire as it is laid into the cable.

The parts to be considered in proportioning a suspension bridge are

The anchoring masonry,
The anchor chains,
The towers and plate,
The suspension cables,
The suspending rods,
The stiffening arrangement,
The road-way.

The data given in the construction of a bridge of this description are

The span,
The load to be supported.

The assumed data

The varied line of the cable,
The width.

And the required elements

The length of cable,
Lengths of suspending rods,

Angle of tangent of cable at point of suspension with axis of tower,
Tension upon the cables,
Section of the anchor irons,
Amount of anchoring masonry,
Size of the towers,
Dimensions of trussing and of road-way.

OF THE CABLES.

225. The curve formed by the cable of a suspension bridge lies between the parabola and the catenary. When loaded the curve is nearly the former, and when unloaded the latter.

Problem 1.

Given the horizontal distance between the points of suspension and the versed-sine, to find the length of the cable, fig. 103.

Fig. 103.

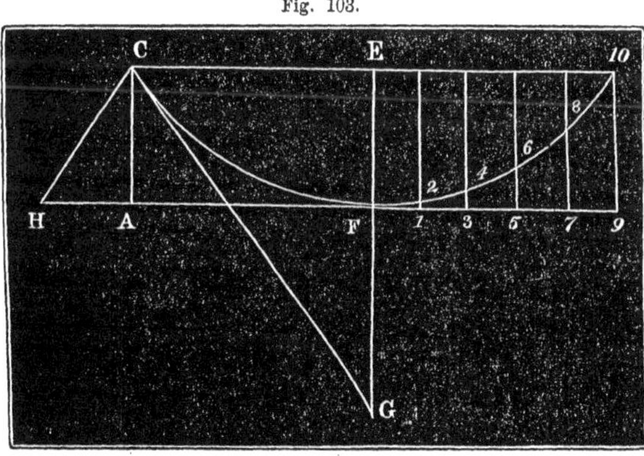

Represent C E by b, and E F by a, and the length of the semicurve is

$$L=b\left[1+\frac{2}{3}\left(\frac{a}{b}\right)^2\right].$$

Let the half span be five hundred feet, and the versed-sine or deflection eighty feet, the formula becomes

$$L = 500\left[1 + \frac{2}{3}\left(\frac{80}{500}\right)^2\right] = 500 \times 1.0171 = 508.55 \text{ feet},$$

which is the half length of cables between towers.

Problem 2.

226. To find the length of the suspending rods. Calling E the horizontal distance between the vertical suspenders, we have the formula

$$X = \frac{Y^2}{b^2} \times a,$$

in which we place E, 2 E, 3 E, etc., in place of Y, thus calling the rods one hundred feet apart, we have

Centre.	Rod 1.	Rod 2.	Rod 3.	Rod 4.	Rod 5.
0	$\frac{E^2}{b^2} \times a$	$\frac{4\,E^2}{b^2} \times a$	$\frac{9\,E^2}{b^2} \times a$	$\frac{16\,E^2}{b^2} \times a$	$\frac{25\,E^2}{b^2} \times a$
0	$\frac{100^2}{500^2} \times 80$	$\frac{200^2}{500^2} \times 80$	$\frac{300^2}{500^2} \times 80$	$\frac{400^2}{500^2} \times 80$	$\frac{500^2}{500^2} \times 80$
0	3.20	12.80	28.80	51.20	80.00

Problem 3.

227. To find the angle E C G, fig. 103. The formula for the angle between the axis of the tower, and the tangent to the curve of the cable at the point of suspension is

$$\text{tang}\ a = \text{E C G} = \frac{2\,a}{b}.$$

Span being one thousand feet, b is five hundred; and a being eighty feet, we have

$$\text{tang } E\,C\,G = \frac{160}{500} = \log 160 - \log 500:$$

$$\text{or } 2.204120 - \dot{2}.698970 = \text{tang } 9.505150 = 17^\circ\, 45' = E\,C\,G.$$

$$\text{Also, } 90^\circ - 17^\circ\, 45' = 72^\circ\, 15' = \text{angle } G\,C\,A, \text{ or } A\,C\,H.$$

When the points of suspension are not at the same elevation, we proceed in the same manner: only using F G, G E, in place of E F, E C, in fig. 103 A.

Fig. 103 A.

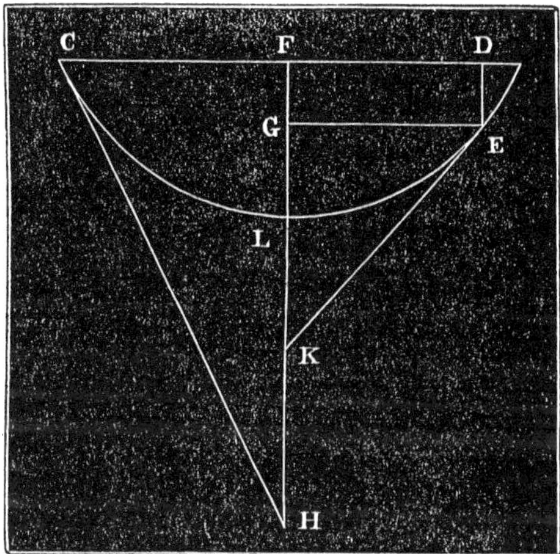

That the resultant of the forces acting upon the top of the tower may be vertical, the angles G C A, and A C H, fig. 103, must be equal; if not, the masonry must be so arranged as to cause the resultant to pass through the centre of gravity. When more than one span is used, and the openings are unequal, that the intermediate pier or piers shall not be pulled over, the cable of the largest, and consequently heaviest span, must have a greater inclination from the horizontal than that of the shorter span; the product of the tensions by their respective inclinations must be equal. Mr. Roebling's plan in connecting several spans, is to attach the cables of adjacent spans to a pendulum upon the pier, by which arrangement the difference in tension upon the different cables swings the pendulums, without racking the masonry.

Problem 4.

228. Given the weight per foot of bridge and load, to find the tension at the lowest point of the curve. The formula for the minimum tension, that at the vertex F of the curve, is

$$T=\frac{p\,h^2}{2f};$$

where p is the weight per foot of bridge and load, h the half distance between the points of suspension, and f the versed-sine. Thus the span beirig one thousand feet, the versed-sine eighty feet, and the load per lineal foot six thousand lbs., the formula becomes

$$T=\frac{6000\times 500^2}{160}=9375000 \text{ lbs. or } 4185 \text{ tons.}$$

The maximum tension is at the points of support, and is expressed by the formula

$$T=\frac{p\,h}{2f}\left[h^2+4f^2\right]^{\frac{1}{2}}:$$

which, in the case before us, becomes

$$T=\frac{6000\times 500}{160}\left[500^2+4\times 80^2\right]^{\frac{1}{2}}=4395 \text{ tons.}$$

229. The object of the anchoring is to connect the cable with a resistance upon the land side, which shall more than balance the weight and momentum of the bridge and load upon the opposite side. The anchoring of the Niagara bridge consists of an iron chain made of flat links, 7 feet long, 7 inches wide, and 1.4 inches thick; the chain links consist alternately of six and of seven of these bars; see fig. 104.

Fig. 104.

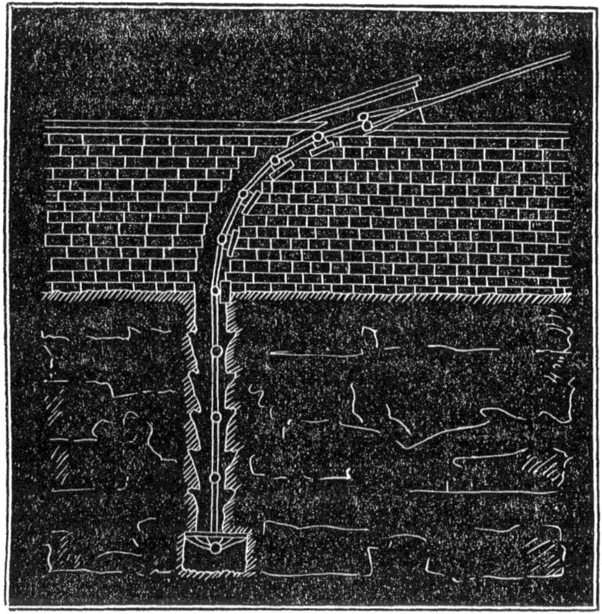

In the Fribourg bridge (Switzerland) the anchorage is made as in fig. 105, (see p. 220,) by a cable in place of the chain. In M. Navier's suspension bridge at Paris, over the Seine, the anchorage depended somewhat upon the natural cohesion of the earth forming the bank of the river, and this being destroyed by the bursting of a water-pipe in the vicinity, the bridge fell. When there is no natural rock for an anchorage, the masonry of the shaft must, by its own weight, resist the tension.

230. The height of the towers must be at least as much as the versed-sine of the cable. Their duty is to support the whole bridge and load. The breadth and thickness of these columns must be determined more with a view to opposing lateral, than downward strains. The former result from the horizontal vibrations of the bridge caused

by the action of the wind. Tremor and vibration caused by a passing load, tend to pull the towers into the river. The section for weight only might be very small. From the practice of the best builders, a mean section of one fifth of the height seems to give the best results; thus, if a tower is sixty feet high, the mean thickness should be twelve feet; or the top being 8×8 feet, the bottom should be 16×16 feet.

If the bridge is so little braced laterally as to swing, a dangerous momentum will be generated which would very much increase the strain, both upon the masonry and upon the cables.

231. The object of the stiffening truss is to transfer the weight applied at any one point over a considerable length, and to prevent vibration. Its dimensions should, therefore, be those of the counterbracing in an ordinary truss.

Any applied load produces a certain depression in the bridge: to use the words of Mr. Roebling, "every train that passes over the bridge causes an actual elongation of the cables, and consequently produces a depression. If the train is long, and covers nearly the whole length of the bridge, and is uniformly loaded, the depression will be uniform. If the train is short, and covers only a part of the floor, the depression will be less *general* and more *local;* and will be the joint result of an elongation of the cables, and of a disturbance of the equilibrium. Depressions will be in direct proportion to the loads, and indirectly as the length of train." The amount of depression depends on the elongation of the cables; the elongation upon the length. The depression is shown by the formula

$$f' = \frac{\pi F}{4 p h},$$

where f' is the depression, π the weight producing it, p the weight per foot of bridge and load, and h the half distance between the points of suspension.

The effect of heat, by expanding the cables, is also to depress the road-way; the amount being shown by the expression

$$f'=\frac{3h}{4f}c,$$

where c is the elongation of the half length of cable.

Upon the top of the towers is placed a pair of cast-iron plates separated by rollers; the upper plate (the saddle) is thus enabled to move over the lower one when pulled either way by the movement of the cables.

The length of the half cable between towers being generally greater than the distance from the top of the tower to the anchoring, expands more, when the saddle moves towards the land side. The dimensions of these castings must be sufficient to resist the whole weight of bridge and load.

232. As an example of the preceding formula, take the following:—

Assume the span as	1,000	feet.
Height of towers	100	"
Deflection of cables	90	"
Weight per foot (lineal) of bridge . .	2,500	lbs.
Weight per foot (lineal) of load . . .	2,000	"
Whole weight per foot	4,500	"
Total weight	4,500,000	"

CABLES.

The formula for the half length of cables between tops of towers is

$$L=b\left[1+\frac{2}{3}\left(\frac{a}{b}\right)^2\right],$$

which becomes

$$L=500\left[1+\frac{2}{3}\left(\frac{90}{500}\right)^2\right]=510.69,$$

which doubled, is 1021.38. To this add double the distance from the top of tower to the anchorage, (see page 206,) which is found as follows:—

$$\text{tang. E C G}=\frac{2\,a}{b}.$$

Also, tang E C G = log 2 a — log b, or 2.255273 — 2.698970 = tang 9.556303 of which the angle is 19° 48′ and 90° — 19° 48′ is 70° 12′ = angle G C A or A C H.

The height of the tower being one hundred feet, and the angle at the tower 70° 12′, we have

Sin 19° 48′	9,529,864
Sin 90° 00′	10,000,000
log height (100)	2,000,000
log distance (295.2)	2,470,136

which double, and we have 590.4; finally, add twice the breadth of the tops of the towers, and the whole length of cable is, from anchorage to anchorage,

$$1021.38+590.40+16=1627.78 \text{ feet.}$$

The formula for the maximum tension, (that at the point of suspension,) is

$$T=\frac{p\,h}{2f}\sqrt{h^2+4f^2},$$

which becomes

$$T=\frac{4500\times500}{180}\sqrt{250000+32400}=2966 \text{ tons.}$$

Number 10 iron wire (20 feet per lb.) will support 1,648 lbs. per strand; this is the ultimate strength; the maximum load for safety is 400 lbs. per strand; whence 2,966 tons, or 6,642,500 lbs. will require 16,606 strands; and if we use two cables, each must have 8,303 wires; or four cables of 4,151 each. The permanent load on suspension bridges should never be more than *one sixth* of the ultimate strength; *one eighth* is a good standard. The accidental load should never exceed one fifth of the whole strength of the cables. The permanent weight supported by the Niagara bridge is only one twelfth of the ultimate strength of the cables.

ANCHOR CHAINS.

The maximum tension being 6,642,500 lbs. the whole section of the four anchorings will need to be

$$\frac{6642500}{15000} = 443 \text{ inches,}$$

or 111 square inches for each shaft; which is obtained by eleven links ten inches wide and one inch thick. If we so attach the anchor chains to the masonry as to reduce the tension one fourth at the first arch, (see Fribourg anchoring,) we may fasten three bars of the chain at that point, and descend from the first to the second arch with eight bars; and leaving two bars at that point, proceed to the bottom with the remaining six.

Where there is no natural rock to build the masonry into or against, enough artificial stone must be put down to balance the bridge and load.

ANCHORING MASONRY.

The entire weight of the bridge and load being 4,500,000 lbs. and the whole tension, as above found, 6,642,500 lbs., or upon each tower 1,660,625 lbs.; this is the tension tending to draw the masonry out of each shaft. This tension must be reduced on account of the inclination of the pulling force. The tower is one hundred feet high. The distance on the line of tension from the top of the tower to the anchoring, as already found, is 295.2 feet; whence the actual effort to move the anchor masonry, is thus,

295.2 to 100 as 1,660,625 to the effort or 561,527 lbs. If rock weighs 160 lbs. per cubic foot, this is resisted by a cube of 3,570 feet, or a mass $10 \times 10 \times 35.7$ feet.

TOWERS.

The height of towers being one hundred feet, and the mean thickness being one fifth of the height, we have mean section 20×20; or top 12×12, and base 28×28.

SUSPENDING RODS.

Assuming the horizontal distances between the centres of the vertical suspenders as five feet, their lengths, then, will be found by formula

$$X = \frac{Y^2}{b^2} \times a;$$

and placing for Y^2 the distances 5, 10, 15, 20, etc., we have, commencing at the centre,

Centre.	5	10	15	20	25
0	$\frac{5^2}{500^2} \times 90$	$\frac{10^2}{500^2} \times 90$	$\frac{15^2}{500^2} \times 90$	$\frac{20^2}{500^2} \times 90$	$\frac{25^2}{500^2} \times 90$
0	.009	.036	.081	.144	.225

TABLE — *Continued.*

Centre.	30	35	40	45	50	d
0	$\frac{30^2}{500^2} \times 90$	$\frac{35^2}{500^2} \times 90$	$\frac{40^2}{500^2} \times 90$	$\frac{45^2}{500^2} \times 90$	$\frac{50^2}{500^2} \times 90$	$\frac{d^2}{b^2} \times a$
0	.360	.490	.576	.729	.900	h

and so on, until we arrive at the tower. Whatever distance above or below the vertex of the curve the road-way is placed, is of course constant, to be added to or taken from the above lengths.

The manner of putting in any camber is simple both in theory and practice. The strain upon the suspenders is merely the direct weight of the road-way and load. If this is 3,500 lbs. per foot, the five feet supported by two rods (one each side) will weigh 17,500 lbs.; each rod or wire rope must hold 8,750 lbs.; this can be done by a section of one half inch area. For extra strains, however, on so large a span as 1,000 feet, one inch of area is not too large.

OF THE STIFFENING TOWERS, GIRDERS, AND STAYS.

The object of the girders supporting the rails is to diffuse the applied weight; these girders may be made of a Howe truss four or five feet deep, by trussed girders, only simply deep and stiffly framed track strings. They should be able to distribute the load applied at one point at least fifteen or twenty feet. The side trusses transfer to a still greater extent any applied load. Mr. Roebling estimates the combined effect of trusses and girders in the Niagara bridge as transferring the weight of a locomotive over a length of two hundred feet. This transferring counteracts the *local* depression. The Niagara truss is formed by a system of vertical posts, five feet apart, and diagonal rods passing from the top of the first post to the foot of the fifth; the inclination being 45°, spreads the weight placed upon any one pair of posts over twice the height of the truss, or about forty feet. As to the actual dimensions of the girders supporting the rails, if we intend them to spread an applied weight over forty feet, they must be as stiff as a bridge of forty feet span. And as regards the truss, if we would effectually distribute the applied weight and check vibration, the trussing should be as strong as the counterbracing in a large span upon the ordinary plans. The principle of trussing a suspension bridge may be thus explained. See fig. 106. Suppose that in place of supporting the three trusses D *s w*, *s m m′*, and *m′ m d*, upon piers at *w* and *m′*, we suspend these points from the cable A *c* B. The cable is flexible, and when we apply a load at *m*, the truss will assume the position D *s c n d*, but between D and *s*, *s* and *n*, *n* and *d*, the truss will be quite stiff. What we require, then, is to make the figure *o p m m′*, incapable of changing its form, which is done by diagonal bracing.

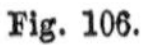
Fig. 106.

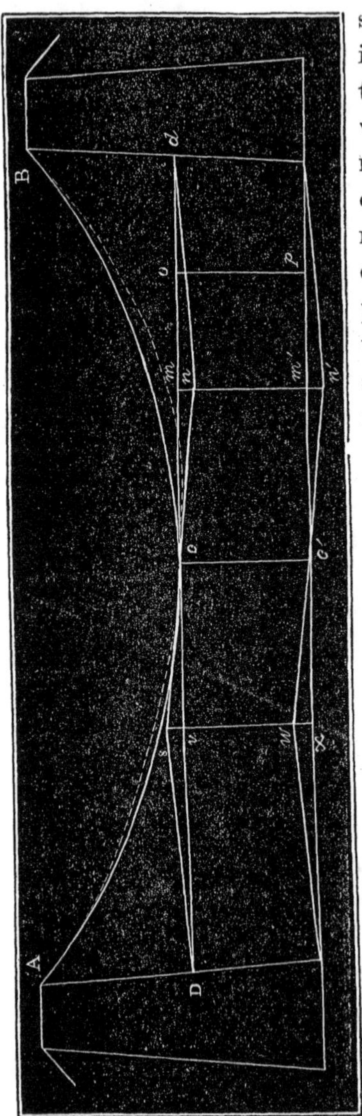

233. Undoubtedly the finest specimen of a bridge of large span upon the suspension principle, or indeed upon any principle, is that built by John A. Roebling, across the Niagara River, a short distance below the falls. The dimensions below of this admirable structure are from the final report of the above-named engineer.

Length of bridge from centre to centre of tower	821′ 4″
Length of floor between towers	800 ft.
Number of wire cables	4
Diameter of each	10″
Solid wire section of each cable	60.40 sq. in.
Total section of four cables	241.60 "
Whole section of lower links of anchor irons	276 "
Whole section of upper links of anchor irons	372 "
Ultimate strength of chains	11,904 tons.
Whole number of wires in cables	14,560
Average strength of a wire	1,648 lbs.
Ultimate strength of four cables	12,000 tons.
Permanent weight supported by cables	1,000 "
Resulting tension	1,810 "
Length of anchor chains	66 ft.
Length of upper cables	1,261 "
Length of lower cables	1,193 "
Deflection of upper cables (mean temperature)	54 "
Deflection of lower cables (mean temperature)	64 "
Number of suspenders	624
Aggregate strength of suspenders	18,720 tons.
Number of overfloor stays	64
Aggregate strength	1,920 tons.
Number of river stays	56
Aggregate strength	1,680 tons.
Elevation of grade above mean water	245 ft.
Depth of river	200 "
Cost of the bridge	$400,000.

19

234. The following items are extracted from the report above referred to:—

"The trains of the New York Central, and Canada Great Western Railroads have crossed regularly at the rate of thirty trips per day for five months. (At present over two years.)

"A load of forty-seven tons caused a depression at the centre of five and a half inches.

"An engine of twenty-three tons weight, with four driving wheels, depressed the bridge at the centre 0.3 feet. The depression immediately under the engine was one inch; the effect of which extended one hundred feet.

"The depression caused by an engine and train of cars is so much diffused as scarcely to be noticed.

"A load of three hundred and twenty-six tons produced a deflection of 0.82 feet only. The Conway tubular bridge deflects 0.25 feet under three hundred tons; the span being only one half that of the Niagara bridge.

"The specified test for the wire was, that a strand stretched over two posts four hundred feet apart should not break at a greater deflection than nine inches; also, that it should withstand bending square and rebending over a pair of pliers without rupture. This test corresponds to a tensile strain of 90,000 lbs. per square inch, or 1,300 lbs. per wire of twenty feet per pound."

The wire is preserved from oxidation by coating with linseed oil and paint. Upon the durability of wire cables employed for suspension bridges the following fact came to light: Upon taking down the cables of the footbridge, put up in 1848, by Mr. Ellet, the wire was found so little impaired that Mr. Roebling did not hesitate to work it into the new cables; also, the original oil was found to be still soft and in good condition, having been up six years.

That iron-work lying under ground has been completely covered with cement grout, as this is found by the above-named engineer to be an effectual guard against oxidation.

Engineers wishing to study the details of the Niagara bridge, will find the final report of Mr. Roebling full of valuable matter, both as regards the making of cables, anchoring, stiffening, and the effect of passing trains.

NOTE. — This engineer is at present engaged upon a still greater work, namely, a railroad suspension bridge across Kentucky River, of 1,224 feet span, 300 feet above the water. There is no lower road-way in this bridge, the cross section being a triangle base upwards.

235. NOTE. — The Britannia tubular bridge, across the Menai Straits, is doubtless a great work, and also an enormously extravagant one. If no other structure were possible it would be admissible; but it is equalled in strength and by far surpassed in economy by Mr. Roebling's system of trussed suspension bridges. The cost of material alone in one span of the Britannia bridge, of 460 feet, exceeds the entire cost of the Niagara bridge of 800 feet span; add to this that we are sure of the strength of wire cables, but not of tubes, and that the 800 feet span of the Niagara bridge weighs only 1,000 tons in itself against 1,400 in a 460 feet span of tube, and it will not be difficult to prove the superiority of the suspension over the tubular system; thus,

A suspension bridge of 800 feet span costs $400,000.
A tubular bridge of 460 feet span costs $500,000.

When we double the linear dimensions we increase the weight by the cube; and the cost of a tube is very nearly as the weight; whence a tubular bridge of 800 feet span will cost 2 × 2 × 2, or eight times 500,000, or $4,000,000 against $400,000. Thus,

Suspension	400,000	1
Tubular	4,000,000	10

Fig. 105.

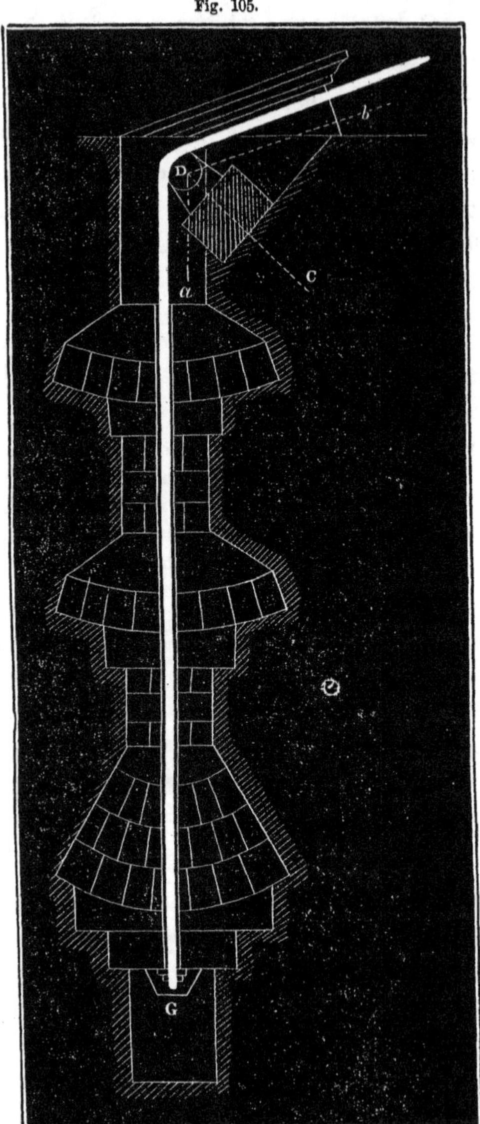

Fig. 105, shows the anchoring of the Fribourg bridge.

Fig. 107.

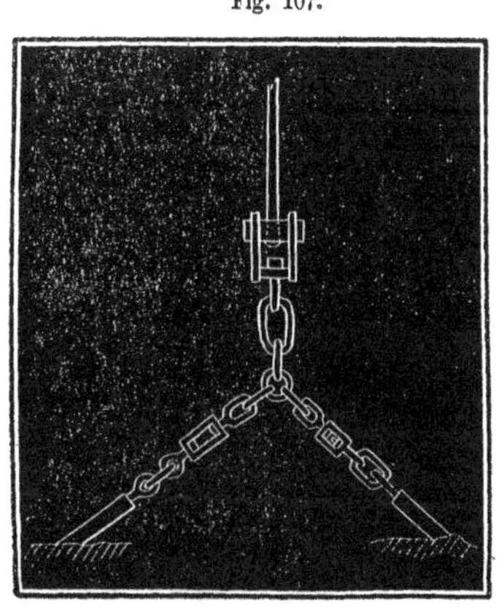

Fig. 108.

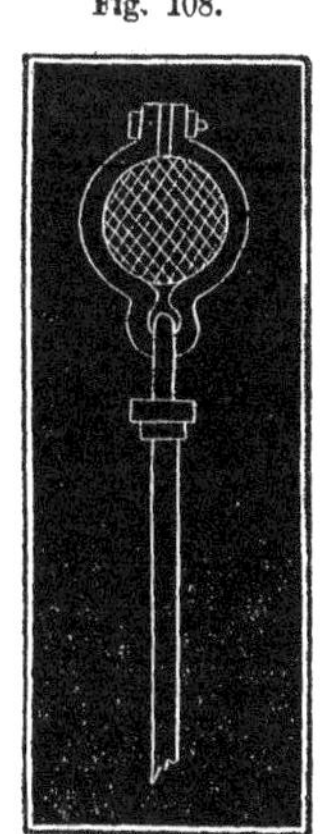

Fig. 107, the manner of fastening the ground stays of the Niagara bridge.

Fig. 108, connection between cable and suspender.

Fig. 109.

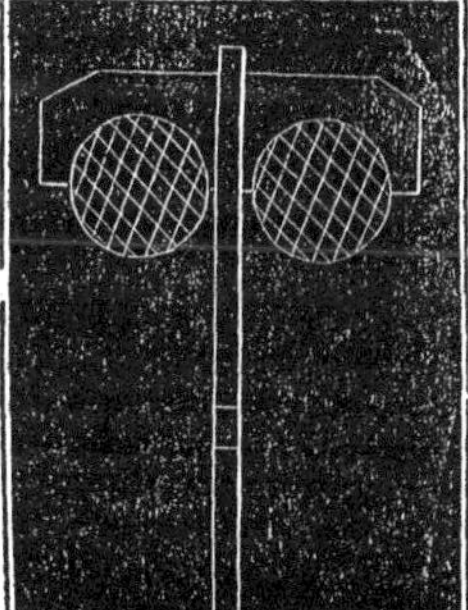

Fig. 109 A.

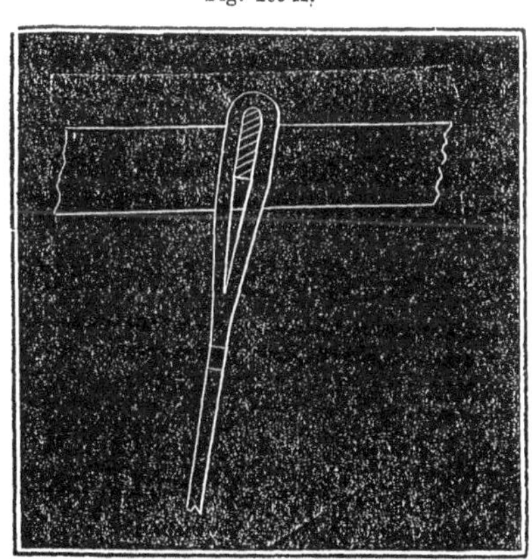

Figs. 109, 109 A, another method of effecting the same.

Fig. 110. Fig. 111. Fig. 112.

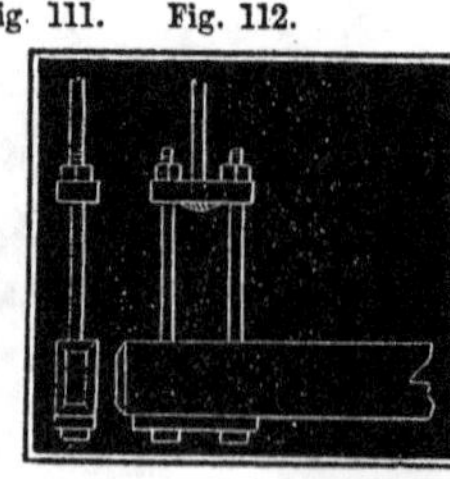

Fig. 110, floor beam attachment to suspender.

Figs. 111, 112, floor beam attachment in Niagara bridge.

Fig. 113.

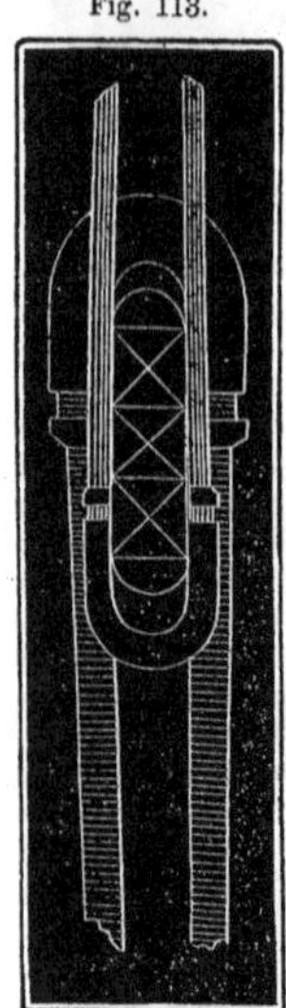

Fig. 114.

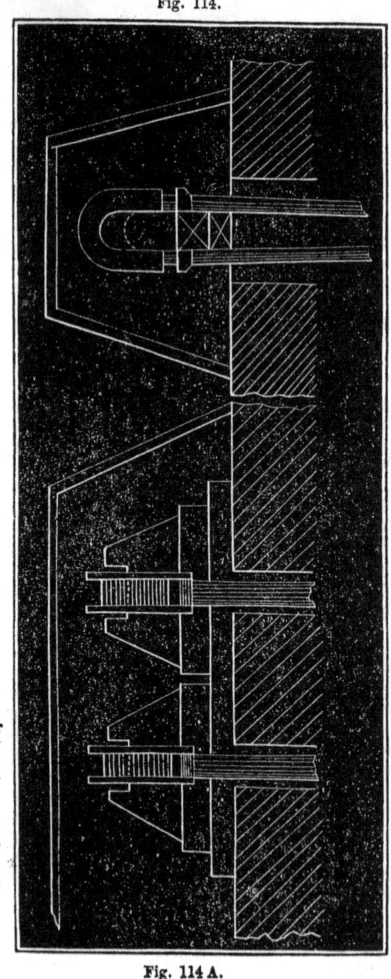

Fig. 114 A.

Fig. 113, connection of land and water cables in Fribourg bridge.

Figs. 114, 114 A, fastening of cables at G, (fig. 105).

Fig. 115, Mr. Roebling's pendulum connection for the cables of two adjacent spans.

Fig. 115.

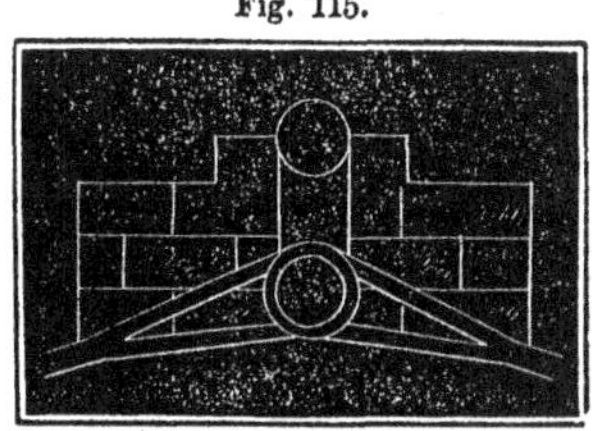

BOILER PLATE BRIDGES.

Spans from 25 to 100 feet.

236. These structures fulfil every requirement of safe, durable, and rigid bridges; being open however to the contingency attendant upon all similar structures of wrought iron, namely, the becoming crystalline when exposed to vibration. Time only will show whether this is a sufficient cause for their non-adoption.

Each side truss consists as it were of a top and bottom chord connected by a vertical web. The whole being of wrought iron, requires that the section of the upper chord should be to that of the lower, as ninety to sixty-six.

The general plan of such bridges is shown in fig. 116. This is the patent wrought iron girder bridge of Mr. Fairbairn. The upper chord is formed by connecting the four plates *a a a a*, by angle irons. The web is formed either by a single or a double plate, stiffened laterally by T iron placed at the vertical plate joints, as shown generally at B, and detailed at C and D; or by a pair of plates separated by a space as at B′, thus forming a rectangular tube. The lower chord is made by bending horizontally the lower part of the web, and to the flanges thus formed riveting the plate *m m*. The suspending rod *f f* is applied to the upper chord by a washer as at E.

The central connecting web, acting as do the braces and ties in a wooden truss, should be more stiff at the ends of

Fig. 116.

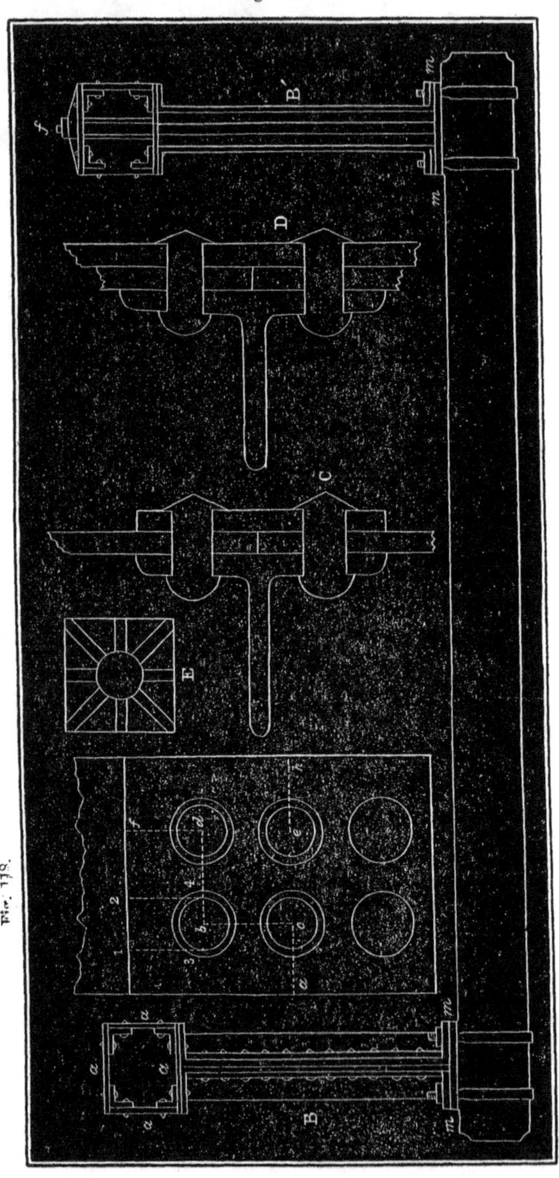

the span than at the centre. This is easily effected by joining the web plates towards the end by stronger T irons than at the centre. The joints for the rib, or the vertical plates, either single or double, are shown in figs. C and D.

An example of the need of such increased stiffness towards the ends, was given to the experimenters upon the Britannia model tube, which (tube) was found to yield by buckling near the ends of the span sooner than elsewhere. Thus advised, the vertical plates were made thicker as the end of the span was approached. Examination of the principles of proportioning a common wooden truss would have shown this without experiment.

The tensile and compressive strength of rolled boiler plates (by the table on page 194,) is, extension 12,740 lbs. per square inch, compression 7,500 lbs. The strength of such work depends in a very great measure upon the size and disposition of rivets. In plates exposed to compression, the strength is not so much affected by riveting as in those subjected to tensile strains; as to whatever amount the plate is cut away, by the same amount is the resistance to tension reduced.

237. Mr. Fairbairn found that to obtain the maximum strength of riveted plates, the section of the rivets should equal that of the plates, that is, in a plate four inches wide, if there are two rivets, the area of each must be one inch; or the diameter $1\frac{1}{8}$ inches; thus leaving a section of

$$4 - 2\frac{1}{4} = 1\frac{3}{4} \text{ inches,}$$

which divided by four gives seven sixteenths of an inch as the distance from the edge of the plate to the side of the first rivet; and seven eighths of an inch between rivets. If the bolt yields by shearing, the rim is destroyed by *detrusion*, or crushing across the fibres. That the rivets and plates may be equally strong, their products of area of section by the actual strength per unit of area must be equal. The detrusive strength of wrought iron (see page 128) is 12,500 lbs. per inch, whence the proportion

$$12{,}500 : 15{,}000 :: 1 : d :$$

where 1 is the resisting length of the plate at right angles to tension, and d, the sum of rivet diameters. Thus suppose we have a plate 13.2 inches wide, to be fastened with nine rivets of 0.8 inch diameter; we have

$$9 \times 0.8 = 7.2 = d,$$

and the above proportion becomes

$$15{,}000 : 12{,}000 :: 7.2 \text{ to } 6 \text{ inches},$$

which is the length of plate section at right angles to tension. As there are nine rivets, there will be eight spaces between them, and one space at each edge of the plate, half as large as those between; or reducing all to the same size,

$$8 \times 2 = 16,\ 16 + 2 = 18;$$

and as the whole plate section after punching is six inches,

$$\frac{6}{18} = .33 \text{ or } \tfrac{1}{3} \text{ inch}$$

for the edge space, and two thirds inch between rivets. Proceeding thus, the result compares with the practice of Mr. Fairbairn as follows:—

	Diameter of rivet.	Distance between rivets.
Mr. Fairbairn	$\frac{5}{8}$ inch, or 0.625 inch,	0.8
Handbook	$\frac{2}{3}$ inch, or 0.666 inch,	0.8

The difference between the results, or 0.041 inch, less than one sixteenth inch, will be partially absorbed by the remark of Mr. Fairbairn that the area of the rivet should be *nearly* as much as that of the plate, and partly by the difference in results showing the detensional force of iron.

238. In experimenting to determine the resistance of rivets, Mr. Fairbairn found that by the common plan of riveting, fig. 117, the strength of plates when whole, single, and double riveted, was as follows, the section of the punched plate being in each case equal to that of the whole one.

Fig. 117.

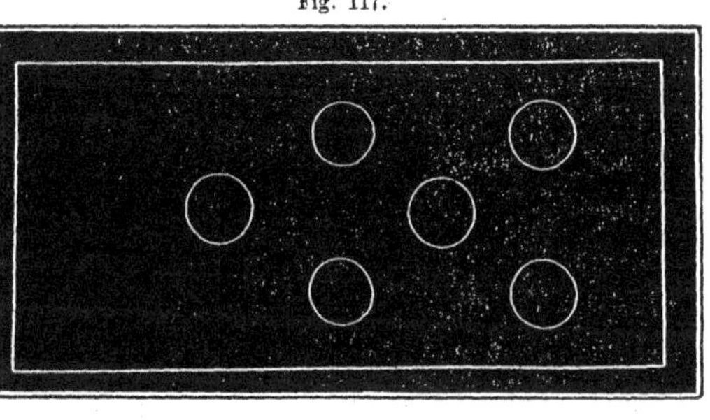

Whole plate, ...	100.
Single riveted, ...	56.
Double riveted, ...	70.

This loss of strength made him fearful of the ability of the tension plates of the Britannia bridge to do their duty; and he was led to adopt what he terms "chain riveting," which consists in placing the rivets as in fig. 118, or *in the same line of tension.* The strength of plates thus made he considers as great at the joints as elsewhere.

239. As to the diameter of rivets, we have the following results of the practice of the best English engineers.

Thickness of plate,	$\frac{1}{4}$,	$\frac{5}{16}$,	$\frac{3}{8}$,	$\frac{7}{16}$,	$\frac{1}{2}$,	$\frac{9}{16}$,	$\frac{5}{8}$,	$\frac{11}{16}$,	$\frac{3}{4}$.
Diameter of rivet,	$\frac{5}{8}$,	$\frac{6}{8}$,	$\frac{7}{8}$,	1,	1,	$1\frac{1}{8}$,	$1\frac{1}{4}$,	$1\frac{3}{8}$,	$1\frac{1}{2}$.

240. As to the distance *in the direction of the force* from rivet to rivet, also from the first rivet to the plate end, we

gather the following from the best executed works in boiler plate. See fig. 118.

Plates exposed to compression,

$$c\,b = 2 \text{ diam.}, \; d\,f = 1\tfrac{1}{2} \text{ diam.}$$

Plates exposed to extension,

$$c\,b = 2\tfrac{1}{2} \text{ diam.}, \; d\,f = 2 \text{ diam.}$$

the diameter being that of the rivet.

The distance at right angles to the force has already been given.

241. If we knew the lateral adhesion of rolled plates, that is, the resistance of the fibres to sliding horizontally past each other; we should determine the distance of rivets in the direction of tension as follows:—

Let R, equal the resistance per unit of area for *detrusion* or shearing, R^1 the lateral adhesion of rolled plates, and we should have

$$R \times d = R^1 \times (2d' + d);$$

also

$$2\,d' + d = \frac{R \times d}{R^1};$$

and

$$2\,d' = \frac{R \times d}{R^1} - d;$$

whence

$$d' = \frac{\left[\frac{R \times d}{R^1} - d\right]}{2}$$

and finally

$$d' = \tfrac{1}{2}\left[\frac{R \times d}{R^1} - d\right]$$

supposing the piece 1, 2, 3, 4, fig. 118, to split out.

The diameter of the semi-spherical head of the rivet should be three times the thickness of the plate to be riveted; that of the conical head four times; and the height of both of the heads, once and one half the plate thickness.

242. Examples of the application of the preceding remarks.

Suppose we wish to build a boiler plate bridge of one hundred feet span, twelve feet rise, weight of bridge and load 3300 lbs. per lineal foot. The tension by formula

$$T = \frac{WS}{8h} \text{ (see Chap. VIII.)}$$

becomes

$$\frac{33000000}{96} = 343{,}750 \text{ lbs.}$$

Each side truss will bear one half of this or 171,875 lbs., and as wrought iron resists eleven thousand pounds of compression per square inch, the required section of the top chord will be

$$\frac{171875}{11000} = 15.6 \text{ square inches.}$$

Also the lower chord resisting fifteen thousand pounds per square inch, must have

$$\frac{171875}{15000} = 11.5 \text{ square inches}$$

of area nearly.

If we make the tube at top of one fourth inch iron, and 8 $\times$ 10 inches; fastening the plates by one fourth inch angle iron, four inches on the side, the section becomes

One top plate	$10 \times \frac{1}{4} = 2\frac{1}{2}$	square inches.
One bottom plate	$10 \times \frac{1}{4} = 2\frac{1}{2}$	"
Two side plates	$8 \times \frac{1}{4} = 4$	"
Four angle irons	$\frac{1}{4} \times 8 = 8$	"
	In all, 17	"

In the lower chord, if we bend the web plates (of $\frac{3}{8}$ inch)

so as to form a flange of eighteen inches in width, and to that rivet a bottom plate 18 × ¼, we shall have

In the flanges, ...	$18 \times \frac{3}{8} = 6\frac{3}{4}$
Bottom plate, ...	$18 \times \frac{1}{4} = 4\frac{1}{2}$
In all,	$11\frac{1}{4}$

The web acting as both ties and braces, must be able to support the following load.

Whole weight of bridge and load is, in round numbers,	344,000 lbs.
One half, ...	172,000 "
And upon each end of the truss, ...	86,000 "

to resist which, at eleven thousand pounds per square inch, requires eight inches nearly, regarding the plate as a brace.

Now the side of the bridge being one hundred feet long, and twelve feet wide, will contain any system of bracing that we choose to draw thereon. Suppose, for example, that we chalk a line upon the erected bridge representing an arch-brace, extending from the end to the centre. Such a brace has actually existence in the bridge; and the same idea holds good for any system of braces that may be assumed. We ought, therefore, to take the most disadvantageous system that can have place, and giving such a good bearing upon the abutment, estimate its width and thickness. Suppose that we draw a natural size representation of Howe's bridge, the end braces must support a load of eighty-six thousand pounds, which at eleven thousand lbs. per inch, requires a section of nearly eight inches; and if the plate is one half inch thick, the brace must be sixteen inches deep. The manner, however, in which the plate would yield is by bulging laterally; which is to be checked by the before-mentioned T connecting irons at the sides. It may be thought that the above method of considering the plates as braces, would give very little thickness by assuming very wide plates. The answer to this is, that the side plates must not be so thin as to need more stiffening angle irons by weight, than a thicker plate with less stiffening. Of course the weight should be minimum.

243. As an actual example of this plan we have the following, built by Mr. Fairbairn for the Blackburn and Bolton Railroad, across the Leeds and Liverpool Canal.

Span, ...	60 feet,
Length, ...	66 "
End bearings, each, ...	3 "
Rise, ...	5 "
Width, ...	28 "

for a double track. Top chord of three eighths iron, web of five sixteenths, lower flange of three eighths, and vertical web plates stiffened by T irons.

This bridge was tested as follows: —

Three engines, weighing twenty tons each, running from five to twenty-five miles per hour, deflected the bridge .025 feet. Two wedges, one inch high, being placed upon the rails, and the engines being chopped from that height, the bridge was deflected at the centre .035 ft.; with wedges of one and one half inches the deflection was .045 ft. The cost of this bridge (in England) was estimated by Mr. Fairbairn at $4,500, while that of a cast-iron bridge of the same span was $7,150.

244. *Example* 2. — Manchester, Sheffield, and Lincolnshire Railroad (England) Bridge, at Gainsborough, on the river Trent. Two spans, each one hundred and fifty-four feet. Rise twelve feet. Top chord, double rectangular tube, 36¾ × 16 inches, vertical web as before, and horizontal plate for the lower chord. The floor beams are wrought

iron girders, cruciform in section, ten inches wide, and one foot three inches (15″) deep, placed four feet apart.

245. *Example* 3.—Fifty-five feet boiler plate bridge, built by James Millholland, in 1847, for the Baltimore and Susquehanna Railroad Company. Each truss consists of two vertical plates 55 × 6 feet, formed of plates thirty-eight inches wide by six feet deep, the plates being fastened together by bolts passing through cast-iron sockets. The lower chord is formed by riveting two bars 5 × ¾ inches to each side of each truss plate; making in all eight. Top chord—one bar of the same size on each side of each plate, compression being made up by a wooden chord between the plates. Height of bridge, six feet; length, fifty-five feet; width, six feet; weight, fourteen tons; cost, $2,200, or forty dollars per foot. The inventor thinks thirty dollars per foot enough when a considerable amount of such bridging is wanted.

NOTE.—White, buff, or some light color should be used in painting iron bridges, as such throw off, and do not absorb heat from the sun.

CHAPTER X.

STONE BRIDGES.

A COMPLETE treatise on stone bridging would be of little practical value to the American engineer, and would occupy too much of the necessarily small space allowed here. The object in the present chapter is to give the manner of dimensioning stone arches of from ten to sixty feet span, and of proportioning retaining walls, piers, and abutments.

CONTRACTION OF THE WATER-WAY.

246. In building a bridge across a stream, we must be careful not to obstruct the water-way so as to prevent free passage to the highest floods. Regard must be had to this in fixing the size of the spans, and the thickness and number of the piers. By contracting the width of the stream the velocity is increased beneath the arches, the same amount of water being obliged to pass through a smaller space, and when the bottom is of such a nature as to yield to this action, there is danger of the foundation being undermined. If the form and size of the piers be so arranged as not to increase the velocity, such danger will be avoided and floods will pass without harm. In bridges crossing

20*

navigable streams, if the bottom is not destroyed the velocity may be made so great as to impede navigation.

247. The following table is from Gauthey, *Construction des Ponts*, showing the velocities which are joint in equilibrium with the material composing the bottom of the stream.

State of the water.	Velocity in feet per second.		Nature of bottom.
Torrents,	10′	0″	Large rocks.
Floods,	3′	3″	Loose rocks.
Common,	3′	0″	Gravel and stones.
Regular,	2′	0″	Fine gravel.
Moderate,	1′	0″	Sand.
Slow,	0′	6″	Clay.
Very slow,	0′	3″	Common earth.

248. If b represents the width of the natural water-way; c, that as reduced by the structure; V, the velocity of the stream in the natural state; then the augmented velocity is expressed by

$$W = m\,V\frac{b}{c};$$

$$\text{and } c = \frac{m\,b\,V}{W};$$

where m is a constant quantity expressing the contraction which takes place in passing the narrow place, which, according to Du-Buat, is 1.09; but depending somewhat upon the form of the bridge piers; adopting which value, we have

$$W = 1.09\,V\frac{b}{c};$$

$$\text{and } c = \frac{1.09\,b\,V}{W}.$$

Example. — Let the bottom be gravel, the width of the

natural water-way one hundred feet, the velocity one foot per second: now for a gravel bottom the velocity must not exceed two feet per second, whence

$$c = \frac{1.09 \times 100 \times 1}{2} = 54\tfrac{1}{2} \text{ feet};$$

which is the width of the contracted water-way; and $100 - 54\frac{1}{2}$, or $45\frac{1}{2}$ feet may be occupied by piers or other obstructions.

The amount of fall which the water suffers in passing the pier is found by the following formula, the notation being the same,

$$\text{fall} = \frac{\overline{V^2 m^2 b^2 - c^2}}{64 c^2}.$$

Thus the velocity being one foot per second, m being 1.09 and $b = 100$; also, $c = 54\frac{1}{2}$, we have

$$\text{fall} = \frac{\overline{1 \times 1 \times 1.09 \times 1.09 \times 100 \times 100 - 54\frac{1}{2} \times 54\frac{1}{2}}}{64 \times 54\frac{1}{2} \times 54\frac{1}{2}} = 0.016 \text{ ft}.$$

The velocity of a river is greatest at its surface and at the centre of the stream. In the same river the velocity is nearly as the square root of the depth; thus the surface velocity being known, that for any other depth may be easily found. The velocity of streams should always be noted at the times of the highest floods. For measuring the velocity of running water a bottle enough filled with water to maintain an upright position, with a small rod placed through the stopper having a red flag upon the upper end, answers very well. Velocities of undercurrents may also be measured by so loading the bottle as to cause it to float two, four, six, or ten feet below the surface.

OF THE FORM OF THE ARCH.

249. There are three general forms which may be given to the intrados of a stone arch.

Semicircular, or one hundred and eighty degrees.

Segmental, less than one hundred and eighty degrees.

Basket handle, nearly elliptical, being formed by a number of circular curves.

Full centre (semicircular) arches offer the advantages of great solidity and care of construction; but unless the springing lines are high, contract considerably the water-way.

Segmental arches give the freest passage to the water, are easily built, but throw a great horizontal strain upon the abutments.

The basket handle gives free passage to the water, when not too flat are very strong, are easily adjustable to different ratios between the span and the distance between grade and the spring line, and except making the centres, are easily built. Whatever the form of the arch, the line of arch springing should not be below high water.

The manner of tracing the full centre and segmental curves is too simple to need remark.

250. In tracing the basket handle curve, the following conditions must be observed:—

The tangents at springing must be vertical.
The summit tangent must be horizontal.
The curve at springing must inclose the ellipse.
The radius of summit must not be greater than the span.

The number of arches composing the curve must not be less than three, nor more than eleven; and must be uneven. Perronet's fine bridge of Neuilly, over the Seine at Paris, has eleven centres. In spans of sixty feet and under, it is unnecessary to use more than five centres.

Fig. 119.

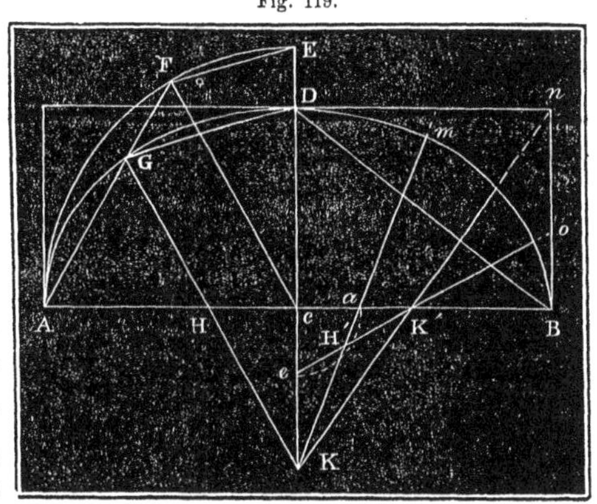

251. The three centred curve is described as follows, fig. 119: —

Let A B represent the span, and *c* D the rise, with *c* as a centre and *c* A as radius, describe the quadrant A F E; make the angle A C F 60°. Parallel to F E draw D G, and parallel to F C draw G K. H is the centre, and A G the arc of the springing curve; also G D is the arc, and K the centre of the summit curve.

THE FIVE CENTRED CURVE.

252. The common construction of the five centred curve leaves the radii of the extreme curves to be assumed. The following method fixes all of the dimensions when the span and rise are given: —

Let *c* B be half the span and *c* D the rise.
Join D B.
Draw *n* K through *n* perpendicular to D B.
Make B *a* equal to *c* D.
Also *c e* to *c a*.
Draw *e* K′ *o* and K *a m*.
K H′ and K′ are the centres, and H′ *m* and H′ *o* the lines representing the several curves.

For spans of from twenty-five to one hundred feet, the five

centred arch answers every purpose; making a strong and well proportioned structure.

THICKNESS OF VOUSSOIRS, (RING STONES).

253. The thickness of the voussoir, or arch stone, depends upon the form and size of the arch, the nature of the masonry, and the character of the stone. No authority gives more reliable results than Gauthey, who, for stone of average quality, with hammer dressed beds, laid in cement, gives the following proportions between the span and depth of key:—

For spans *under six feet* the depth should be *thirteen inches.*
From six to fifty feet, 13 inches plus $\frac{1}{48}$ of the span.
From fifty to one hundred feet, $\frac{1}{24}$ of the span.
For over one hundred feet, $\frac{1}{24}$ of 100 plus $\frac{1}{48}$ of the remainder.

Thus for a span of one hundred and ninety-six feet we have

$$\frac{100 \times 12}{24} + \frac{96 \times 12}{48},$$

or, $50 + 24$ equal in all to seventy-four inches, or six feet and two inches; whence the following table:—

Span of arch in feet.	Thickness of voussoir in inches.
6	$13 + 0 = 13$
8	$13 + 2 = 15$
10	$13 + 3 = 16$
12	$13 + 3 = 16$
15	$13 + 4 = 17$
18	$13 + 5 = 18$
20	$13 + 6 = 19$
25	$13 + 7 = 20$
30	$13 + 8 = 21$
35	$13 + 9 = 22$

Span of arch in feet.	Thickness of voussoir in inches.
40	$13+10=23$
45	$13+11=24$
50	$13+13=26$
60	$=30$ inches.

THICKNESS AND FORM OF ABUTMENTS.

254. The above depend upon the span and form of the arch, the height of the abutment, and character of the masonry.

Different methods of determining the thickness of an abutment have from time to time been given; several very correct rules have been arrived at, but difficult of application. The most simple rule is given by Hutton in the course of mathematics edited by Rutherford; it is as follows: —

Fig. 120.

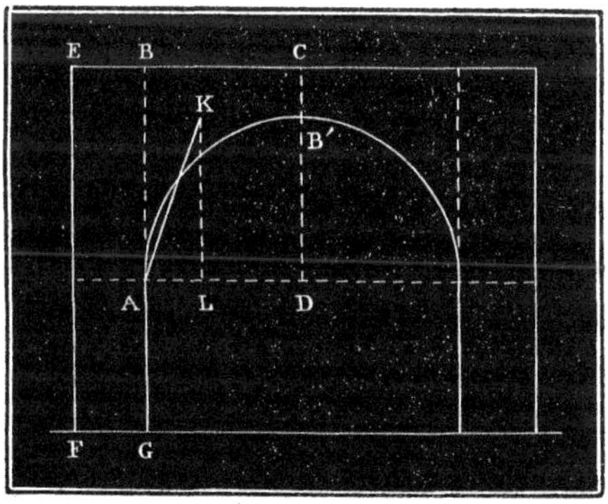

Let A B, C D, fig. 120, be one half of the arch, and A G F the abutment.

From the centre of gravity K of the arch, draw the vertical K L; then the weight of the arch in the direction K L will be to the horizontal thrust, as K L to L A. For the weight of the arch in the direction K L, the horizontal thrust L A, and the thrust K A will be as the three sides of the triangle K L, L A, K A; so that if m denotes the weight of the arch,

$$\frac{LA}{KL} \times m,$$

will be its force in the direction L A, and

$$\frac{LA}{KL} \times GA \times m$$

its effect on the lever G A to overturn the wall, or cause it to revolve about the point F.

Again, the weight or area of the pier is as E F × F G, and therefore E F × F G × ½ F G, or ½ F G² × E F, is its effect upon the lever ½ F G, to resist an overthrow. Now that the abutment and the arch shall be in equilibrium these two effects must be equal to each other; whence we must have

$$\tfrac{1}{2} F G^2 \times E F = \frac{LA}{RL} \times GA \times m;$$

whence

$$FG = \sqrt{\frac{2\,GA \times AL}{EF \times RL} \times m.}$$

The following table has been calculated for the use of builders and engineers, giving the thickness of abutments for different spans and heights.

255. THICKNESS OF RECTANGULAR ABUTMENTS.

	Semicircular arch.				Basket-handle arch.			
	The height being.							
Span.	5	8	10	15	5	8	10	15
6	3	3	3¼	3½	3½	4	4	5
8	3½	4	4¼	4½	4	4½	5¼	6
10	4	5	5	5	4½	5¾	6¼	7
15	4½	5¼	5½	6	5	6½	7¼	8
20	5	5½	6	7	6	7¼	8	9
25	5½	6	6½	7¼	7	7½	8¼	9½
30	6	7	8	8½	8	8½	9¼	10
35	6½	7	8¼	9	9	9¼	10	11
40	7	7½	8¾	9½	9½	10	11	12
45	7½	8¼	9¼	10	10	10¾	11½	12½
50	8	9	10	11	10¼	11½	12¼	13

256. The form of a bridge abutment will depend upon the localities and upon the use to which the bridge is to be put, whether used for a railroad, or for common travel; whether near a large city, or in a location where appearance need not be regarded. Where a river acts dangerously upon a shore, wing walls will be necessary. These wings may be curved or straight, and may be simply the abutment produced, or may be swung around into the

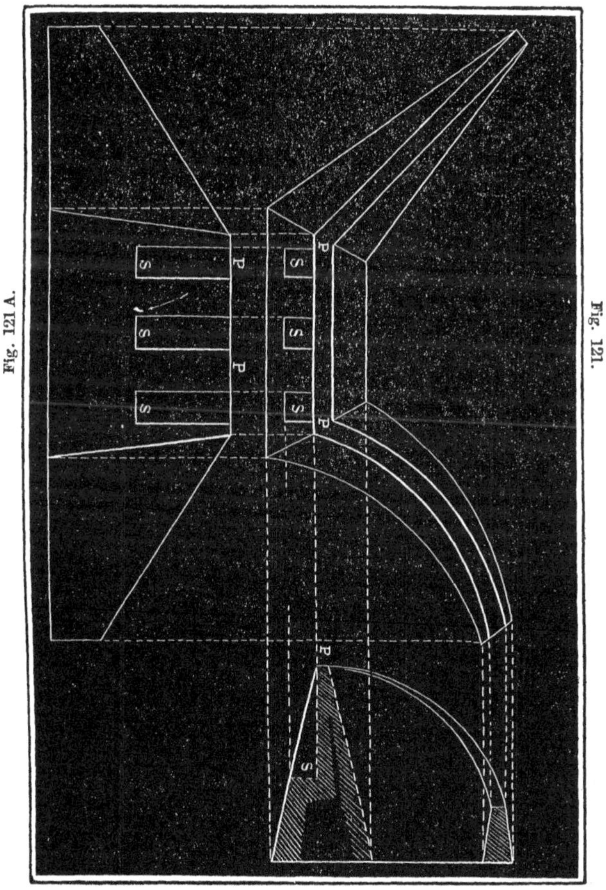

Fig. 121 A.

Fig. 121.

Fig. 121 B.

bank at any required angle, until the winged abutment, as in figs. 121, 121 A, 121 B, becomes the U abutment, fig. 124; or by moving the walls, W and W, parallel to themselves, takes the form of the T abutment, fig. 122.

Fig. 122.

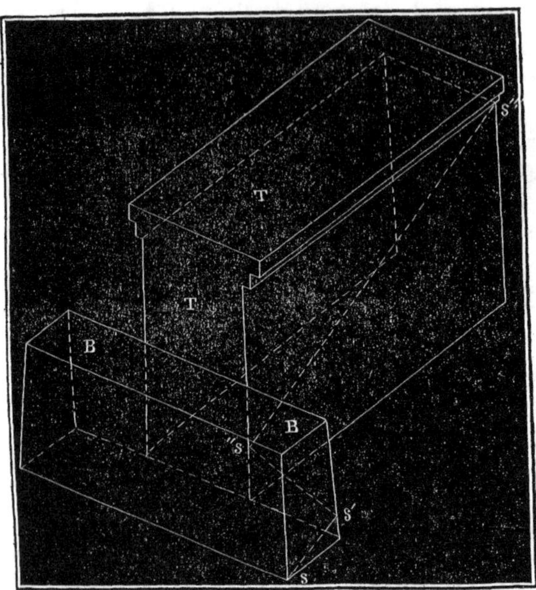

The curved wing, in fig. 121, being arched, requires a little less thickness, but at the same time is longer. B B, show the bridge seats, and *c e*, the parapets. The slope of the wings may be battered with an inclined coping, or off-setted at each course. Wing walls, subjected to special strains or to particular currents of water, require positions and forms accordingly. In skew bridges, as in Chap. V., the wing, at the acute angle, is longer and inclines less from the face of the abutment than that at the obtuse angle. The more the wing departs from the face line and swings round into the slope, the greater the thrust becomes upon it, as the centre of pressure is raised; the thrust becomes a maximum when the wing is inclined from forty-five to seventy degrees from the face of the abutment. The body of an embankment, as well as any other retaining wall, may be much stronger by giving it a rapezoidal instead of a rectangular section, as the resisting leverage is thereby much increased. Abutments may be to advantage buttressed in order to resist special strains, as in case of the arches or braces of wooden bridges.

Fig. 123.

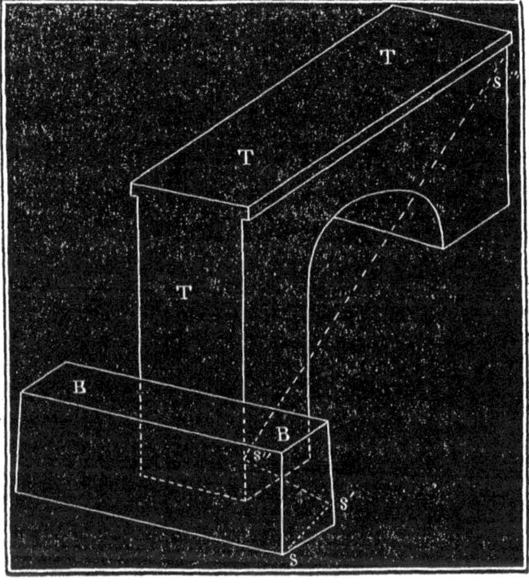

Fig. 124.

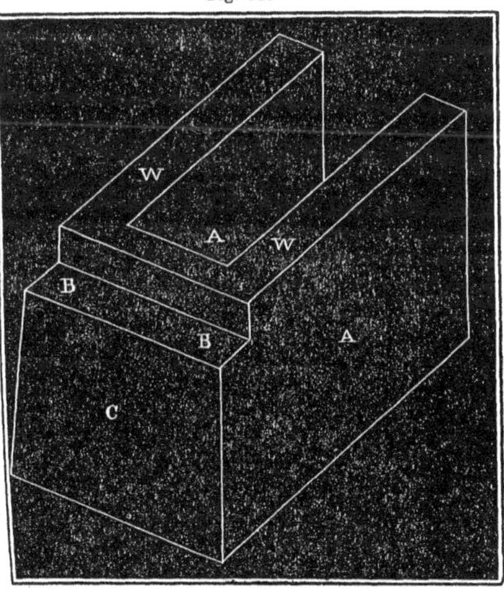

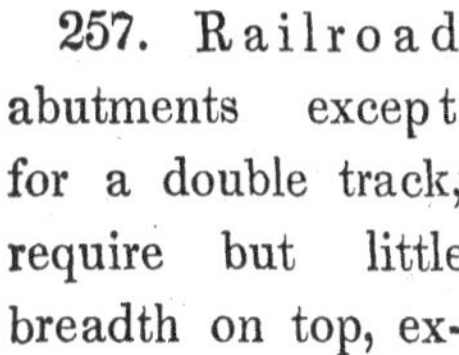

257. Railroad abutments except for a double track, require but little breadth on top, except where the truss itself rests. The common T abutment

originated by Captain John Childe, and now in very extensive use, seems to fulfil any requirement of a good abutment, see fig. 122, page 242. B B is the bridge seat, and the mass T T takes the place of wings. The difference of level of the top and of the bridge seat depends upon the difference between the height of the bearing of the lower chord of the bridge, and grade. The line of contact between the earth and the wall is shown by $s\,s'\,s''\,s'''$. The length of the top of the masonry is thus. Suppose the slope to be one and one half to one, and the whole height thirty feet, the whole horizontal length of slope is then forty-five feet; from this we take the sum of the horizontal distances, $s\,s'$ and $s'\,s''$, and suppose these to be, respectively, six and eight feet, we have the whole operation thus:—

$$30 \times 1\tfrac{1}{2} - 6 + 8 = 45 - 14 = 31 \text{ feet.}$$

It may be advisable in very high abutments to lighten the masonry by an arched opening as in fig. 123. The walls, also, of the U abutment (see fig. 124), when large, may be pierced with arches to save masonry.

Probably the cheapest mode of bringing a bridge to the embankment is that shown in fig. 125; A being the bridge seat for the main truss, and B that for the trussed girder.

Fig. 125.

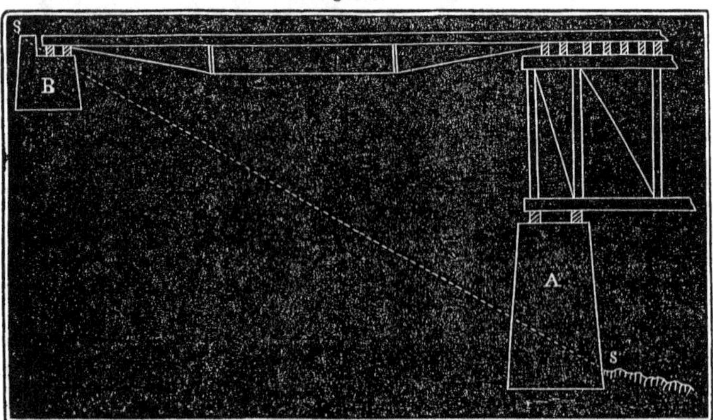

PIERS.

258. The thickness of a pier may be considered either as depending upon the weight of the superstructure, or as resisting the thrust of arches or braces. For the first requirement, very little thickness would suffice; for the second, it may require to be considerable. The objection to thick piers is the expense, and the contracting too much the water-way; the benefit, a large bearing surface, and in stone bridges where there are several continuous spans, a saving of centring; as where the piers are not able to resist the thrust of the arches, they must all be carried up at once.

259. Piers supporting truss bridges, require very little thickness provided a good foundation is obtained. The following table shows the sufficient dimensions for the piers of wooden or iron trussed bridges, when the masonry is good. (See First Class Masonry, specification, Chap. IV.) From ten to twenty feet in height the latter is assumed at one twelfth; from twenty to fifty feet in height at one twenty-fourth.

Span.	Length of bridge seat.	Width of seat.
20 to 40 feet,	20 feet,	4 feet,
40 to 60 "	20 "	4½ "
60 to 80 "	22 "	5 "
80 to 100 "	23 "	5½ "
100 to 125 "	23 "	6 "
125 to 150 "	24 "	6½ "
150 to 200 "	24 "	7 "

260. Upon the form of the up-stream end of the pier, or the starling, depends, in a considerable degree, the contraction of the water-way. In sluggish water the form is not of much importance, but in swift flowing rivers a great deal depends upon the choice. The forms in use are the rectangle, the rectangle terminated by right-lined triangles, and

the same terminated by curved-lined triangles, and finally the ellipse.

The latter is that which causes the least disturbance to the water, but is also the most costly.

The effect of gyration at the shoulder, deserves notice, as it may be the cause of the ruin of the foundation when the bottom is of yielding material.

River beds being porous, springs work up through them with a force equal to the whole depth of water; and whenever there is a means of escape for such, its pressure will act upwards against any structure that comes within its reach; and if four or five feet deep, is capable of moving enormous weights. Such springs gave a great deal of trouble at the foundation of the United States Dry Dock, at Brooklyn, N. Y. When checked in one place they burst up in another, and to proceed with the work it was necessary to allow them a passage through which to flow.

261. However proper it may be to give to piers the proper form to cause as little contraction as possible to the water, it is no less necessary to give them strength to oppose the

Fig. 126.

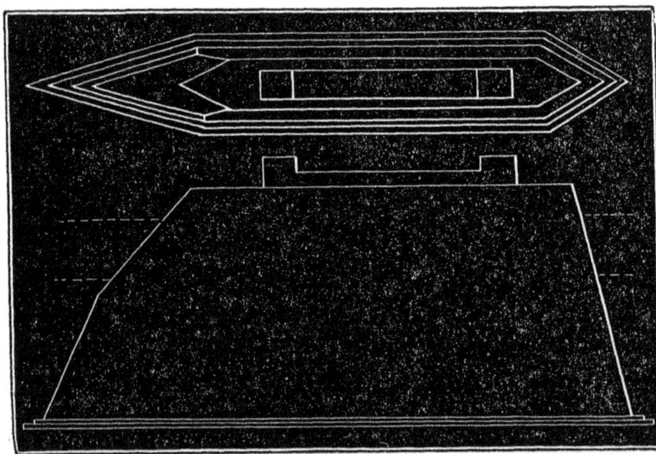

shocks to which they are subject from floating ice, timber and shipping. The best method of breaking up ice, when it comes in large masses, is by inclining the front of the pier, as shown in fig. 126. The angle of the front being inclined from 30° to 50°. The ice running up this slope breaks by its own weight, and falls off on either side.

The foundations of piers may be protected by sheet piling, (see chap. XII.,) or the bottom, if soft, may be dredged out for a few feet and filled in with loose rock.

The form of the down-stream end is not of so much importance as of the upper one, but deserves consideration; as when the water is swift or the bottom soft and yielding, the eddies caused by sharp angles wear upon the soil in a dangerous manner.

CHAPTER XI.

MASONRY.

STONES.

262. THE varieties of this material most commonly used in engineering operations are granites, limestones, sandstones, slates, brick, and artificial stones; the latter being made by compounding clays, limes, and cements.

Rock taken from the surface, which has been exposed to the atmosphere, is of an inferior quality to that found at a depth where it has been exposed to a strong pressure; and is consequently denser. Therefore, in opening a quarry it is advisable to excavate upon a hill-side and come at once to the sound stone. Rock is generally found in beds, divided by joints or seams, at which the natural adhesion is broken and the layers are easily separated. When the quarry shows no natural line of separation, one may be produced by drilling a line of holes at equal distances from each other, into which conical steel pins are driven, and the stone splits; the pins being placed in the plane of the required seam.

263. Stone is used almost entirely to resist a compressive strain; as in the voussoirs of an arch, or in the courses of a pier. The resistance of stone to crushing, is as follows:—

	Pounds per square inch.
Granite	10,000 to 16,000
Limestone	12,000 to 14,000
Sandstone	10,000
Marble	9,000 to 14,000
Firm, hard burned brick	2,600
Yellow burned brick	1,500
Red brick	1,200
Pale-red brick	900
Chalk	750

264. When stone cannot be found, brick forms an excellent substitute; being made from clay earths, which can be found in almost any locality. Bricks are well fitted for nice work, are cheap, and easy of transport. The French, at Algiers, have used concrete, rammed in boxes so as to make large cubes and other shapes. The structures built of this material are found to be very nearly if not quite as strong as those of natural rock.

LIMES, CEMENTS, MORTARS, AND CONCRETES.

265. Nothing is more important in the construction of masonry than good cement; and generally, no part of construction is intrusted to more ignorant persons. Under the above head are to be considered limes, cements, sands, common hydraulic mortar, and concrete.

266. Lime is obtained by burning off the carbonic acid from the pure limestones; when it is put up in air tight barrels and is unslacked lime. Natural cements are composed of pure lime mixed with argyle magnesia, iron, and manganese. Artificial cements are prepared by mixing with pure lime, calcined clay, forge scales, powdered bricks which are underburnt, and other materials of like nature. Cements made thus artificially, are as good as those naturally hydraulic.

Lime is termed rich, poor, hydraulic, and eminently hydraulic, according to its properties.

Rich or fat limes are those which double their volume in slacking and dissolve in fresh water to the last particle. They absorb about 300 per cent. of their weight of water.

Poor limes do not much increase their volume, do not dissolve completely, and absorb 200 per cent. of water.

Hydraulic limes set in fifteen or twenty days after immersion, and continue to harden as they grow older. After one year their consistency is about that of hard soap.

Eminently hydraulic limes set in five or six days, and continue to harden.

Limes are said to set when they will bear, without depression, a rod of $\frac{1}{20}$ of an inch diameter loaded with ten or twelve ounces.

Note.—The following test was applied to every tenth cask of Rosendale cement used upon the masonry of the United States Dry Dock at the Brooklyn (N. Y.) Navy Yard. Cakes two inches in diameter and three fourths of an inch in thickness, after being immersed five days, were required to bear a rod of one twenty-fourth of an inch diameter loaded with fifty lbs. Two bricks united with the cement and immersed five days, were required to resist one hundred lbs. before separating. The following shows the progress of hardening. The force required to thrust a rod one twenty-fourth of an inch in diameter through a cake three fourths of an inch in thickness, was, after

24 hours,	65 lbs.
48 "	70 "
72 "	75 "
15 days,	150 "
50 "	390 "

SAND.

267. Sand is the product of the decomposition of granitic and schistose rocks, and weighs, per unit of bulk, somewhat less than one half of the rock producing it; owing to the spaces between the grains. The amount of lime necessary

to fill these spaces must be known before we can form a solid mass with the least lime. The amount of void may be found by filling a measure with sand, and then pouring in water: the volume of water is that of the spaces. In pebbles of one half inch in diameter the void amounts to about one half, in gravel about five twelfths, in common sand two fifths, and in very fine sand, one third. Clean sharp sand obtained from the beds of rivers is the best for mortars.

268. In mixing the ingredients for mortar, the lime is first spread on a platform and wet by sprinkling with water, which causes it to give off a great deal of heat and vapor, and fall into a powder. The sand is then applied, and the whole brought with water to a consistent paste.

The proportions for common mortar for dry work are

Sand, . .	$7\frac{1}{2}$ to 2
Lime, . . .	1

It is well always to use a small quantity of cement; the parts which have in practice been found perfectly satisfactory are

Cement, . . .	1
Lime, ...	3
Sand, . . .	6

For hydraulic mortar the following proportions have been used with success:—

Cement, . . .	2
Sand, ...	3

269. Concrete is made by mixing broken stone, brick, or shells, with cement mortar; it is used for foundations, backing of arches, and for making artificial stone. The common proportions are

Cement, . .	1 or 2
Sand, . . .	$1\frac{1}{2}$ or 3
Broken stone, .	5 or 10

The cement and sand are first mixed as for cement mortar; the broken stone is added and the whole well mixed and immediately applied before it has time to set. Both concrete and cement mortar should be made as required for use, and in no case applied after standing over three hours.

FLASHING MORTAR.

270. Flashing consists of a thin coat of cement mortar made with a very large part of cement. It is used to protect the face of walls exposed to the wet; such as the top of arches. Stone liable to disintegration may be protected by flashing.

POINTING MORTAR.

271. Pointing is used to protect the joints of masonry, and is made by mixing cement and sand with a minimum of water. The joint is first cut out to the depth of from one half to one inch, carefully brushed clean, moistened with water, and filled with the mortar, which is well rubbed with a steel tool. To give architectural effect, plaster of Paris (Gypsum) is sometimes used in pointing.

GROUT.

272. Grout is thin-tempered mortar, composed almost entirely of cement and water. It is run into the joints, and is useful in filling crevices in masonry which cannot be filled with mortar.

CONSTRUCTION OF ARCHES.

273. The foundations being secured, and the piers and abutments being carried up to the springing line of the arch, the centres are carefully adjusted to their places and the arch is commenced. When the voussoirs begin to bear upon the centre (which is when the angle of the joint with the horizontal is greater than the angle of repose of one stone upon another), the frame is liable to change of form, (particularly when the arch is flat,) which must be provided for by counter loading the centre in various points as the work proceeds. Great care should be taken to make each stone point in the direction of the radius of the arch. To do this effectually, their thickness should be marked upon the outer rib of the centre. The line of the joint may then be fixed by a straight-edge placed both on the centre and the rib mark, or by a template so cut that when one side is level the other shall stand at the proper angle. Excess of weight upon one side of the centre causes a depression at that point, and a corresponding rise at the opposite side of the arch. Both sides being loaded, the haunches settle, and the crown rises. The point where the centre is first loaded will determine the point where the frame is to be temporarily weighted. Such precautions, however, need only to be taken in arches of over fifty feet span, unless the curve is quite flat. The keystone should be put into the proper place, but not driven until the rest is finished. The back joints are then closely wedged and cemented with thin tempered mortar, and the whole is left to set. The masonry of the spandrels is brought up to about one fourth the height of the arch, or enough to prevent by their weight any change of form of the curve. The centres are then struck and the soffit and voussior joints cleaned and pointed. The facing and road-way may next be carried up; the parapet

Fig. 127. Fig. 128.

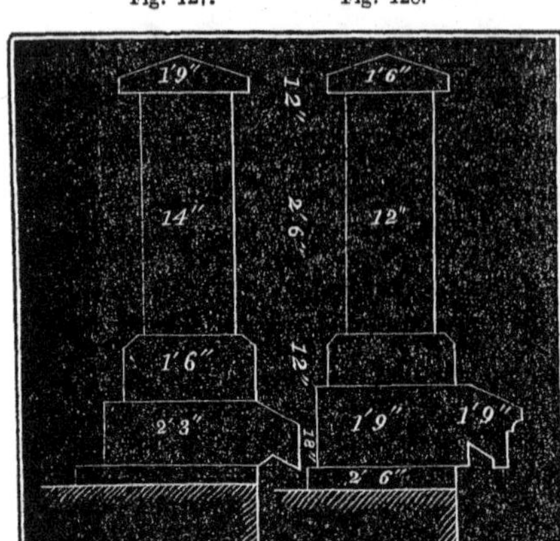

coping and drains finished off; and the whole pointed. Parapets are shown in figs. 127 and 128. The spandrels, fig 129, may be carried up solid or hollow; their weight must be enough to stiffen sufficiently the arch. It should, at least, be carried up solid to the line *c c c*;

Fig. 129.

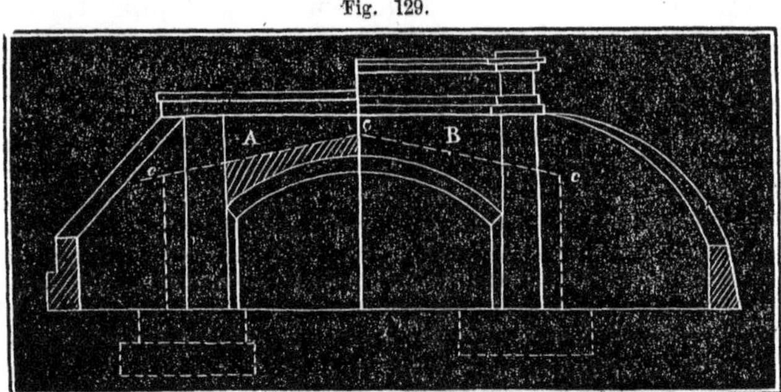

the shaded mass being of well-cemented rubble. Above this the filling may be of masonry, solid or arched, or even of well-rammed layers of earth. The road-way should, in all cases, be well drained, that the water may not sink through to the masonry.

The apparatus for handling stone (cranes, lewises, and derricks) is much better understood by inspection than by description.

Wherever walls support masses of earth, the thrust may be somewhat lessened by ramming the earth behind the wall in layers inclining backward. In laying up the corners each should be well cleaned and moistened before the mortar is laid upon it. When a stone has been once placed upon the mortar bed, it should not be moved at all *laterally*, but may be gently mauled on top.

CULVERTS AND DRAINS.

274. Small culverts are made by covering two side walls with large flat stones; the bottom being paved with stone at least nine inches deep, laid dry. The general dimensions of such structures depend somewhat upon the class of masonry, but as this is generally the *third* or *fourth*, will not vary much.

Opening.	Side walls.	Cover.	Heads.
2 × 2	3 × 2	12	2 × 10
2 × 3	3 × 3	12	3 × 10
3 × 3	3 × 3	12	3 × 11
3 × 4	3½ × 4	15	4 × 12
4 × 4	3½ × 4	15	4 × 13
4 × 5	3½ × 5	18	5 × 15
5 × 5	4 × 5	18	5 × 16
5 × 6	4 × 6	18	6 × 18

Figs. 130, 131, and 132, show plans for culverts of from 5 to 25 feet span.

Fig. 130.

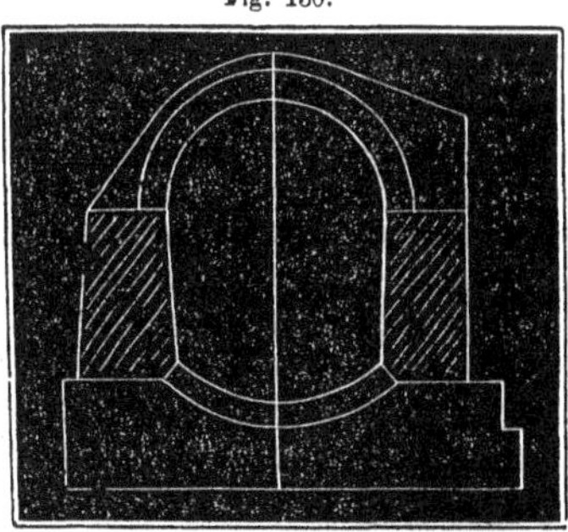

Fig. 131. Fig. 132.

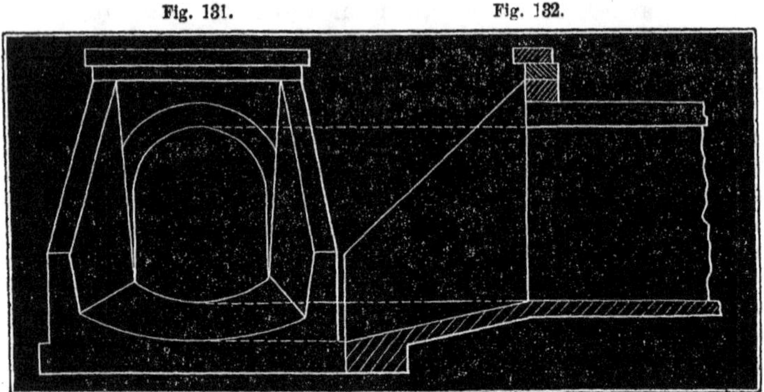

RETAINING WALLS.

275. A wall made to sustain a mass of earth or water, to resist overthrow, requires a certain thickness. A body of earth assumes what is termed the natural slope, the inclination of which depends upon the adhesion of the soil, but may be taken as one and one half horizontal, to one vertical, ($1\frac{1}{2}$ to 1), as an average.

The problem is, knowing the height of the wall and the form of the mass of earth to be supported, to find the thickness of the wall.

Let A B 6 F, represent the thickness of the wall. Its centre of gravity is at O, and is horizontally projected at *m*. The centre of gravity of the thrusting triangle of earth, B 4 6, is C, (formed by the cutting of lines joining any two angles to the centre of the opposite sides,) is horizontally projected at C^a, and the horizontal component of the thrust is exerted at 2, tending to overthrow the wall with a leverage, 6 2.

Fig. 133.

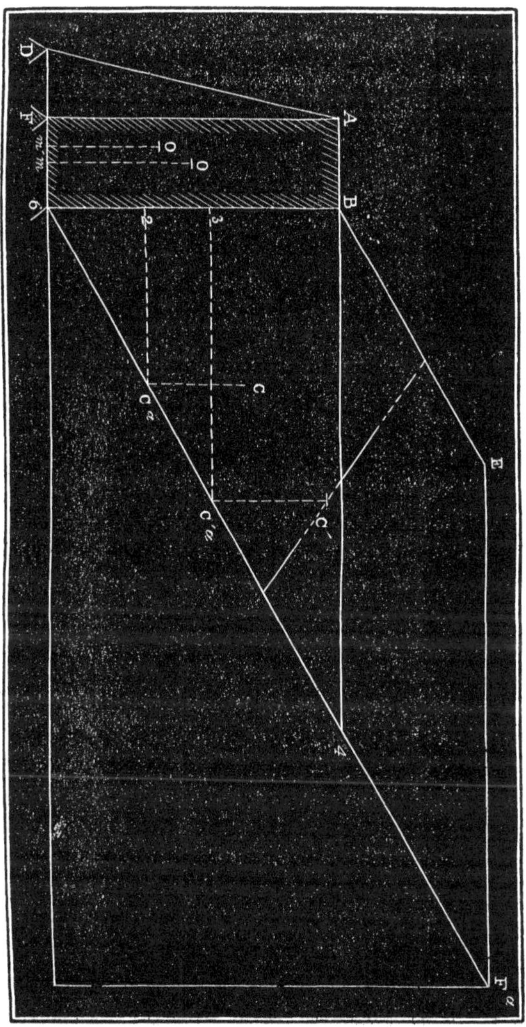

The overthrowing power is, then, the area of the triangle B 4 6 × the weight of the unit of area × the leverage 6 2. And the resisting power, the area A B × B 6 × the weight of a unit of area by one half breadth, or *m* 6; or, calling *w*

the weight of the wall, and w' that of the triangle, B 4 6, and L and L' the leverage respectively of the wall to resist and of the earth to overthrow; we must have at least

$$w\,L = w'\,L',$$

and to insure stability,

$$w\,L > w'\,L'$$

or,

$$L = \frac{w'\,L'}{w},$$

and as $L =$ half base finally, the thickness, or

$$2\,L = \frac{2\,w'\,L'}{w}.$$

276. *Example.* — Let the height of wall be twenty feet, slope one and one half to one; if a cubic foot of earth weighs one hundred lbs., and of masonry, one hundred and sixty lbs., we have the overthrowing force,

$$\tfrac{20}{2} \times 15 \times 1 \times 100 \times \tfrac{20}{3},$$

and the resisting force, (assuming the thickness as eight feet, in order to get the area),

$$20 \times 8 \times 1 \times 160 \times \tfrac{8}{2}.$$

Or performing the operations,

For overthrowing, ...	100,000 lbs.
For resisting, ...	102,400 lbs.

If the wall in place of retaining only the mass B 4 6, retains the bank B E F^a, the pressure will evidently be increased. The centre of gravity of the trapezoid B E F^a 6 is at C′, which is horizontally projected at C'^a, and the horizontal component of the thrust acts at 3 with the leverage 6 3.

Any superincumbent load, as a train of cars at E F^a, will again increase the pressure, not only by reason of weight, but from shocks and vibration.

For resisting lateral pressure, the beds of masonry are best when rough dressed. For vertical loads, hammer dressed beds are the best.

The leverage of resistance is very much increased by battering the wall in front, as at A D. The centre of gravity is then horizontally projected at m', but the distance D m' is much greater than F m.

The amount of masonry remaining the same, by decreasing the top, and increasing the base, the strength is very much increased.

When retaining walls are exposed to shocks or pressures in special directions, they may be very much aided by buttresses opposing directly such forces, as in fig. 134.

The increase of strength thus made by a small bulk of masonry is very great.

All abutments, wing-walls, and side walls of culverts, come under the head of retaining walls.

When the face of the wall does not by its position admit of buttresses, as in fig. 134, it may be dovetailed into the earth; the latter being firmly rammed around the masonry, as in fig. 135.

Fig. 134.

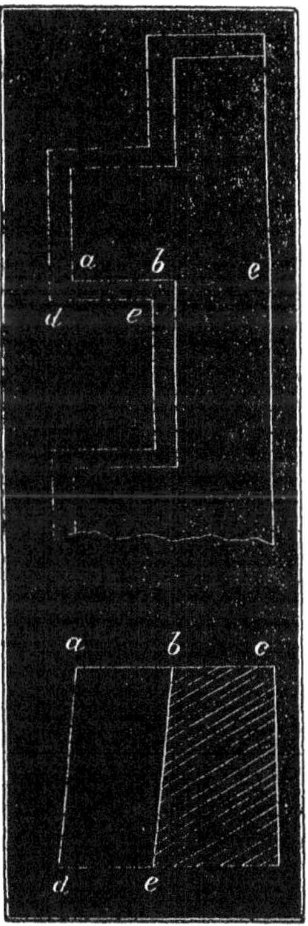

Fig. 135.

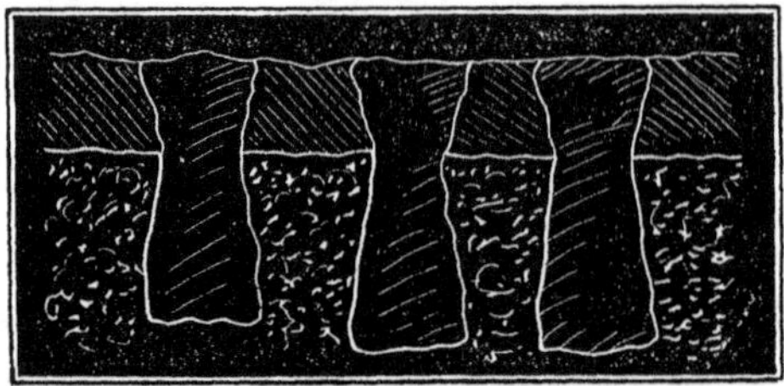

277. The weight of the different earths and stones are shown in the following table.

Name of material.	Weight per cubic foot.
Brick, common	97 to 125
Brick, stock	115 to 135
Brickwork, (average,)	90 to 95
Chalk, ...	144 to 166
Granite, ...	164 to 187
Marble, ...	111 to 117
Mortar, (hair,) dry	80 to 86
Puzzolano, ...	160 to 178
Slate, ...	157 to 180
Stone, (average,)	140 to 150
Clay, (common,)	110 to 125
Clay and gravel, ...	150 to 170
Earth, common, ...	95 to 126
Gravel, ...	100 to 110
Quick-lime, ...	50 to 55
Quartz sand, ...	170 to 175
Common sand, ...	88 to 93
Shingle, ...	88 to 92
Earth, loose	90 to 95
Stone work, (hewn,) in wall, . . .	160 to 175
Stone work, (unhewn,) in wall, .	125 to 140

CHAPTER XII.

FOUNDATIONS.

---

278. FOUNDATIONS may be divided into four classes.

Those on *firm* dry land.
Those on *unfirm* dry land.
Those on *solid* bottom, under water.
Those on *unfirm* bottom, under water.

Foundations upon firm dry land require only to be placed at a sufficient depth to be out of the way of frost; varying from one foot in the Southern, to two and three feet in the Middle, and four and five feet in the Northern States. The first course should consist of small, flat stones placed dry, but well packed by hand, upon the bottom; upon the top of this layer, the mortared or cement masonry should be commenced. The object of the first course of small stones is to apply the weight of the superincumbent masonry as equally as possible to the ground. All boulders and rounded stones should be carefully kept out of the foundation.

Unfirm soils are prepared by driving piles, upon which a platform holding the masonry is placed; or by placing the lower courses directly upon the heads of the piles.

Sand piles are made either by driving and withdrawing a wooden pile and filling the hole thus made with sand; or by digging trenches and filling such with sand. The applied weight is thus spread over the entire surface of the sides and bottom, instead of being placed upon the bottom only. When the weight of a heavy structure is thrown upon a few small points of support, they may be made the piers and abutments of a series of inverted arches, by which the whole surface beneath the structure is made to assist in bearing the load. Foundations upon yielding or sandy and wet soils may be secured by piling around the whole structure; by which the earth is kept from spreading. Foundations upon dry land do not generally give much trouble to the engineer; but operations carried on under water require all the science and patience that he is master of.

279. Three methods of founding under water may be noticed,

By driving piles.
By coffer-dam.
By caisson.

In very shallow water, where no danger arises from contracting the water-way, we may throw in loose stones until the surface is reached; and commence thereon the lower courses of the masonry. This is termed "Enrockment."

PILE DRIVING.

This operation has for its object the consolidation of naturally weak bottoms; for piles driven close together tend to prevent that compression that might take place under a heavy structure. Piles may resist either by friction against the soils through which they are driven, or by bearing upon a firm superstratum at too great a depth to be reached by uncovering. Piles driven in clay have sometimes acted as a conductor to water, which, insinuating itself along the side of the wood, produced settling which would not otherwise have taken place.

Experience has shown that four feet apart from centre to centre, when there is a good substratum, is near enough to bear the heaviest loads.

The fact that a pile refuses to enter further, does not show that it has reached a bed strong enough to bear the required load; for though it may bear upon a solid bottom, or resist penetration by side friction, when the load has been for some time upon the pile, it may be found too weak to stand. Piles have in some cases refused to enter the ground from the blow of a 1,500 lbs. ram, falling twenty feet, when first driven, and have afterwards gone down three feet from a ram of 1,000 lbs.

The following formula, showing the resistance which a pile should offer, is given by *Weisbach* in Mechanics of Engineering, Vol. I. p. 285. First, when the ram remains upon the pile after the blow,

$$Ps = \frac{G'^2 \times H}{G + G'}.$$

And, second, when the ram does not remain upon the pile,

$$Ps = \left(\frac{G'}{G + G'}\right)^2 \times GH.$$

Example.— A pile weighing five hundred lbs. is driven two feet, by forty blows of a 1,000 lbs. ram falling six feet. Required the weight which may be safely supported by the pile without further penetration.

The notation in the formula above is thus,

$G =$ the weight of the pile.
$G' =$ the weight of the ram.
$H =$ the fall of the ram.

s = penetration per blow.
P = the weight in lbs.

The penetration per blow will be $\frac{2}{40}$ or .05 feet; and the formula for the second case

$$\left(\frac{1000}{1000+500}\right)^2 \times \frac{500 \times 6}{.05} = 26,667 \text{ lbs.}$$

Of which *one tenth* or *one twelfth* only is the maximum load which should be placed upon the pile permanently. The surest test of the power of a pile is to load it temporarily, when the time and place admit.

Perronet considered fifty tons, or 112,000 lbs. as not too great for a twelve inch pile; and allowed twenty-five tons for a pile of nine inches in diameter.

That the point of the pile may not be shattered by contact with the hard earth, an iron shoe is sometimes fitted to the lower end; and that the head may not split, an iron ring is driven on to the top.

The force of the blow given by a ram depends upon the weight of the ram or monkey, and upon the velocity at which it strikes the pile; the velocity depends upon the height from which it falls. The velocities of bodies falling freely being as the times, and the spaces fallen through as the squares of the times, we have the following rules; and from them the table succeeding.

Given the *velocity* of a body to find the *space* through which it must fall,

$$\left(\frac{\text{Velocity in feet per second}}{8}\right)^2 = \text{space in feet.}$$

Thus a weight to acquire a velocity of two hundred feet per second, must fall through a height of

$$\left(\frac{200}{8}\right)^2 = 625 \text{ feet.}$$

Given the *space* fallen through, to find the *velocity*.

$$\sqrt{\text{height in feet} \times 64.3} = \text{velocity in feet per second.}$$

Thus the velocity of a body falling twenty feet will be

$$\sqrt{20 \times 64.3} = 36 \text{ feet per second.}$$

Momentum is the product of weight by velocity; therefore, to find the force of the blow given by a ram of given weight, falling a given height, we find, first, the velocity by rule two. Also, given the weight of ram, the necessary velocity to produce any required effect being found, it is easy to find the height, and the reverse.

Examples.— Suppose we have a ram weighing 2,000 lbs. and wish to strike a blow of 25,000 lbs.; the velocity must be

$$\frac{25000}{2000} = 12\tfrac{1}{2} \text{ feet per second;}$$

and to acquire that velocity, the height fallen must be (rule one)

$$\left(\frac{12\frac{1}{2}}{8}\right)^2 = 2.43 \text{ feet.}$$

Again, if we have a pile-engine which admits of a fall of fifteen feet, and we wish to strike a blow of 18,000 lbs., we first find the velocity (rule two) thus:—

$$\sqrt{15 \times 64.3} = 31 \text{ feet per second nearly,}$$

whence the weight

$$\frac{18000}{31} = 581 \text{ lbs.}$$

The form of the common pile-engine is too well known to need description.

Mr. Nasmyth's system of pile-driving consists in forcing the pile into the ground by a great number of blows following each other in rapid succession. Piles were driven by his engine at the United States Dry Dock, at Brooklyn, (N. Y.,) as follows: A pile was sunk fifty-seven feet by a hammer of 4,500 lbs.; it was driven forty-two feet in seven minutes by three hundred and seventy-three blows.

MITCHELL'S SCREW PILE.

Mitchell's screw pile is a cast-iron column, around the lower part of which is a spiral flange. It is screwed into the ground, and offers great resistance to vertical pressure, on account of the large bearing surface obtained.

DR. POTTS'S ATMOSPHERIC SYSTEM.

280. All methods of placing foundations in difficult positions must yield to the above plan, which consists in exhausting the air from a hollow cast-iron cylinder; when the pressure upon the surface of the ground, outside of the cylinder, forces the earth immediately under the pile to its interior; at the same time the pile sinks into the opening thus made, both by its weight and by the atmospheric pressure from the outside. The earth is moved from the interior of the pile; and when sunk to the necessary depth, the interior is filled with concrete.

A very successful application of the above system was made at the Godwin Sands, at the mouth of the Thames River, (England). There, sands change their position with every violent storm, and are yet so compact that a steel bar could be driven only eight feet with a sledge hammer; and a pointed rod three inches in diameter, when sunk thirteen feet deep, required forty-six blows from a one hundred lbs. ram falling ten feet to drive it one inch. But a hollow pile two and a half feet in diameter was sunk seventy-eight feet, at the rate of ten feet per hour for a part of the time. In case of meeting with rock, the pile may be converted into a diving-bell, and the obstruction moved.

The pile is cast in lengths of ten or twelve feet, and flanged together with cemented joints.

In founding a bridge at Rochester, (England,) a pile of this nature was loaded with thirty tons of iron rails, which caused a settlement of three fourths of an inch. The rails being removed and the air exhausted, by a single effort the pile descended six and a half feet. One hundred tons of rails were then placed upon the pile, when the settlement was again three fourths of an inch. (This small depression was owing to the compression of the soil.)

The piles supporting the Shannon bridge, on the Midland Great Western Railroad, (England,) were sunk by this system; and are ten feet in diameter, and filled with concrete.

After wooden piles have been driven, they are cut off at the bottom to receive the lower courses of the masonry. In some cases square timber caps are placed upon the pile heads, and thereon a plank floor. In others, the spaces between the piles are filled with cement and concrete.

COFFER-DAM.

281. In founding in water from five to twenty-five feet deep, a contrivance called a "coffer-dam," is sometimes used. It is formed by driving a double or triple row of piles around the foundation; which rows are made water tight, either by tongued and grooved square piles, or by round

piles, to which is fastened a sheathing of plank. The space between the courses of piling is emptied of water and packed closely with clay or other material impervious to water. The interior of the dam is then pumped dry and the masonry laid as on dry land. The thickness of the dam depends upon the depth of water; the pressure upon the lower part being of course much greater than that at the upper. If it was considered as a mass resisting by its weight, overthrow from the pressure of the water, the thickness would be easily calculated. Thus, if the water is twenty feet deep the whole hydrostatic pressure upon each lineal foot of the dam is $20 \times 1 \times 10 \times 62\frac{1}{2} = 12{,}500$ lbs.; and as the weight of water increases in the order of the terms of an arithmetical progression, as also the pressure, it may be expressed by the elements of a triangle, of which the height is the depth; and as the centre of gravity of a triangle is at two thirds of the height from the vertex, the pressure may be regarded as concentrated at one third of the depth from the bottom; and the leverage of the above 12,500 lbs. is

$$\frac{20}{3} = 6.67 \text{ feet};$$

and the overthrowing force is 83,375 lbs. The resisting force of a clay dam twenty feet high and ten feet thick, would be

$$20 \times 10 \times 110 \times \frac{10}{2} = 110{,}000 \text{ lbs.}$$

Determining the thickness thus, would make the dam, when in deep water, very thick; and it is generally best to brace the inside against the ground, and when the masonry will admit, against that.

Dams of the following thickness have proved perfectly secure:—

Depth of water.	Thickness.
6 feet.	3 feet.
10 "	5 "
15 "	8 "
20 "	12 "
25 "	14 "

The best form for a large coffer-dam is circular, or elliptical; as the pressure is thus resisted more equally in all places than when there are flat sides and angles in the plan.

To keep the dam dry while the work is going on, pumps are rigged along one side of the dam the lower ends of which are placed in a trench or well which drains the bottom.

The piers of the Victoria bridge at Montreal, (Canada,) are put down by coffer-dams. Some of the piers being in but few feet of water, and upon a rocky bottom, which did not admit of the driving of piles; the dams for such were built in sections, floated to the site and anchored.

FOUNDATION BY CAISSON.

282. In deep water the coffer-dam becomes very expensive, on account of the size and length of the piling, and the quantity of bracing required. In such cases recourse is had to the caisson; which is simply a box in which the masonry is built, and afterwards sunk to the proposed site. The manner of putting down a piece of masonry by caisson will best be shown by an example.

Suppose we wish to sink a pier thirty feet long, twenty feet high, and six feet wide, in twenty feet of water.

Let the caisson bottom be of two courses of square 12×12 timbers, fastened strongly at right angles to each other. Let the courses of masonry be two feet thick. Assume the weight of a cubic foot of stone as one hundred and sixty lbs., a cubic foot of wood at thirty, and of water sixty-two lbs. per foot.

Every floating body will sink until it has displaced a quantity of water equal to its own weight.

If the bottom is ten feet wide and thirty-five feet long, it will weigh

$$35 \times 10 \times 2 \times 30 = 21{,}000 \text{ lbs.}$$

one course of masonry weighs

$$30 \times 6 \times 2 \times 160 = 57{,}600 \text{ lbs.}$$

one course of side timbers, 12×12, which are laid upon the sides of the raft,

$$(2 \times 35 + 2 \times 8) \times 30 = 2{,}580 \text{ lbs.}$$

Now load the bottom with one course of masonry and three courses of side timbers, and we have

Stone	57,600 lbs.
Bottom of caisson . .	21,000 "
Three side courses . .	7,740 "
In all	86,340 "

which divided by 62, gives 1,392; which divided by the area of the caisson bottom, gives

$$\frac{1392}{350} = 3.98,$$

or nearly four feet, for the depth at which the caisson will float. This leaves the sides one foot above the water surface.

Putting on a second course of masonry and three more side courses of timber, we have

Floor	21,000 lbs.
Two courses masonry .	115,200 "
Six side courses . . .	15,480 "
In all	151,680 "

which divided by 62, and by 350, gives seven feet very nearly; leaving the top one foot above the surface.

In the same manner we proceed until the caisson grounds upon the bed, which has been previously prepared, either by pile-driving or by dredging. The bottom being reached, the sides are taken off, and the masonry remains upon the floor. The caisson may at any time be grounded by filling with water, and may be raised again by pumping out. The masonry may be laid either from barges or rafts at the site, or at the shore. Guide piles are necessary to insure the descent in the proper manner, and to prevent overturns.

In laying stone under water, it is to be remembered that masonry submerged loses $\frac{62}{160}$ nearly of its weight, and is consequently more liable to be injured by shocks than when above the surface.

CHAPTER XIII.

SUPERSTRUCTURE.

283. Nothing aids more the proper accomplishment of any object than a correct idea of what is wanted. The following definition is given by Mr. W. B. Adams, of what good superstructure should be:—

"The principal requirements of permanent way are: That it shall be well drained, especially in contiguity to the substructure; that the weight and damaging power of the locomotives and rolling stock should be considered the data for calculation; that the strength, hardness, and tenacity of rails, and the immobility of the substructure should be adapted to the hardest work to which the railway is to be subjected; that the substructure should have an amount of bearing surface proportioned to the load to be borne, and the nature of the rail and ballast; and a sufficiently fair hold in the ground to prevent looseness or lateral motion, from the side lurches of the engines and trains; that the rails should possess so much vertical and lateral stiffness, either in themselves or in their fastenings, as to prevent all deflection; and have sufficient hardness of surface not to laminate or to disintegrate beneath the rolling loads; also, to have sufficient breadth or tread surface to diminish the crushing effect of the wheels.

"They should be as smooth as possible, to prevent concussion, and be laid at the proper angle, and the curves regularly bent, so as to insure the accurate tread of the wheels. The joints should be so made that the rails may practically become continuous bars, yet with freedom to contract and expand without being too loose. And with all this there should be interposed between the rails and the solid ground, some medium sufficiently elastic to absorb the effect of the blows of the wheels, without being crushed or forced down into the ballast, and yet stiff enough to keep the upper surface of the rails in a uniform plane."

TIMBER-WORK.

284. The timber-work supporting the rails consists either of cross ties of wood, hewn flat on top and bottom, of dimensions from 6 × 7 to 7 × 9, and 2½ or 3 feet longer than guage; or of longitudinal sawed timbers rectangular in section, placed directly beneath the rail, and giving it a bearing throughout the whole length.

Longitudinal bearings seem to possess no advantage over cross ties, but are subject to some decided disadvantages. In case of removal, two rails at least must be taken up to admit of the replacing a timber; while with cross ties any one may be taken out and replaced without even affecting the immediate passing of a train. A continued bearing is no better than a broken one, as the strength of the timber itself offers very little resistance to the weight of a locomotive. Strength is not to be expected in the timber-work; it is only the elastic medium between the rail and the ground serving to maintain the rail in a proper position. The strength is in the rail. The distance at which to place cross ties depends upon the weight of engines traversing the road, the nature of the ballast, and the strength of the rail; somewhere between two and four feet from centre to centre.

The amount of superficial bearing which the timber-work ought to give per lineal foot of rail, is differently estimated by different engineers.

Upon the 4′ 8½″ guaged roads of America, 1¾ square feet per lineal foot of rail has been allowed.

Several of the English roads give the following:—

Name of road.	Guage.	Square feet per lineal foot of rail.
London and N. W. Railway,	4′ 8½″	3
Great Western,	7′ 0″	2½
S. and W. of Ireland,	5′ 3″	3⅔
Midland G. W. of Ireland,	5′ 3″	2 7/12

If ties are made eight inches wide, and eight feet long; we have the following amounts of bearing surface per lineal foot of the rail with different distances of the ties.

Distance C to C of tie.	Superficial feet per lin. foot.
2	2.66
2½	2.13
3	1.78
3½	1.53

Of course the longer the tie is made the greater may be the distance between, provided the rail will bear it. Mr. Peter Barlow, in his report of August, 1835, to the directors of the Liverpool and Manchester Railway, fixes the following dimensions for superstructure.

	Distance between insides of ties being				
	3′	3′ 9″	4′	5′	6′
Weight in lbs. per yard.	50	59	61	67	79
Depth of rail in inches.	$4\frac{1}{2}$	$4\frac{5}{8}$	$4\frac{3}{4}$	5	$5\frac{5}{10}$

At the time these dimensions were given, however, much less weight was applied to the rails than at the present day. As the bearing is increased, the rail must become heavier and more expensive; but the number and cost of the ties is lessened. The report above referred to, concludes that five feet bearings, involving heavier rails, would cost no more, after the road bed is consolidated, than shorter ones; but that on embankments and soft subsoils, it would be at first somewhat more expensive.

285. The object of the ballast is, first, to transfer the applied load over a large surface; second, to hold the timber-work in place, horizontally; and third, to carry away the rain water from the superstructure; it also furnishes the means of adjusting the timber-work to the proper position. It should be at least one half way up the depth of the tie, and deep enough below the under surface to prevent the timber being forced down by the passing weight. From various observations it appears that there should be one and a half times the depth of the tie of ballast, beneath the under surface; or the whole depth of ballast should be from two to two and one half times the depth of tie.

For ballast, broken stone, gravel, or other dry, durable, and porous material, is suitable.

A perfectly inelastic road bed is not to be desired. Something is necessary to absorb the shocks given by the wheels, and prevent their reaction against the machinery. To supply this amount of elasticity, and to transmit the weight evenly to the ground, is the duty of the ballast and timber-work.

Of late years there has been applied, in England, cast-iron hemispherical bowls, designed to take the place of both tie and chair. Such answers very well when there is no lack of ballast, and where wooden ties are worth from seventy-five cents to one dollar each.

SECTION OF THE RAIL.

286. A good rail must be able to act as a girder, or supporter, between the ties, as a lateral guide upon curves; and must possess a top surface of sufficient hardness and size to resist the rolling wear of the wheels.

			Lbs. per yard.	Tons per mile. (2,240 lbs.).
One square inch of rail section weighs,			9.9	15.72
Two inches	"	"	19.8	31.42
Three inches	"	"	29.7	47.14
Four inches	"	"	39.6	62.84
Five inches	"	"	49.5	78.56
Six inches	"	"	59.4	94.28
Seven inches	"	"	69.3	110.00
Eight inches	"	"	79.2	124.50
Nine inches	"	"	89.1	140.01
Ten inches	"	"	99.0	155.57
			Single line of rails.	Double line of rails.

Thus, at sixty dollars per ton, each square inch of section costs $943.20 per mile, or $94,320 per one hundred miles, whence the necessity of rolling the rail to the form which shall give the greatest strength with the least weight.

The sections most in use in America are shown in fig. 136, and 137.

Fig. 136.

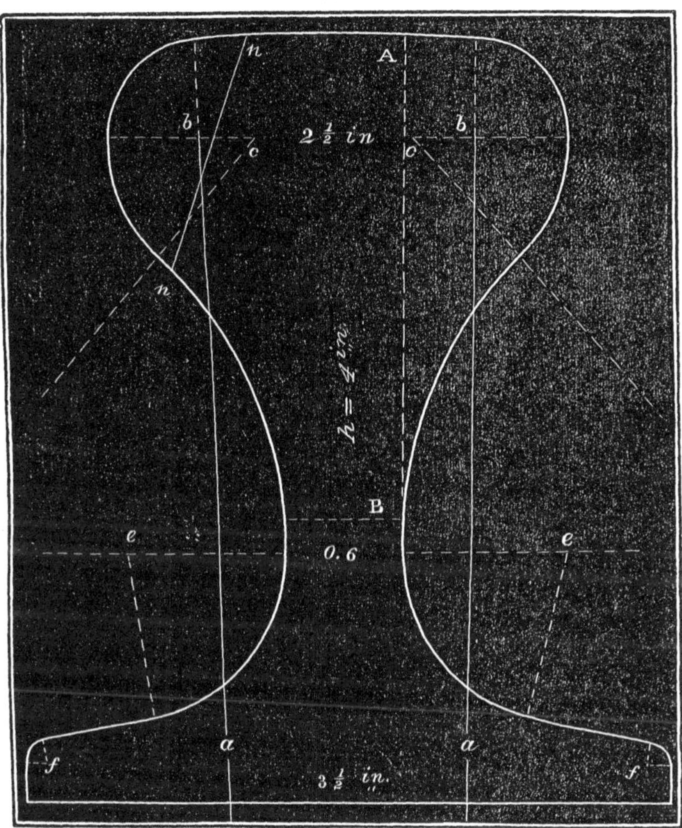

Fig. 136 gives the most direct bearing, is compact, and brings the fibres at top and bottom more directly in opposition with the compressive and extensive strains. The top of the rail being curved to a radius of ten or twelve inches, the load is applied nearly to a single point; whence the whole resistance in fig. 137, depends upon the lateral resistance of the piece *a b c d* to being pushed down.

An objection is sometimes made to fig. 136, on the ground that it splits off on the line *n n*: this will not be the case when the head is joined to the web by a proper curve, as in

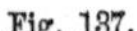

Fig. 137.

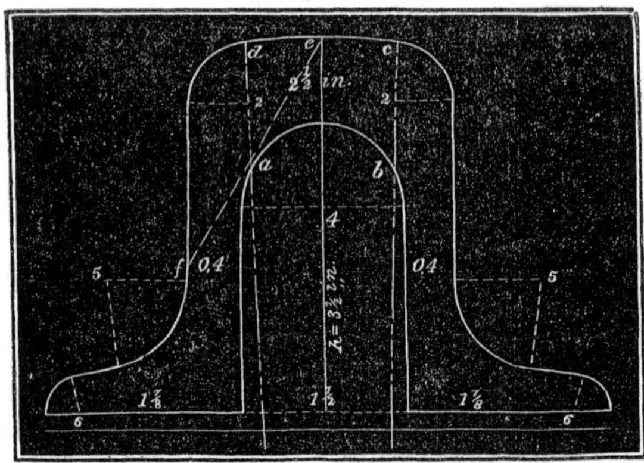

fig. 136. This splitting off happens full as often in fig. 137, as may be seen where it is in use; and it might be supposed to act in that manner; because if the weight is transferred at all from the point of application to the web, it must be in the direction *ef*.

The rails in present use upon our roads, weigh from fifty to seventy-five lbs. per lineal yard; and are laid upon cross ties placed at a distance of from two and one half to four feet from centre to centre.

OF THE ACTUAL DIMENSIONS OF RAILS.

Digesting carefully the results of the experiments of Barlow, Fairbairn, and Hodgekinson, and the experience of Mr. W. B. Adams, and other English engineers; also the conclusions arrived at by the Berlin Convention of 1850, appointed to determine the best form of section, we come to the following limiting dimensions.

THE HEAD.

Mr. Barlow limits the width of head at two and one half inches as the maximum; the Berlin Convention, at two and one fourth inches; W. B. Adams, at two and one half; and all of the above recommend supporting the edges of the head well from the rib.

THE VERTICAL RIB.

The experiments of the Prussian engineers fix the thickness for a rail four inches high, at one half of an inch, and a rail four and one half inches high, at 0.6 or $\frac{6}{10}$ inch. Mr. Barlow makes it six tenths of an inch for a four and one half inch rail, and 0.75, or three fourths inch for a rail four and five eighths inches high, and for four and three fourths inches high, 0.8 eight tenths inch.

THE BOTTOM FLANGE.

The use of this is more for bearing and fastening, than for supporting strength. The Prussian engineers make three and one half inches an ample base for a rail five inches high. The edge for one half or three fourths of an inch, should be nearly horizontal, or parallel with the base, to allow the spike to have a good bearing.

OF THE INCLINATION.

As the tread of the wheel is conical, the top of the rail must be inclined to fit this cone, otherwise the wear will come upon the inner edge of the rail only. This may be done in two ways; by placing the rail base level, and inclining the vertical axis of the cross section of the rail, and making the tread square with that axis; or by making the rail section true, and inclining the base, either by cutting the tie, or by a wedge placed between the rail and the tie.

OF THE HEAD CURVATURE.

If the top surface of the rail were perfectly flat, and the

wheel tire does not happen to fit it exactly, (from want of the proper position of the rail, by settling, or other cause,) the wheel will bear entirely upon one edge, and would soon destroy the rail. To remedy this, a slight convexity is given to the top. Mr. Clark (in R. R. Mach.), recommends the top to be curved to a radius of *ten* or *twelve* inches.

OF THE VERTICAL DEPTH (HEIGHT) OF THE RAIL.

Mr. Barlow's general results are as follow:—

Distance from inside to inside of tie.	Height of rail.
3′ 0″	4 1/2″
3′ 9″	4 5/8″
4′ 0″	4 3/4″
5′ 0″	5″
6′ 0″	5 1/10″

In the London edition (1836) of Barlow's Strength of Materials, page 402, in a report to the London and Birmingham Railway Co., upon the best form and upon the strength of rails; after a carefully conducted set of experiments, and an elaborate theoretical deduction of results, the writer comes to the following five sections of rails possessing the maximum strength, with the least weight.

Dimensions.	No. 1.	No. 2.	No. 3.	No. 4.	No. 5.
Height,	4 1/2	4 5/8	4 3/4	5	5 5/10
Breadth at top,	2 1/4	2 1/4	2 1/4	2 1/4	2 1/4
Depth of top,	1	1	1	1	1
Thickness of rib,	0.6	0.75	0.8	0.85	1.0
Width of lower flange,	1 1/4	1 1/2	1 1/2	1 2/3	1 2/3
Depth of lower flange,	1	1	1	1 1/8	1 1/2
Weight per yard,	51.4	58.8	61.2	67.4	79
Distance C. to C. of ties,	3′	3′9″	4′	5′	6′

This table shows the ratio of material which should be placed in the top and bottom.

With the above dimensions, and joining the curve of the head to the rib at two and one fourth inches from the top of the head, we obtain a strong and well-shaped rail, with the least material possible. See fig. 136.

As an example of the application of the above, the table below has been formed, showing four standard forms, which will be found to unite all of the requirements of good rails; the general form being that of fig. 136.

Dimensions.	The weight of the rail being, in lbs., 60	65	70	75
Width of head,	2½	2½	2½	2½
Rad. of top,	12	12	12	12
Height of rail,	4	4¼	4½	4¾
Thickness of rib,	0.6	0.6	0.65	0.7
Breadth of base,	3½	3½	3¾	4
Depth of head at point A B,	2¼	2¼	2½	2½
Thickness at edge of lower web,	½	½	½	½

and the following figures show the weights which should be applied to differently spaced sleepers.

Distance centre to centre of tie.	Distance clear.	Weight of rail, in lbs., per yard.
1½ feet,	1 feet,	60 lbs. per yard.
2 "	1½ "	60 "
2¼ "	1¾ "	60 "
2½ "	2 "	60 "
2¾ "	2¼ "	65 "
3 "	2½ "	65 "
3¼ "	2¾ "	70 "
3½ "	3 "	75 "

The amount of inclination or bevel to be given to the cross section of the rail, depends *directly* upon the curve of the wheel, and *indirectly* upon the gauge of the track. (See Chapter XIV. part 2.) The radius of curvature being averaged at 2°, or 2,865 feet,

	Feet or	Inches.
For the 4′ 8½″ gauge it should be	.0017	.020
For the 5′ gauge,	.0017	.020
For the 5½′ gauge,	.0019	.022
For the 6′ gauge,	.0021	.025

in the width of the rail, or two and one half inches.

The above dimensions embrace all of the best results of experiment and experience, and at the same time satisfy the conditions demanded by the mechanical and physical nature of the material — iron.

CHAIRS AND JOINTS.

287. The chairs most common at present are made of a wrought iron plate, with two lips, either cut and punched up, or forged up, to hold the lower web of the rail. Such chairs weigh from six to ten pounds each, and are less liable to break than the common form of cast-iron chairs. It is probable that a cast-iron chair may be made, however, with properly shaped lips, and so hollowed out as to be at once strong and light. (See Clarke's R. R. Machinery, "Permanent Way.")

Of late the chair of Mr. Daniel L. Davis, of Dedham, Mass., has attracted considerable attention, and bids fair to be the means of obtaining a better rail surface than has heretofore been possible. This gentleman has been for twenty years Road-master of the Boston and Providence Railroad, and has had ample opportunity for considering the subject of track laying in every respect. The rail bears upon a cup of wrought iron, which rests upon a piece of rubber, lying in the chair. The testimony of the leading managers of the New England Railroads bears witness of the excellence of the arrangement.

The practice of notching *each end* of the rail causes the expansion to be exerted directly *against* the fastenings, which should not be the case. Some point should be *fixed longitudinally*, to resist the end shocks from the wheel. This point should be either the *centre* or *one end* of the rail. End chairs may hold the rail laterally, and vertically, but not longitudinally.

The weakest part of the track is that, where, to resist the concussions of the wheels it should be strongest, namely, at the joint: here we lose the strength of the rail and depend entirely upon the tie. The flattened ends of rails which have been laid for a few years show the bad effect of the common joint. The complete remedy for this is, so splicing the rail that it is as strong at the joint as elsewhere. The method termed "fishing," is not much more expensive than the ordinary method of jointing, it is perfectly effectual, and has had the test of long and successful use. It consists in bolting a plate two and one half feet long, two and one half or three inches wide, and from one third to one half inch thick, to the ends of both rails making the joint; one plate being placed on each side. The plates are convexed a little from the rail as in fig. 138, so that being sprung by screwing on the nuts, the latter shall not work loose by the vibration of the rail.

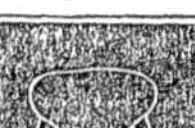

Fig. 138.

In the above arrangement there is no tie below the joint, but the latter lies midway between two sleepers.

Another method of "fishing" is, to place a piece of H or T iron beneath the rail, bolting it firmly to the lower flanges.

In bolting rails together at the ends, the bolt holes must be cut a little larger than the bolt, to allow for the expansion of the iron.

The effect of the joint upon the passing carriage, is the

jumping motion; the middle of each rail being a summit, and the end a depression, (the strength at the joint being taken away); and if the joints are not opposite to each other, there is generated a very injurious and dangerous side rocking. Figs. 138, 138 A, and 138 B, show the methods of fishing.

Fig. 138 A.

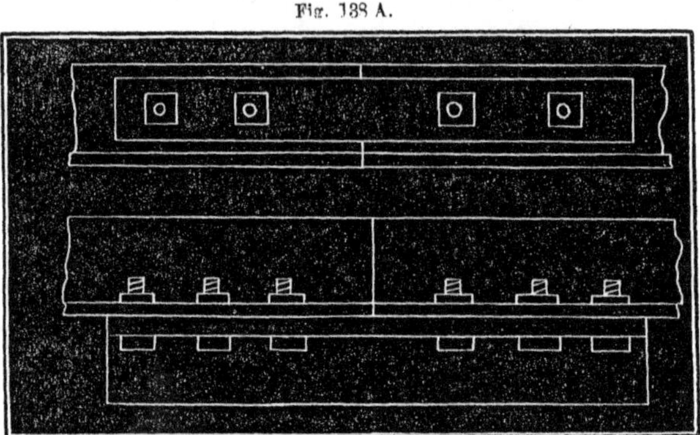

Fig. 138 B.

To avoid the wear caused by frequent joints, various forms of compressed rails have been proposed; consisting of two or more parts breaking joint. One form has been contrived in which the section is vertically halved; another of three parts, a head placed on top of a double vertical web. Fig. 139 shows what would seem to answer any purpose (if compound rails are at all allowable). The joint is here divided into four parts, so that the strength of the bar at any point is reduced only one fourth. In bolting the parts together the joints should be left open enough (see in advance) to allow for contraction; and the bolt-holes, as before noticed, should be longer than the bolts. (This enlargement, extending only in the direction of contraction, and not in the line of the force.) The upper part of such a rail should be

Fig. 139.

hardened to resist the rolling of the wheels, while the webs must possess the strength to act as a girder.

It is questionable whether, by dividing the rail, particularly when it is done horizontally, we do not prevent the mutual extension and compressive actions which ought to have place in the top and bottom; for we cannot make the bolts perfectly tight because of expansion.

Some of the compressed rails which have been laid in America have given good results, others have not.

Mr. W. B. Adams observes, that a compressed rail to be as strong as a sixty pound whole rail, must weigh ninety lbs. per yard.

Some engineers have proposed such a rail that when one side becomes worn it may be turned over so that the lower may become the upper table. This is quite wrong in principle; as when the lower fibres have been subjected for some time to extension, they are entirely unfitted to oppose compression.

OF THE LIFE OF RAILS.

288. The time which a rail will last, depends upon the form and weight, and *on the quality of the iron;* and upon the number, weight, and speed of engines and cars passing over it.

NOTE. — The effect of *quality* is altogether too little regarded in America. How worthy of attention it is may be seen by the following.

Upon the same road were used two kinds of seventy-two pound rails, each five inches deep, and having a bearing surface of 2.7 inches in width. The one was worn out with a tonnage of 41,000,000 tons, the other of 22,000,000 tons; the difference being entirely in the *quality* of the iron.

Upon the Philadelphia and Reading Railroad there have been used forty-five pound rails of reheated and refined iron, which have lasted for eighteen years; and that with a very heavy traffic upon them. While upon other American roads, English sixty pound rails have required renewing in one, two, three, and four years.

The durability of rails is practically independent of time, and depends entirely upon the amount of work done. The repairs of iron, depending upon flaws and other physical defects, will be greater at the commencement of operations than afterwards. After the first one or two years the regular depreciation begins. The first Liverpool and Manchester rail weighed thirty-five lbs. per yard, and the locomotive seven and a half tons. As the traffic increased, so did the necessary weight of engines, and a corresponding increase in the strength and weight of rails was also rendered necessary. In 1831, the average weight of engines with tenders was eighteen tons. In 1855, the maximum engine with tender, fuel, and water weighed sixty tons; and in like manner the rails increased from thirty-five to eighty-five lbs. per yard.

Messrs. Stephenson and Locke, in a report to the London and North-western Railroad Company, in 1849, recommend the adoption in future of an eighty-five lb. rail.

Upon the roads of Belgium are used rails of fifty-five and sixty-four lbs. per yard; but it is asserted that an eighty lb. rail would allow of ten times more traffic.

For the average of American roads, when the iron is good, (*in quality,*) fifty-five, sixty, and at most sixty-five lbs., will probably be found ample for the heaviest traffic: the rail being of the form already given, and supported on ties not more than two and a half feet from centre to centre.

Mr. Belpaire, (of the Belgium engineers,) concludes, from many experiments, that in sixty miles, each engine abrades 2.2 lbs.; each empty car 4½ oz.; and each ton of load 1.4 oz.; the amounts being in direct ratio to the several weights.

Captain Huish, of the London and North-western Railroad, (England,) estimates (Report of April, 1849) that fifty trains per day, or 18,250 trains per annum, for twenty years, would wear out a seventy lb. rail.

The Belgian engineers have concluded that 3,000 trains per annum, for one hundred and twenty years, would wear out a fifty-five lb. rail.

Now $120 \times 3{,}000 = 360{,}000$ Belgian, and $20 \times 18{,}250 = 365{,}000$ English, a very satisfactory coincidence, as the different observers did not know of each other's proceedings. The difference, 5,000 trains, being accounted for by the use of heavier engines upon the roads of England.

From the above results the following table is formed, showing the life of rails under from two to one hundred trains per day. American roads being less nicely finished, as regards the road-bed, will of course wear out rails faster than the roads of Europe. The table will serve as a base for estimates.

Trains per day.	Trains per year.	No. of years' life of rails.
2	600	604
4	1,200	302
6	1,800	201
8	2,400	151
10	3,000	121
12	3,600	100
14	4,200	86
16	4,800	75
18	5,400	67
20	6,000	60
30	9,000	40
40	12,000	30
60	18,000	20
80	24,000	15
100	30,000	12

Probably one half of the above numbers of years would show the full life of rails upon American roads.

As those rails which are most used wear out the soonest, they should be made accordingly heavier. Such are those at depot grounds and at sidings.

NOTE.—From the reports of the Reading (Penn.) Railroad it appears that in 1846 $\frac{153}{209}$ of the damaged rails were split; and that in 1845 $\frac{285}{295}$ were split.

As regards the *quality* of railroad iron, it is generally notoriously bad, and its makers know it as well as those who buy it. Railroad companies are not willing to pay for good iron. Comparisons between American and English iron amount to little. First rate iron can be made in England or in America, and so can that which will last about two years. Time will convince companies that the most expensive iron is the cheapest.

TABLE OF THE WEIGHT PER MILE OF DIFFERENT RAILS.

Weight in lbs. per yard.	Tons per mile. (2,000 lbs.)	Tons per mile. (2,240 lbs.)
50	44.00	39.29
55	48.00	43.21
60	52.80	47.19
62	54.56	48.71
64	56.32	50.28
66	58.05	51.86
68	59.84	53.43
70	61.60	55.00
72	63.36	56.57
74	65.12	58.14
76	66.88	59.71
78	68.64	61.28
80	70.40	62.86

TRACK-LAYING.

289. As wrought iron expands 0.0000068 of its length per degree (Fahrenheit) of heat, a change of 130° will cause the following expansions:—

In a 15 feet rail .0135 ft.
" 18 " " .0162 "
" 20 " " .0176 "

and that the track may be kept in the right vertical and horizontal line, rails laid in cold weather must not be placed in contact; but separated by space enough to allow expansion to take place. In hot weather they may be placed close together. Calling 100° the maximum and —30° the minimum, we form the following table for the average lengths of rail, (20 feet).

At —30° place the rails in contact.

—20°	at a distance of		.00136	feet	.016	inches.
—10°	"	"	.00272	"	.032	"
0°	"	"	.00408	"	.049	"
10°	"	"	.00544	"	.065	"
20°	"	"	.00680	"	.082	"
30°	"	"	.00816	"	.092	"
40°	"	"	.00952	"	.114	"
50°	"	"	.01088	"	.131	"
60°	"	"	.01224	"	.147	"
70°	"	"	.01360	"	.163	"
80°	"	"	.01496	"	.179	"
90°	"	"	.01632	"	.196	"
100°	"	"	.01768	"	.212	"

Fig. 140.

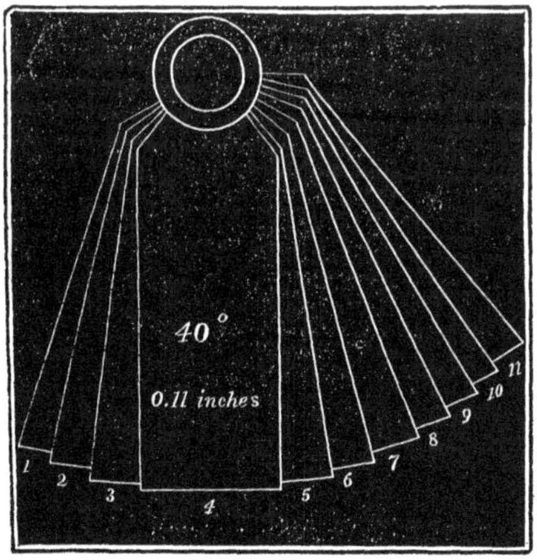

The proper distance of rails may be fixed by the use of the steel plates shown in figs. 140 and 140 A, which are marked with the temperature, according to their thickness, as in the above table.

To incline the rail base may be used, when the rail is not levelled, wedges one

Fig. 140 A.

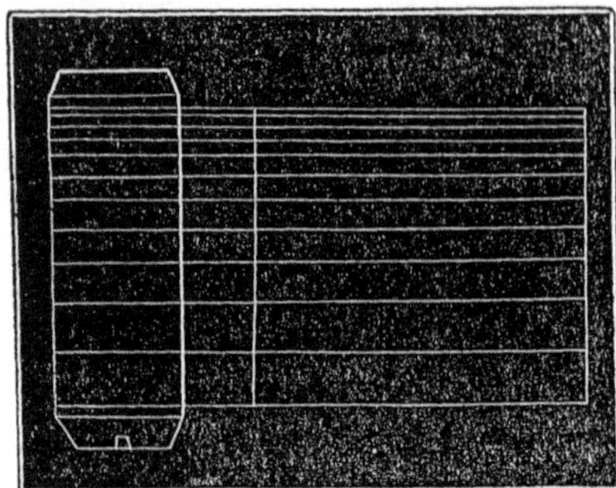

foot long and six inches wide, spiked with the rail to the tie. When the chairs are of cast-iron, they may be cast to the required slope.

FROGS.

290. When one line of rail crosses another, a contrivance called a frog is used; see figs. 141 and 142.

Fig. 141.

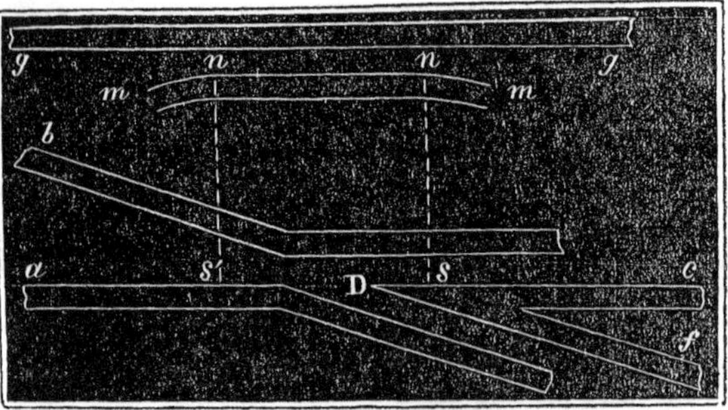

That the wheel may run smoothly from *a* to *c*, fig. 141, the rail *b f* must be cut at D, and the rail *a c* must be cut at the same point. Cutting the two gives the form shown in the figure, and further developed in fig. 142.

In order that the flange of the wheel shall not leave the line *a c*, when at the break D, the guard rail *m m* is used to confine the opposite wheel. It should be placed at a distance of two inches from, and parallel with, the main rail *g g*, from opposite six inches below the frog point at *s*, to six inches above the shoulder at *s′*. From the ends of the parallel line *n n* the guard rail should gently curve away at both ends. Thus the wheel will be gradually brought into the right line, kept so until the break in the rail is passed,

Fig. 142

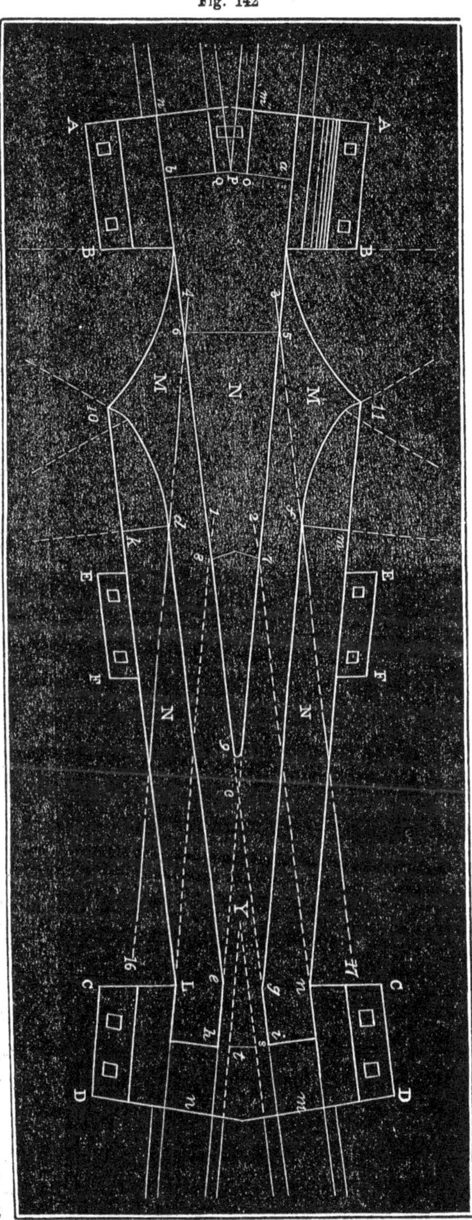

and finally easily released. To place and maintain the guard rail in the right position, it is well to put both it and the main rail into a double chair, which is spiked to the sleeper.

The form and dimensions of the cast-iron frog depends upon the angle at which the cutting rails cross, and upon the size of the wheel tire.

To draw the frog, proceed as follows:—

Let *a c b* be the angle. Parallel with and two inches from *b c* draw *d e*, *e* being in *a c* produced. In the same manner fix the point *g*. At the width of the rail head (from $2\frac{1}{4}$ to $2\frac{1}{2}$ inches) draw, parallel to *a c*, 4. 8. The point

Fig. 142 A.

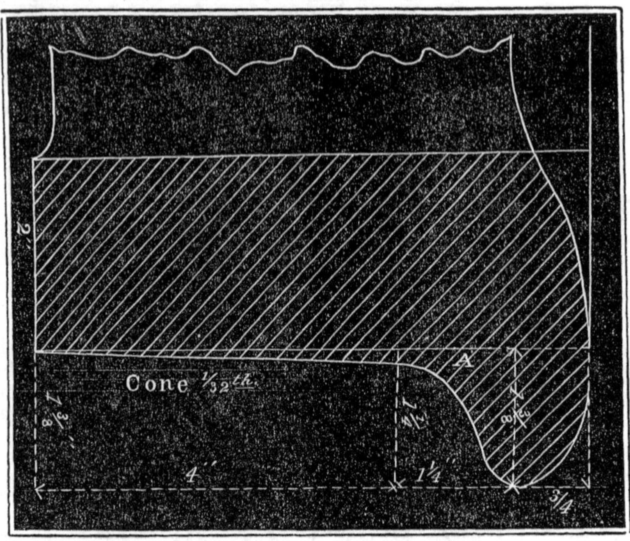

8 is the limit to the solid steel. At double the rail width, or 4½ inches, draw, also, parallel to *a c*, 16. 6; 5. 6 is the limit of the flat steel, generally about half an inch in thickness. This is the least amount of steel allowable; it is best to steel the whole tongue, and all of that part of the wings acted upon by the wheels. The geometric point is generally very thin, and is omitted to a distance far enough back to make the point a third or half an inch wide, which is rounded off; *e h* and *d k* are made two and a half inches; as also *f m* and *g n*; *k* 10 and *m* 11 are made six or seven inches, and joined to *d* and *f* by a curve, abrupt at first, but afterwards more gentle. The distances, 5 *a* and 6 *b* must be such that *a* 9 is three and one eighth inches, (depending upon the breadth of rail base,) *o m''* is from three to four inches. At the other end of the frog *e h* must be enough to make *s t* at least an inch, when *e h* and *i g* are from three to four inches; *i m'* being, as at

the other end, three or four inches. The steel plates N N are one half inch in thickness. The surface, N, is two inches above the bottom, M. The lower plate, M, is two inches thick. A B, C D, and E F are six or seven inches wide, and one inch thick. The spike holes $\frac{11}{16}$ square, the spike being one half inch. The sharp edges, *i g*, *e h*, *b b*, 8, 9, A *s* 79, should be rounded off to fit the wheel at A, fig. 142 A. The surface of the tongue N 9 should be formed to a double incline to fit the wheel cone.

NOTE.—Fig. 142 A gives the shape and dimensions of the largest tires.

Another method of making a frog is to cut and weld the rails *a* and *b* of the track, as in fig. 143. The continuations of these rails are bent as shown in the figure.

Fig. 143.

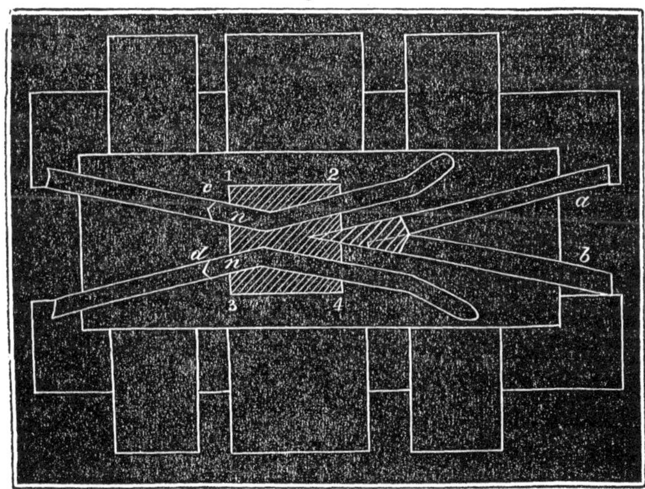

The whole angle is placed upon a firm wooden bearing. There is no weaker part of the track than the frog. To make up the strength at such places a heavy longitudinal timber twelve feet long will answer a good end.

Fig. 144.

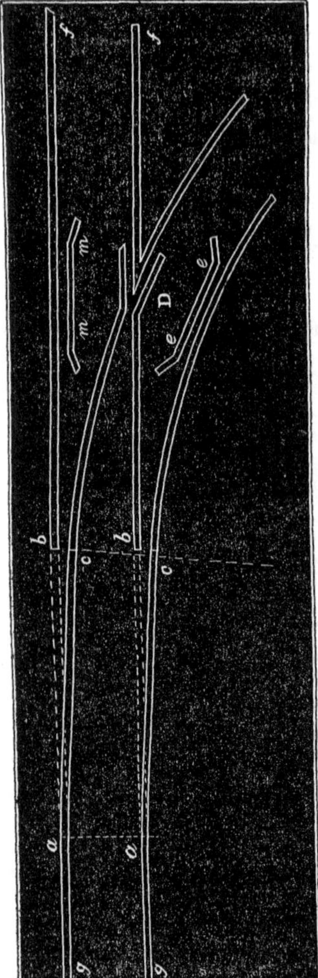

SWITCHES.

291. The object of the switch is to adjust a single line of rails to two or more pairs, so that any two lines may be made continuous. The form in general use consists of two rails, as at *a b*, *a b*, fig. 144, moving upon *a* and *a* as centres. Here the tangent point of the turnout curve is at *c*. The data given for the switch are the length of switch rail and the motion at the toe (*c*) (which determine the direction of the starting tangent) and the radius of curvature of the turnout curve. The required elements are, the angle of frog at *b* and the distance from *a* to the point of the frog.

The following formula and table are by Josiah Hunt, Esq., (at present chief engineer of the Hannibal and St. Joseph Railroad, Mo.). The formula was first published in Appleton's Mechanics' Magazine, vol. 1, p. 575.

$$D = 2\,(g - s) \times \frac{\text{cot.}\,S \times \text{cot.}\,F}{\text{cot.}\,S + \text{cot.}\,F}.$$

Where $S =$ angle of switch.
$F =$ angle of frog.
$s =$ the movement.
$g =$ the gauge.

Example. — How far from the toe of the switch is the point of the frog, the gauge being 4′ 8½″, the rail twenty feet long, and moving five inches; the frog being six feet long, six inches wide across the head, and three inches at the mouth?

We have

$$D = 2\,(4.708 - .417) \times \frac{\frac{240}{5} \times \frac{72}{6+3}}{\frac{240}{5} + \frac{72}{6+3}};$$

$$\text{or, } D = 8.582 \times \frac{48 \times 8}{48 + 8} = 58.85 \text{ feet.}$$

In laying the rails, the distance from the point to the end of the frog (towards the switch) is to be taken from the above.

Table showing the distance between the frog and switch, gauge 4′ 8½″, movement of switch-rail five inches. Frog six inches across head, and three inches at mouth. Main track being straight.

Length of frog.	LENGTH OF SWITCH RAIL.					
	12	14	16	18	20	22
3	29.1	29.7	30.1	30.4	30.7	30.9
3½	33.3	34.0	34.5	35.0	35.3	35.6
4	37.3	38.2	38.8	39.4	39.8	40.2
4½	41.1	42.2	43.0	43.7	44.3	44.7
5	44.8	46.1	47.1	47.9	48.5	49.1
5½	48.3	49.8	51.0	51.9	52.7	53.2
6	51.7	53.4	54.8	55.9	56.8	57.6
6½	55.0	56.9	58.5	59.8	60.8	61.7
7	58.1	60.3	62.1	63.4	64.7	65.7
7½	61.2	63.6	65.6	67.2	68.5	69.6

292. When the switch rail is short, the angle between the main line and the switch rail, when switched, is considerable; and causes quite a shock to the passing engine. The switch shown in fig. 145 remedies the evil, makes the ma-

Fig. 145.

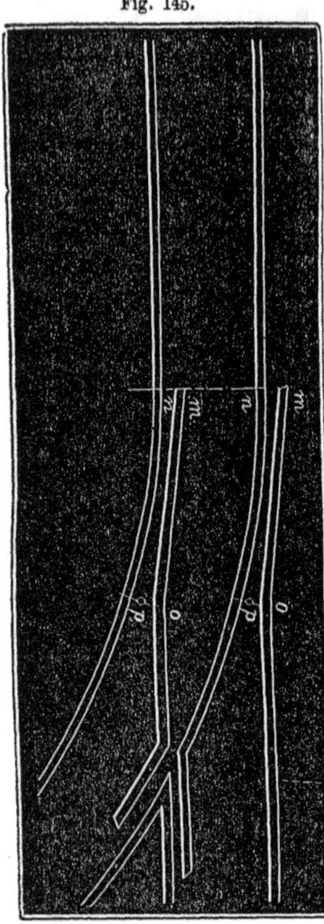

chinery compact, and the calculation simple. The tangent point of the turnout curve is at *n n* (the usual heel). In place of adjusting the single to the double line of rails, the double is adjusted to the single line. The data given are the gauge and radius of curve; and, as before, the elements required the frog angle and distance from switch to frog point.

Now

$$\text{Rad.}^2 - \overline{\text{Rad. less gauge}}^{\,2} = \text{distance}^2,$$

$$\text{or } R^2 - \overline{R - 8}^{\,2} = D^2,$$

$$\text{and } D = \sqrt{R^2 - (R - g)^2}.$$

The angle of frog is also

$$\text{Sin angle of frog} = \frac{\text{Sin } 90 \log D}{\log R}.$$

The length of this switch rail depends upon the radius of curvature. The distance between the two rails at S must be enough to admit the wheel flange, that is, at least two inches.

Let A B, fig. 146, be the straight rail; E D the curved one. Draw G H parallel with and two inches distant from the inner edge of A B. No point of the curved rail must fall within G H; whence E is the turning-point, and E D the length, found as follows.

Let R equal the radius of curve to outside of outer rail; d equal two inches plus width of rail, or $i\,e$, and D equal $D\,E$.

Fig. 146.

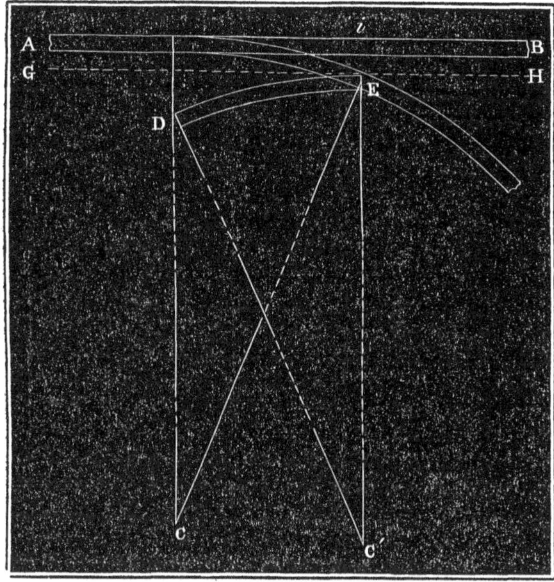

Then

$$D = \sqrt{R^2 - (R - d)^2}.$$

Example.— Let the radius of outer rail be five hundred feet, and the gauge five feet. We have, then, the distance

(A.) $D = \sqrt{500^2 - 495^2} = 72$ feet, very nearly.

$$\text{Also, Sin } E\,C\,D = \frac{\text{Sin } 90 \log D}{\log R},$$

(B.) $$\text{or } \frac{\text{Sin } 90 \log 72}{\log 500} = 8^\circ\ 17',$$

and the length of switch

(C.) $\sqrt{500^2 - 499.65^2} = 18\frac{3}{4}$ feet nearly.

Five hundred feet is, therefore, about the longest radius for which such switches should be used.

Crossings occur where two tracks cross, and consist of four frogs, with the corresponding guard rails, as in fig. 147.

Fig. 147.

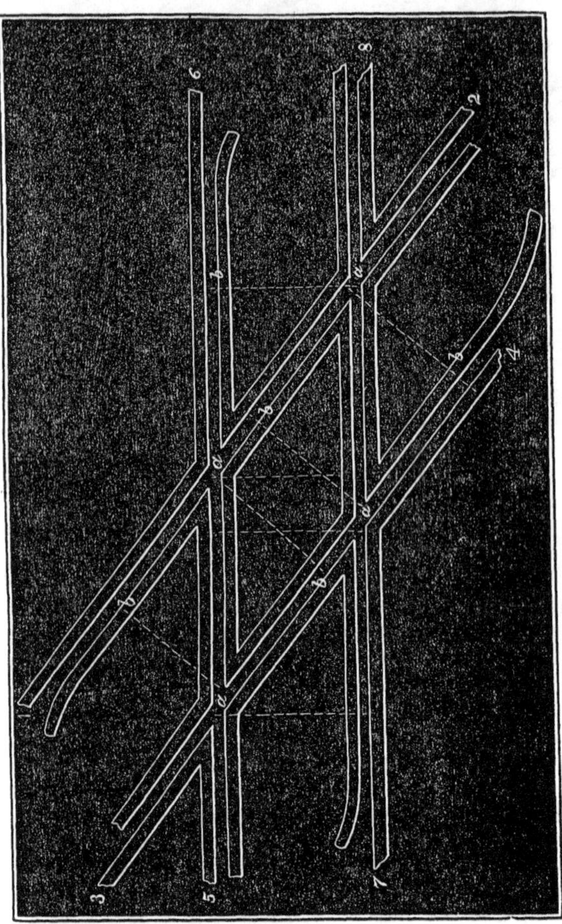

ELEVATION OF THE EXTERIOR RAIL.

293. The motion of a train of cars around a curve is accompanied by a tangential force, depending in amount

upon the velocity of the train and the radius of curvature. This force tends to throw the cars from the track; and is counteracted by elevating the exterior rail.

The centrifugal force of any body in motion in a curved line is shown by the formula

$$\frac{W V^2}{32 R}.$$

Where W is the weight in lbs.
V the velocity in feet per second.
R the radius of curvature.
and 32 the accelerating force of gravity.

The force tending to throw the car from the rail is not *centrifugal* but *tangential*, but it matters not whether the body is kept in position by *tension* upon the *inside* or by *compression* on the *outside;* the amount of the force is the same.

Fig. 148.

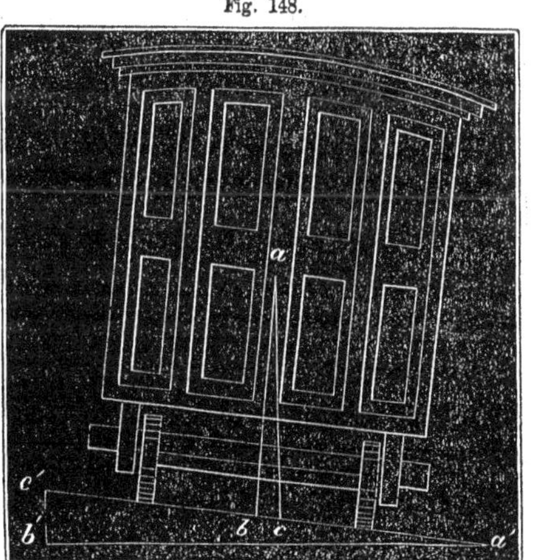

The horizontal projection of the centre of gravity of the car, when at rest, is at c, fig. 148, and when in motion the direction of the weight should be $a\,b$; and the inclination, $c'\,a'\,b'$, must be such that $a\,b$ will be perpendicular to $c'\,a'$; to effect which, $c'\,b'$ should be to $a'\,b'$ as the weight to the tangential force; or E being the elevation of the rail, g the gauge, W the weight, and c the tangential force; we have

$$E : g :: c : W,$$

$$\text{or } E = \frac{c\,g}{W}, \text{ and } c \text{ being} = \frac{W\,V^2}{32\,R};$$

$$\text{finally } E = \frac{\left(\frac{W\,V^2}{32\,R}\right)g}{W} \text{ or } \frac{V^2\,g}{32\,R} = E.$$

Fig. 149.

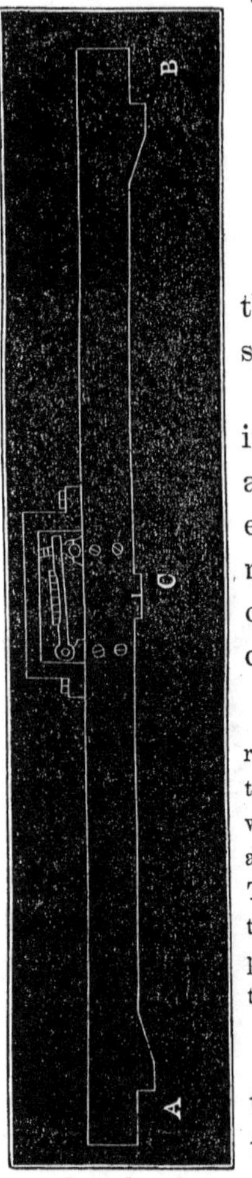

Where W = weight of a car.
V = speed of train in feet per second.
g = gauge of road.
R = radius of curve.
E = elevation of outer rail in feet and decimals.

g and R are the only fixed quantities in the formula; and the average weight and speed of a car must be assumed.

Examination of the formula shows how important it is that all trains should run at such a velocity as to demand the same elevation of rail. The absolute elevation must be arranged to meet the requirement of the fastest trains; and other trains must conform, even at a disadvantage.

NOTE. — The subject of the mechanics of traversing railroad curves, is yet quite in the dark. The action of the train, as caused by its own momentum, is *tangential;* while the action of the engine tends to pull the cars against the *inner* rail, being *opposed* to the first motion. This might require a reduction of the elevation given by the formula when the engine is exerting a strong tractive power, but when running without steam the full elevation is needed, (see chapter III.)

In laying and maintaining the rails to the proper elevation, a clinometer attached to a rail gauge, as in fig. 149, answers a good end: the small arc being graduated according to the different elevations required by curves of different radii. Thus the index of the level being placed at 2°, when the rails are fitted to A and B, the elevation is correct for a 2° curve; or for a curve of 2,865 feet radius.

The difference in gauge of one foot makes a difference in the elevation of but 0.009 feet, or about $\frac{1}{10}$ of an inch.

The following table is calculated for the average of the different gauges in use, thus, —

$$\begin{array}{r} 4.7 \\ 5.0 \\ 5.5 \\ \underline{6.0} \\ 4)\overline{21.2} \\ \end{array}$$

Average gauge, 5.3 feet.

TABLE OF ELEVATION OF OUTER RAIL.

Radius of curve in feet, being	ELEVATION OF OUTER RAIL IN FEET AND DECIMALS, THE VELOCITY IN MILES PER HOUR BEING					
	10.	15.	20.	25.	30.	40.
250	.130					
500	.070					
1,000	.037	.079				
2,000	.018	.040	.074	.111		
3,000	.013	.026	.048	.074	.106	
4,000	.009	.020	.037	.058	.079	.154
5,000	.007	.016	.031	.045	.065	.119
6,000	.006	.013	.024	.037	.053	.095
7,000	.005	.011	.021	.033	.046	.086
8,000	.004	.010	.018	.029	.039	.077
10,000	.003	.008	.010	.022	.032	.059

CHAPTER XIV.

EQUIPMENT.

PART I.

LOCOMOTIVES.

As the locomotive engine is the power by which railroads are worked, and as its proportions and dimensions are so intimately connected with the physical character of the road, it is thought proper to take space enough at this point to examine the general principles of its construction, and of its adaptation to the work required of it upon railroads.

Under the general principles, we recognize the production and consumption of steam, the disposition of weight upon the several pairs of wheels which shall secure the necessary adhesion, the application of the power generated in the boiler to the moving of the wheels, and that general arrangement of parts which shall render the use of power economical.

BIRTH AND GROWTH OF THE LOCOMOTIVE.

294. The first idea of the application of steam to locomotion, is due to the unfortunate Solomon de Caus, of Nor-

mandy (France), who was confined in a madhouse for insisting that steam could be made to move wheeled carriages.

295. In the year 1784, William Murdoch, the friend and assistant of James Watt, built a non-condensing steam locomotive engine, on a scale of about one inch per foot, having

Cylinders, ...	$\frac{3}{4} \times 2$ inches,
Wheels, ...	$9\frac{1}{2}$ inches,
and Weight, ...	10 lbs.

This little engine, however, accomplished the speed of ten miles per hour.

296. In 1802, Richard Trevethick patented the application of the non-condensing steam-engine to the propelling of carriages on railroads; his engine was fitted with one horizontal cylinder, which applied its power to the wheels by means of spur gear.

297. In 1825, the truck was first applied, to relieve the driving wheels of a part of the weight, and to enable the engine to pass freely around curves.

298. In 1827, Timothy Hackworth applied the blast pipe, for the purpose of draft. He applied, also, spring balances to the safety-valves, and used the waste steam to heat the feed water. This engine drew one hundred tons, at five miles per hour, and forty-five tons on a fifty feet grade.

299. In 1828, M. Leguire (France) introduced the multitubular boiler.

300. In 1829, the directors of the Liverpool and Manchester Railroad offered a premium for the best locomotive, which should draw three times its own weight, at ten miles miles per hour. The "Rocket," by Robert Stephenson, of Newcastle on Tyne, was the successful competitor, and drew the load required, seventy miles, at an average speed of 13.8 miles per hour; its maximum velocity was twenty-

nine miles per hour; it evaporated 5.4 lbs. of water per pound of coke, and 18.24 cubic feet per hour.

301. From 1830 to 1840, the changes that were made were rather those of dimension, proportion, and arrangement, than of essential elements of steam producing.

302. In 1840, several truck frame engines were sent to England from the Norris Works of Philadelphia. These locomotives would draw a load of one hundred and twenty tons over a sixteen feet grade, at the rate of twenty miles per hour.

303. In 1845, the Great Western Railroad, of England, was supplied with an engine of twenty-two tons weight, having cylinders $15\frac{3}{4} \times 18$, wheels 7 feet, heating surface 829 square feet. This locomotive carried seventy-six and one half tons at a velocity of fifty-nine miles per hour. The consumption of coke was 35.3 lbs. per mile, and of water, 201.5 cubic feet per hour.

THE ENGLISH LOCOMOTIVE OF 1850.

304. The "*ne plus ultra*" for the seven feet gauge (Great Western Railway) by Gooch, has inside cylinders 18×24 inches, one pair of eight feet driving wheels, grate area twenty-one square feet. Fire-box surface, one hundred and fifty-three feet. Three hundred and five two inch tubes, giving 1,799 feet of surface. Total heating surface, 1,952 square feet. Weight of engine, empty, thirty-one tons; of tender, eight and one half tons; whole weight with wood and water, fifty tons. Evaporating power, three hundred cubic feet of water per hour. This engine can draw two hundred and thirty-six tons, at forty miles per hour.

The maximum for the London and North-western Railroad, four feet, eight and one half inches gauge (Crampton's patent), has cylinders 18 × 24 inches; wheels, eight feet; two hundred two and three sixteenths inch (outside diameter) tubes; grate, twenty-one and one half square feet; fire surface, one hundred and fifty-four feet; tube surface, 2,136 feet; whole heating surface, 2,290 square feet; weight, loaded, thirty-five tons; twelve tons upon driving wheels; tender, twenty-one tons, loaded; whole weight, fifty-six tons.

THE AMERICAN LOCOMOTIVE OF 1855.

305. The engine "Charles Ellet, Jr.," drew on the 9th of August, 1854, forty tons, over a grade of two hundred and seventy-five feet per mile, and over grades of two hundred and thirty-eight feet, upon curves of three hundred feet radius. This engine has wheels four and one half feet in diameter coupled seven feet apart; cylinders 14 × 26 inches; and weighs, including wood and water, 53,058 lbs. This is a tank locomotive, the tender is dispensed with, and in its room a tank containing one hundred cubic feet of water, and one cord of wood is used. This engine was built by Richard Norris and Son.

An engine built by the Cuyahoga Steam Furnace Co. of Cleveland, Ohio, performed the following feat.

An ordinary passenger train was carried one hundred and one miles, over a total ascent of 1,255 feet of grades, making twenty stops, at an average speed of twenty-five miles per hour, with a consumption of only ninety cubic feet of wood.

The same engine drew an average load of three and one third cars four hundred and thirty miles, making seventy-five stops, surmounting a total ascent of 5,439 feet, averaging twenty-five miles per hour, with one tender full of wood only.

In the months of July and August, 1856, two engines upon the Pacific Railroad (Missouri), one by R. R. & G., and one by Palm & Robertson, ran each one hundred and twenty-five miles, with three passenger and one baggage cars, using only one cord of wood.

NOTE.—For an interesting example of what can be done by the American locomotive, and an illustration of engineering peculiarly American, the reader is referred to a description of the "Mountain top track" at the Rock-fish Gap crossing of the Blue Ridge (Va.), by the Virginia Central Railroad, given by the engineer under whose direction the work was proposed and executed (Charles Ellet, Esq.), from which is extracted the following:—

"The eastern slope is 12,500 feet long, and rises 610 feet; the average grade being $257\frac{4}{10}$ feet, and the maximum $295\frac{68}{100}$ feet per mile. The least radius of curvature 234 feet; upon which curve the grade is $237\frac{6}{10}$ feet per mile. The western slope is 10,650 feet long, and falls 450 feet; the average grade being $223\frac{1}{10}$, and the range $279\frac{84}{100}$ feet per mile.

"The engines, which have taken loads ranging from twenty-five to fifty tons up one slope at seven and one half miles per hour, and down the opposite one at six miles per hour, making four trips of eight miles per day for three years, were designed and built by M. W. Baldwin & Co., Philadelphia, and have three pair of forty-two inch wheels all coupled, the flange base being 9′ 4″, cylinders $16\frac{1}{2} \times 20$ inches, weigh, with wood and water, 55,000 lbs., or twenty-seven and one half tons. They run without a tender, the engine carrying its own feed; thus gaining the double advantage of increasing the adhesion of the engine, and avoiding the resistance of a tender."

GENERAL DESCRIPTION.

306. The locomotive is a non-condensing, high pressure engine, working at a greater or less degree of expansion, according to the labor to be performed, and placed upon wheels which are so connected with the piston, that any motion of the latter is communicated to the former, by which the whole is moved.

The power exerted in the cylinder and referred to the circumference of the driving wheel, is called *traction;* its amount depends upon the cylinder diameter and steam pressure, upon the diameter of wheel and stroke, this latter being the distance between the wheel centre and point of application of power.

The means by which the "traction" is rendered available for moving the engine and its load, is the resistance which the wheel offers to slipping on the rail, or its bite, and is called adhesion; it is directly as the weight applied to the wheels, but depends also upon the state of the rails. It varies from nothing, when there is ice on the rail, to one fifth of the weight upon the driving wheels when the rail is clean and dry, and in some cases has reached as high as nearly one third. It should be enough to resist the maximum force of traction, that is, the wheel should not slip when the engine is doing its greatest work.

Steam producing, *Traction*, and *Adhesion*, are the three elements which determine the ability of an engine to perform work. The proportions and dimensions of the machine depend upon the duty required of it; sufficient adhesion for a required effect should be obtained rather by a proper *distribution*, than by *increase* of weight.

Fig. 150 shows the relative position of parts in the locomotive engine as at present constructed in America.

1 2,	Grate upon which the fuel is placed.
1 2 3 4,	Interior fire-box.
5 6,	Exterior fire-box.
7 7 8 8,	Shell of the boiler.
9 9,	Boiler flues.
10 11 12 13,	Exhaust chamber, or smoke box.
14,	Steam dome, entrance to steam pipe.
15,	Steam pipe.
16,	Piston.
18,	Piston rod.
19,	Connecting rod.

Fig. 159.

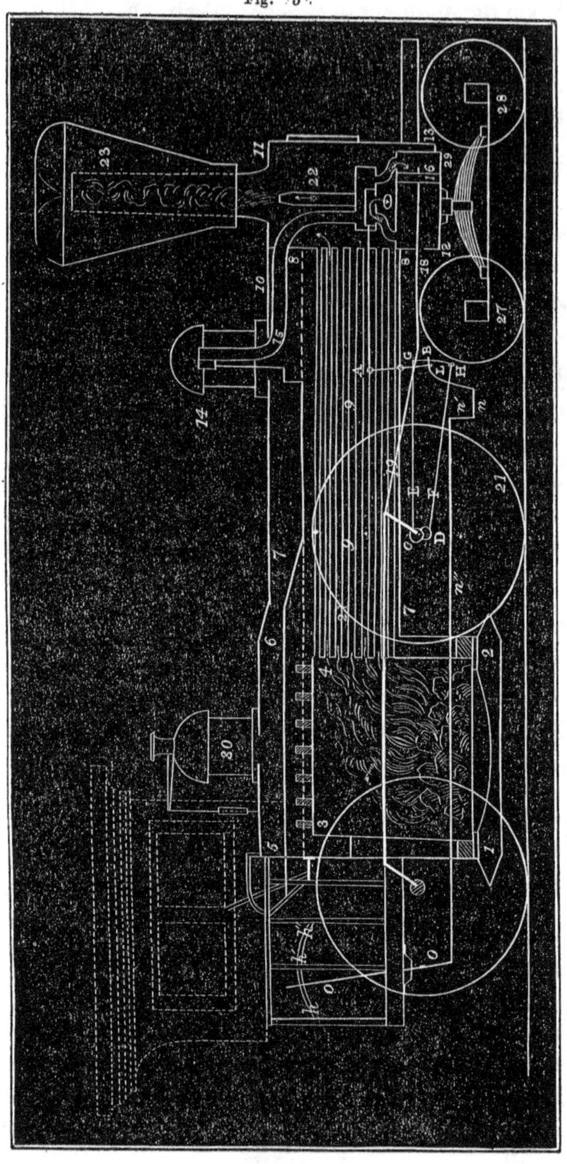

20,	Crank.
21,	Driving wheel.
22,	Blast pipe.
23,	Chimney.
27 28,	Leading wheels, supporting the front end of the engine, turning on a swivel, 29.
30,	"Blow off" safety-valve.

307. The operation of generating and applying steam for the production of motion is as follows: —

The boiler and the space between the two fire-boxes being filled with water, (high enough at least to cover the flues and the top of the inner box,) fire is applied to the fuel placed upon the grate; the heat which fills the fire-box and tubes, is communicated to the water and converts the same to steam; which entering the mouth of the pipe, 15, flows to the cylinder, where it forces the piston to the end of the stroke. This motion is transferred through the connecting rods and cranks to the wheels, which revolving, move the engine upon the rails. At the same time the eccentrics, placed upon the driving axle, give a motion to the valve gear, and thence to the valves, by which the admission of steam is stopped at the first end of the cylinder, and commenced at the other. The volume of steam which entered during the first half stroke is forced out of the cylinder by the returning piston, up the blast pipe, and out at the chimney, where a vacuum is produced, which can be supplied with air only from the chamber 10 11 12 13; after a few strokes the air is exhausted from the *chamber*, which can be refilled only by the external air *drawn through the fuel, furnace, and tubes.* The more complete this vacuum, the stronger the current of air drawn through the fire, which (current) is the draft. The admission of fresh air is regulated by a damper placed at 2. The fuel is placed upon the grate by means of a door in the rear of the fire-box.

The necessary height of water is maintained in the boiler by pumps worked by the engine, in such a manner as to secure at all times the proper supply. The proportions and dimensions of the boiler, the engine, and the carriage, with the rules for obtaining the same will be considered shortly.

DUTIES EXPECTED OF LOCOMOTIVE ENGINES.

308. The work required of any engine depends upon the nature and amount of traffic, and upon the physical character of the road.

The nature of the traffic, whether bulky or compact, and whether requiring quick or slow transport, determines somewhat the number and size of the trains, and consequently the number and power of the engines.

A road with steep grades and sharp curves, with the same amount of traffic, will need stronger engines than a road with easy grades and large curves.

The amount of motive power and cost of working it, depends in a great degree upon the disposition of grades as regards the direction of the traffic movement. The most economically worked road will be either a level one, or one where the bulk of the traffic is moved *down* hill.

The mineral, commercial, or agricultural nature of the country, determines the direction of the traffic, and the physical nature, the arrangement of the grades.

The different kinds of labor required of locomotives, necessitate the employment of engines of different proportions; and the different classes of railways, require engines possessing different amounts of power.

309. The classification of locomotives should be determined according to the following relations.

Department depends upon commercial duty.
Division depends upon character of road.

Order depends upon weight of trains.
Class depends upon speed of trains.

NOTE. — The general classification is given at the end of this chapter.

High rates of speed are generally combined with light loads, and heavy trains are required to move at the lower velocities.

Great speeds require the rapid production and consumption of a large bulk of steam of but little density; large wheels and short stroke, that the ratio of velocities of piston and wheel may be as great as possible.

Heavy trains consume less steam by bulk, per mile, but of a much greater density, and combine a long stroke with a small wheel, by which great leverage is obtained.

In general, engines for winter use should be heavier than those for summer, upon the same ground, as natural causes are more liable to resist adhesion in the winter.

The locomotive engine may be so proportioned as to run at any speed from ten to sixty miles per hour, over grades from ten to two hundred feet per mile, and to carry loads from two hundred to two thousand tons.

The rules by which the necessary dimensions to perform any required duty are fixed, depend upon the very simplest mechanical laws.

NOTE. — The formulæ expressing the most proper relations to exist between the several steam-producing and steam-consuming parts are more reliable than the assertions of any machinist in America, and though taken from books, are the result of the experience of the most able and practical men for twenty years. Operatives are too apt to despise book knowledge, forgetting that the very knowledge so despised is the result of more practice than a lifetime can afford them. Railroad managers are too apt to receive as indisputable, the opinions of men who are *practical*, simply because they understand nothing of *principle*.

Since the work of D. K. Clark (England) has appeared, any dimension from the beginning to the end of a locomotive may be fixed, to the eighth of an inch, with absolute correctness, and there is no excuse for departing from the proper proportions. It does not follow that because a locomotive does actually start off and draw the train, that it is properly made. A race-horse can draw a plough, and a yoke of oxen a "trotting buggy," but this is by no means the correct adaptation of power.

310. The elements which govern the requirements of power are

The maximum grades.
The weight of the train.
The required speed.

And the elements which govern our ability to produce the power needed,

The grate area.
The heating surface.
The cylinder diameter.
The steam pressure.
The stroke.
The diameter of wheels.
The weight upon driving wheels.

MECHANICAL AND PHYSICAL PRINCIPLES GOVERNING THE CONSTRUCTION OF THE LOCOMOTIVE ENGINE.

RESISTANCE TO THE MOTION OF RAILROAD TRAINS.

311. The exact resistance to the motion of a railroad train cannot be determined, as some of the elements are so variable; for example, the state of the weather. An approximate estimate, near enough for practice, is easily obtained. To arrive at correct data the observations must be made upon trains working under the same conditions that they are subject to in practice.

The whole resistance is made up of several partial resistances, some of which are constant at all speeds, and some of which increase with the velocity.

The engine and tender resistance is composed of the friction of pistons, cross heads, slide valves, cranks, eccentrics, pumps, the back pressure of the blast, and various erratic movements, rolling, twisting, and pitching together with both wheel and axle friction, which is common to the engine and tender.

The atmospheric resistance is not due to the direct action of the air upon the front and sides of the train entirely, but chiefly to the exhausting action in the rear. The train has, as it were, to pull along a large column of air like the water in the wake of a ship; form or amount of frontage has little or no effect. The resistance depends upon the bulk of the train and its velocity. A train with the same frontage offers more resistance as its bulk increases.

Oscillatory resistance is caused by irregularities in the surface of the rails, and increases with the velocity, and also with increase of height of the centre of gravity of the car or engine.

Frictional resistance may be divided into wheel and axle friction. That of the axle is composed of two parts, the direct vertical friction on the journal, and the side friction on the collar, consequent upon lateral motion. The vertical friction is independent of the surface pressed or of velocity, but is directly proportional to the pressure, and the same remark applies to that of the collars. As the diameter of wheel increases, the oscillation is increased, the centre of gravity being raised. The direct cause of the vertical friction is the weight of the car or engine, and of the lateral irregularities in the surface of the rails, which cause the car to sway from side to side. Wheel friction which acts between the periphery of the wheel and the surface of the rail increases with the load, and decreases as the wheel diameter augments.

For the total resistance to the motion of a railroad train, D. R. Clark gives the following formula: —

$$\frac{V^2}{171}+8=R,$$

Where R is the resistance in lbs. per ton,
and V the velocity in miles per hour.

From this expression we form the following table: —

Velocity in miles per hour.	Resistance in lbs. per ton.
10	8,585
12	8,842
15	9,315
20	10,339
25	11,655
30	13,263
40	17,356
50	22,620
60	29,052
100	66,480

From a great number of experiments made by Mr. Clark, the relative resistance to the motion of inside and outside connected engines is as follows: —

Inside connections	17
Outside connections	14

The effect of curves, bad state of the road, and adverse winds, amounts (according to the same author) to the following percentages: —

Bad state of the road	40
Curves	20
Strong head and side winds	20
In all	80

The resistance due to grades depends entirely upon the rate of incline, and is quite independent of all other considerations. The *relative* effect of grades decreases with the absolute increase of resistance on a level. Thus common roads admit of steeper grades than do railroads, because the level resistance is much more upon the former than on the latter.

The exact determination of the resistance due to any grade depends upon the very simple mechanical principle, regulating motion upon the inclined plane. For each foot rise of grade per mile, the resistance per ton is

$$2240 \times \frac{1}{5280}.$$

Thus the resistance to one ton upon a forty feet grade is

$$2240 \times \frac{40}{5280} \text{ or } 17 \text{ lbs.}$$

And if we are moving at thirty miles per hour the sum of all other resistances is, by the formula, or the table at the end of Chapter XIV., part I., 13.3 lbs. per ton; whence the whole resistance to the motion of one ton, at thirty miles per hour, upon a forty feet grade, is

$$17 + 13.3 \text{ or } 30.3 \text{ lbs.}$$

and one hundred tons would be one hundred times as much. Table 1, at the end of Chapter XIV., part I., gives the whole resistance to the motion of trains of from fifty to one thousand tons, moving at speeds varying from ten to one hundred miles per hour, and table 2 gives the resistance upon grades from ten to one hundred feet per mile.

TRACTION AND ADHESION.

312. The whole steam pressure upon both pistons, referred by means of the crank, connecting, and piston rods, and wheel, to the rail, is called "traction." It is the *drawing* power of the engine. Its amount depends upon the diameter of cylinder, steam pressure, stroke, and diameter of wheel.

By increasing the steam pressure, we increase the power. By increasing the cylinder diameter, we increase the power. By increasing the stroke, we increase the power. By decreasing the wheel diameter, we increase the power. And by adjusting the dimensions of the above parts, we may give any desired amount of power to the engine.

The formula expressing the tractive power of an engine, of any dimensions, is

$$\frac{(2A)\,P.2\,S}{C}.$$

Where $A =$ the area of one piston.
$P =$ the steam pressure in cylinder per square inch.
$S =$ the stroke in inches.
$C =$ the circumference of the wheel in inches.

The formula is expressed verbally as follows: Double the stroke and multiply it by the total steam pressure on both pistons; divide the product by the circumference of the driving-wheel in inches.

ADHESION.

313. As observed on page 307, the adhesion or the bite of the wheels upon the rail is, as an average, from one fifth to one sixth of the weight; one fifth when the rail is in a good state, and less when wet or greasy; we cannot depend upon more than one sixth in practice. Therefore, if the

tractive power of an engine is 3,000 lbs. we must, to make it available, place 3,000 × 6 or 18,000 lbs. upon those wheels which are connected with the machinery, (driving wheels).

FUEL.

314. The fuels employed in the locomotive engine for the evaporation of water are wood, coal, and coke. In England the latter is used exclusively. In America the first has, on account of its cheapness, been quite generally adopted; but of late railroad companies have been turning their attention to coal and coke.

The immense beds of coal distributed throughout the United States will furnish fuel to railroad companies almost without limit. Its position as well as its amount will render its adoption practicable in nearly all of the States. Ohio alone contains more coal than all of Great Britain. The following table is from the iron manufacture of Frederick Overman.

Name of State.	Area of Coal-fields.
Georgia	150 square miles.
Maryland	550 " "
Alabama	3,400 " "
Tennessee	4,300 " "
Michigan	5,000 " "
Missouri	6,000 " "
Indiana	7,700 " "
Ohio	11,900 " "
Kentucky	13,500 " "
Pennsylvania	15,437 " "
Virginia	21,195 " "
Illinois	44,000 " "
In all	133,132 " "

315. The following table (also from the works of Overman) gives the nature and evaporative power of the different American coals.

Name of Coal.	State where found.	Percentage of carbon.	Steam of 212° evaporated per lb.	Quantity of heat by volume.	Percentage of coke by weight.
Anthracite.					
Beaver Meadow,	Pa.	88.9	10.4	94	
Forest Improvement,	Pa.	90.7	10.8	94	
Lehigh,	Pa.	89.1	9.6	94	
Lackawanna,	Pa.	87.7	10.7	94	
Coke.					
Midlothian,	Va.		10.3	92	.66
Cumberland,	Md.		10.3	92	.75
Bituminous.					
Maryland,	Md.	73.5	11.2	85	
Cumberland,	Md.	74.3	11.0	85	
Blossburg,	Pa.	73.4	10.9	85	.83
Karthans,	Pa.	73.8	9.8	85	.88
Cambria County,	Pa.	69.4	10.2	85	
Clover Hill,	Va.	56.8	8.5	85	.68
Tippecanoe,	Va.	64.6	8.5	85	
Pittsburgh,	Pa.	55.0	8.9	85	.68
Missouri,	Mo.				.57

316. The employment of the several varieties of wood depends more upon the commercial than the chemical character. The following table shows the specific gravity, the nature and the evaporative value of the different species.

Species.	Specific gravity green.	Specific gravity air dried.	Specific gravity kiln dried.	Degrees of heat which may be generated.	Percentage of Charcoal.	Quantity of heat as to volume.	Weight of one cord in lbs.	Relative value as fuel.	Species.
Hickory,				3000	44.69	25	4469	1.00	Hickory.
White Oak,	1.07	0.71	0.66	3000	21.62	25	3821	0.81	White Oak.
Black Oak,				3000	23.80	25	3254	0.71	Black Oak.
Red Oak,	1.05	0.68	0.66	3000	22.43	25	3254	0.69	Red Oak.
Beech,	0.98	0.59	0.58	3000	32,36	25	3236	0.65	Beech.
Birch,	0.90	0.63	0.57	3000		25			Birch.
Maple,	0.90	0.64	0.61	3000	27.00	25	2700	0.57	Maple.
Yellow Pine,				2800	24.63	23	2463	0.54	Yellow Pine.
Chestnut,				3000	25.25	25	2333	0.52	Chestnut.
Pitch Pine,				2800	19.04	23	1904	0.43	Pitch Pine.
White Pine,	0.87	0.47	0.38	2800	18.68	23	1868	0.42	White Pine.

Of the relative value of wood and coal, we have the following results of experience.

In the engines of the Baltimore and Ohio Railroad 2.55 lbs. of pine wood were found equal to one pound of Cumberland coal.

On the Reading Railroad, three pounds (Pennsylvania) of pine wood equal to one pound of Anthracite coal.

Mr. Haswell estimates the best varieties of wood fuel to contain twenty per cent. of carbon.

Walter R. Johnson found that one pound of wood, upon an average, evaporated two and one half pounds of water.

The average percentage of coal from American bituminous coal from the above table is seventy-three per cent., and the average percentage of carbon, sixty-seven and one half per cent.

317. The following table shows the relative properties of good coke, coal, and wood.

Name of fuel.	Weight per cubic foot, in lbs.	Degrees of heat generated.	Percentage of carbon, in the fuel.	Economic bulk, or cubic feet required to stow one ton.	Economic, or stowage weight per cubic foot.	Cubic feet of air to evaporate one lb. of water.	Equivalent economic bulk, to evaporate the same weight of water.	Weight of water evaporated per lb. of fuel in ordinary practice.	Relative value as fuel, disregarding the actual cost.
Coke.	63	4300	95	80	28	22.4	13	8½	100
Coal.	80	4000	88	44	51	32.0	10	6	71
Wood.	30	2800	20	107	21	16.0	60	2½	29

The power of fuel depends upon the amount of carbon in it.

Pure coke is solid carbon.

Hence its superior value as a heat generator.

OF THE PROCESS OF COKING.

318. Anthracite coal is used for locomotive fuel in its natural state. It is employed chiefly upon those roads on the eastern slope of the Alleghanies. The bituminous coal lies in the Mississippi valley, and may be found anywhere between the summits of the Alleghanies and the Rocky

Mountains. This, in its natural state, contains so much pitchy matter as to render it unfit for locomotive purposes. Upon being heated, it melts, runs into a mass, and clogs the grate; requiring frequent poking and a strong draft. But when the bitumen is burnt off by slow and careful baking, (as described below,) no fuel equals it.

Just as carbonized wood is charcoal, so carbonized coal is coke. Coke is bituminous coal deprived of its bitumen, the raw coal being baked in ovens having vents so regulated as to admit air enough to char, without consuming the coal. The ovens being closed at the proper time, the fire is gradually extinguished, and the coke, compacted into large masses, requiring to be broken up before taken out. Coal may be coked by piling loosely in heaps, covering with earth, and firing through openings, which, after forty or fifty hours, are closed. In preparing coke, however, in the large quantities required for railroads, and that it may be of the very best quality, a good deal of care must be taken.

Probably in no place more or better coke is made, or the operation more skilfully carried on, than at the Camden-town station of the London and North-western Railroad, (England).

The company have built eighteen ovens, in two rows, all discharging their volatile gases into a horizontal flue terminating in a chimney one hundred and fifteen feet high; having an internal diameter of eleven feet, and being three feet thick, (making the external diameter seventeen feet). The ovens are elliptical, 11×12 feet inside, with walls three feet thick. The height is ten feet, the first three feet from the ground being solid, and furnished with a fire brick floor, on which the coal is placed. Each oven communicates with the flue by an opening in the top two and one half feet by twenty-one inches; which opening is closed by an iron damper, to regulate the draft. The openings for the doors are three and one half feet square outside, and two and three fourths inside, being closed with iron doors four and one half by five feet, lined with fire brick, and balanced in opening by counterweights. (The object of the chimney and horizontal flue is to carry the smoke and unburned gases so far up that they shall not be a nuisance. In America we might allow the smoke of each oven to escape through a low chimney of its own, (ten or twelve feet high,) and save the cost of a large stack; like the coking ovens in our foundries).

The operation of coking is carried on as follows: — Each alternate oven is charged between eight and ten A. M. every day, with three and one half tons of good coals. A whisp of straw is then thrown in, which takes fire from radiation from the top, and inflames the smoke then arising from the surface, by the reaction of the hot sides and bottom upon the body of the fuel. In this way the smoke is consumed at the very point of the process, where it would otherwise be the most abundant. The coking process is a complete combustion of the volatile principles of the coal. The mass of coal being first kindled at the surface, where it is supplied with an abundance of oxygen, because the doors in front and vents in the rear are open, no more smoke goes from the chimney than from that of a common kitchen fire. The gas generated from the slightly heated coal cannot escape destruction in passing up to the bright flame of the oven. Any deficiency in oxygen for consuming the smoke is supplied by the air entering the grooves of the dampers.

As the coking process advances most slowly from the top to the bottom, only one layer is consumed at a time; while the surface is covered with red-hot cinders, ready to consume any particles of carburetted or sulphuretted hydrogen gases which may escape from below. The greatest mass cannot emit more gases than the smallest heap.

The coke being perfectly freed from all smoky and volatile matters, by a calcination of forty hours, is cooled down to a moderate ignition by sliding in the dampers and opening the doors, which had been partly closed during the latter part of the operation.

The coal is now converted into a clean, crystalline, porous, columnar mass, of a steel-gray color, and so hard as to cut glass. This is broken up and taken out — coke. It is sometimes extinguished by a watering-pot. This is wrong, it ought not to be wet, and even more, ought to be immediately shut up in fire-proof boxes and bins. Even left to itself in the air, it absorbs moisture rapidly, which must be burned off in the boiler; it should by all means be kept in a dry place. Mr. Woods (England) observes, that coke may absorb as much as eight per cent. of water in going from the oven to the storehouse. The amount of absorption depends upon the nature of the coke. D. K. Clark records the following, the coke being immersed in water.

No. 1. Close-grained and good, absorbed 14.5 per cent. of water.
No. 2. Porous and ordinary, absorbed 21 per cent.
No. 3. Very close-grained and good, 9 per cent.

The time of coking may be stated generally as fifty hours, though it is somewhat improved by being allowed forty hours more; this gives time for a better consolidation, and gives a firmer, brighter, and more crystalline mass.

Mr. Gooch, of the Great Western (England) Railroad, experimented upon the time of coking with the following results.

In oven.	Yield per ton of coal.	Water evaporated per lb. of coke.	Result.
48 hours	12.71 cwt.	7.1 lbs.	902.
72 "	12.00 cwt.	7.7 lbs.	924.

Thus, though the yield per ton is decreased by a greater

time, the value of the coke per pound is augmented, and the increase overbalances the decrease.

Firstrate coal gives from seventy-five to eighty per cent. by weight, of compact glistening coke, weighing about 14 cwt. per chaldron, (thirty-six bushels). The bulk is increased from ten to fifty per cent.

In breaking out the coke from the ovens, a great deal is unavoidably reduced too fine for use in the locomotive furnace under a strong draft; such may, however, be used in firing up, in standing still, and at the stations.

In taking the coke from the ovens it should be separated into the three following classes.

Large coke.	Cubes of	9	inches	to the side.
Medium coke.	"	6	"	"
Small coke.	"	3	"	"

Pittsburgh coal carefully coked for forty-eight hours, gives seventy-five per cent., by weight, and one hundred twenty-five per cent. by bulk, of firstrate, firm, bright, clean coke.

The best test for coke is to place it in water. Water, weighing sixty-two and one half pounds per cubic foot, should not float good coke, which ought to weigh sixty-three pounds per cubic foot, therefore if the coke floats it is too light.

Much of the bituminous coal in the Mississippi valley does not coke, but burns up. A large part cokes moderately well, but not so well as the Pittsburgh coal. In estimating for a comparison of fuels, the particular coal of any location must be tested.

OF THE COMPARATIVE VALUE OF WOOD, COAL, AND COKE.

This question divides itself into two parts,

The relative cost of the different fuels,
and The relative power to produce heat.

319. It does not follow that because coke in England, anthracite in Pennsylvania, or wood in New England, is the most economical fuel, that either of the above will be so in Ohio, Indiana, or Illinois, or because wood is the cheapest in some parts of a State, that it is so throughout, or even that one fuel should be applied to the whole length of a single road.

The heat used to evaporate water in the locomotive boiler is developed by combustion; combustion is produced by chemically combining the oxygen of the air with the carbon of the fuel; whence, that material containing in a given cost the largest amount of carbon will produce heat the most economically.

From the table on page 320, we see that, by bulk, thirteen of coke are equal to sixty of wood; that one pound of coke evaporates eight and one half pounds of water; that one pound of wood will evaporate two and one half pounds of water. Tables of specific gravity give as an average weight per cubic foot of hard wood, thirty pounds. A cord of wood, by very careful measurement, contains one hundred cubic feet *solid*, or one hundred twenty-eight feet *as piled*, taking the average size of wood; whence a cord will weigh three thousand pounds. And we have as the relative evaporative efficiency of a cord of wood and a ton of coke,

$$2240 \times 8\tfrac{1}{2} = 19040,$$
$$3000 \times 2\tfrac{1}{2} = 7500.$$

Now if the cost of a cord of wood is to the price of a ton of coke as 7,500 to 19,040, it is immaterial which we use.

As an example of the use of the above proportion, when

the absolute cost of wood, coal, coke, and labor are known, take the following.

If wood, cut and ready for burning, costs $3.00 per cord, how much may be given for a ton of coke?

As 7,500 is to 19,040, so is 300 to 762, or $7.62.

From the same proportion we form the following table.

Cost per cord of wood ready for burning. (Cents.)	Price that may be paid per ton for coke. (Cents.)
200	508
225	571
250	635
275	698
300	762
325	825
350	877
375	952
400	1016
425	1079
450	1143
475	1206
500	1270

In the comparison above, the maximum evaporative power of wood has been used, 2½ lbs., and the ordinary power of coke, 8½ lbs. of water per pound of fuel.

320. In making coke in large quantities, the ovens should be at the mines, as we thus save transporting the extra weight of coal over coke.

The cost of making coke, exclusive of the cost of the coal, is approximately as follows: —

10 ovens capable of making annually 5,000 tons of coke,	$5,000
Sheds, and apparatus to correspond,	3,000
In all,	8,000

Annual interest at 6 per cent.,	480
Annual cost of attendance, 2 men,	1,000
The sum of which is,	$1,480
And the cost per ton,	$0.29\frac{6}{10}$

or in round numbers, thirty cents per ton; and if coal is $1.50 per ton, adding twenty-five per cent. we have $1.87 as the cost of coal that will make one ton of coke, to which add the cost of making per ton, thirty cents, and we have as the whole cost of one ton of coke $2.17; and from the rule on page 327 we see that wood must not cost over $0.85 per cord to be as economical as coke at $2.17; of course inferior qualities of coal will give less good coke and change the comparison.

COMBUSTION.

321. The combustible element in all fuels is carbon; the heat necessary for steam producing, is obtained by combining the carbon of the fuel with the oxygen of the air, forming carbonic acid gas.

Carbonic acid gas consists of

Oxygen	16	Parts by weight.
Carbon	6	

Atmospheric air consists of

Oxygen	8	Parts by weight.
Nitrogen	28	

Whence, for the combustion of one pound of carbon, we require

Carbon	1.00
Oxygen	2.66

But to obtain 2.66 of oxygen from the atmospheric air, we also use nitrogen in the proportion of 28 nitrogen to 8 oxygen; whence, for converting one pound of carbon to carbonic acid, we require

Oxygen . .	2.66
Nitrogen . .	9.31
Or . .	11.97 lbs. of atmospheric air.

From careful observations on the gases passing through the chimneys of well-constructed boilers, oxygen is found free, varying in amount from one quarter to one half of the quantity necessary for combustion; this is owing to the mechanical obstructions to the perfect conversion of the air arising from leakage through the fuel.

More than the above 11.97 lbs. of air should, therefore, be applied to the fire for each pound of carbon consumed. Twenty-five per cent. is found by experience to be a sufficient surplus allowance to convert the carbon.

Whence, to	11.97
add	3.03
and we have	15.00 lbs. of atmospheric air per lb. of carbon.

Air weighs .075 lbs. per cubic foot, whence $\frac{15}{.075}$ or 200 cubic feet of air are necessary for the proper combustion of one lb. of pure carbon.

Knowing the necessary amount of air for one lb. of carbon, and also the percentage of carbon in the different kinds of fuel, it becomes a simple arithmetical operation to fix the bulk of air required for any species of coal, coke, or wood. The result of such a calculation is shown in the seventh column of the table on page 320.

"There are two causes why all the heat which fuel may furnish is not obtained. First, that the inflammable gases evolved by the heat are not all consumed from want of a sufficient supply of oxygen, the air drawn through the fire being only sufficient to decompose more fuel than when decomposed it could burn, or supply with oxygen. The thick smoke that escapes from a chimney when fresh fuel is thrown on a hot fire, is unconsumed gas; decomposed from the fuel, but without oxygen enough to burn—although there may have been a sufficient supply of heat. From this cause it is, perhaps, that flame is seen coming from the top of a steamboat chimney which appears to be continuous from the furnace; but which, in fact, is ignited by contact with the air, having retained sufficient heat for that purpose.

"All smoke-consuming furnaces are simply means of admitting fresh air to the unconsumed gases above the fire, which, in a common chimney, will effect the object, as so large a mass of smoke retains the necessary amount of heat. This only prevents the nuisance of smoke. To render the gases thus reheated useful in evaporating water, this supply of oxygen must be added while the gases are yet in the flues." This might seem difficult. Mr. McConnell (England) divides the flues of his locomotives into two parts, connecting the front ends of the first part and the back ends of the second part by a space of twelve or fifteen inches, (called by him a 'combustion chamber,') into which he admits any required amount of fresh air. (See appendix E.)

"A second cause why the full value of the fuel produced is not obtained is, that so much is abstracted from the gases in passing through long tubes, that there is not enough left to continue combustion, although the inflammable gas is still there. That a tube or any substance in the way of the hot gases does absorb the heat enough to prevent the burning of the gas, is proved by the action of Davy's Safety

Lamp; this is a common light surrounded by a wire gauze, which so absorbs the heat from the flame as to extinguish the latter at the wire; by applying fire above the gauze, the gas is again kindled, showing plainly that want of heat above had quenched the flame." See Stöckhardt's Chemistry; translation by C. H. Peirce, M. D., Cambridge, Mass., 1852, page 105.

We require, then, in every boiler, first, to have a sufficient supply of oxygen to decompose the fuel; next, a quantity above the fire to consume the produced gases; third, such an arrangement of communicating surface that so much heat shall not be abstracted from the gases as to deaden their combustion, until just as they are discharged, at which period they ought to be consumed. (See appendix E.)

GENERATION OF STEAM.

322. The means of producing the power is of course of the first importance.

The heat generated in the fire-box is conducted through the tubes to the exhaust chamber; during which passage it is imparted to the metal, and from thence absorbed by the adjacent water, which being thereby made lighter, rises to the surface and gives place to a new supply. The duty of the furnace is to *generate*, and of the tubes to *communicate*, heat.

The power of a plain surface to generate steam, depends upon its position and on the ability of the material to transmit heat. An experiment recorded in Clark's Railway Machinery, gave the following results: A cubic metallic box submerged in water and heated from within, generated steam from its upper surface more than twice as fast as from the sides when vertical, while the bottom yielded none at all. By slightly inclining the box the elevated side produced steam much faster, while the depressed one parted so badly with it as to cause overheating of the metal.

Acting upon this result, most builders of engines of the present day give an inclination of from one inch to one quarter of an inch per foot to the sides of the inner fire-box. That the heat should be applied in the most effectual manner to the water, the latter should *circulate* freely around the hot metal, carrying off the heat as soon as it reaches the surface. As the heat is applied to the *inside* of the furnace and tubes, it must, therefore, be the *inside* dimensions which determine the amount of heating surface.

NOTE. — If we multiply the interior surface of a tube by the intensity of heat applied, and divide the product by the exterior surface, we shall have the intensity at the outside. We also *apply more heat* to the *outside* of a tube, which, passing to the inner surface, augments in intensity per unit of area.

The area of the inner fire-box is not all available for heating, but requires to be reduced as follows: —

For the fire-door.
For the ferrule area.
For the top stays.
For the side stay bolts.

The area is, therefore,

Sides, twice length by height, less stay bolts.
Back, twice height by breadth, less fire-door.
Front, twice height by breadth, less ferrule area.
Top, twice length by breadth, less top stays.

TUBES.

323. The tubes or flues, varying in number from one hundred to three hundred, in diameter from one and a half to three inches, and in length from eight to sixteen feet, fur-

nish the real communicating surface. The amount of heating surface thus obtained for any length, number, and diameter, is given in table 10, Chapter XIV., Part I. The surface of a single tube is found by the formula

$$\frac{Ld\,3.1416}{144}.$$

Where $L =$ the length,
and $d =$ the diameter, both in inches.

The efficiency of circular tubes is a matter not yet fully understood. They certainly give a large amount of surface in a small boiler. Pambour considered the value of tube area per unit of surface, in terms of the furnace area, as one third only; that is, three square feet of tube surface as equal to one foot of furnace area, in power of generating steam. D. K. Clark makes no distinction between the two surfaces, but observes "there is reason to believe that in the upper semicircular part of each tube the efficiency principally resides. The winding progressive motion, observable in tubes of considerable diameter, confirms this conclusion, as it is with much probability due to the cooling of the upper portion of the gases of combustion, which, as they cool also, become heavier and descend laterally, to make room for the hotter smoke next the bottom of the flue; the general result of which is the spiral motion of the current in its progress onwards." Certainly the upper half of the tube would part much easier with the steam than the under one, even supposing the applied heat to be the same.

At page 340 of "Overman's Mechanics," is the following: "The application of heat to a *concave* surface is wrong in principle. The heat in gases is conducted to other bodies, and among themselves by *convection* only. This quality of gases causes the convex form of a vessel to be the most profitable in absorbing the heat of ascending gases, because the motion of the gas causes a constant change of particles on the convex body. On a *concave* surface exposed to the influence of moving gases, but little effect is produced; because the particles of gas in the concavity are at rest. A plane surface is for the same reason an imperfect form for absorbing heat; it must be exposed at an angle of 45° to obtain the best effect of the heating gases. In all cases if we wish to obtain the best effect from the fuel, we should expose a convex surface to the current of hot air. The direction of the motion of the hot gases decides the position of the metal which is to absorb the heat; if the current is horizontal the pipes must be vertical. Gases do not convey heat by radiation. Tubes and other vessels containing water must be so placed that the hot gases play around the outside.

"If we lead a current of hot air around a cylinder we shall observe that a particle of air plays but a short time upon its surface, when it gives way to another; the particles play almost around the cylinder, and a concentration or increase of density behind the pipe is the result. The relative position of pipes in the range is not indifferent, and the distance of one from the other must be related to their diameter."

The conducting power of the metal composing the fire-box and tubes, is one condition which limits the rate of evaporation, when the heat is abundant on the one side and circulation free on the other, as the water certainly carries off the heat as fast as it arives at the outer surface.

All the heat should be extracted if possible from the gases before they enter the smoke box. We should so arrange the flues, that without so much contracting the passage for the exit of the gases as to need too strong a blast, yet to confine the gases until their full value is extracted.

Several attempts have been made to apply the ideas of Clark and Overman, but as yet they have been very indirect and have met with only moderate success. (See Appendix, E.)

EVAPORATION, PRESSURE, TEMPERATURE, AND DENSITY.

324. The character of work to be done determines the nature of the steam to be used.

The quantity of work to be done shows the amount of steam to be produced.

The amount and character of the steam required, fixes the dimensions and proportions of the boiler.

A cubic foot of water, at a temperature of 62°, weighs 62.321 lbs.

A cubic foot of steam, generated at 212° Fahrenheit, under the atmospheric pressure (44.7 lbs. per square inch) weighs .03666 lbs.

Whence one cubic foot of water boiled at 212°, makes 1,700 cubic feet of steam.

The total heat of saturated steam (steam produced in contact with the water), consists of two parts at all temperatures; the *latent* and the *sensible.* The sensible heat is that shown by the thermometer, and varies with the pressure. The latent heat absorbed during the generation of steam, amounts to three fourths of the whole. As the temperature at which the steam is produced increases, the bulk produced from a given unit of water *decreases*, but the pressure and the total heat increase. (See C. R. M. p. 59, 61, Regnault's experiments.)

Table 8, Chapter XIV., Part I., gives the properties of saturated steam, produced under pressures varying from fifty to one hundred and fifty pounds per square inch.

The steam produced over water is called saturated, and

an application of heat to an isolated volume of this steam, raises both the temperature and pressure, the volume and density remaining the same. The saturation is then no more, and the steam is surcharged. If the heat be withdrawn, pressure and density fall, and a precipitation of water takes place. The priming of steam in a cylinder is an illustration of this. D. K. Clark, in Railway Mechanics, urges the necessity of thoroughly drying the steam before applying it to the pistons; in this manner, he says, ten per cent. may be gained at two velocities, and in some cases forty per cent. at high speeds.

MOTION OF STEAM IN PIPES.

325. Steam may flow from any vessel into a vacuum, into the open air, or into steam of a less density. The velocity of efflux of steam is the same as that of a stream of water flowing under a pressure equal to that of the steam. Steam flowing into the atmosphere of course has 14.7 lbs. per inch resistance to meet, which is equivalent to a reduction of 14.7 lbs. of its pressure. The following numbers show the velocity of efflux of steam into the open air under different pressures.

Pressure.	Velocity, in feet, per second.
50	1791
60	1838
70	1877
80	1919
90	1936
100	1957
110	1972
120	1990
130	2004

LOSS OF PRESSURE CAUSED BY THE MOTION OF STEAM.

326. The loss of power suffered by the steam during its motion from the boiler to the cylinder is caused by condensation in passing through cold pipes, and by friction and sharp bends. The total fall that may be caused by a combination of circumstances is from ten to fifteen per cent. at low velocities, and from fifty to sixty per cent. at high speeds. The fall of pressure decreases as the square of the velocity of motion, that is, the fall at a velocity of 1,600 feet per second is four times as great as the fall at a velocity of eight hundred feet. By well protecting the steam pipes and cylinders, and by drying, it may be worked at nearly its initial pressure.

APPLICATION OF STEAM.

327. The steam being generated in the boiler, and conveyed to the cylinders, is admitted alternately to the opposite sides of the piston, by which its reciprocations are produced. The first valve applied to regulating the admission of steam to the cylinder was so arranged that the steam was admitted during the whole stroke; at the end of which, ingress stopped and egress commenced at the first end, and ingress commenced at the second end simultaneously; this caused an unnecessary resistance to the return movement, by preventing the quick escape of the first cylinder-full, which had to be *pushed* out, instead of *flowing* out. The continuance of the full pressure upon the piston also, until the end of the stroke, caused a dangerous momentum to be given to the reciprocating machinery.

These evils are obviated by causing the exhaust passage to open, and the entering part to close a little *before* the end of the stroke. This is effected by moving the valve bodily forward.

Now it is well ascertained, that with very free steam entrances, if we allow the cylinder to be only partially filled, and then cause the steam to expand itself, more work is accomplished with a given bulk than when the cylinder is completely filled. That the steam may have time thus to expand itself, the return of the piston must not take place until after the suppression (the stopping of admission).

328. There are four positions of the valve during each half stroke, and three distinct actions of steam in the same period, which are as follows: —

Position of valve.	Action of steam.
Admission (A).	
	Entrance.
Suppression.	
	Expansion.
Release.	
	Compression.
Admission (B).	

The longer the time between suppression and release, of course the more complete will be the expansion. The entire force of the steam should not (even if possible) be extracted, as a certain force is necessary to produce a blast.

The time of expansion is regulated by the proportions of the valve cover; which may be so adjusted as to fix suppression or release at any desired part of the stroke.

By the above means any rate of expansion may be established, but when once fixed will remain the same, the valve being invariably connected with the eccentric, and thus partaking of its motion.

329. The great step which has been taken in locomotive construction since 1840 is the invention of the "link mo-

tion," by Williams, which, perfected by Howe, admits of varying the travel of the valve, and thus using the steam under any desired rate of expansion. By this arrangement, the power of regulating the force applied to the piston, according to the work to be done, is placed in the engineer's hands, to be used at any time under whatever conditions the engine may be working.

By this arrangement, two eccentrics to each cylinder are required, (and in some dispositions of the link, only one). Fig. 150 shows the general plan of varying the expansion. A fixed relation evidently exists between the points A and B, two distinct motions are communicated by the eccentrics C and D through the rods E and F, to the two ends G H, of the curved link L; the eccentrics are so adjusted upon the driving axle as to cause the two ends of the link to move in opposite directions, whence at some point midway there is no motion; the link is movable (vertically) upon the suspended point L, so that by bringing L to one end or the other, the motion given to the rod *m* partakes of the motion of that eccentric which is nearest to it. Thus the movement of the valve may be checked, or even reversed in a second, while the engine is in motion, and that without sudden shocks.

The link is moved by the levers *n n' n''* terminating in the bar O, placed at the foot board of the engine in reach of the engineer. Applied to this is an iron sector *h h' h''*, made fast to the frame of the engine. Now when the point L is in such a part of the link as to place the valve in a position admitting steam for any fraction of the stroke, let the point at which the bar O stands upon the sector be marked for that admission; and so also for any number of different degrees of expansion. It is plain that the engineer may thus, by fixing the lever O, use any percentage of admission that is required; and may always know just what duty the engine is doing. Five minutes' examination of the reversing gear upon an engine will render the operation plain.

330. If we cut the steam off at half stroke and then allow it to expand, of course the mean pressure during the whole stroke is less than that at entering. The effective mean pressure obtained by any degree of expansion is shown by the following formula, deduced from a mean of forty-nine experiments with the Great Britain locomotive, (Great Western Railroad, England,) having cylinders 18×24.

$$13.5\left(\sqrt{a}-28\right)=\text{mean pressure}$$

where a is the percentage of admission.

From this formula, table 11 is made.

331. Mr. Clark deduces as general results, from a very extensive and carefully conducted system of experiments, the following.

That the maximum useful admission is seventy-five per cent.

The minimum useful admission ten per cent.

The greatest possible gain by working expansively is one hundred per cent., which is effected by an admission of ten per cent.

The best admission for engines having ports $\frac{1}{14}$ of the area of the piston, and blast area from $\frac{1}{13}$ to $\frac{1}{16}$ of piston, at high speeds (from thirty to sixty miles per hour) and with considerable loads, is from sixty to sixty-six per cent. With a wider port and blast area, the best admission is seventy-five per cent.

The resistance due to the back pressure of the blast, varies as the speed squared, and inversely as the square of the area of blast orifice.

332. From the experiments made by Daniel Gooch, with the engine "Great Britain," the following results appear.

The loss of fuel at seventy-five per cent. admission, the blast orifice being from $\frac{1}{10}$ to $\frac{1}{11}$ of piston at sixty miles per hour, is from $\frac{1}{8}$ to $\frac{1}{10}$; at thirty or forty per cent. admission, the loss is from $\frac{1}{8}$ to $\frac{1}{50}$; and at thirty miles per hour, (seventy-five per cent. admission,) from $\frac{1}{11}$ to $\frac{1}{40}$.

The resistance from steam compressed in the cylinder, increases with the speed, and also with the degree of expansion; it varies from eight per cent. in full gear, (seventy-five per cent.,) to twenty-eight per cent. at an admission of forty per cent.

At the highest velocities, the whole resistance from back pressure is nearly the same for all expansions; for compression increases as blast pressure decreases.

The above deductions hold good for speeds under forty miles per hour, with steam ports at least $\frac{1}{14}$, and blast orifice from $\frac{1}{12}$ to $\frac{1}{15}$ of the piston area.

OF BOILER PROPORTIONS.

333. The dimensions of American locomotives seem to depend more upon the shop whence they come, than upon any special duty required of them. It is not surprising that the utmost economy is seldom attained when a railroad president orders a lot of locomotives, from the cheapest builder, to suit his own ideas of an engine; or when engines are ordered by a superintendent of machinery who does not know the difference between a sixty foot grade and a level. It is the affair of the company's agent and not of the machinist to know just what a railroad needs. It is a common, and most absurd practice, for a man who is completely ignorant of machinery to order five or ten engines, without the least regard to the character of the road or of the traffic.

334. The particular characteristics of each class of en-

gines is entirely a matter of figures. There is no reason why a general table should not be formed embracing all divisions, orders, and classes of locomotives, in which the requirements and general dimensions corresponding thereto should be laid down for machine shop reference. Such a table would at once establish a mutual understanding between railroad companies and builders. Such a general classification is shown hereaftar. The dimensions of engines are not given, as it was thought best to let each person fill it up according to his own ideas. By so doing some valuable general properties may be arrived at.

335. Thus far experience has been the only guide to proportion (in America at least). Practice, in many things, is the only correct path to the right results, but locomotives are too expensive for philosophical apparatus; correct experiments upon imperfect machines will lead to the means of avoiding errors. The following is the *modus operandi* of D. K. Clark in his "Railway Machinery."

A number of engines of different proportions are chosen, and observations made upon the amounts of fuel and water consumed upon the work done, and under what conditions. These results are so tabulated as to show the effect in difference of construction upon the performance of the engine, whence the proportioning of parts becomes a simple arithmetical operation. The reduction of experiments to tables, and the deduction from tables of formulæ, is a simple operation compared with the skill and care required in observing the operation of a machine, subject to so many disturbances as a locomotive engine in rapid motion. None have had a better opportunity of observing, have conducted experiments with more care, or have obtained results which show fewer discrepancies than the English engineers Clark and Gooch, and the French and German observers Le Chatlier and Nollan.

336. Three essential parts of the locomotive are the *grate area*, *heating surface*, and *cylinders*. No two writers upon this subject arrive at the same dimensions to perform the same work. They not only differ, but differ widely. They cannot all be right; all but one, or all must be wrong. American builders have fixed the dimensions of their engines by observing the performance of constructed machines, not by rules deduced from any systematic experiments, but upon a system of remedying visible errors. If a chimney diameter of ten inches is found too small and twenty too large, fifteen has been assumed as about right.

337. As an example of the difference in the results obtained by different authors, take the following: —

An engine to do the same work must have, according to

Zerah Colburn.[1]	Norris.[2]	D. K. Clark.[3]	D. K. Clark.[4]	
18 × 22	18 × 22	18 × 22	18 × 22	Cylinders.
5	5	5	5	Wheels.
13.00	13.86	14.00	19.60	Grate area.
1114	812	1327	1327	Heating surface.
250	324	134	134	Area of chimney.
4	23	28	28	Area of blast.
59	73	——	——	Steam room.
100	73	——	——	Water room.

From these figures, the work done being the same, Mr. Clark gives forty per cent. more grate area than either Colburn or Norris, an easier blast, and greater heating surface. Norris makes the steam and water room equal, while Colburn makes the latter almost double the former. It is to

---

[1] Colburn on the Locomotive Engine.

[2] Norris's Handbook for Locomotive Engineers and Machinists.

[3] D. K. Clark's Railway Machinery, calculated for coke.

[4] D. K. Clark's Railway Machinery, calculated for wood.

be observed that Colburn gives only rules adopted by different builders, not vouching for their correctness, while Norris lays down his rules as fixed and right. The engines used by the English experimenters in their observations, vary in dimension between the following wide limits, whence the universal application of their results.

Grate area	9 to 24	square feet.
Fire surface	50 to 100	" "
Tube surface	400 to 1,000	" "
Whole surface	450 to 1,100	" "
Blast orifice	10 to 20	sq. inches, area.
Speed of engine	12 to 20	miles per hour.

338. The result of some sixty experiments upon forty-five different engines (detailed in Clark's Railway Machinery, page 156), gives the following formula, expressing the relations which ought to exist between grate area, heating surface, and consumption of water; that evaporation may be carried on in the most economical manner.

$$S = \sqrt{ac} \times 21.2 = \text{surface.}$$

Where S is the heating surface in square feet.
a is the grate area in square feet.
c is the hourly consumption of water in cubic feet.

From which we deduce the value of a or c thus,

$$a = \frac{\left(\frac{S}{21.2}\right)^2}{c} = \text{grate area;}$$

$$\text{and } c = \frac{\left(\frac{S}{21.2}\right)^2}{a} = \text{hourly water consumption.}$$

The maximum evaporation which should be carried on per square foot of grate is found, by Mr. Clark, to be sixteen cubic feet per hour. Thus, if we wish to evaporate 160 cubic feet of water per hour, we must have a grate area of at least $\frac{160}{16}$ or ten square feet.

339. The above formula for the grate area gives the dimension for a coke-burning furnace. Locomotives burning wood or coal require a modification of the above, as follows:—

To produce a given amount of heat, a certain amount of carbon must be burnt. As wood contains much less carbon than coke, a correspondingly larger bulk must be burnt, and a larger grate is necessary; not, however, larger in proportion to the larger bulk of fuel, as we may have a deeper wood than coke fire. The relative depth of fire being as the stowage bulk, and the actual depth of a coke fire being 1.9 feet, that of a wood fire will be 2.5 feet.

Now let A be the number of lbs. of coke per foot of water evaporated.

B the number of lbs. of coal per foot of water evaporated.

C the number of lbs. of wood per foot of water evaporated.

Call d the depth at which it is the most economical to burn coke; d' the same depth for coal, and the depth for wood d''. Then will the area of a coke grate be

$$\frac{A}{d};$$

Of a coal grate

$$\frac{B}{d'};$$

And of a wood grate

$$\frac{C}{d''}.$$

To be able to fix the proper grate area for any fuel, we must know its evaporative power, and a depth of a layer in the furnace. Knowing the absolute value for coke, it remains only to obtain the relative value for any other. Thus far we have disregarded the difference in *time* of burning wood and coke. To produce a given amount of heat, we burn a certain chemical value of fuel; a much larger bulk of wood than of coke is needed. If we burn wood and coke *at the same depth* and *in the same time*, the grate areas would be proportional to the bulks of fuel to produce the same heat; but, *first*, we burn fuel in a depth proportioned to the economic stowage bulk, or as 2.5 to 1.9, which decreases the wood area; and, *second*, a layer of coke 1.9 feet deep burns in one hour, while a layer of wood 2½ feet deep burns in fifteen minutes; whence 60 m. divided by 15 m. = 4 layers of 2½ feet deep each, or in all ten feet, which into the bulk (equal to a mass of coke 1 foot square × 1.9 high) or 1 foot square by 14 high, gives 14 ÷ 10 = 1.4; or, finally, the area of the wood grate should be 1.4 times that of a grate to burn coke.

OF THE SIZE AND USE OF THE SMOKE BOX.

340. The smoke box is the general termination of the flues, and the place where the vacuum is produced, which causes the draft. The size of the boiler being the same, the vacuum varies directly as the blast pressure. The power of the blast is of course affected by the capacity of the smoke box. Mr. Clark fixes the capacity of the exhaust chamber at three cubic feet per square foot of grate. The vacuum in the furnace varies from one to two thirds of that in the smoke box. The less the resistance to the hot gases experienced in the flues, the less may be the vacuum Upon the vacuum depends the amount of air drawn

through the grate; upon the bulk of air drawn through the grate depends the combustion; upon the combustion the evaporation. Whence the evaporation *cet. par.* depends the vacuum in the smoke box.

The velocity of any fluid depends upon the power applied to it, (being as the square root,) the pressure applied to the gases in the furnace of a locomotive is the vacuum in the smoke box; thus the combustion or rate of evaporation is as the square root of this vacuum. To double the evaporation it is necessary to quadruple the vacuum.

BLAST PIPE.

341. The blast pipe conducts the waste steam from the cylinder, which drives the air from the chimney and produces the vacuum in the smoke box; its form should permit the freest escape of the steam from the cylinder. The blast pipe area should nowhere be smaller than the exit part, except at the construction at the top. "Too much care," says Mr. Clark, "cannot be taken to adjust the blast pipe concentrically with the chimney; one half inch has been known to spoil the draft of a locomotive." "The area of orifice is the most critical and most important item in the composition of the locomotive."

For the form, dimensions, and influence of this important member, the reader is referred to Clark's Railway Machinery.

As the grate area increases, the blast may decrease. The greater the flue area the easier may be the blast; decrease of smoke box capacity and of chimney diameter, both allow a milder blast.

342. The following proportions are collected from the work of Mr. Clark. The order in which the different parts of the engine stand in importance with relation to the blast.

is shown in column 1. The figures show the ratios (the best) which may be had under the most favorable circumstances.

Grate area	1
Ferrule area (area of section of tubes at back flue sheet)	$\frac{1}{5}$
Tube, sectional area	$\frac{1}{4}$
Capacity of smoke box, cubic feet	3
Chimney, height four diameters, area of section	$\frac{1}{15}$
Blast orifice	$\frac{1}{75}$

The vacuum in the smoke box is somewhat regulated by a damper placed in front of the ash pan, by a valve in the chimney, or by a venetian blind covering the front ends of the tubes.

TUBE SECTION AND LENGTH.

343. The section of the tubes (crosswise) is the space through which the hot gases pass off. By increasing the length or decreasing the diameter, we of course require a stronger blast.

That the steam may escape as soon as generated, there must be a certain clearance between the tubes, which Mr. Clark fixes as follows:—

Divide the number of tubes by thirty and the result is the clearance in eighths of an inch; or algebraically

$$C = \frac{\left(\frac{N}{30}\right)}{8} = \text{clearance in inches;}$$

Or otherwise

$$C = \frac{N}{240} = \text{clearance in inches.}$$

PROPORTIONS OF CYLINDERS AND WHEELS.

344. The above proportions depend entirely upon the nature and amount of work to be done, and upon the character of the road. Small wheels and long stroke are to be applied to heavy trains and steep grades. Short stroke and large wheels to fast trains and level roads.

There are some advantages in a long cylinder, even with a constant ratio between the stroke and wheel diameter. The steam has more time to expand; the action of the machinery is slower, and the erratic movements of the engine caused by the movement of the reciprocating machinery are lessened, at the same time the centre of gravity is raised and oscillation increased.

OF THE CARRIAGE.

345. The arrangement of the wheels, axles, springs, and draw-link, and the distribution of the weight of the engine upon its several bearings so as to provide the necessary adhesion, and to run steadily upon the rails, is a matter well worthy of more attention than is commonly given to it.

The frame is the base of the engine, to which every thing should be attached. The cylinders and the wheel both being attached to it, it of course becomes the counterpart to the piston and connecting rod; the former holding the cylinder and wheel together, while the latter pushes them apart. The frame *should* form a rigid connection between the piston and the wheel; and its strength must be able to resist the whole power of the engine, applied alternately as compression and as extension.

The wheels of a locomotive answer three several purposes, and are classed as follows:—

Leading wheels.
Driving wheels.
Trailing wheels.

The duty of the driving wheels is to transfer the power of the engine to the rails, by which the motion is produced. That of the leading wheels, to guide the engine; and that of the trailing wheels, to support the after end of the engine.

The weight upon the driving wheels must be enough for sufficient adhesion. That upon the leading wheels, sufficient to guide the engine upon curves, (decreasing as their distance from the centre of gravity becomes greater, and increasing with the speed.)

The centre of gravity of an engine is generally at a distance of from one quarter to one sixth of the length of the barrel from the furnace horizontally and forwards, and in the lower part of the barrel, vertically.

The weight upon any one pair of wheels is as their distance from the centre of gravity; by changing their position we change the applied weight.

The flange base[1] must increase as the engine becomes heavier, when applied to fast trains, as more leverage is necessary to keep it on the rails. Heavy freight engines with four or five pairs of wheels, and no truck, wear the rails and strain themselves very much. We should make the wheels of such very small and near together, in order to contract the flange base.

---

[1] *Wheel base,* — Horizontal length between centres of extreme wheels. *Flange base,* — Horizontal length between centres of extreme fixed flanged wheels.

DISTRIBUTION OF WEIGHT.

346. Suppose the whole load upon the wheels is 60,000 lbs. If the centre of gravity is half-way between the wheels (there being two pairs), each will support 30,000 lbs. If the centre of gravity is twice as near to one axle as to the other, the furthest one will support 20,000 lbs.; and the nearest one 60,000 — 20,000, or 40,000 lbs.

Suppose the engine has six points of support, or three points in the side elevation, (the ordinary four driving wheels and a truck engine). Let the centre of gravity be one foot behind the middle axle and the distances between the wheel centres eight feet.

The weight upon the middle axle being *H*, that upon the hind axle is $\frac{H}{7}$, because that axle is seven times more distant from the centre of gravity than the middle one, and for the same reason the weight upon the front axle is $\frac{H}{9}$.

$$\text{Now } H + \frac{H}{7} + \frac{H}{9} = 60{,}000 \text{ lbs.}$$

$$\text{Whence } H = 47{,}976 \text{ lbs.}$$

$$\text{Also, } \frac{H}{7} = 6{,}853 \text{ lbs.}$$

$$\text{And } \frac{H}{9} = 5{,}331 \text{ lbs.}$$

And the same laws (see article Lever, in any work on Mechanics) apply to any arrangement of wheels and to any position of centre of gravity.

Springs are employed to absorb the shocks received by the wheels from irregularities in the surface of the rails. They must be equally stiff on both sides of the engine, or lateral rocking will be generated.

When, as is generally the case, the springs are connected by compensating levers, their stiffness being as the load upon them, the arms of the connecting lever must be inversely proportional to the applied weights. The shock received by one wheel is by the lever communicated to the whole four, (or even more when there are such). The truck springs of some builders are also connected by an equalizing lever.

According to Mr. Clark, not more than twelve tons should ever be placed upon one axle; whence engines requiring a tractive power of twelve tons and less may be of the form shown in fig. 151. Between twelve and twenty-four tons, of the form fig. 152; and over twenty-four of the forms figs. 153, 154, and 155.

Fig. 151.

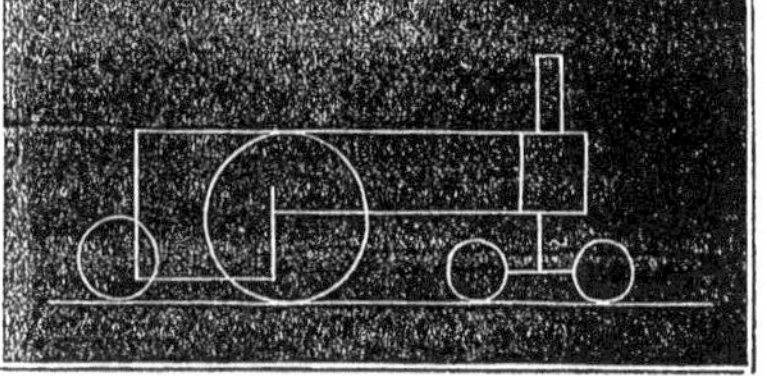

The weight upon the leading wheels of fast passenger engines should be as much as one fifth of the whole weight. Upon freight engines it need not be more than one sixth.

Fig. 152.

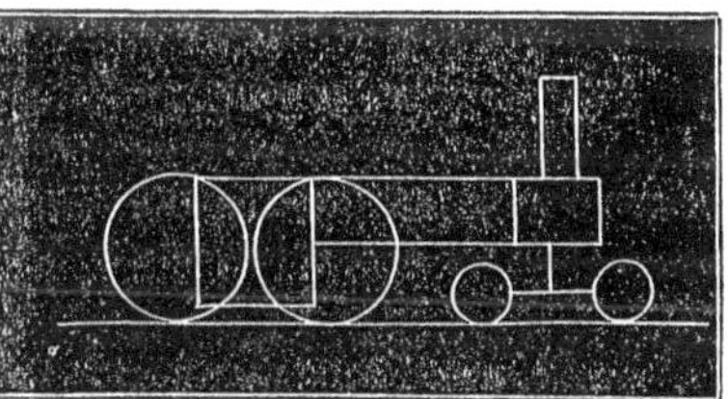

The line of traction of a locomotive ought to be as near as possible at the same vertical height as the driving wheel centres. If much below this the load will tend to lift the engine off from the leading wheels, upon the drivers as a fulcrum, thus increasing the adhesion and lessening the leading power.

Fig. 153.

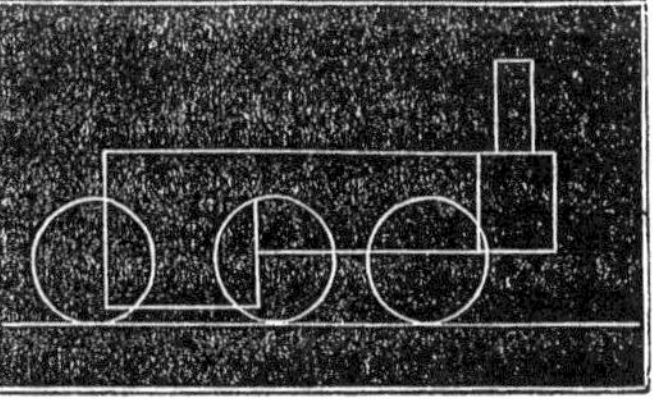

Fig. 154.

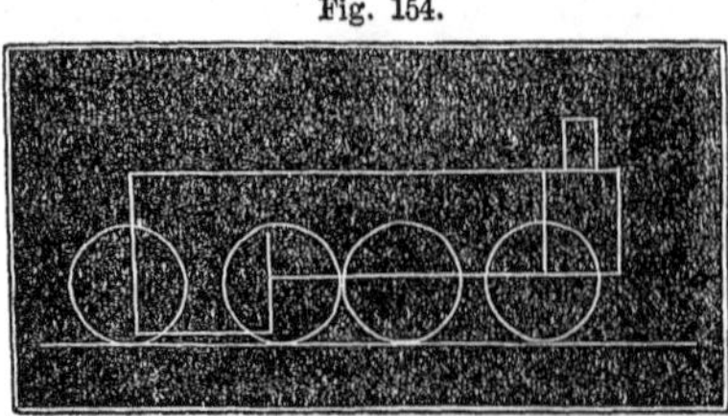

Fig. 155.

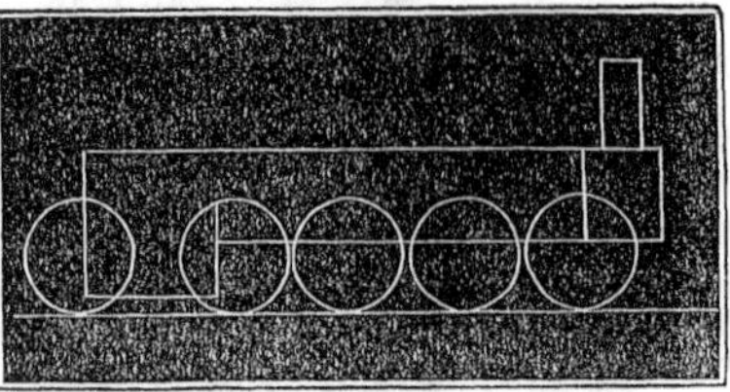

If the traction bar (draw link) is above the wheel centres, it will tend to lift the rear of the engine from the rails.

The general form of engines used in America are shown in figs. 151, 152, 153, 154, and 155.

Fig. 151 is the express passenger locomotive.

Fig. 152 is the ordinary passenger, mail, and mixed engine.

Fig. 153 is the heavy freight engine.

We have, also, engines with three, four, and five pairs of small wheels without a truck, for heavy grades and large amounts of work.

OF ERRATIC MOVEMENTS.

347. The erratic movements of a locomotive in motion are due to three separate causes.

To the motion of the machinery.
To the arrangement of the frame and wheels.
To the state of the surface of the rails.

Those caused by the motion of the machinery are as follows: *Longitudinal fore and aft movement*, generated by the reciprocations of the piston rod, cross head, connecting rod, and crank; and depending in amount upon the weights of the moving parts, steam pressure, and velocity of motion. *Pitching* of the engine, arising from the oblique action of the cross heads upon the guides, which tends to lift the front end of the engine from the rails; and depends in amount upon the ratio between the stroke and length of connecting rod. *Rocking* laterally, arising from the difference of time of action of the cross heads; one acting with its greatest vertical power, when the opposite one acts with none. *Vibration in plan* about the centre of gravity of engine, produced by the pressure between the piston and crank pin, and by the momentum of the reciprocating machinery. This last, combined with lateral rocking, produces *sinuous* or *spiral* motion.

The amounts of these several irregularities depend considerably upon the arrangement of carriage; that is, upon the position of wheels; being less as the base included by the bearing points is greater.

The influence of the state of the rails is shown by the vertical and lateral shocks arising from the rail joints and from bad adjustment, both horizontally and vertically.

The amounts of these irregularities increase very rapidly with the speed. Le Chatelier's experiments make them increase nearly as the square of the velocity.

Longitudinal fore and aft motion is nearly balanced by applying a counterweight to the wheel, opposite the point to which the connecting rod is attached. The remedy for pitching consists in placing the guide bars under the heaviest part of the engine; by which, a great weight is opposed to the vertical action of the cross heads. Crampton's engine is quite free from this disturbance, as the guide bars are almost directly under the centre of gravity.

The only counteracting effort (remedy it is not) for sinuous motion yet applied, is extension of wheel and flange base, thus giving the guiding wheels more control over the mass of the engine.

The remedy, however, which applies at once to all of the

erratic movements, is reduction of speed, as when we divide the velocity by two we decrease the disturbances nearly fourfold.

REVIEW OF THE FORMULÆ AND FORMATION OF THE TABLES.

No. 1.

348. Given the weight and velocity of a train, to find the necessary traction on a level.

Formula.

$$W \times R,$$

W being the weight of the train in tons, and R the resistance in lbs. per ton; found by the formula

$$\frac{V^2}{171} + 8 = R.$$

By this formula is formed table 1, giving the traction required to move trains of from fifty to one thousand tons weight, at speeds from ten to one hundred miles per hour.

No. 2.

349. To find the traction due to a grade.

Formula.

$$\frac{W.R}{L},$$

where W is the weight of the train in tons, R the rise, and L the length of the incline. By this rule is formed table 2, giving the necessary traction to overcome grades from ten to one hundred feet per mile, with loads from one to one thousand tons.

To obtain the whole traction required, add the amounts taken from tables 1 and 2; thus the traction necessary to draw five hundred tons at twenty miles per hour over fifty feet grades is,

By table 1, ...	6,300 lbs.
By table 2, ...	10,605 "
In all, ...	16,905 "

or, algebraically,

$$(W \times R) + \left(\frac{W R}{L}\right) = T,$$

the letters standing for the same quantities as above.

No. 3.

350. To find the weight to place on the driving wheels.

Formula.

$$6\,T,$$

where T is the whole tractive power. (Table 3.)

Nos. 4 and 5.

The tractive power of an engine is expressed by

$$T = \frac{(2\,A)\,P.\,2\,S}{C}.$$

Where T is the tractive power.
P, steam pressure in lbs. per square inch.
S, stroke in inches.
C, circumference of wheel in inches.
A, area of one piston in inches.

From this formula we get the values of the several factors as follows: —

The steam pressure, or $P=\frac{T\,C}{(2\,A)\,2\,S}$. (A.)

The stroke, or $S=\frac{C\,T}{(2\,A)\,(2\,P)}$. (B.)

The piston area, or $A=\frac{T\,C}{4\,S\,P}$. (C.)

The wheel circumference, or $C=\frac{2\,A\,.\,P\,.\,2\,S}{T}$. (D.)

And from (C) we get the diameter of piston by the following: —

$$d=\sqrt{\frac{\text{area}}{.7854}}.$$

And in like manner from (D) the diameter of wheel by

$$d=\frac{c}{3.1416}.$$

(See tables 4 and 5.)

No. 7.

351. To find the capacity of cylinders of any dimension.

Formula.

$$\frac{D^2 \times .7854 \times \text{Stroke}}{1728}.$$

This gives the capacity in cubic feet. The dimensions above (see D and S) being in inches. (Table 7.)

No. 6.

352. To find the hourly steam consumption in terms of the capacity of one cylinder, (that is, the number of cylinderfuls per hour).

Formula.

$$N\frac{5280}{c} \times 4,$$

where N is the number of miles per hour, c the wheel circumference. (Table 6.)

No. 8.

353. Knowing the hourly consumption of steam, to reduce it to water.

Formula.

$$\frac{B}{N},$$

B being the bulk of steam in cubic feet, and N the relative volume of steam and water. (The values of N are given in table 8.)

No. 9.

354. Knowing the hourly water consumption, to find the grate area and heating surface.

First, $\frac{\text{Cubic feet of water per hour}}{16} = \text{grate area in square ft.}$

Second, $S = \sqrt{a\,c} \times 21.2 = \text{heating surface},$

where a is the grate area, and c the hourly consumption of water in cubic feet.

From the same formula,
Grate area, or

$$a = \frac{\left(\frac{S}{21.2}\right)^2}{c}.$$

Also water consumption, or

$$c = \frac{\left(\frac{S}{21.2}\right)^2}{a}.$$

(See table 9.)

No. 10.

355. To find the necessary number of tubes to give any amount of heating surface.

Formula.

$$N = \frac{S}{L d \pi},$$

when N is the number, S the required surface, L the length, d the diameter, both in feet, and $\pi = 3.1416$. (See Table 10.)

No. 11.

356. To find the mean cylinder pressure for any percentage of admission.

Formula.

$$13.5 \sqrt{a} - 28,$$

where a is the percentage of admission. (See Table 11.)

As to the internal arrangement of the barrel of the boiler, we must of course have the length of tubes the same as that of the barrel, (that is, in the general plan of boiler, some makers have moved the back flue plate ahead). The length of tubes will of course be the same as the distance between the tube sheets. The number is governed by their diameter and by the proper clearance, which is found by the formula,

$$\frac{\frac{N}{|30|}}{8} \text{ in eighths of inches, or } \frac{N}{240} \text{ in inches,}$$

The upper fifteen to eighteen inches of the barrel must be left for steam room.

OF THE DIAMETER OF BARREL.

357. To find the diameter of a barrel to contain a given number of tubes,

Represent the inside diameter of boiler by	D,
Diameter of one tube	d,
Clearance between tubes	c,
Number of tubes	n,
Sectional area of boiler, in inches	A,
Water section, in inches	B,

we shall have as the area of water room per tube,

$$(d+c)^2,$$

and the whole area of water room,

$$(d+c)^2 \times n,$$

the whole section of the barrel,

$$\frac{A}{B}\left[(d+c)^2 n\right],$$

and the diameter of that area,

$$D=\sqrt{\frac{\left[(d+c)^2 n\right]\frac{A}{B}}{.7854}}$$

which is the boiler diameter in inches, to which add $\frac{D}{16}$ on each side, or in all $\frac{D}{8}$ as the room to be left between the sides of the boiler and first tube.

The *diameter* finds its maximum limit in the gauge less the two half breadths of tire, and two or three inches allowance for attachment to the frame and other mechanical incidentals. The *length* must be enough to carry the leading wheels a sufficient distance from the centre of gravity of the engine.

ADAPTATION OF THE LOCOMOTIVE ENGINE TO THE MOVEMENT OF RAILWAY TRAINS.

358. First, as regards the nature of the traffic.

There are certain necessary causes of a bad application of power upon railroads; for example, when the trains are very much heavier in one direction than in the other, as we are obliged to use the same engine both ways, because when it arrives at one end of the road it must go back to start again. Where the traffic requires to be worked chiefly up hill, we use an engine much heavier to *ascend with the load* than is necessary to *descend without a load.* Different objects of transport require different speeds. Perishable freight, such as ice, beef, pork, cattle, &c., requires to be moved in much less time than grain, lumber, flour, coal, and manufactured articles. As a general thing, the difference between the characters of freight engines, as regards the nature of the traffic, can be adapted only with a view to amount, disregarding the nature.

With passenger traffic, however, there is a great variety of speeds made use of, and consequently may be a greater difference in the proportions of engines depending entirely upon the nature of the traffic.

ADAPTATION AS REGARDS THE PHYSICAL CHARACTER OF THE ROAD.

The best adaptation of locomotive power to any system of grades, would be that which should render the mileage a minimum; and this will be done, as nearly as possible, by applying engines, the strength of which shall be proportional to the resistance to be overcome. The best mode of comparing different adaptations of power is by reducing the grades to a level; or by equating for grades by means of the capacity of motive power.

This is done as follows:—

The length of an incline being . . . . . L,
The resistance on a level being . . . . . R,
The ratio of the resistance due to the grade to the resistance on a level by . . . . . r,
The equivalent horizontal length by . . . . L',

and we shall have,

$$(R+r)L=L'.$$

Example.—Let the length of a grade be seventy-five miles; the value of

$$r=\frac{R}{3};$$

and we have

$$\left(\frac{3}{3}R+\frac{R}{3}\right)L=\left(\frac{4R}{3}\right)75=100 \text{ miles.}$$

Let us now compare the mileage of some of the large roads of America, as given by a good, and also by a bad adaptation of power.

The Massachusetts Western Railroad may be divided into the four sections below (including the Boston and Worcester road).

	Length miles.	Maximum grade.
Boston to Worcester, ...	44	30
Worcester to Springfield, ...	$54\frac{1}{2}$	50
Springfield to Pittsfield, . . .	52	83
Pittsfield to Albany, ...	$49\frac{1}{2}$	45

Assume the speed of freight trains as fifteen miles per hour, the resistance on a level will be 9.3 lbs., or for simplicity call it ten pounds per ton.

The resistance due to a	30	feet grade is	13	lbs. per ton.
" "	50	"	21	"
" "	83	"	35	"
" "	45	"	19	"
And the value of r for a	30	"	$\frac{13}{10}$	"
" "	50	"	$\frac{21}{10}$	"
" "	83	"	$\frac{35}{10}$	"
" "	45	"	$\frac{19}{10}$	"

And the relative length of the several sections will be,

Boston to Worcester,	$\frac{10}{10}+\frac{13}{10}=\frac{23}{10}$ of 44	$=101$
Worcester to Springfield, . .	$\frac{31}{10}$ of $54\frac{1}{2}$	$=169$
Springfield to Pittsfield, . . .	$\frac{45}{10}$ of 52	$=234$
Pittsfield to Albany, . . .	$\frac{29}{10}$ of $49\frac{1}{2}$	$=144$
And the sums,	200	648

the equated distance being $3\frac{1}{4}$ times the actual length. This length assumes the resistance of the several sections to be for their whole length that given by their maximum grade. This might seem erroneous; but its correctness will be seen when it is remembered that the greatest load that can be taken over any section is limited by its maximum grade.

Now suppose that the engine employed is of the following dimensions (as it is very nearly).

Cylinders, . . .	16 × 20 inches,
Wheels, ...	54 inches.

Assume the cylinder pressure 110 lbs., and the tractive power of the engine is 5,287 lbs.

A load of 500 tons, upon a 30 feet grade, requires a traction of	11,500 lbs.
Upon a 50 feet grade, ...	15,500 lbs.
Upon an 83 feet grade, ...	22,500 lbs.
Upon a 45 feet grade, ...	14,500 lbs.
To move the above load from Boston to Worcester we should require	2 engines,
From Worcester to Springfield, ...	3 "
" Springfield to Pittsfield, ...	5 "
" Pittsfield to Albany, ...	3 "

And the products of the number of engines by the lengths of the corresponding divisions, are

Boston to Worcester, . .	44 × 2 = 80
Worcester to Springfield, . . .	$54\frac{1}{2} \times 3 = 103\frac{1}{2}$
Springfield to Pittsfield, . .	52 × 5 = 260
Pittsfield to Albany, . . .	$49\frac{1}{2} \times 3 = 148\frac{1}{2}$
	660

Suppose that by making the engines on the several sections strong in proportion to the resistance of those sections, one engine is capable of taking the whole load over all of the grades. The mileage becomes as follows: —

Boston to Worcester, . .	44 × 1 = 44
Worcester to Springfield, . . .	$54\frac{1}{2} \times 1 = 54\frac{1}{2}$
Springfield to Pittsfield, . .	52 × 1 = 52
Pittsfield to Albany, . . .	$49\frac{1}{2} \times 1 = 49\frac{1}{2}$
	200 miles.

The mileage before was . . . 660 miles,
And the saving therefore . . . 400 "

or about 70 per cent. of the first mileage.

359. From a recent report of the New York and Erie Railroad it appears that the same power will draw

28 tons on the Western division,
80 " Susquehanna division,
85 " Delaware division,
and 20 " Eastern division,

neglecting the assistance required from Susquehanna to Deposite. In the following table are given the actual lengths of the several divisions, and the sum of the products of three lengths both by the relative and a uniform resistance on each.

Division.	Length.	Miles run by an engine not adapted.	Miles run by an engine adapted.	Difference.
Western,	128	128 × 3.04	128 × 1.0	201.12
Susquehanna,	139	139 × 1.06	139 × 1.0	8.35
Delaware,	104	104 × 1.00	104 × 1.0	0.00
Eastern,	88	88 × 4.25	88 × 1.0	286.00
Sum of differences,				555.47 miles,

that is, the miles run by engines adapted to the work on the several divisions will be 555.47 less than the miles run by engines not adapted. (See Appendix F.)

PENNSYLVANIA CENTRAL RAILROAD.

360. The physical character of this road is as follows:—

	Length.	Max. grades.
Philadelphia to Harrisburg, .	106	45
Harrisburg to Altoona, ...	131	21
Altoona to Johnstown, . .	48½	92
Johnstown to Pittsburgh, . . .	78½	53

The value of r will be here

45 feet grades, ...	$\frac{19}{10}$
21 feet grades, ...	$\frac{9}{10}$
92 feet grades, ...	$\frac{39}{10}$
53 feet grades, ...	$\frac{25}{10}$

Whence the equation,

$$
\begin{aligned}
106 &\times \left(\tfrac{10}{10} + \tfrac{19}{10}\right) = 307 \\
131 &\times \left(\tfrac{10}{10} + \tfrac{9}{10}\right) = 249 \\
42\tfrac{1}{2} &\times \left(\tfrac{10}{10} + \tfrac{39}{10}\right) = 208 \\
78\tfrac{1}{2} &\times \left(\tfrac{10}{10} + \tfrac{25}{10}\right) = 275 \\
\text{Sum, } 358 & \qquad\qquad \text{Sum, } 1039,
\end{aligned}
$$

and $1039 - 358 = 681$.

361. On the Baltimore and Ohio Railroad we have,

	Miles.	Max. grade.
Baltimore to Harper's Ferry, .	80	82
Harper's Ferry to Cumberland, .	98	40
Cumberland to Raccoon, . .	88.2	116
Raccoon to 148⅔ miles, . . .	60.5	40
148⅔ miles to Wheeling, . .	51.3	80

And as before,

$$
\begin{aligned}
80 &\times \left(\tfrac{10}{10} + \tfrac{35}{10}\right) = 360 \\
98 &\times \left(\tfrac{10}{10} + \tfrac{17}{10}\right) = 265 \\
88.2 &\times \left(\tfrac{10}{10} + \tfrac{49}{10}\right) = 520 \\
60.5 &\times \left(\tfrac{10}{10} + \tfrac{17}{10}\right) = 163 \\
51.3 &\times \left(\tfrac{10}{10} + \tfrac{35}{10}\right) = 231
\end{aligned}
$$

Sum of Col. 1 = 378, Sum of Col. 3 = 1539; difference 1161.

Thus by the most correct adaptation of power, upon the above-named railroads, the following percentages of mileage may be saved.

Massachusetts Western,	70
New York and Erie,	$55\frac{1}{2}$
Pennsylvania Central,	68
Baltimore and Ohio,	75

Of these roads the Baltimore and Ohio is that which has actually the best adaptation; and the Western road of Massachusetts that which has the worst.

362. To determine the actual dimensions of the engines which should be used upon any road, from the tables, proceed as follows: — Let the load be one hundred tons, the maximum grade thirty feet per mile, and speed twenty-five miles per hour.

Referring to the tables in succession we have,

By table 1, Traction for 100 tons, on a level, at 25 miles per hour,	1,550 lbs.
By table 2, Traction for 100 tons, on a 30 feet grade,	1,273 "
Whole traction required,	2,823 "

By the formula, table 3, the weight upon the drivers must be

$$2823 \times 6 = 16938 \text{ lbs., or 8 tons.}$$

By table 4, with a wheel five feet in diameter, and a stroke of twenty inches, we have the decimal .2122.

By table 5, the mean cylinder pressure being sixty pounds per inch, and piston twelve inches in diameter, we have as the total pressure

On both pistons,	13,572 lbs.
And finally, 13572 × .2122 =	2,880 "
The requirement being	2,823 "

By table 6, we see that five feet wheels at twenty-five miles per hour, use 33,600 cylinders of steam per hour.

By table 7, the capacity of a cylinder 12 × 20 is 1.31

cubic feet; also $33600 \times 1.31 = 44016$ cubic feet of steam per hour.

Assuming the mean cylinder pressure at sixty pounds, and the entering pressure at eighty pounds, also the loss in passing from the boiler at twenty pounds, we must generate the steam at one hundred pounds per square inch.

By table 8, we see that when steam is produced under one hundred pounds pressure per inch, each cubic foot of water makes 293 cubic feet of steam; whence

$$\frac{44016}{293} = 150,$$

is the number of cubic feet of water to be evaporated per hour. At sixteen cubic feet of water per hour per square foot of grate, we thus require

$$\frac{15.0}{10} \text{ or } 9.4 \text{ feet, nearly;}$$

and by table 9, we find the heating surface necessary to evaporate 150 cubic feet of water per hour, with nine square feet of grate surface, to be 779 square feet; and by the formula, with 9.4 square feet, we have,

$$S = \sqrt{9.4 \times 150} \times 21.2 = 797 \text{ square feet,}$$

the fuel being coke; for wood, multiply the grate area (as mentioned before) by 1.4 and the grate area will be $1.4 \times 9.4 = 13.16$. The tube surface of course remains the same, as, when the necessary amount of heat is developed, the same surface only is enough to apply it to the water.

To obtain 779 square feet of heating surface, we see, by table 10, that it is given by

100 tubes 17 feet long and $1\frac{3}{4}$ inch diameter,
or 100 " 16 " $1\frac{7}{8}$ "

or 100 tubes	15	feet long and	2	inch diameter,
or 100 "	14	"	$2\frac{1}{8}$	"
or 100 "	$12\frac{1}{2}$	"	$2\frac{3}{8}$	"
or 100 "	12	"	$2\frac{1}{2}$	"

or by consulting the table, and having given the number and length, the number and diameter, or the length and diameter, we may easily find the third factor of the surface. Thus the length being eleven feet, and diameter two inches, 779 feet is obtained by

$$\frac{779}{11 \times 3.1416 \times 167} = 135 \text{ tubes.}$$

To obtain the diameter of barrel to contain 135 two inch tubes, we use the formula

$$D = \sqrt{\frac{\frac{A}{B}\left[n(d+c)^2\right]}{.7854}}.$$

We have already found $d=2$ inches, $u=135$, whence c will be by formula,

$$c = \frac{N}{240} = 0.54,$$

and

$$d + c = 2.54,$$

also,

$$(d+c)^2 = 6.45,$$

and

$$135 \times 6.45 = 871 +;$$

and allowing three fourths of the boiler cross section to be filled with tubes, we have,

$$\tfrac{4}{3} \text{ of } 871 = 1161;$$

also,

$$\frac{1161}{.7854} = 1478,$$

the square root of which is 38.5 nearly, to which add $\frac{38.5}{8}$

or 4.8 inches, (see page 359), and we have

$$38.5 + 4.8 = 43.3 \text{ inches,}$$

as the inside diameter of boiler, whence the following locomotive to meet the requirement as stated.

Weight upon driving wheels,	16,938 lbs.,
Cylinders, . . .	12 × 12 inches,
Wheels, ...	5 feet,
Tubes, ...	135 — 11 feet × 2 inches,
Grate, ...	13.16 square feet,
Barrel, (inside diameter,)	43.3 inches,

and under the most favorable circumstances, the chimney may be 40 inches high, 12.7 inches in diameter; the blast orifice 5.8 inches in diameter; and the capacity of smoke box 39½ cubic feet.

363. We may vary the tractive power of an engine by using the steam at a greater or less degree of expansion, but the adhesion remains the same. If an engine was built able to work a road partly level, and partly on steep grades, varying the power simply by varying the expansion, it would be unnecessarily heavy for the easy parts of the road. The expansive principle may be advantageously employed in adjusting the power to the difference of resistance on any one division of a road, and also to the varying load which each day's traffic will present.

Suppose we would move a load of two hundred tons over the road below; and suppose, also, that we require the cylinder pressures set opposite the several divisions.

10 miles, level,	. . . . .	60 lbs.,
"	10 feet per mile, . . .	80 "
"	20 " . . .	100 "
"	30 " . . .	120 "

The boiler pressure being 150 lbs., and the pressure at entering the cylinder 145 lbs.,

An admission of	71	per cent.	gives a	mean pressure of	120	lbs.,
"	55	"	"	"	100	"
"	40	"	"	"	80	"
"	28	"	"	"	60	"

And if the	1st	notch	of the sector	admits,	75	feet,
"	2d	"	"	"	70	"
"	3d	"	"	"	65	"
"	4th	"	"	"	60	"
"	5th	"	"	"	55	"
"	6th	"	"	"	50	"
"	7th	"	"	"	45	"
"	8th	"	"	"	40	"
"	9th	"	"	"	35	"
"	10th	"	"	"	30	"

We should work the engine as follows: —

From	0 to 10	miles,	use the	10th	notch,
"	10 to 20	"	"	8th	"
"	20 to 30	"	"	5th	"
"	30 to 40	"	"	2d	"

APPLICATION OF LOCOMOTIVE ENGINES TO RAILROADS.

364. *Department* 1. *Freight.*

GENERAL CLASSIFICATION.

Number of division.	Maximum grades.	Designation of parts.	Order 1 50 tons.	Order 2 100 tons.	Order 3 250 tons.	Order 4 500 tons.	Order 5 750 tons.	Order 6 1,000 tons.
1	Level.	Grate area. Tube surface. Cylinders. Wheels. Weight.						
2	10 feet per mile.							
3	20 feet per mile.							
4	40 feet per mile.							
5	60 feet per mile.							
6	80 feet per mile.							
7	100 feet per mile.							

The speed is assumed from twelve to fifteen miles per hour. The mean cylinder pressure is assumed at sixty lbs. per square inch; the initial pressure at ninety pounds, and the boiler pressure at 120 lbs. per square inch. The grate areas are designed for coke; for wood multiply the same by 1.4.

365. *Department* 2. *Passenger.*

Classification.		Order 1 50 tons.	Order 2 100 tons.	Order 3 150 tons.	Order 4 200 tons.	Designation of parts.
Division 1 Level.	25 miles per hour.					Grate area. Tube surface. Cylinders. Wheels. Weight.
Division 2 20′ grades.	25 miles per hour.					
Division 3 40′ grades.	25 miles per hour.					
Division 4 60′ grades.	25 miles per hour.					
Division 5 80′ grades.	25 miles per hour.					
Division 6 100′ grades.	25 miles per hour.					

The engines in the Northern States require more power in winter than in summer.

To the above classification might be added, an engine for "making up trains," and similar station work; such an engine should be able to start easily the extreme weights of trains, from fifty to one thousand tons, and should be fitted with a power of varying its adhesion.

FORMULA.

$$W \times \left[\frac{V^2}{171} + 8\right] = R.$$

Example.

The speed being thirty miles per hour, and load 250 tons.

$$R \text{ will be} \left[\frac{30 \times 30}{171} + 8\right] \times 250 = 3315 \text{ lbs.}$$

366. Table 1. Showing the required traction on a level for loads from fifty to one thousand tons, and for velocities from ten to one hundred miles per hour.

Velocity.	50 Tons.	75 Tons.	100 Tons.	250 Tons.	500 Tons.	750 Tons.	1000 Tons.
10	429	643	858	2146	4292	6435	8585
12	442	663	884	2210	4421	6630	8842
15	465	698	931	2328	4657	6982	9315
20	517	773	1034	2585	5170	7735	
25	582	874	1165	2912	5825		
30	663	994	1326	3315	6630		
40	868	1302	1736	4340			
50	1181	1696	2262	5655			
60	1452	2180	2905				
100	3324	4986	6648				

FORMULA.

$$\frac{W R}{L}.$$

Example.

The tractive power to overcome the resistance of 750 tons upon a sixty feet grade is

$$750 \times \frac{60}{5280} = .19090.$$

367. Table 2. Showing the tractive power necessary to overcome grades from ten to one hundred feet per mile with loads from one to one thousand tons.

Grade.	1 Ton.	50 Tons.	75 Tons	100 Tons.	250 Tons.	500 Tons.	750 Tons.	1000 Tons.	Grade.
10	4	212	318	424	1061	2121	3181	4240	10
20	8	424	636	848	2122	4242	6362	8480	20
30	13	636	955	1273	3170	6363	9545	12730	30
40	16	848	1272	1696	4244	8484	12724	16960	40
50	20	1060	1590	2120	5305	10605	15905	21200	50
60	26	1272	1910	2546	6340	12726	19050	25460	60
70	30	1500	2240	3000	7500	15000	22400	30000	70
80	33	1697	2545	3393	8489	16969	25459	33950	80
100	40	2120	3180	4240	10610	21210	31810	42400	100
Grade.	1 Ton.	50 Tons.	75 Tons.	100 Tons.	250 Tons.	500 Tons.	750 Tons.	1000 Tons.	Grade.

FORMULA.

$6\,T.$

Example.

Required traction 5,000 lbs.; upon driving axles the weight is $5000 \times 6 = 30{,}000$ lbs.

368. **Table 3.** Giving the weight which should be placed upon the driving axles to secure any amount of adhesion; the latter being one sixth of the weight.

Required traction.	Weight in pounds.	Weight in tons.
500	3000	1.34
1000	6000	2.69
2000	12000	5.36
3000	18000	8.04
4000	24000	10.80
5000	30000	13.40
6000	42000	16.07
7000	42000	18.75
8000	48000	21.43
9000	54000	24.11
10000	60000	26.80.
12000	72000	32.14
14000	84000	37.50
16000	96000	42.86
18000	108000	48.22
20000	120000	53.60

FORMULA.

$$\frac{2S}{c}.$$

Where S = stroke.
c = circumference of wheel, (both in inches.)

Example.

Let stroke be twenty inches, and diameter of wheel five feet, the ratio will be

$$\frac{40}{188.4} = 0.2122.$$

369. Table of decimals, which, multiplied by the total piston pressures (table 5) will give the traction in pounds, or ratio between double stroke and wheel circumference. Table 4.

Wheel.	STROKE IN INCHES.										Wheel.
	18	20	22	24	26	28	30	32	34	36	
3½	2728	3031	3334	3638							3½
3¾	2553	2837	3120	3404	3688						3¾
4	2386	2652	2918	3182	3444	3708					4
4¼	2250	2500	2750	3000	3250	3500	3750				4¼
4½	2151	2390	2593	2830	3071	3294	3529	3764			4½
4¾	2012	2235	2459	2682	2905	3129	3352	3575	3800		4¾
5	1910	2122	2334	2546	2766	2979	3192	3405	3617	3830	5
5½	1736	1929	2122	2315	2500	2692	2885	3077	3273	3473	5½
6	1591	1768	1945	2122	2321	2500	2678	2857	3036	3215	6
6½	1468	1632	1796	1958	2131	2295	2459	2623	2790	2951	6½
7	1364	1516	1667	1819	1970	21.21	2273	2424	2576	2727	7
7½	1272	1414	1556	1691	1831	1972	2114	2254	2394	2535	7½
·8	1194	1326	1417	1592	1688	1818	1948	2078	2208	2337	8
Wheel.	18	20	22	24	26	28	30	32	34	36	Wheel.
	STROKE IN INCHES.										

FORMULA.

$$2\,(d^2\,.7854 \times p) = P.$$

Where d = diameter.
p = pressure per inch.

Example.

The whole pressure at one hundred pounds per inch on two sixteen inch pistons will be

$$2\,[16 \times 16 \times 0.7854 \times 100] = 40212.$$

370. Table 5. Total pressures upon pistons from ten to twenty-four inches in diameter, and for steam pressures from fifty to one hundred and fifty pounds per square inch.

Diam. of cyl'r.	Area of one piston.	WHOLE PISTON PRESSURE ON BOTH PISTONS, AT A PER INCH PRESSURE OF											Diam. of cyl'r.
		50	60	70	80	90	100	110	120	130	140	150	
10	78.5	7950	9420	10990	12560	14130	15700	17270	18840	20410	21980	23550	10
11	95.0	9500	11400	13300	15200	17100	19000	20900	22800	24700	26600	28500	11
12	113.1	11310	13572	15834	18096	20358	22620	24882	27144	29406	31768	33930	12
13	132.7	13270	15924	18564	21232	23906	26540	29194	31848	34502	37156	39810	13
14	153.9	15390	18468	21546	24624	27702	30780	33858	36756	40014	43092	46170	14
15	176.7	17670	21204	24738	28272	31806	35340	38874	42408	55942	49476	53010	15
16	201.1	20110	24132	28154	32176	36198	40220	44242	48264	52062	56308	60330	16
17	227.0	22700	27240	31780	36320	40860	45400	49940	54480	59020	63560	68100	17
18	254.5	25450	30540	35630	40720	45810	50900	55990	61080	66170	71260	76350	18
19	283.5	28350	34020	39690	45360	51030	56700	62370	68040	73710	79380	85050	19
20	314.2	31420	37704	43988	50272	56556	62840	69124	75408	81692	87976	95260	20
21	346.4	34640	41568	48496	55424	62352	69380	76208	83136	90064	96992	103920	21
22	380.1	38010	45612	53214	60816	68418	77020	83622	91224	98826	106428	114030	22
23	415.5	41550	49860	58170	66480	74790	83100	91410	99720	108030	116340	124650	23
24	452.4	45240	54288	63336	72384	81432	90480	99528	108576	117626	126672	135720	24

FORMULA.

$$N = \frac{5280}{c} \times 4.$$

Where $N =$ the number.
$c =$ wheel circumference.

Example.

Speed twenty-five miles per hour, wheels four and a half feet, the number of cylinders per hour is

$$\frac{5280}{4\frac{1}{2} \times 3.1416} \times 4 = 37300.$$

371. Table 6. Showing the hourly consumption of steam in terms of the capacity of one cylinder, with wheels from three and a half to eight feet, and speeds from ten to sixty miles per hour.

Wheel.	Wheel in inches.	Revolutions per mile.	NUMBER OF CYLINDERS PER HOUR AT A VELOCITY OF								
			10	12	15	20	25	30	40	50	60
3½	42	480	19200	23040							
3¾	45	449	17960	21552	26940						
4	48	421	16840	20208	25260	33681					
4¼	51	397	15880	19056	23820	31760	39700				
4½	54	373	14920	17904	22380	29840	37300				
4¾	57	361	14440	17328	21660	28880	36100				
5	60	336			20160	26880	33600				
5½	66	306			18360	24480	30600	36720			
6	72	281				22480	28100	33720	44960		
6½	78	259				20720	25900	31080	41440	51800	62160
7	84	240				19200	24000	28800	38400	48000	57600
7⅛	90	224					22400	26880	35840	44800	53760
8	96	211					21109	25320	33760	42200	50640

FORMULA.

$$\frac{D^2 .7854 \times \text{Stroke}}{1728} = C.$$

Example.

Cubic content of a cylinder 15×24 is

$$\frac{15 \times 15 \times 0.7854 \times 24}{1728} = 2.44 \text{ cubic feet.}$$

372. Table 7. Capacity of cylinders in cubic feet of from ten to twenty-four inches in diameter, and from eighteen to thirty-six inches stroke.

Diam. of cyl'r.	CAPACITY OF CYLINDERS IN CUBIC FEET, STROKE BEING										Diam. of cyl'r.
	18	20	22	24	26	28	30	32	34	36	
10	082	091	100	109	118	127	136	145			10
11	093	104	115	126	137	148	159	170	181		11
12	118	131	144	157	170	183	196	209	222	235	12
13	133	149	165	181	197	213	229	245	261	277	13
14	160	178	196	214	232	250	268	286	304	322	14
15	184	204	224	244	264	284	304	324	344	364	15
16	208	232	255	278	301	324	347	370	393	416	16
17	235	263	289	315	341	367	393	419	445	471	17
18	263	294	323	352	381	410	439	468	497	526	18
19			361	394	427	460	493	526	559	592	19
20			400	437	474	511	548	585	622	659	20
21				481	521	561	601	641	681	721	21
22				528	572	616	660	704	748	792	22
23					625	674	723	772	821	876	23
24					681	733	785	837	889	941	24

373. Table 8. Giving the volume, pressure, temperature, and density of steam.

Steam pressure.	Relative volume or cubic feet of steam, water being 1.	Temperature.	Total heat.	Weight of a cubic foot.	Steam pressure.
50	552	281	1200	1129	50
60	467	293	1203	1335	60
65	434	298	1205	1436	65
70	406	303	1206	1535	70
75	381	307	1208	1636	75
80	359	312	1209	1736	80
90	323	320	1212	1929	90
100	293	328	1214	2127	100
110	269	335	1216	2317	110
120	249	341	1218	2505	120
130	231	347	1220	2698	130
140	216	353	1221	2885	140
150	203	358	1223	3070	150

FORMULA.

$$S = \sqrt{ac} \times 21.2.$$

Where S = surface.
a = grate area.
c = cubic feet of water per hour.

Example.

Grate area sixteen square feet, cubic feet of water per hour two hundred, surface is

$$\sqrt{16 \times 200} \times 21.2 = 1199.92.$$

374. Table 9. Showing the necessary amount of grate area and heating surface for any hourly consumption of water.

Cubic ft. of water evap'd per hour.	GRATE AREAS IN SQUARE FEET.																						
	7	8	9	10	11	12	13	14	15	16	17	18	19	20	21	22	23	24	25	26	27	28	29	30
	HEATING SURFACE CORRESPONDING TO ABOVE GRATE AREAS AND TO SIDE COLUMN.																							
100	561	599	636	670	703	734	764	793	821	848	874	900	924	948	972	995	1017	1039	1060	1081	1102	1122	1142	1161
110	588	628	667	702	737	770	802	831	861	888	916	943	969	994	1018	1042	1066	1089	1111	1133	1155	1176	1197	1217
120	614	657	697	734	770	805	837	869	900	927	957	985	1013	1039	1064	1089	1114	1138	1162	1184	1207	1229	1251	1272
130	639	683	725	764	801	837	871	904	936	965	996	1025	1053	1081	1107	1133	1159	1184	1208	1232	1255	1278	1300	1323
140	663	709	752	793	831	869	904	938	972	1003	1034	1064	1093	1122	1150	1177	1203	1229	1254	1279	1303	1327	1351	1374
150	686	734	779	821	860	900	935	971	1006	1038	1070	1101	1131	1161	1190	1218	1245	1272	1298	1323	1350	1373	1398	1422
160		758	805	848	889	927	966	1004	1039	1073	1106	1138	1169	1199	1229	1258	1286	1314	1341	1367	1393	1419	1444	1469
170		782	829	874	916	957	996	1034	1071	1106	1140	1173	1205	1236	1266	1296	1325	1354	1382	1409	1436	1462	1488	1514
180		805	853	900	943	985	1025	1064	1102	1138	1173	1207	1240	1272	1303	1334	1364	1393	1422	1450	1478	1505	1532	1558
190			877	924	969	1013	1053	1093	1132	1169	1205	1240	1274	1307	1339	1370	1401	1431	1461	1490	1518	1546	1573	1600
200			900	948	995	1039	1081	1122	1161	1199	1236	1272	1307	1341	1374	1406	1437	1468	1499	1529	1558	1586	1614	1642
210			928	974	1019	1064	1007	1149	1189	1229	1264	1298	1336	1374	1408	1441	1473	1505	1536	1566	1596	1625	1654	1683
220				1000	1042	1089	1133	1176	1217	1258	1291	1324	1365	1406	1441	1475	1508	1541	1572	1603	1634	1664	1693	1722
230				1019	1067	1114	1159	1203	1245	1286	1323	1359	1398	1437	1473	1508	1542	1575	1607	1639	1663	1701	1724	1761
240					1091	1138	1184	1229	1272	1314	1354	1393	1431	1468	1505	1541	1575	1609	1642	1675	1692	1738	1754	1799
250					1111	1162	1208	1254	1298	1341	1380	1422	1458	1499	1533	1572	1606	1642	1675	1709	1733	1774	1797	1836
260						1184	1232	1278	1323	1367	1406	1450	1484	1529	1560	1603	1636	1675	1708	1743	1774	1809	1840	1872
270						1207	1256	1303	1349	1401	1433	1478	1515	1557	1592	1634	1668	1692	1741	1776	1808	1843	1875	1908
280							1279	1327	1374	1435	1460	1505	1546	1586	1624	1664	1700	1738	1774	1809	1842	1877	1910	1943
290							1302	1351	1400	1452	1486	1532	1573	1614	1653	1693	1729	1754	1804	1841	1873	1910	1939	1977
300								1374	1425	1469	1512	1558	1600	1642	1682	1722	1758	1799	1834	1872	1904	1943	1968	2011
320									1469	1516	1564	1610	1654	1696	1738	1778	1816	1859	1894	1932	1970	2008	2024	2078
340										1564	1612	1658	1704	1748	1792	1833	1872	1915	1954	1993	2032	2069	2096	2141
360											1658	1706	1754	1800	1844	1886	1928	1971	2012	2050	2090	2128	2166	2204
380												1753	1802	1848	1894	1938	1982	2025	2066	2107	2148	2187	2226	2264
400												1800	1848	1900	1944	1990	2034	2077	2120	2162	2204	2244	2284	2322
425														1950	2014	2056	2077	2142	2187	2226	2268	2317	2353	2396
450														2014	2056	2120	2150	2190	2200	2300	2332	2374	2417	2459
475																2175	2210	2268	2310	2353	2416	2445	2480	2523
500																		2332	2370	2412	2459	2523	2565	2608

FORMULA.

$$N = \frac{S}{L d \pi} \text{ or } \frac{S}{L d 3.1416}.$$

Where $S =$ whole surface,
" $L =$ length,
" $d =$ diameter, in feet,
" $\pi = 3.1416$,
" $N =$ the number.

Example.

Diameter two inches, surface 1466, length fourteen feet, we have,

$$N = \frac{1466}{14 \times 0.167 \times 3.1416} = 200.$$

375. Table 10. Giving the number and dimensions of tubes to obtain any given amount of surface.

L'gth.	Diam. 1½	Diam. 1¾	Diam. 1⅞	Diam. 2	Diam. 2⅛	Diam. 2¼	Diam. 2⅜	Diam. 2½	L'gth.
8	314	336	397	419	445	471	504	523	8
8½	334	389	422	445	473	500	535	556	8½
9	352	411	447	471	507	530	566	588	9
9½	372	435	471	497	523	559	597	621	9½
10	392	457	496	524	556	589	628	655	10
10½	411	480	521	549	584	618	659	687	10½
11	431	503	545	576	612	647	690	720	11
11½	451	526	570	602	640	677	721	753	11½
12	471	549	595	628	667	705	752	786	12
12½	490	572	620	654	695	735	783	818	12½
13	510	595	645	681	723	764	814	851	13
13½	530	617	669	707	750	793	845	884	13½
14	549	640	695	733	778	823	876	916	14
14½	569	663	719	759	806	852	907	949	14½
15	589	686	744	785	834	882	938	982	15
15½	608	708	769	811	861	911	969	1015	15½
16	628	731	794	837	889	941	1000	1048	16
16½	648	754	819	863	917	971	1031	1081	16½
17	668	777	843	889	945	1000	1062	1114	17

FORMULA.

$$13.5\sqrt{a} - 28,$$

where a is the percentage of admission.

Example.

What is the mean pressure, with an initial pressure of one hundred pounds, and sixty per cent. admission.

$$13.5\sqrt{60} - 28 = (13.5 \times 7.7) - 28 = \tfrac{76}{100} \text{ of } 100, \text{ or } 76 \text{ lbs.}$$

376. Table 11. Showing the mean cylinder steam pressure for any percentage of admission, the initial pressure being from 50 to 150 lbs. per inch.

Initial pressure in pounds.	MEAN CYLINDER PRESSURE, ADMISSION BEING IN HUNDREDTHS OF THE STROKE.													
	10	15	20	25	30	35	40	45	50	55	60	65	70	75
50	7	12	16	20	23	26	28	31	33	36	38	40	42	44
60	9	14	19	24	28	31	34	37	40	43	46	49	51	53
70	10	17	22	28	33	36	40	43	47	50	54	57	59	62
80	12	19	26	32	38	42	41	49	54	58	62	65	68	71
90	13	22	29	36	42	47	51	54	60	65	69	73	76	80
100	15	24	32	40	47	52	57	62	67	72	77	81	85	89
110	16	26	35	44	52	57	63	68	74	79	85	89	93	98
120	18	29	38	48	56	62	68	74	80	86	91	97	102	107
130	19	31	42	52	61	68	74	81	87	94	99	105	110	116
145	21	34	45	56	65	73	80	87	94	101	107	113	119	125
160	22	36	48	60	70	78	85	93	100	108	114	121	127	134

PART II.

CARS.

WHEELS AND AXLES.

377. Of the mechanical details of car building it is not necessary here to speak; but of those matters which fit a car for special duty, and depend upon particular characteristics of any road, such as the gauge, something must be said.

The trend of the wheel tire, as remarked in Chapter XIII., is not turned cylindrical, but conical. A perfectly straight road would of course require no cone upon the wheels; the object of the latter being to vary the wheel diameter when upon curves. The general practice is to give a certain standard cone to all wheels, for all gauges. This is quite wrong, as will be seen by the following formula, which is from "Pambour on the Locomotive Engine."

Fig. 156.

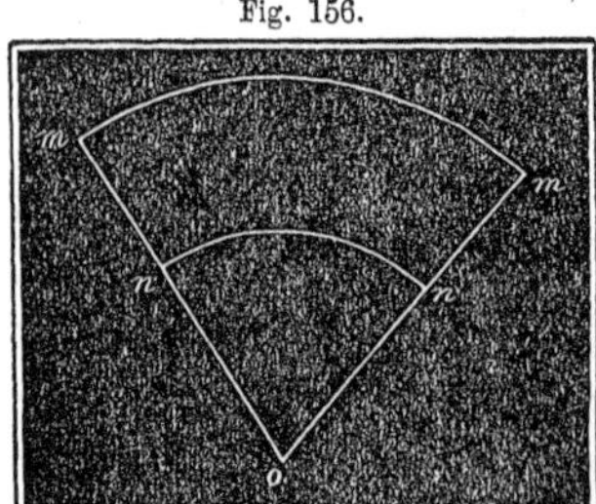

Let $m\,m'$, fig. 156, represent the outer rail, and $n\,n'$ the inner one. The circumferences upon the same axles must evidently vary as the length of these curves, which are included between the same radii.

Let D, be the diameter of the first wheel, and d, that of the second; and we shall have,

$$\frac{m\,m'}{n\,n'} = \frac{\pi\,D}{\pi\,d},$$

or otherwise

$$m\,m' = 3.1416\,D,$$

and

$$n\,n' = 3.1416\,d.$$

We have also,

$$\frac{m\,m'}{n\,n'}=\frac{m\,o}{n\,o}.$$

Expressing the radius of curvature by r, and the half gauge by e, the above proportion may be expressed by

$$\frac{m\,m'}{n\,n'}=\frac{r+e}{r-e},$$

and also

$$\frac{D}{d}=\frac{r+e}{r-e},$$

and finally

$$D-d=\frac{2\,e\,D}{r+e}.$$

This equation shows the difference in diameters that ought to exist between the inner and outer wheels, that the required effect, (no dragging of the outer and no slipping of the inner wheel,) is produced.

Example.

Let the radius of curvature be	1,000 feet,
The gauge of the road, ...	6 "
The wheel diameter, ...	4 "

And the formula becomes

$$\frac{2\,e\,d}{r+e}=\frac{24}{1003}=.024 \text{ feet},$$

or .288 inch on both wheels, or 0.144 inch for each wheel; which for four inches breadth, gives a curve of $\frac{1}{28}$ of the width, or decimally, 0.144, and vulgarly, $\frac{1}{7}$ of an inch. For a three feet wheel, the rule gives a cone of 0.11 inch.

Note.—Messrs Bush and Lobdel cone their wheels 0.08 inches in a four inch tire; or $\frac{1}{4}$ inch per foot. The formula above for a three feet wheel, and 4′ 8½″ gauge, gives a curve of 0.09 inches.

The wheel most used upon American roads is made of cast-iron, in one piece, and consists either of two side plates, connected by a hub and rim, or of a central plate ribbed on the sides. Messrs Whitney and Son, (Philadelphia,) pass all their wheels through an annealing process, which renders them much less liable to fracture from shocks and from cold than when the wheel is allowed to cool at once, when hot from the foundery.

The wheels used upon English roads are made with a wrought iron rim and spokes, with a cast hub, the tire being put on separately. Such wheels are less liable to fracture, but cost more than the American wheel.

378. A very frequent cause of accident upon railroads, is the breakage of axles. Experiments made at Wolverhampton, (England,) upon differently formed axles, show very plainly that it is quite wrong to reduce the diameter of the axle at the middle. That if any variation exists it should be in making the middle the largest. That the effect of a shoulder behind the wheel was to decrease very much the strength. Probably the strongest and most economical railroad axle, would be a wrought iron tube. Certainly a hollow axle is much stronger in resisting tension than a solid one containing the same amount of material.

NOTE 1.—Thomas Thorneycroft, of Wolverhampton, England, an educated man, and a manufacturer of railway axles, observes:—That the various forms of axles, as generally made, possess within themselves the elements of destruction. That there are certain fixed principles to be observed in proportioning axles, and that just as such principles are departed from, just so much is liability to failure increased.

He says:—It is doubtful whether the wheel is the support and the journal the loaded part, or the reverse. If the latter is the case, then the cone of the wheels causes a lateral strain, tending to bend the axle; and should that bending extend no further than one half of the elastic limit, if long continued, fracture must result; and should the elastic limit be exceeded, the plane of the wheel will be removed from that in which it ought to revolve.

The object of the first experiment was to determine the effect of the form of the longitudinal section of the axle upon its elastic limit.

By reducing the diameter of the axle from $4\frac{5}{16}$ inches at centre, to $3\frac{3}{4}$ inches; the limit of elasticity was reduced from .343 to .232 inches; and the load, to produce that elasticity, from fourteen to seven tons.

Experiment second was to ascertain the effect of a reduction of diameter at the centre, upon the ability to resist sudden shocks. One half of the axle was made $4\frac{1}{2}$ inches in diameter from middle to end, and the other half was reduced from $4\frac{1}{2}$ to four inches at centre. The wheel being fixed, and a ram allowed to fall upon the journal, when the following result was obtained. Under forty-six blows, the unreduced end was bent to an angle of eighteen degrees. Under sixteen blows, the reduced end was bent to twenty-two degrees.

Experiment third was to ascertain the effect of a shoulder behind the wheel, one end being turned with a shoulder of one eighth of an inch, as a stop to the wheel, the other end turned plain. Tested by hydraulic pressure, the shouldered end broke with sixty tons, the plain end with eighty-four tons.

The object of the fourth experiment was to find the influence of the position of the wheel, as regards the end of the journal. An axle was fastened into a cast-iron frame, in a line with the neck of the journal, when the latter was broke with seven blows of a ram falling ten feet. The other end was keyed into the frame, with the neck of the journal projecting $1\frac{1}{2}$ inch, and broke at the twenty-fourth blow of the same ram, falling ten feet.

The results of the trials are thus summed up by the experimenter: — That axles should never be smaller at the centre than at the ends, but on the contrary, that if a difference in size is made, the centre should be the largest.

The best authorities on the strength of materials, give the hollow tube as three times stronger in resisting twisting, than the solid bar possessing the same weight. Thus an axle with an external diameter of five inches, and an internal diameter of $3\frac{3}{4}$ inches, is three times as strong as a solid axle of $3\frac{3}{4}$ inches diameter.

Note 2. — The following experiments were prepared by M. Bourville, and executed by the Austrian government. The apparatus consisted of a bent axle, which was firmly fixed up to the elbow in timber, and which was subjected to torsion by means of a cog-wheel connected with the end of the horizontal part. At each turn the angle of torsion was twenty-four degrees. A shock was produced each time that the bar left one tooth to be raised by the next. An index adapted to the apparatus, indicated the number of revolutions and shocks. Seven axles, submitted to this trial, presented the following results: —

1st. The movement lasted one hour; 10,800 revolutions and 32,400 shocks were produced. The axle, two and six tenths inches in diameter, was taken from the machine and broken by an hydraulic press. No change in the texture of the iron was visible.

2d. A new axle, having been tried four hours, sustained 129,000 torsions, and was afterwards broken by means of an hydraulic press. No alteration of the iron could be discovered, by the naked eye, on the surface of rupture; but tried with a microscope, the fibres appeared without adhesion, like a bundle of needles.

3d. A third axle was subjected, during twelve hours, to 388,000 torsions, and broken in two. A change in its texture, and an increased size in the grain of the iron, was observed by the naked eye.

4th. After one hundred and twenty hours, and 3,888,000 torsions, the axle was broken in many places; a considerable change in its texture was apparent, which was more striking towards the centre; the size of the grains diminished towards the extremities.

5th. An axle, submitted to 23,328,000 torsions during seven hundred and twenty hours, was completely changed in its texture; the fracture in the middle was crystalline, but not very scaly.

6th. After ten months, during which the axle was submitted to 78,732,000 torsions and shocks, fracture, produced by an hydraulic press, showed clearly an absolute transformation of the structure of the iron; the surface of rupture was scaly like pewter.

7th. Finally, as a last trial, an axle submitted to 128,304,000 torsions; presented a surface of rupture like that in the preceding experiment. The crystals were perfectly well defined, the iron having lost every appearance of wrought iron.

CLASSIFICATION OF CARS.

379. Railroad cars come under three general heads,

Those for passenger transport,
Those for freight traffic,
Those for repairs of the road.

380. The American passenger car consists of a body about fifty feet long, ten feet wide, and seven feet high, containing seats for about sixty passengers, being cushioned, warmed, lighted, and ventilated. Except for emigrants, second and third class cars are but little used in America.

House, box, or covered freight cars, differ from the "flat," or platform car, only in having a simple rectangular house, about six feet high and nine feet wide, built upon the floor.

This is used for the protection of such freight as will not bear exposure; as furniture, books, dry goods, hardware, and small machinery. Carriages, boxes, bales, masts, lumber, and fuel are carried by platform cars. Bulky machinery, and first and second class freight too large for the box cars, should be protected by tarpaulins.

381. The general arrangement of wheels, springs, and brakes, is the same for the several classes of cars, the chief difference being in the ease of springs. Each car rests upon two "trucks," consisting of four, six, or eight wheels, so connected by levers and springs, as best to absorb shocks, and connected with the body by a pin only, by which the passage of curves is made quite easy.

Cars used for the movement of earth are so arranged as to allow the body to be tipped up, that the contents may be quickly "dumped," either at the sides, ends, or middle, as desired.

382. Upon some roads, a continuous draw bar is passed under the whole train, the several cars being attached to it, and to each other by safety chains only. By adopting this, and at the same time by springing the buffer beams tight upon each other, the whole train becomes one piece; and the jerks at stopping and at starting are in a great measure avoided.

As lightness combined with strength is a desideratum in all cases, it will be found best to truss the longitudinal frame pieces of the car with rods, rather than to use large and heavy beams, as done by many builders.

383. As regards the mode of retarding trains of cars, the practice of applying blocks to the wheels is justly considered by many as quite wrong. The brake should be applied to the rail and not to the wheel. Blocks drawn against the wheel are supplied with friction by means of levers worked

by a brakeman, who can at pleasure cause the wheels to slide upon the rail. A shoe, sliding upon the rail, may be supplied with friction from the whole weight of the car. The retarding force should be applied at once to every car alike; if too much in front, the rear cars are driven against those in advance; if too much behind, the train is liable to break.

The proper place for the brakeman is upon the top of the train, where all signals may be quickly seen.

CHAPTER XV.

STATIONS.

---

384. The entire establishment of buildings for operating a railroad, consists of the

Terminal, { Passenger, Freight, } Stations.

Way, { Passenger, Freight, } Stations.

Engine houses.
Repair shops, (for engines).
Repair shops, (for cars).
Wood sheds.
Water tanks.

And appertaining to these, scales for the weighing of cars and freight; turntables, transfer tables, switch and gate houses.

385. The location of the several buildings mentioned above will depend upon the situation of the terminus, the character of the traffic, and the number of trains arriving and departing.

386. The passenger house should be at the most convenient point of access to the persons using it. The freight

buildings should be at the most convenient point for receiving, shipping, and distributing merchandise.

The engine and car houses, with the shops for repair, may be placed where the land is cheap, and so distant from dwelling-houses as not to cause inconvenience to the inmates thereof by smoke and noise. The wood sheds, tanks, turntables, etc., etc., are generally at the engine houses; weigh scales, etc., at the freight buildings.

387. A railroad which connects the interior with a seaport, would probably bring two classes of freight; one for export and one for home consumption. The first should be carried at once to the wharves and loaded into the ships with one transshipment; while the second should be delivered as near as possible to the centre of home trade.

The departments of arrival and departure should be kept quite distinct, when the amount of business transacted is considerable; otherwise operating will become complicated. The arrival part of a large passenger house requires a great number of doors, that exit may be easy to the large number of passengers that arrive at once. The departure rooms require few doors, as departing passengers come singly or in small bodies. Thus, in large cities the front of a long rectangle is given to departure, while a long side, communicating with an outside platform, forms the arriving room.

One thing in particular ought to be looked to by American railroad companies, — the arrangement of public vehicles that shall secure travellers from the impositions and extortions of hack-drivers. No person whatever should have access to any building except passengers and the railroad officials. The places of the several carriages, and the rates of pay for the same, should be fixed by the company; the fare being paid by checks bought by the traveller from a company agent at the station.

388. The terminal freight house should contain all of the apparatus necessary for receiving and embarking freight. When the central part of the building is occupied by tracks, and the sides by platforms, the landing platform should incline gently from the car to the door; and that for loading, from the door to the car. This arrangement facilitates the handling of freight. The interior of the building may be divided into departments, either according to the destination or the class of the freight.

389. A terminal engine house, with a table in the centre, to contain

10 engines,	must be	145	feet	in diameter.
15 "	"	150	"	"
20 "	"	167	"	"
25 "	"	183	"	"
30 "	"	200	"	"
35 "	"	217	"	"
40 "	"	233	"	"
45 "	"	250	"	"
50 "	"	267	"	"

The diameter of the table being forty-five feet, and the engine occupying, when off from the table, fifty feet. Again, thirty-two engines would require a diameter of

$$\frac{32 \times 10}{3.1416} + (2 \times 50) = 207 \text{ nearly.}$$

The engines within the house may be supplied with water from small tanks between each alternate pair of pits, (each tank holding five thousand gallons,) or the entire building may be furnished from a cast-iron pipe running around the whole, and being in connection with a large tank. In such pipe there should be a gate over the centre of each pit, and near its upper end. It may be convenient to connect all to a series of small tanks, by a pipe, that the water level may be kept nearly constant.

Repair shops for engines and for cars, may be plain, rectangular buildings, so arranged as to accommodate the necessary machinery.

Turntables consist of simply a circular framework of wood or iron, placed at the centre upon a solid iron pintle which bears the whole weight, and guided at the circumference by a series of fifteen, eighteen, or twenty wheels fourteen or fifteen inches in diameter. The wheels are placed in an independent spider frame, and run upon a curved rail placed on the bottom masonry, and the table runs upon the top of the wheels, so that the motion of the circumference of the table is double that of the wheels.

The frame consists, first, of a pair of timbers ten or twelve inches wide and fifteen or sixteen inches deep, upon which the rails are placed, strongly trussed so as to throw the load upon the centre. At right angles to these are placed, at a distance of eight or ten feet, timbers 5×10, also trussed, which serve to connect the load more completely with the wheels. The whole is stiffened by diagonal bracing, and is strongly floored. The table is turned by a pinion upon itself, working into a rack fastened to the foundation or to the side masonry. The trusses, as also the centre bearing, should be capable of adjustment vertically.

The cost of the table, exclusive of masonry, is from $1,200 to $1,800.

Weigh scales are made similar to, but stronger than, the ordinary hay-scales, being rigid and strong enough to bear the weight of a locomotive. Every car (freight) placed upon the road should have the number and the exact weight painted upon it in some conspicuous place, so that the contained load may, at any time, be found by placing the car upon the scale.

At *way* stations the freight and passenger houses, wood and water station, may all be combined; the plan and size depending upon the location and importance of the station. The relative position of the tank, wood shed, and passenger house should be such that when the tender is at the proper place for receiving its supplies the centre of a passenger train of ordinary length shall be at the passenger door.

OF THE WATER SUPPLY.

390. The number of engines leaving the terminus of a road determines the amount of water necessary at the *principal* stations; and the character of the road and of the traffic fixes the location and size of the *way* water stations. The amount of traffic being pretty equally distributed over the length of the road, the tanks should be placed at equal equated distances; thus the engines will need to water at closer points upon steep grades than upon level roads. Generally, however, the water is taken where it can be got, the location of streams and springs fixing the place. Steam, hydraulic, wind, human, or animal power may be employed to raise the water to the tank. Oftentimes high springs will fill the tanks without the application of artificial power. As we find the liquid water in nature it is more or less impregnated with vegetable, gaseous, and saline matter, which often impairs its fitness for mechanical purposes. These admixtures are derived from the rocks and ground over or through which the water flows. The incrustations which form in boilers are caused by the precipitation of the impurities in consequence of the concentration of water in the boiler. They may be effectually removed, no matter what their nature, by boiling charcoal in the water. If the water, previous to filtration, can be heated, to expel all the air and carbonic acid gas, which is often the solvent of the foreign

matter, the filtering process will be accelerated, and will be more effectual. Rain water is more pure than any other; practically, perfectly so. River water comes next to it. Spring water is generally adulterated with basic salts in various forms, most of which may be precipitated by gently heating and filtering through charcoal.

391. Fig. 157 shows a convenient form for a tank house, with pump and heater.

Fig. 157.

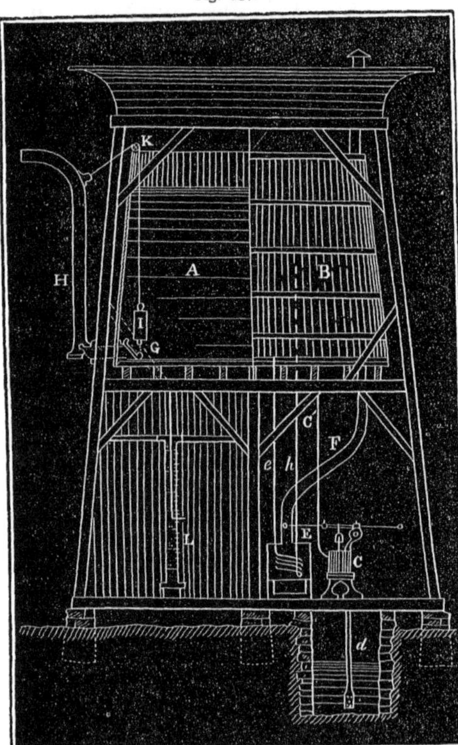

A shows half interior section of the tank.

B, half elevation of tank.

C, pump; C′, supply pipe; *d*, suction pipe and strainer.

E, heater.

e, the short, and *h*, the long pipe.

H, the discharge pipe.

G, discharge valve.

I, counter weight for discharge pipe.

K, wheel for weight rope.

L, scale showing amount of water in the tank.

The heater shown in the cut is made of a coil of two inch pipe of iron. The short pipe descends from within six inches of the bottom of the tank to within two or three feet of the floor; then bending four or five times around spirally, turns up through the centre of the coil, and runs three or four feet into the tank. A small grate is placed in the lower part of the coil, and the whole apparatus is cased in sheet iron. By such an arrangement of pipe, circulation is obtained, and the water in the tank is kept quite warm. The following rules and tables may be found convenient.

392. The velocity of water in any pipe necessary to discharge a given quantity, in a fixed time, is expressed by

$$\frac{144\,C}{a}.$$

Where C is the number of cubic feet per hour, and a the area of the pipe.

393. The head necessary to send water through a given length of pipe, of any diameter, is shown by the formula

$$\frac{C}{D+C'}=H.$$

Where $C=$ a constant.
$C'=$ constant for diameter of pipe.
$D=$ diameter of pipe.
$H=$ heads required.

The experimental values of C and C' are as follows: Let V equal the velocity in feet per minute, and we have

V.	C.
60	8.62
70	11.40
80	14.58
90	17.95
100	21.56
120	29.70
140	38.90
150	44.00
180	62.13

Also, the values of C' are

Diameter of pipe.	C′.
2	.000
3	.006
4	.028
5	.053
6	.078
7	.104
8	.134

EXAMPLE OF USE OF PRECEDING RULES.

Required the head of water necessary to send 1,333 cubic feet of water, or 10,000 gallons per hour, through an eight inch pipe one thousand feet long.

The velocity by rule *one* will be

$$\frac{1333 \times 144}{8^2 .7854} = 3840 \text{ feet per hour, or } 64 \text{ feet per minute.}$$

By rule *two* (the value of C for 60 being 8.62, and for 70 11.40, that for 64 is 10 nearly), we have

$$\frac{10}{8 + 0.134} = 1.23,$$

which multiplied by ten (the number of times that one hundred is contained in one thousand feet, the distance), gives the result, twelve inches or one foot, which is the required head; and if the entrance to the tank is twenty feet high, we have, as the necessary head, $20 + 1 = 21$ feet.

394. The formula expressing the power of an engine to raise a given amount of water is

$$\frac{W\,V}{33000}.$$

Where W is the weight of a column of water, and V the velocity in feet per minute; also 33,000 the expression of a horse-power. For example, how many horse-power must an engine possess to raise one thousand cubic feet of water per hour through a six inch pipe fifty feet high?

The velocity will be

$$\frac{1000 \times 144}{6^2 \times 0.7854} = 5000 \text{ feet per hour,}$$

or eighty-three feet per minute. The weight of a column of water fifty feet high and six inches in diameter is

$$\frac{62 \times 0.7854 \times 50 \times 12}{1728} \times 62\tfrac{1}{2} = 612\tfrac{1}{2} \text{ lbs.}$$

Also,

$$\frac{612\frac{1}{2} \times 83}{33000} = 1\tfrac{1}{2} \text{ horse-power nearly.}$$

395. Among the pumps now in use for raising water at railroad stations are Carpenter's rotary, Worthington's, McGowan's, and that of Messrs. Perkins and Bishop, either of which answers every purpose.

396. TABLE SHOWING THE WEIGHT AND COST PER FOOT OF CAST-IRON PIPE.

Diameter of bore. Inches.	Thickness of metal. Inches.	Weight of pipe per lineal foot. Lbs.	Cost of pipe per lineal foot. Cents.
1	$\frac{1}{4}$	3.06	15
$1\frac{1}{4}$	$\frac{1}{4}$	3.67	18
$1\frac{1}{2}$	$\frac{1}{4}$	4.29	21
$1\frac{3}{4}$	$\frac{3}{8}$	7.81	39
2	$\frac{3}{8}$	8.73	44
$2\frac{1}{4}$	$\frac{3}{8}$	9.65	48
$2\frac{1}{2}$	$\frac{1}{2}$	14.70	73
$2\frac{3}{4}$	$\frac{1}{2}$	15.93	80
3	$\frac{1}{2}$	17.15	86

The weight of a cubic foot of cast-iron being 450 lbs., and the price being five cents per lb.

TABLE SHOWING THE CAPACITY OF McGOWAN'S DOUBLE ACTING PUMPS.

Explanation.	No. 1.	No. 2.	Time required to fill a 6600 gallons tank.	
			Hours.	
			Small pump, No. 1.	Large pump, No. 2.
Stroke in inches,	5	$8\frac{1}{2}$		
Diameter of plunger,	$2\frac{5}{8}$	$3\frac{1}{8}$		
Area of plunger,	5.278 in.	7.70 in.		
Cube of half stroke in gallons,	0.114	0.283		
Discharge in gallons per hour. / Full strokes per minute.				
At 10	136.8	339.6	49	19
" 20	273.6	679.2	24	10
" 30	410.4	1018.8	16	7
" 40	547.2	1358.4	12	5
" 50	684.0	1698.0	10	4
" 60	820.8	2037.6	8	$3\frac{1}{2}$
" 70	957.6	2377.2	7	3
" 80	1094.4	2716.8	6	$2\frac{1}{2}$
" 90	1231.2	3058.4	5	$2\frac{1}{4}$
" 100	1368.0	3396.0	5	2

CHAPTER XVI.

MANAGEMENT.

All that is required to render the efforts of railroad companies in every respect equal to that of individuals, is a rigid system of personal accountability through every grade of service. — *D. C. McCallum.*

ORGANIZATION OF EMPLOYEES.

397. RAILROAD management may be divided into two grand departments, —

Financial management.
Operating management.

The first of these does not properly come into a work of the present kind. It embraces the entire system of accounts. Its officers are a president, secretary, treasurer, attorney, and directors.

398. The operating management is subdivided as follows: —

The mercantile department.
The mechanical department.

The first embracing every thing relating to the adjusting of tariffs, the transport of passengers and freight, the em-

35*

barking and delivering of goods, and the weighing and measuring, ticket and receiving offices, steamboat, stage, and railroad connections. The second, the maintaining the road-bed, superstructure, bridging, masonry, buildings, and fixed stock in working order; making all repairs, renewals, enlargements, and alterations, and the purchase, inspection, maintaining, and operating of the rolling stock. These departments are again divided and subdivided until we come to the minutest details.

NOTE.—That part of Chapter XVI. in italics is extracted, by permission, from the elaborate Report of D. C. McCallum to the stockholders of the New York and Erie Railroad, (March 25, 1856).

399. The following general principles govern the formation of an efficient system of operations.

First. A proper division of responsibilities.

Second. Sufficient power conferred to enable the same to be fully carried out, that such responsibilities may be real in their character.

Third. The means of knowing whether such responsibilities are faithfully executed.

Fourth. Great promptness in the report of all derelictions of duty, that evils may at once be corrected.

Fifth. Such information to be obtained through a system of daily reports and checks that will not embarrass principal officers nor lessen their influence with their subordinates.

Sixth. The adoption of a system, as a whole, which will not only enable the general superintendent to detect errors immediately, but will also point out the delinquent.

400. *A system of operations to be efficient and successful should be such as to give to the principal and responsible head of the running department a complete daily history of details in all their minutiæ. Without such supervision the procurement of a satisfactory annual statement must be re-*

garded as extremely problematical. The fact that dividends are made without such control does not disprove the position, as in many cases the extraordinarily remunerative nature of an enterprise may insure satisfactory returns under the most loose and inefficient management.

All subordinates should be accountable to, and directed by, their *immediate superiors only.* Each officer must have authority, with the approval of the general superintendent, to appoint all persons for whose acts he is held responsible, and to dismiss any subordinate when in his judgment the interests of the company demand it.

401. The following table shows the rate and direction of subordination for a first class railroad:—

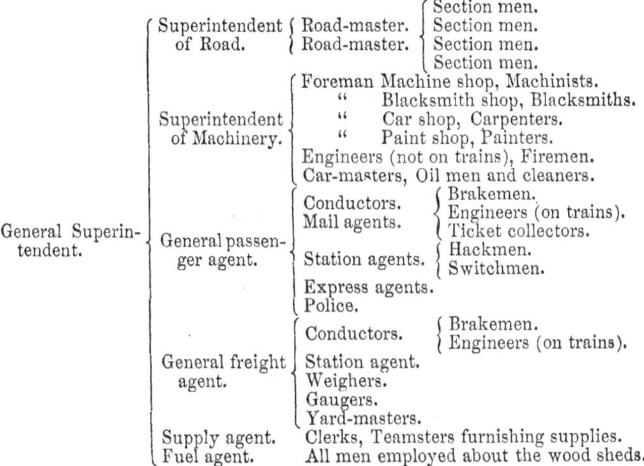

General Superintendent.	Superintendent of Road.	Road-master.	Section men.
			Section men.
		Road-master.	Section men.
			Section men.
	Superintendent of Machinery.	Foreman Machine shop, Machinists.	
		" Blacksmith shop, Blacksmiths.	
		" Car shop, Carpenters.	
		" Paint shop, Painters.	
		Engineers (not on trains), Firemen.	
		Car-masters, Oil men and cleaners.	
	General passenger agent.	Conductors. Mail agents.	Brakemen.
			Engineers (on trains).
			Ticket collectors.
		Station agents.	Hackmen.
			Switchmen.
		Express agents.	
		Police.	
	General freight agent.	Conductors.	Brakemen.
			Engineers (on trains).
		Station agent.	
		Weighers.	
		Gaugers.	
		Yard-masters.	
	Supply agent.	Clerks, Teamsters furnishing supplies.	
	Fuel agent.	All men employed about the wood sheds.	

DUTIES OF EMPLOYEES.

402. *The General Superintendent* has entire control of all of the heads of departments; he issues his orders to the heads only, and is the main agent for transferring the resolves of the directors to the operating department, and

the channel through which the reports of the departments go to the directory.

The Superintendent of the Road has complete charge of the road-bed, superstructure, bridging, masonry, and buildings; also all removals, enlargements, and alterations. He should be a thorough civil engineer, able in every respect to build a railroad from beginning to end.

The Superintendent of Machinery has charge of the purchase, inspection, repair, and operating of all of the rolling and fixed machinery, of shops, engine houses, turntables, tanks, and weigh scales. He is responsible for the good condition, proper adaptation and efficiency of the entire equipment of engines and cars.

The General Passenger Agent fixes, under the direction of the president and general superintendent, the prices of passenger transportation, has charge of all conductors, ticket sellers, station police, mail and express agents, of stage, steamboat, and railroad connections, and of all operations incident to transporting passengers.

The General Freight Agent has charge of all persons occupied at all of the stations in forwarding and receiving merchandise, in measuring and weighing, in receiving money, and bookkeeping, station agents, and train hands. He makes and regulates, with the approval of the president and general superintendent, the tariff for freights; contracts with connecting roads, and insures the benefits of such agreements, examines all claims for damages to freight, and sees that such are properly settled.

The Agent for Wood contracts, with the approval of the general superintendent, for the supply of the necessary amount of fuel; attends the measurement, inspection, and delivery at the proper places; registers each month the amount of fuel supplied and used, and the location and amount on hand.

The Supply Agent has charge of the supply of all materials in use in all departments; iron, timber, engines, rails, bridges, and every thing in use upon the road; charging each department with its correct quantity and quality of material received.

Road-masters will have charge, under the superintendent of the road, of the maintenance of the road-bed and superstructure of divisions of from twenty-five to fifty miles in length, depending upon the care that the road-way may need. They will have charge of gravel trains, and of wood trains, which run under the orders of the superintendent of the road. They should pass over their divisions at least once per day. Under them are placed section men, having care of ten miles each, being supplied with the proper tools and signals. They must pass over their respective sections at least once per day in a hand car. They should see that every switch, frog, chair, and rail on their section is in proper order, and report at once any defects, which cannot be remedied by them, in the track, to the road-master.

Engineers are subject to the superintendent of machinery when off, and to the conductor when on, the trains. None but a man well acquainted with the details of machinery, and who has served in a locomotive machine shop, and is in every respect temperate and steady, should fill this berth.

Foremen of the blacksmith, machine, carpenter, and car shops, are subject to the superintendent of machinery, and have charge of the repairs and cleaning of the engines, cars, and other machinery.

Car-masters have charge of the men employed in cleaning, oiling, and examining the cars and their wheels. The cars should be thoroughly examined at the end of each trip, and at each stop, by an inspector who accompanies the train and looks to the wheels, axles, boxes, and brakes.

Conductors. — A conductor of a train should be a machinist, a prompt, active man, who should station himself on the top of the cars in such a position as to see the whole train, and able at any moment to communicate with the engineer. He should direct the running of the train, and control the engineer and the person who takes the fares. The latter should confine himself to the inside of the cars.

NUMBER OF TRAINS TO BE USED.

403. This is determined by the quantity and quality of the material to be transported, and by the character of the road. The train should not be so heavy as to be beyond the power of the engines upon the steepest grades, nor so light as to increase unnecessarily the number. A road doing a large passenger business must accommodate the public as far as possible as regards the time of departure and arrival, and the connections with other roads. A freight road must regard more the character of the road. Some classes of freight (ice, beef, etc.) do not admit of delay. As we increase the number of trains, the ratio of time employed in actual work to the whole train under steam is decreased, as there must be much time lost on sidings in waiting for trains to pass. Liability to accidents is also incurred. Commercial circumstances, more than any other, will determine the proper number and class of trains.

AMOUNT OF SERVICE OF ENGINES.

404. This is much less than is generally supposed. The number of engines required to perform any amount of work is considerably greater than the number actually in motion,

because of liability to accident, time required for cleaning and repair. The New York State Engineer's Report for 1854 gives, as the number of engines on 2,500 miles, 668, or one engine per $3\frac{3}{4}$ miles. Also, 668 engines run per annum 11,393,000 miles, or 17,055 miles per annum per engine; thus requiring .00005863 of an engine per mile run per annum.

This is very nearly fifty-five miles per day, (313 days per annum). Also, $\frac{968}{2500}$ gives $\frac{27}{100}$ of an engine per mile of road, and the same report gives the following: —

> One locomotive for $3\frac{3}{4}$ miles of road.
> One passenger car for $2\frac{1}{2}$ miles of road.
> One freight car for $\frac{32}{100}$ miles of road.

Or each mile needs

> $\frac{27}{100}$ of a locomotive.
> $\frac{40}{100}$ of a passenger car.
> 3 freight cars.

Or to one engine $7\frac{81}{100}$ passenger cars, and $10\frac{72}{100}$ freight cars. From Lardner's Railway Economy it appears that the average daily run of an engine is forty-two miles, or seventy-five miles per day, working four days in the week. That the daily service is two hours working, and three and three quarters hours standing with steam up. The maximum annual mileage mentioned by Lardner is that upon the Belgium lines, and was 21,737. The maximum in America has been, as far as we have been able to ascertain, 22,000, and this for eighteen years.

NOTE 1. — Two little eight ton, four wheeled, Stephenson engines, cylinders 10 × 16, four and a half feet drivers, inside connection, copper fire-boxes, have averaged 22,000 miles per annum, with trains weighing forty tons exclusive of engine and tender, for eighteen years, costing about $700 per annum each for repairs, or $3.18 cents per mile run, upon the Bangor and Oldtown Railroad (Maine).

NOTE 2.—In the Report of the Railroad Commissioners of the State of New York for the year ending September 30, 1855, is the following:—

One engine is required for each three and a half miles; or one engine in constant use for five and a quarter miles. The average run per annum by each engine in actual use is 22,823 miles; or 16,302 to all of the engines. Also, as regards the work done by cars.

	Effective in constant use.	Miles per car.	Distance run per annum per car.
Passenger,	650	4	45.126
Baggage,	246	11	———
Freight,	7500	0.35	11.970

the number of miles being 2,615.

EXPENSES, RECEIPTS, PROFITS.

EXPENSES.

405. American railroad reports as a general thing do not analyze the cost of working. The gross expense is given, and in some cases is primarily divided. Besides the retrospective use of a minute division of expenses, which enables us to see what system is the most economical, there is a prospective use, namely, the formation of estimates for future operations and a correct base for establishing tariffs. If the circumstances of the traffic remain the same, an estimate of what the cost will be at any time is easy; but if they change, the data for the estimate change also. That we may at all times possess these data, we should know every year just the cost of working each article of traffic. It is not enough that the gross receipt exceeds the whole expense; even then the road may be working unprofitably. Unless each item of transport pays for itself, we are taxing unjustly some other item, (except, indeed, in such cases as adopting low rates in order to fill trains running in one direction which would otherwise run empty). An analysis of cost will also show whether or not it is best to attract an increased amount of business by a reduction of rates.

406. The whole cost of operating and of maintaining a railroad may be generally and specially divided as follows: —

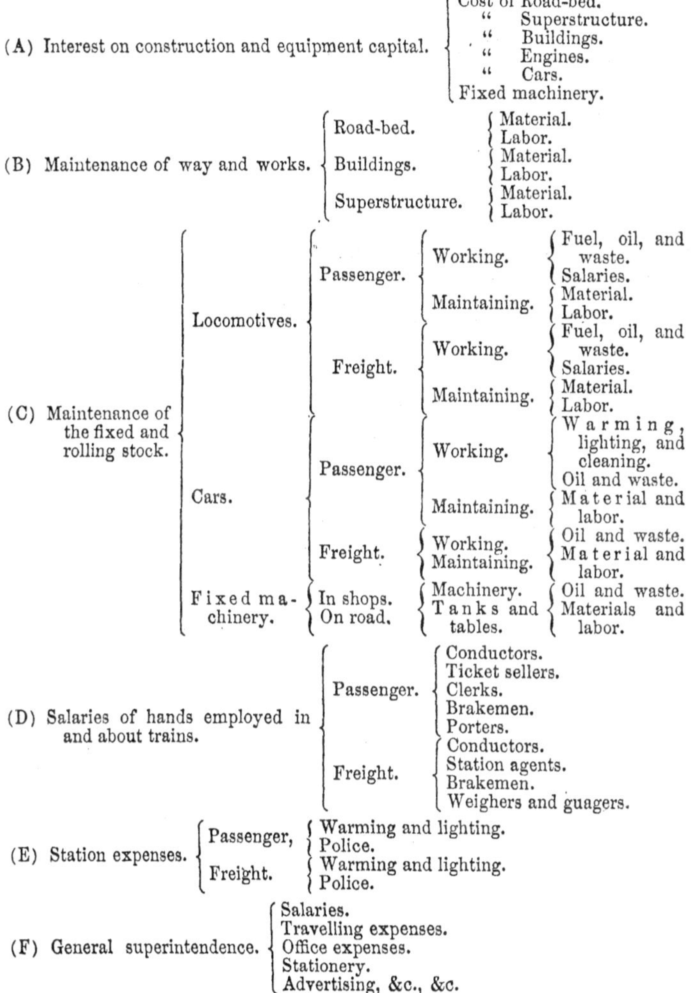

- (A) Interest on construction and equipment capital.
  - Cost of Road-bed.
  - " Superstructure.
  - " Buildings.
  - " Engines.
  - " Cars.
  - Fixed machinery.
- (B) Maintenance of way and works.
  - Road-bed. — Material. Labor.
  - Buildings. — Material. Labor.
  - Superstructure. — Material. Labor.
- (C) Maintenance of the fixed and rolling stock.
  - Locomotives.
    - Passenger.
      - Working. — Fuel, oil, and waste. Salaries.
      - Maintaining. — Material. Labor.
    - Freight.
      - Working. — Fuel, oil, and waste. Salaries.
      - Maintaining. — Material. Labor.
  - Cars.
    - Passenger.
      - Working. — Warming, lighting, and cleaning. Oil and waste.
      - Maintaining. — Material and labor.
    - Freight.
      - Working. — Oil and waste.
      - Maintaining. — Material and labor.
  - Fixed machinery.
    - In shops. On road.
      - Machinery. — Oil and waste.
      - Tanks and tables. — Materials and labor.
- (D) Salaries of hands employed in and about trains.
  - Passenger. — Conductors. Ticket sellers. Clerks. Brakemen. Porters.
  - Freight. — Conductors. Station agents. Brakemen. Weighers and guagers.
- (E) Station expenses.
  - Passenger, — Warming and lighting. Police.
  - Freight. — Warming and lighting. Police.
- (F) General superintendence.
  - Salaries.
  - Travelling expenses.
  - Office expenses.
  - Stationery.
  - Advertising, &c., &c.

The actual *general* decision of the operating expenses

upon the New York State system of roads was, for 1854, as follows. (See State Engineer's Report).

Way and works,	1,123	dollars per mile of road.	
Machinery,	2,072	"	"
Salaries on and about trains,	640	"	"
Stations,	30	"	"
General superintendence,	333	"	"
Total,	4,198	"	"

That the detailed expenses may be charged to the proper departments, and that we may be able to take out the exact cost of working any one class of trains, or of carrying any article of transport, the following form should be filled.

407. TABLE SHOWING THE GENERAL AND DETAILED EXPENSES OF WORKING AND MAINTAINING THE RAILROADS OF NEW YORK STATE, FOR 1854, AND THE NEW YORK AND ERIE RAILROAD FOR THE YEAR ENDING SEPTEMBER 30, 1855.

	WAY AND WORKS.				LOCOMOTIVE ENGINES, CARS, AND FIXED MACHINERY.												
					LOCOMOTIVE ENGINES.												
Nature of the item is shown in horizontal columns.					Passenger Locomotives.						Freight Locomotives.						Total count of passengers and freight.
Name of railroad.	Road-bed.	Superstructure.	Buildings.	Total.	Fuel.	Oil and waste.	Salaries.	Whole.	Repairs.	Total.	Fuel.	Oil and waste.	Salaries.	Whole.	Repairs.	Total.	
Cost, in dollars, per mile, upon N. Y. State Railroads.	351 453	140 88	22 27	F. 513 P. 568	395	50	140	585	237	822	202	31	122	355	191	546	1368
Cost in cents, per ton, or per passenger per mile run, N. Y. and Erie Railroad.	.020 .035	.161 .207	.010 .011	F. .191 P. .253	.157	.021	.107	.285	.109	.394	.205	.018	.080	.303	.081	.384	.778
NOTES.					RECAPITULATION.												SUMMARY.

TABLE, CONTINUED.

LOCOMOTIVE ENGINES, CARS, AND FIXED MACHINERY.									Station expenses.	Salaries of employees in and about trains.	General superintend'nce.	Grand total.
CARS.							FIXED MACHINERY.	Whole cost of machinery oiling on the road.	Repairs and material. Warming and lighting.	Conductors. Brakemen. Weighing. Loading. Porters. Watchmen.	Stationery. Salaries. Offices. Travelling. Advertising. Agencies.	Cost per passenger or per ton, per mile run, or count per mile of road.
Passenger cars.			Freight Cars.			Total count of cars.	Repairs, oil and waste, labor, and machinery.					
Operating.	Maintaining.	Total.	Operating.	Maintaining.	Total.							
50	145	195	45	206	251	446	44 F. 55 P.	841 1072	—— ——	371 246	180 170	1905 2056
.020	.079	.099	.022	.045	.067	.166	.015 F. .018 P.	.466 .511	.023 .026	.240 .159	.045 .053	.965 1.002
SUMMARY.				DEDUCTIONS.								

408. The following general measures are recommended by Lardner in his Railway Economy, as being the means of obtaining increased economy in the working of railroads.

1st. So to manage the traffic as to cause the cars to carry more complete loads.

2d. To encourage the transport to long distances.

3d. To regulate the tariff so as to give the largest possible number of cars to each engine.

4th. To adjust the tariffs where the business is chiefly in one direction, so as to attract return traffic, that the cars may not run without a load.

5th. Not to increase the number of trains beyond a reasonable accommodation of traffic.

6th. To diminish as far as possible express trains, if it be not practicable to abolish them altogether.

RECEIPTS AND PROFITS.

409. The distribution of expenses, as we have seen, is somewhat complicated, and is systematically done upon a very few roads. The classification of receipts is, however, very easy, and is properly detailed in nearly all railroad reports. Upon the New York State railroads, the following was the division for the year 1854.

Average receipts per mile of road,

Passengers, ...	$4,074.16
Freight, ...	3,776.72
Extras, ...	427.28
Whole, ...	$8,278.16
Whole expense, ...	$4,710.14

or fifty-seven per cent. of the receipts.

Receipts per mile run by trains,

Passengers,	$1.32
Freight,	2.02
Extras,	1.67
Whole,	$5.01
Average,	1.67
Whole expense per mile run by train,	$0.97

Average receipts per passenger and per ton, per mile,

Passenger,	1.95 cents,
Ton,	2.79 "
Average of passenger or ton,	2.37 "
Average expense of passenger or ton,	1.38 "

410. Upon the New York and Erie Railroad for the y ending September 30, 1856.

Receipts per mile of road,

Passengers,	$3,397.34
Freight,	7,143.42
Express and mail,	397.84
Whole,	$10,938.60
Whole expense per mile of road,	5,263.00

or forty-eight per cent. of the receipts.

Receipts per mile run by trains,

Passengers,	$1.16
Freight,	2.13

Average receipts per passenger and per ton, per mile,

Passenger,	2.02 cents,
Ton,	2.37 "

411. Upon the New York State roads,

Average number of passengers per mile run, . .	57.4
Average distance travelled by passengers, . . .	81.4
Average tons per mile run, ...	90.0
Average distance, whole number of tons carried, . .	177.0

Length, ...	496	miles,
Freight tonnage, ...	150,673,997	"
Passenger, ...	84,069,398	"

412. It is of course an object on every railroad to make the gross receipts overbalance the gross expense by the largest possible amount. The elements which determine the gross receipts are,

The charge per mile, for transport,
The number of units transported,
The distance carried,

of which the company's directors can control the first only, except as adjustment of rates may attract business.

Reduction of tariff, to a certain degree, has the effect of increasing the receipts by augmenting the number of fares; but the reduction may be carried too far. So, also, for a certain distance, increased rates will increase the whole receipts; but in this case, also, the extreme must be avoided. The point to be arrived at is, evidently, that at which the difference of expense and receipt is the greatest, and this is not necessarily when receipts are the greatest.

We can make the receipts nothing either by making the charges so large that nothing can bear them, or so small as to vanish. Even when the receipts are 0, we still have the expense of moving the empties.

By forming a table in which one column shall show the different charges, and the second the corresponding amounts transferred, with the consequent receipts and cost of working, which shall find which rate of charge will give the greatest difference between expense and receipt.

EXPRESS TRAINS.

413. Express trains are a source of vast expense, directly and indirectly, which can never be repaid by any practicable tariff to be levied upon them.

Dr. Lardner, (1850):—Resolved, That this meeting recommend the adoption of a higher rate of fare upon express passenger trains, corresponding in some degree to the increased cost of such trains.—American Railroad Convention of 1854.

INCREASED COST OF WORKING.

This is due to the extra wear and tear of engines, cars, and road, from increased speed, and also to the delays occasioned to other trains in motion at the same time.

The influence of express trains is felt not only by themselves, but by nearly all the trains upon the road.

NOTE.—To determine the most economical speed, regard need only be had to the variable elements of cost, namely: cost of power, and maintenance of superstructure, and rolling stock; assuming the power expended as the resistance, and the cost of repairs of machinery and superstructure as the velocity, we form the following table:—

Velocity in miles per hour.	Resistance in pounds per ton.	Hours con. in going 300 miles.	Product of column 2 × 3.	Cost of repairs.	Result.
10	8.6	30	258	100	358
15	9.3	20	186	150	336
20	10.3	15	154	200	354
25	11.6	12	139	250	389
30	13.3	10	133	300	433
35	15.2	8.60	131	350	481
40	17.3	7.50	130	400	530
45	19.8	6.67	132		
50	22.6	6	136		
60	29.1	5	145		
100	66.5	3	200		

The result is found by adding the product of columns 2 and 3, or column 4 to column 5, from which the minimum cost is seen to be produced by a very little more than fifteen miles per hour. The variable (and above assumed) element is the rate of increase of cost of maintenance.

All trains in motion at the same time within a certain distance of the express, must be kept waiting with steam up, or be driven with extra velocities in order to keep out of the way.

Where the time table is so arranged as to call for speed nearly equal to the full capacity of the engine, it is very obvious that the risks of failure in "making time" must be much greater than at reduced rates; and when they do occur, the efforts made to gain time must be correspondingly greater and uncertain. A single example will be sufficient to show this: —

A train whose prescribed rate of speed is thirty miles an hour, having lost five minutes of time, and being required to gain it, in order to meet and pass an opposing train at a station ten miles distant, must necessarily increase its speed to forty miles an hour; and a train whose prescribed rate of speed is forty miles an hour, under similar circumstances, must increase its speed to sixty miles an hour; in the former case it would probably be accomplished, whilst in the latter it would more probably result in failure; or, if successful, it would be so at a fearful risk of accident.

But a failure in either case would have the effect of retarding the movement of the opposing train, deranging the time of those of the same and of an inferior class in both directions, involving, perhaps, on the part of the latter, the necessity of similar struggles for time, and thus may prove the primary cause of accident to all trains whose movements may have been affected thereby.

The first cost of locomotives, (assuming the cost to increase with the weight,) is thirty per cent. greater for express trains, than for those of the second or third class.

The cost of repairs being assumed as the product of the weight by distance run, and this distance being the same, is as the weight, or increased thirty per cent. (This assumes the power to be equally well adapted.)

The cost of cars does not (though it ought), differ much for express or slow trains; the cost of repairs will certainly be increased.

The interest of construction capital to be charged to expresses, will be, their mileage proportion plus any expense which may have been incurred in reducing curves and grades; the proportion of repairs of superstructure, charged to expresses, will depend on their weight. The locomotive causes $\frac{25}{29}$ of the wear of rails, and as the weight of the engines is increased thirty per cent., the increased wear will be $\frac{15}{58}$.

The use of stations and of employees costs no more for express than for accommodation trains.

The repairs of locomotives will be nearly, if not quite, as the product of their weight by the distance run; and this, from the above, will be thirty per cent. greater on an express than on an ordinary train, the distance being the same.

The carriages for express trains ought to be at once stronger and more convenient than those for the slower work, the shocks arising from irregularities in the rails being very much greater as velocity increases; and the runs being very long, passengers require easier seats, even, in some cases, accommodation for sleeping. The cost for repairs, therefore, of express cars, would be somewhat greater than for any others.

COST AND MAINTENANCE OF WAY AND WORKS.

As the speed is increased, the relative effect of grade and curves is lessened, but the absolute danger of passing curves is increased. Express trains require larger radius of curvature, or greater elevation of exterior rail than others, which extra elevation causes an unnecessary resistance to all other trains. The rails to resist large and heavy wheels must be heavier and more firmly fastened. All bridges and viaducts (particularly if on grades or curves), will require more strength to resist the increased shocks to which they will be subject. The wear of rails is nearly as the weight passing over them; the wear of rails consequent upon stopping and starting the trains depends upon the momentum of the train which is to be imparted to them.

The proportion, in which the working expenses are distributed under the several heads on the larger railways of Great Britain, is as follows: —

Direction and management,	7
Way and works,	16
Locomotive department,	35
Cars,	38
Sundries,	4
	100

And the percentage of increase due to fast travelling, to be applied to the several items of expense, with the resulting increase in total expense, is shown below.

Direction and management,	7	0 =	0.0
Way and works,	16	27 =	4.3
Locomotive department,	35	30 =	10.5
Cars,	38	10 =	3.8
Sundries,	4	0 =	0.0
		100	18.6

or 18 per cent. increase, nearly.

Express trains, as worked on many roads, run at an unnecessary speed, to make up for frequent stops. Overcoming a long distance in a short time, depends as much on decrease in the number of stops, as increase in the speed.

The following figures show the effect of decreasing the number of stops.

A train running 400 miles, and stopping once in fifty miles, each stop being five minutes, (including coming to rest and starting,) to pass over the whole distance in eight hours, must run fifty-five miles per hour.

Stopping once in twenty miles, sixty-three miles per hour.

Stopping once in ten miles, eighty-six miles per hour.

The following table shows the velocities of the different classes of trains in England, France, and Belgium, including and excluding stops.

EXCLUDING STOPS.

	Express.	1st class.	2d class.	3d class.	
England,	43.9	32.8	32.8	25.2	miles per hour.
France,	—	27.5	24.3	28.1	"
Belgium,	—	26.2	25.7	27.6	"

INCLUDING STOPS.

	Express.	1st class.	2d class.	3d class.	
England,	36.5	24.8	24.8	17.5	miles per hour.
France,	—	22.1	17.9	19.9	"
Belgium,	—	20.7	19.3	18.1	"

The distances at which the different classes of trains stop in the several countries, are as follows:—

TRAINS STOP ONCE IN

	1st class.	2d class.	3d class.	Express.
England,	8 miles,	8 miles,	5 miles,	24 miles.
France,	10 "	6 "	6 "	— "
Belgium,	6.8 "	5.6 "	5 "	— "

OF THE INCREASED DANGER OF FAST TRAVELLING.

The causes of accident, beyond the control of passengers, are

Collision by opposition.
Collision by overtaking.
Derailment by misplaced switches and draws.
Derailment by obstacles upon the rails.
Breakage of machinery.
Failure of track or bridges.
Fire.
Boiler explosions.

Those *causes* which are aggravated by fast travelling are the first, second, fifth, and sixth; the *effects* of all are worse at high speeds than at low.

The proportion of accidents due to each of these causes, taken at random from one hundred cases on English railways, are as follows: —

Collision,	56
Breaking of machinery,	18
Failure of the road,	14
Misplaced switches,	5
Obstacles on rails,	6
Boiler explosion,	1
	100

In collision by opposition, the engines, tenders, and baggage cars must be demolished before the shock reaches the passengers; in collision by overtaking, the engine of the rear train plunges at once into the last passenger car of the leading train; the force in the last case is the difference of the speeds, in the former the sum. The *increase* of danger from this cause, attendant upon express trains, is due, first, to the longer time required in stopping, and second, in the greater shock if collision occurs.

Breakage of machinery is more liable to take place while wheels are revolving 25,000 times per hour, than when the speed is less.

Failure of the superstructure of bridges, (particularly when on curves or grades,) is more liable to take place at high than at low velocities.

Accidents from obstacles upon the track, from fire, boiler explosions, and misplaced switches, are no more attendant upon express than upon other trains, but the consequences are worse with the high speeds.

From the analysis above, of one hundred accidents, it appears that eighty-eight per cent. of the cases are due to the causes that are aggravated by increase of speed, and if we assume the aggravation of collision, and breakage of machinery, to be (speed being doubled) as two to one, the danger of travelling a fixed distance, by express, is eighty-eight per cent. greater than by a slow train.

COMPARATIVE COST OF WORKING HEAVY AND LIGHT TRAINS.

414. The question is sometimes asked, if it would not be better to run a greater number of trains and reduce the weight of engines. A comparison of cost is easily made.

The cost of working trains consists of

Fuel, oil, and waste.
Engine-men's wages.
Wear of rails.
Conductor and brakemen.
Wear of cars.

Suppose we have to move 1,000 tons per day over any road. If we do it by one engine and 100 cars, the whole cost will be

One Engineer	$2.00
One Fireman	1.50
One Conductor	1.75
Four Brakemen	5.00
	$10.25

And if we move 1,000 tons by *ten* trains of one hundred tons each,

Ten Engine-men at	$2	$20.00
Ten Firemen at	$1\frac{1}{2}$	15.00
Ten Conductors at	$1\frac{3}{4}$	17.50
Ten Brakemen at	$1\frac{1}{4}$	12.50
		$65.00

Difference of salaries in favor of the heavy train, of $54.75.

As the whole weight upon the drivers must be the same to move a given load by either method, the only difference in weights of engines will be that upon the truck. To lead well a truck must have five tons upon it. The whole weight upon *ten* trucks is, then, fifty tons, and that upon *one*, *five* tons, which leaves an excess of forty tons to be daily carried over the road by the small trains. The heaviest freight engine will not cost over $15,000; the cost of an engine to draw one hundred tons cannot be less than $5,000.

10 × 5000 = 50000 less 15000 is $35000. $\frac{6}{100}$ of 35000 is $2100.

Add to this five times as much fuel used in firing up and standing with steam up, ten times as much oiling, cleaning, and repairing, ten times as much engine house and shop accommodation; also that the cars in frequent trains are much less loaded than in seldom ones, increased delay and chance of accident from increased number of trains, and estimating all of them at $170.00 per day, (the cost of the large engine being assessed at $30 per day, and that of each of the small ones as $20, the daily difference is $170,) and we have, as the whole daily increased cost of working ten small over one large train,

$$170.00 + 54.75 \frac{\frac{6}{100} \text{ of } 35000}{313} \text{ or } 6.71 = \$231.46 \text{ per day,}$$

or $72,446.98 per annum, which employs a capital of $1,207,449.

BRANCH ROADS.

415. These lines, when belonging to the main road, are generally worked at a loss; and when independent, are a poor investment. At a meeting of the directors of the Boston and Worcester (Mass.) Railroad in February, 1855, it was declared that out of six branches, but one was profitable. That four of them gave an income upon cost of from one and a quarter to one and three quarter per cent.

Independent branch lines generally share a joint business by the mileage standard; and here is where they lose, for if the branch trains do not traverse the main line, and the tribute passengers help to fill a train which runs at any rate upon the main, then the branch expense of carrying the passengers is to that of the main, as (say ninety to ten), and the branch should take $\frac{90}{100}$ of the receipts. In this case the branch is charged with using both the cars and road of the main. If it runs its own cars over the main, (as when the branch is near the terminus,) it should be charged only with the wear of the road.

In like manner several roads, forming a continuous line,

should not divide the receipts according to the mileage; but according to the cost of working that mileage. Thus if we have the continuous line below, column one shows the length; column two, the cost of building; column three, that of maintaining; and column four, the division of receipts.

Division.	Length.	Construction Capital.	Maintaining Capital.	Result.
1	8	10	4	$10 + 4 = 14$
2	9	6	$3\frac{1}{2}$	$6 + 3\frac{1}{2} = 9\frac{1}{2}$
3	6	7	$2\frac{3}{4}$	$7 + 2\frac{3}{4} = 9\frac{3}{4}$
4	10	4	$1\frac{1}{4}$	$4 + 1\frac{1}{4} = 5\frac{1}{4}$

REPRODUCTION OF ROAD AND STOCK.

416. Besides the annual repairs necessary to maintain a road in proper working order, there is needed a periodic expenditure for *reproduction*. Evidently the time will come, upon all roads, when rails and sleepers, buildings, bridges, etc., need to be replaced. Knowing the life of rails, we also know the annual depreciation, and from that can easily find what sum must annually be laid aside, which being properly invested, shall, at the end of the life of the rail, together with its interest, be equal to the cost of renewing.

RAILS.

Suppose rails to last ten years, the annual depreciation is ten per cent. At sixty lbs. per yard we have one hundred and five tons per mile, which, at $60 per ton, amounts to $6,300. Let the cost of rerolling and relaying be $30 per ton, the depreciation is then $30 per ton for ten years, or $3 per ton per annum, or $315 per mile per annum.

SLEEPERS.

If sleepers last seven years, and cost forty cents apiece, their annual depreciation per mile (at 2,400 per mile) will be $138 per mile (nearly).

BRIDGES.

If wooden bridges cost $30 per lineal foot, and last twenty years, the annual depreciation per foot will be $1.50, and if there is ten feet per mile of road, $15 per annum per mile.

EXTRAS.

Allowing for the annual depreciation per mile of buildings, fences, etc., $33, we have as the whole annual depreciation, $500 per mile; and the amounts which yearly reserved and placed at compound interest for each of the ten years, will pay for reproducing the road, are as follows: —

At the end	of the	1st	year	$298
"	"	2d	"	315
"	"	3d	"	333
"	"	4th	"	354
"	"	5th	"	373
"	"	6th	"	397
"	"	7th	"	417
"	"	8th	"	446
"	"	9th	"	472
"	"	10th	"	500

which, at six per cent., gives, at the end of the tenth year, $500 each.

NOTE. — Reproduction of rolling stock has been proved to be nothing more than repairs, as a locomotive may be fitted with one and another new part until none of the original machine remains. See Lardner's Railroad Economy.

As the business upon a railroad increases, so does the amount of station accommodation necessary, and also of rolling stock, which increase should be debited to capital, and not to revenue.

The permanent investors in a railroad are in favor of having capital maintained, even at the expense of revenue. The temporary shareholders, and the speculators in stock, wish most to produce large dividends, even at a sacrifice of capital, and would charge nothing to revenue.

The rights of both of the above classes are to be regarded, as the road is often built mainly by the efforts of the temporary investors.

WORKING RAILROADS BY CONTRACT.

417. An experiment has lately been tried upon the working of railroads which bids fair to reduce very considerably the cost of operating; and to render the enterprises more profitable, namely, working the several departments by contract; that is, paying certain persons a fixed price for supplying the necessary amount of power, cars, or material per annum, thus bringing into play *private interest* and *individual enterprise*. There is no doubt but that by a judicious system of this kind, correctly applied, many roads which are now worthless could be made to pay, while the value of good roads would be also increased.

CLASSIFICATION OF FREIGHT.

418. Freight is classified according to its nature, the commercial nature of the country traversed by the road, and the direction of the principal market. The distribution adopted upon some of the large roads is as follows: —

CLASSIFICATION OF ARTICLES.

Double First Class.

[Articles marked thus * at owner's risk.]

Baskets, *Band Boxes;
*Camphene;
*Carboys, and contents;
*Demijohns, and contents;
*Eggs;
Feathers, in bags;
Furs;
Hobby Horses;
Musical Instruments;
*Plaster of Paris, (ornaments);
Pictures, in frames;
Teazles, in casks;
Wagons, (children's);
Willow Ware.

First Class.

*Ale, in glass;
*Apples, green, *pre-paid;*
Bacon, loose;
Batting;
Bells;
*Berries, *pre-paid;*
*Blinds, (window) in packages;
Bonnets;
*Books, in boxes;
Boots;
Bran, in bags;
Brass, in sheets and pigs;
Brass Castings;
Brass Vessels;
Bread and Biscuit;
Brooms, in bales or bundles;
Broom Handles, in boxes or bundles;
Brushes;
Buffalo Robes, packed;
Buttons;
*Candies and Confectionary, canvassed;
Cane;
Cards;
Carpeting;
Caps;
China Ware;
Chocolate;
*Cigars, in boxes;
Cinnamon;
*Clocks, in boxes;
Cocoa;
Cassia;
Coffee, ground;
Collars;
Combs;
Copper, in sheets and pigs;
Copper Vessels;
Corks;
*Cotton, in bales;
*Cotton Waste;
Covers and Sieves;
*Cranberries;
*Cutlery;
Deer Skins, in bundles;
Doors;
Dry Goods;
Fancy Goods;
*Figs, in boxes;
Fire-arms;
*Fish, fresh, *pre-paid;*
Flour, in bags;
Forks, hay and manure;
*Fruits, fresh, *pre-paid;*
*Game, *pre-paid;*
Garden Seeds;
Ginger;
*Glass, in boxes;
*Glass Ware, in boxes or casks;
Glue;
*Grapes, *pre-paid;*
Gun Stocks, in boxes or bundles;
Hair, in sacks;
Hams, loose;
Harness;
Hides, dry;
Hoe Handles;
*Hollow Ware;
*Honey;
Hops, pressed;
*Ice, *pre-paid;*
Indigo;
Ink,
Iron Castings, light;
Ivory;
Japan Ware;
Joiners Work;
*Lemons, in boxes, canvassed;
*Looking-glasses, well boxed;
*Machinery, boxed, light;
Marble, wrought, at owner's risk of breakage;
Mats;
Mattrasses, double, at 150 pounds each;
Mattrasses, single, at 100 pounds each;

Mill Stuffs, in bags or casks;
Measures;
* Meat, fresh, *pre-paid;*
Meat, in bulk, salted;
Medicines;
* Melons, *pre-paid;*
Moss, in sacks;
Nuts, in sacks or casks;
* Oranges, in boxes, canvassed, *pre-paid;*
* Oysters, in cans or kegs;
Palm Leaf, in bales;
Paper, brown wrapping and straw, (light);
Paper Hangings;
Pelts;
* Porter, in glass;
* Poultry, dressed, *pre-paid;*
* Prunes;
Rags, (see second class);
* Raisins;
Rake Handles;
Rattan;
Rugs;
Saddle Trees;
Saddlery;
* Sash, in packages;
Scale Beams;
Scythe Snaths;
Shoes;
Shovel Handles;
Soap, fancy;
Soda;
Spices;
* Spirits Turpentine;
Stationery;
Straw Goods;
Teas, (see third class);
Tin Ware, in crates or hhds.;
Toys;
Trunks, empty, 80 pounds each;
Tubs;
Turners' Work;
* Vegetables, *pre-paid;*
Veneering;
Wadding;
Warp, on beams;
Warp Beams;
Waste, woollen;
Wax;
Whalebone;
Wheelbarrows;
Whips;
Wicking;
* Wines, in baskets or boxes;
* Wooden Ware;
Wool;
Woollens.

Second Class.

Alcoholic Liquors;
* Ale, in casks;
Apples, dried;
Alum;
Anchors;
Anvils;
Ashes, pot or pearl;
Axes, in boxes;
Axles, iron;
Bacon, packed;
Bagging;
Barilla;
Bark, tanner's, 1½ cord per ton;
Beans;
* Beef, in casks or boxes;
Beer, in casks;
Bleaching Salts;
Bones;
* Bottles, packed, (empty);
Brimstone;
Burr Blocks;
Burlaps, in original packages;
* Butter, in firkins;
* Candles, in boxes;
Cannon;
Canvas;
Castings, heavy;
Cement;
Chains;
Chalk;
Chair and turned Stuff, in bales or bdls.;
Cider, in casks;
Cheese, in boxes or casks;
Clay, Coal, and Coke, in casks or boxes;
Clover Seed;
Coffee, in sacks;
Copperas;
Cordage;
Crockery Ware, well packed;
Domestics, in original packages;
Dye Stuffs, in woods;
Earthen Ware, well packed;
* Fire Brick;
Fish, dried or salted;
Flax Seed;
Flocks;
Floor Cloth, painted;
Flour, in barrels, 20 barrels or less;
Furnaces;
Grain, of all kinds;
* Grindstones;
Groceries, generally heavy, not otherwise specified;
Gunnies, in bales;
Hoes;
Hams, shoulders or sides, in casks or boxes;
Hardware, except Cutlery;
* Hemp, in bales;
Hemp Seed;
* Hides, green;
* High Wines;
Hoops, shaved or split, 3,000 pounds per cord;

India Rubber;
Iron, pig, bloom, boiler, rod, and bar;
Iron, hoop, sheet, or bolts;
Iron, nuts, rivets, and spikes;
Junk;
Lard, in barrels or casks;
Lead, sheet, pig, or pipe;
Leather;
Liquors, in barrels or casks;
Lime, in barrels or casks;
Marble, unwrought, at owner's risk of breakage;
Meal, in bags or casks;
Molasses;
Moss, pressed;
Nails, in kegs;
Oakum, in bales;
Oil, owner's risk of leakage;
Oil Cake,
Oil Cloth;
* Oysters, in shell;
Paints, dry or in oil;
Paper, (white,) in boxes or bundles;
Paper, (heavy brown and hardware);
Pasteboard;
Pepper;
Peaches, dried;
Peas, in sacks or casks;
Pickles, in casks;
* Pipes, in boxes;
Pitch;
Plaster, in casks or barrels;
Ploughs;
Pork, packed;
* Porter, in casks;
Potatoes, in casks or sacks;
Rags, foreign, pressed;
Rakes;
Railroad Chairs and Spikes;
Rice;
Rope;
Rosin;
Saleratus;
Salt, in bags or casks;
Saltpetre;
Scales, in boxes;
Scythes, in bundles;
Scythe Stones;
Shot, in bags;
Shovels and Spades;
Sizing;
Slate;
Soap, (common,) in boxes;
Soda;
Spelter and Zinc;
Spikes, in kegs;
Spirits, domestic;
Starch;
Steel, in boxes or bundles;
Steel Springs;
Stone;
* Stone Ware, well packed;
Sugar;
Sumac;
Tallow, owner's risk of heat;
Tar;
Tiles;
Tin, metal and plate;
Tobacco, in bales, boxes, or hhds.;
Tow, pressed, (in bales,) owner's risk of fire;
Twine, in bales;
Vegetable Roots, in sacks or casks;
* Vinegar;
Water, Mineral;
Whiskey, in casks;
White Lead;
Whiting;
* Wine, in casks;
Wire, in rolls and casks;
Woods, in shape, unfinished;
Woods, of value, namely, Mahogany, Lignum Vitæ, Rosewood, Cherry, Cedar, Walnut, etc.;
Wool, foreign, pressed, in bales;
Yarn, pressed;
Zinc and Spelter.

Third Class.

Includes the following articles in quantities of 8,000 pounds, and less than 16,000 pounds, in any one shipment from one consignor to one consignee. Same articles shipped in like manner, in quantities of 16,000 pounds and upwards, will be taken at special rates.

Anchors;
Anvils;
Ashes, pot and pearl, in casks;
Axes, iron;
Bacon, packed;
Bark, tanner's, 1¼ cord per ton;
Beans, in sacks or casks;
Beef, packed;
Burr Blocks;
Cannon;
Cement, in barrels or casks;
Chain Cable;
Cider;
Clay;
Coffee;
Copper, in boxes;
Flaxseed, in sacks or casks;
Flour, in barrels;
Grain, of all kinds;
Grindstones;

Hams, packed;	Pork, packed;
High Wines;	Potatoes, in sacks or casks;
Iron, pig, bar, bloom, sheet, hoop, or rod;	Railroad Iron, Chairs and Spikes;
Iron Castings, heavy;	Salt, in sacks and barrels;
Lard, in casks or barrels;	Shot;
Lead, sheet, pig, or pipe;	Slate;
Lime, in barrels;	Spikes, in kegs;
Marble, unwrought, at owner's risk of breakage;	Sugar, in casks;
Molasses;	Teas;
Nails, in kegs;	Tobacco, in boxes or hhds.;
Plaster, in barrels;	Vinegar, in barrels;
	Whiskey, in barrels.

Besides the above regular articles, are the following special objects of transport:—

Stores;	Looking-glasses;
Cabinet Ware;	Trees and Shrubbery;
Brick;	Safes;
Charcoal;	Mill-stones;
Pressed Hay;	Steam-engines;
Broom Corn;	Machinery;
Boxes of Cigars;	Agricultural Implements;
Barrels;	Lumber;
Bags;	Live-Stock;
Corn in the Ear;	Carriages;
Poultry;	Coal and Coke.

TIME TABLES.

Fig. 158, (see end of volume).

419. The most complete graphic valuation of an engineering problem, is doubtless the time table of S. S. Post, Esq., chief engineer of the New York and Erie Railroad. Let the vertical lines represent *time* in spaces of ten minutes each, and the horizontals, distances, the heavy lines representing the several way stations. Suppose now that we leave station A at six, A. M., and wish to arrive at K at two, P. M., stopping ten minutes at each station; the number of way stations being eight, the whole time consumed in stops will be $10 \times 8 = 80$ minutes. From two, P. M., and on the line K, go back eighty minutes or to M, and from A draw A B, in the direction A M, which cuts the line B B at B, which is four miles, or thirteen minutes from A. Now, as

we *wait* ten minutes, pass along *on the line* B B one division (ten minutes) to B′ and start again parallel to A B, arriving at C at one and a half hours from starting. Proceeding thus, we arrive at K at the required time. The inclination of the line shows the speed. Thus, if it passes twenty horizontal spaces in six vertical divisions, we have twenty miles in sixty minutes, or twenty miles per hour.

Suppose now we would start an express train at eight, A. M., from A to arrive at K at one, P. M., (see line 8 F,) it will pass the first train at station F, and will run at the rate of seventeen miles per hour from A to F, at the same rate from F to G, and at *thirteen miles per hour* from G to 1.

Suppose also that we start a train from K at six, A. M., to arrive at A at eleven, A. M., we pass the before-mentioned trains at E and D.

Also a freight train which is required to pass the above-named trains, leaving K at eight, A. M., and arriving at A at one, P. M., will stop ten minutes at G, ten minutes at M, pass the first train at L, wait ten minutes on a siding at two and a half miles from L, and run to A at nearly a uniform rate of speed.

So also may the motion of any train be laid down and traced through the hours of the day upon the table. By plotting the profile of the road upon the line A K, the places are shown at which grades will oblige us to use a less speed. Curves also may be shown by increasing the steepness of the grades; or by making a grade on the profile when the road is level, steep enough to involve an amount of power equal to that consumed by the curve.

LOCOMOTIVE REGISTERS.

420. American railroad reports are, as a general thing, quite destitute of detailed accounts of the performance of

the power. Some of the large roads, indeed, are of late improving in this respect.

That fares and tolls may be properly applied to the different articles of transport, the cost of moving each article should be known.

Such items as the salaries of employees, and repairs of machinery, are easily distributed to the proper heads; but the correct amount of fuel, oil, and waste, to be charged to any department, is not so evident. What we require is, the exact amount of fuel, oil, and waste used, and work done by each engine; to obtain which, some system of registering these quantities must be adopted.

The following five blanks being filled, we have all that is required:—

Number 1 is the engineer's weekly return to the master of machinery, and gives, as seen, the times of arriving at, and departing from, each station. The fuel should always be ready at each station for delivery, in cords and half cords, or in tons and fractions, when coal or coke. It may be delivered either from a small car placed on a pair of rails at right angles to the track, or from a box hung upon a crane, which may be at once swung over and lowered into the tender; the box which is already in, being first removed. The latter method gives the most correct results, as whatever fuel is left at the station may be credited to the engine. The whole operation of wooding would not take longer than it does to describe it, and would lead to a systematic and economical method of working.

The tanks and pumps being charged to construction, we may, without material error, charge the cost of the water supply to the trains according to their mileage.

Number 2 is the wood register, showing the amount of fuel delivered to the several engines from the different stations, and should be weekly signed and returned by the station wood master to the fuel agent. The engineer's fuel receipts (No. 1) check these reports.

Number 3 is the conductor's mileage account, giving the exact weight left at, and taken from, each station; and, consequently, the load carried between stations, which is checked by the station master's return.

Number 4 is the monthly account of the performance of engines, compiled from the weekly return by the superintendent of machinery, and reported to the superintendent.

Number 5 gives the annual performance of each and all of the engines upon the road, and is attained from the monthly reports, and from those of the repair and transportation departments.

The work done by different classes of cars should be registered in like manner.

Knowing the amount of material used, and also the work done, it is easy to find the cost per mile of moving any article of transport, regard of course being had to the character of the parts of the road traversed by the several engines. An engine working a sixty feet grade should be allowed more fuel than one which works a level only.

Number 1.

A. and B. Railroad. Report of amount of material consumed, and of work done by Engine No. 50, during the week ending July 4, 1856.

——, Engineer.

MONDAY.	Name of train.									
	Name of station.									
	Time of arriving.									
	Time of departing.									
	Fuel taken.									
		Whole cost fuel consumed . . . . . . —— Whole time under steam . . . . —— Whole time running . . . . ——								

And the same for each day of the week.

WEEKLY MEMORANDA.

Cords of wood used . . . . . . ——
Gallons oil used . . . . . . ——
Pounds tallow used . . . . . ——
Pounds waste used . . . . . . ——
Miles run . . . . ——
Whole time running . . . . . ——
Whole time under steam . . . . ——
Time under repairs . . . . . ——
Cost of repairs . . . . ——

———, Master of Machinery.

Number 2.

—— RAILROAD. AMOUNT OF FUEL DELIVERED TO ENGINES FROM —— STATION DURING WEEK ENDING ——.

Name of Engine.		A.	B.	C.	D.	E.	F.	G.	H.	K.	Total.
Monday.	Morning.										
	Afternoon.										
Tuesday.	Morning.										
	Afternoon.										
Wednesday.	Morning.										
	Afternoon.										
Thursday.	Morning.										
	Afternoon.										
Friday.	Morning.										
	Afternoon.										
Saturday.	Morning.										
	Afternoon.										
Total to each engine.											

Wood Station Master ——.

NUMBER 3.

A. and B. Railroad. Conductor's mileage return, for week ending July 4, 1856, showing work done by Engine No. 54.

MONDAY.	Train.												
	Station.												
	Cars taken.												
	Cars left.												
	Cars in train.												
	Weight of train.												
	Eq'd distance.												
	Eq'd mileage.												
	Total equated mileage												———

And the same for each day of the week.

NUMBER 4.

A. AND B. RAILROAD. PERFORMANCE OF LOCOMOTIVE ENGINES FOR MONTH ENDING ———.

Number.	Use.	Miles run.	Time.			Wages.		Fuel.		Oil, waste, and tallow.						Repairs.		Totals.		Work done.				Comp. work done.
																				Freight.		Passenger.		
			Working.	At rest.	Under repairs.	Cost.	Cost per mile.	Cords.	Miles per cord.	Gallons oil used.	Miles per pint.	Pounds of waste.	Pounds of tallow.	Cost of oil, waste, and tallow.	Cost per mile of oil, waste, and tallow.	Cost.	Cost per mile.	Cost.	Cost per mile.	Equated freight mileage.	Cost per ton per equated mile.	Equated passenger mileage.	Cost per ton per equated mile.	

———, General Superintendent.

NUMBER 5.

A. AND B. RAILROAD. ANNUAL REPORT OF COST OF MAINTENANCE OF, AND WORK DONE BY THE

Name or number of the engine:	Name of the builder or manufactory from whence bought.	Use to which it is applied.	Date of comme'g work upon the road.	GENERAL CHARACTER AND PRINCIPAL DIMENSIONS OF THE ENGINES.											
				Weights.			Capacity of tender in gallons.	Cylind'rs.		Mode of connection.	Driv'g wheels.		Relative power, or traction at a mean cylinder pressure of 75 lbs.	Boiler.		
				Whole weight of engine with fuel and water.	Weight upon the driving wheels.	Weight of the tender with feed.		Diameter of bore.	Stroke.		Number.	Diameter.		Grate area.	Whole heating surface.	Area of blast orifice.

RECAPITULATION, No. 1.

Cost per equated mile, per ton, of working freight engines.

Engineer and fireman.	Fuel.	Oil, tallow, and waste.	Repairs.	Total.

RECAPITULATION, No. 2.

Cost per equated mile, per passenger, of working engines.

Engineer and fireman.	Fuel.	Oil, tallow, and waste.	Repairs.	Total.

NUMBER 5, Continued.

LOCOMOTIVE POWER, ALSO THE COST PER TON AND PASSENGER PER MILE, TOGETHER WITH THE

Number of miles run.	WHOLE EXPENSE OF WORKING AND OF MAINTAINING THE LOCOMOTIVES, AND EXPENSE PER MILE.														TIME OF	
	Cost of engine-men and firemen.	Cost of oil, waste, and tallow.						Cost of fuel.			Repairs.		Total.		Time, in days, of active s'vice.	Time, in days, at rest.
		Gallons of oil used.	Miles run to one pint of oil.	Pounds of waste used.	Pounds of tallow used.	Cost for oil, waste, and tallow.	Cost per mile run for oil, waste, and tallow.	Cords of fuel used.	Cost of fuel.	Cost per mile run for fuel.	Cost of repairs of engine.	Cost per mile run for repairs of engine.	Total cost.	Total cost per mile run.		

RECAPITULATION, No. 3.

Of —— freight engines —— are in working order, or —— per cent. of the whole. Average work of an engine is —— days per annum, and for each day at work —— days repairing and —— at rest.

RECAPITULATION, No. 4.

Same as 3; for passenger, in place of freight engines.

Number 5, Continued.

NATURE AND AMOUNT OF REPAIRS, THE DIMENSIONS, & THE PRESENT STATE OF THE STOCK, 1856.

SERVICE.	RECEIPTS, OR AMOUNT OF WORK DONE BY LOCOMOTIVES.											
	Passenger.		Merchandise.				Mixed trains.					
Time while under repair.	Cars carried one mile.	Cost per car per mile.	Freight cars carried one mile.	Cost per mile for freight cars.	Tons of freight carried one mile.	Cost per ton per mile for freight.	Mileage of mixed trains.	Cost per ton (gross) per mile for mixed trains.	Total equated mileage of engines.	Comparative effect of engines.	Nature of repairs.	Present condition of machinery.

Recapitulation, No. 5.

Relative cost per equated mile of gross to net tons of freight carried. Relative cost per equated mile of gross to net tons of passengers carried.

____

Gen'l Superintendent.

TELEGRAPH.

421. The magnetic telegraph has lately come into use as a means of communication along the lines of long railroads, and nothing serves better the purposes of adjusting the movement of trains, of transmitting orders, and of keeping the general superintendent informed at all hours, of the exact condition in detail of the whole road, and of all its trains. The following is extracted from Mr. Mc'Callum's Report, before referred to:—

"A single track railroad may be rendered more safe and efficient, by a proper use of the telegraph, than a double track railroad without its aid,—as the double track can only obviate collisions which occur between trains *moving in opposite directions*, whilst the telegraph may be used effectually in preventing them, either from trains moving in an *opposite, or the same direction;* and it is a well established fact deduced from the history of railroads, both in Europe and in this country, that collisions between trains moving in the same direction have proved by far the most fatal and disastrous, and should be the most carefully guarded against. I have no hesitation in asserting, that a single track railroad, having judiciously located turnouts, equal, in the aggregate, to one quarter of its entire length, and a well-conducted telegraph, will prove to be a more safe and profitable investment than a much larger sum expended in the construction of a *continuous* double track, operated without a telegraph.

"Collisions between fast and slow trains, moving in the same direction, are prevented by the application of the following rule:—'The conductor of a slow train will report himself to the superintendent of the division, immediately on arrival at a station where by the time table he should be overtaken by a faster train; and he shall not leave that station until the fast train passes, without special orders from the superintendent of the division.' A slow train under such circumstances, may, at the discretion of the division superintendent, be directed to proceed. He, being fully apprised of the position of the delayed train, can readily form an opinion as to the propriety of doing so, and thus, whilst the delayed train is permitted to run without regard to the slow train, the latter can be kept entirely out of its way.

"NOTE.—In moving trains by telegraph, nothing is left to chance. Orders are communicated to the conductors and engineers of the opposing trains, and their answers returned giving their understanding of the order before either is allowed to proceed.

"Their passing place is fixed and determined, with orders *positive* and *defined* that neither shall proceed beyond that point until after the arrival of the other; whereas, in the absence of a telegraph, conductors are governed by general rules and their individual understanding of the same; which rules are generally to the effect, that in cases of detention, the train arriving first at the regular passing place, shall, after waiting a few minutes, proceed cautiously, 'expecting to meet the other train,' until they have met and passed, the one failing to reach the 'half way post' between stations being required to back (always a dangerous expedient), and the other permitted to proceed; the delayed train being subjected to the same rule in regard to all other trains of the same class it may meet, thus pursuing its hazardous and uncertain progress during the entire trip. The history of such a system furnishes a serious commentary on the imperfection of railroad regulations.

"The liability to collision under the system referred to has prompted the invention of various expedients for suddenly arresting the progress of trains; and which seem to have been conceived under the impression, more imaginary than real, that the difficulties they were designed to obviate, are unavoidable in their character; but which may, by the exercise of ordinary care and the use of the telegraph, be subjected to perfect control. Some of these inventions undoubtedly possess sufficient merit to entitle them to adoption under any circumstances, whilst others, for the above reasons, are entirely valueless — indeed it is questionable whether a reliance on their use may not in many cases lead to danger, *by producing recklessness, and thus increase instead of diminish the evils sought to be avoided.*"

NEW YORK AND ERIE RAILROAD.

422. As a fine specimen of American railroad engineering, and American railroad management, stands the above-named line, extending from Jersey City to Lake Erie, at Dunkirk; embracing with its branches 496 miles of road, employing over 1,000,000 dollars worth of labor per annum, upwards of 200 locomotive engines, and about 3,000 cars; earning annually over 5,000,000, and expending 2,680,000 dollars.

The whole cost of the road up to September 30, 1855, was, with the equipment, nearly $33,750,000. There are 129 truss bridges, amounting in all to 15,692 feet in length; 64 trestle, stringer, and pile bridges, of 5,489 feet total length; 3 viaducts, of length 1,274 feet in all; 167 arch culverts, of from 3 to 30 feet span; 527 box culverts, from 1 to 12 feet span; 92 wood sheds, 14,200 feet total length; 435 buildings; 433 switches, of 387,914 feet available length, and 504,205 feet total length.

Notwithstanding the immense amount of business transacted by such a road, so complete is the organization and management of employees, that the general superintendent, sitting in his New York office, can at any moment tell, within one mile, where each car or engine is, what it is doing, with what loaded, the consignor and consignee, and the time of arriving and departing the several stations, and other trains; and thus at any moment may perceive and correct faults and remissness, and in reality *control* the whole road.

APPENDIX.

A.

DECIMAL ARITHMETIC.

The advantage of a Decimal system of Arithmetic and of mensuration, as applied to engineering, can hardly be overstated. Civil and mechanical engineers both use "per force" some decimal expressions, as 0.7854, 3.1416, etc., etc. Why not adopt the system entirely? All calculations are much easier made decimally, and mensurements made with more exactness. The most perfect system of weights and measures is doubtless that of the French. All lengths are based upon the *meter* as a unit, and whether the mechanic is making a watch or a locomotive his scale is metrical. The meter is exactly $\frac{1}{10000000}$ of the distance from the pole to the equator, and was found, by measuring a meridian line from Rhodes to Dunkirk (France), 570 miles long. The metrical scale is thus,

Millimetre	.001 or $\frac{1}{1000}$
Centimetre	.01 or $\frac{1}{100}$
Decimetre	.1 or $\frac{1}{10}$
Metre	1.
Decametre	10.
Hectametre	100.
Ridometre	1000.
Myriametre	10000.

The metre is 3.280899 ft., or 39.370788 English inches. The English and American foot is $\frac{1}{3}$ of the yard; the yard is $\frac{360000}{391393}$ of a pendulum vibrating seconds at the latitude of London, at the level of the sea, in a vacuum. The standard American scale is an eighty-two inch bar made by Troughton of London for the United States Coast Survey. In civil engineering the decimal division is almost entirely adopted; indeed, any other would lead to almost endless calculation. The chain is one hundred feet long and divided into one hundred links. The tape is graduated to feet, tenths, and hundredths. The levelling rod to feet, tenths, hundredths, and thousandths. As the English foot is so universally adopted, and as it may at any time be got from a pendulum, it might not be best to attempt to introduce the metre, but the foot should certainly be divided decimally. The division should be thus,

.001 or $\frac{1}{1000}$
.01 or $\frac{1}{100}$
.1 or $\frac{1}{10}$
1.
10.
100.
1000.

thus preserving a constant ratio, and not changing the proportion at each increase or decrease as follows:—

$\frac{8}{8}$ = 1 inch.
12 inches = 1 foot.
$16\frac{1}{2}$ feet = 1 rod.
40 rods = 1 furlong.
8 furlongs = 1 mile.
3 feet = 1 yard.
6 feet = 1 fathom.

B.

ALGEBRAIC FORMULÆ.

As this work may come into the hands of those who are unacquainted with the solution of algebraic problems, it was thought best to give the following: —

$a + a$, signifies a added to a, or $2\,a$.

$a - a$, denotes a less than a, or o.

$a \times a$, a multiplied by a, or a square, a^2 (see below).

$a \div a$, or $\frac{a}{a}$, } a divided by a, or 1.

a^2, the square of a, or $a \times a$.

a^3, the third *power* of a, or $a \times a \times a$.

$\sqrt{a}$, the square root of a, or $a^{\frac{1}{2}}$.

$\sqrt[3]{a}$, the cube or third root of a, or $a^{\frac{1}{3}}$.

$\frac{a + b + c}{d}$, shows that the sum of a, b, and c, is to be divided by d.

$(a + b + c)\,d$ or $\overline{a + b + c} \times d$, denotes that the *sum* of a, b, and c, is to be multiplied by d.

Generally in place of writing $a \times b$ to express multiplication, we put simply $a\,b$.

The above signs may be compounded in any manner; thus,

$$\sqrt[4]{\frac{\left[\frac{(a+b)\,c}{d}\right]\frac{3}{4}}{m}}.$$

Here we have, first, the product of c by the sum of a and b; this is divided by d, and three quarters of the quotient is divided by m; and, finally, the fourth root of the last result is extracted, which is the value of the expression.

The following examples show the use of formulæ. See Chapter VI., on Earthwork, art. *Average Haul*: —

Required the average haul of several masses of earth. Let m m' m'' m^n represent the several masses, and d d' d'' d^n the respective hauls; S the sum of the masses, D the average haul, and we have

$$D = \frac{m\,d + m'\,d' + m''\,d'' + m^n\,d^n}{S}.$$

If we make the values $m = 100$ also $d = 100$
$m' = 200$ $d' = 50$
$m'' = 300$ $d'' = 75$
$m^n = 400$ $d^n = 200$

the sum is 1000, and we have

$$D = \frac{100 \times 100 + 200 \times 50 + 300 \times 75 + 400 \times 200}{1000} = 122 \text{ ft.}$$

In Chapter VIII., *Wooden Bridging*, we have the expression

$$S = \frac{4\,b\,d^2}{l};$$

and if $b = 10$
$d = 12$
and $l = 20$

S becomes

$$\frac{4 \times 10 \times 144}{20} = 288.$$

In Chapter IX., *Iron Bridges*, we have

$$T = \frac{p\,h}{2\,f}\sqrt{h^2 + 4f^2};$$

and making $p = 4000$
$h = 500$
$f = 80$

we have

$$\frac{4000 \times 500}{2 \times 80}\sqrt{500^2 + (4 \times 80^2)} = 6249900.$$

In Chapter XIII., *Elevation of Exterior Rail,*

$$E = \frac{\left(\frac{W\,V^2}{32\,R}\right) g}{W},$$

and when $W = 50$
$V = 20$
$g = 5$
$R = 2000$

we have

$$E = \frac{\left(\frac{50 \times 400}{32 \times 2000}\right) 5}{50} = 0.03.$$

And finally, in the latter part of Chapter XIV., we have the formula

$$D = \sqrt{\frac{\left[n\,(d + c)^2\right] \frac{A}{B}}{0.7854}},$$

and making $n = 200$
$d = 2$
$c = 1\frac{1}{2}$
$A = 4$
$B = 3$

we have

$$D = \sqrt{\frac{\left[200\,(2 + 1\frac{1}{2})^2\right] \frac{4}{3}}{0.7854}}.$$

Now $2 + 1\frac{1}{2} = \frac{5}{2}$ and $\left(\frac{5}{2}\right)^2$ is $\frac{25}{4}$,

also, $200 \times \frac{25}{4} = 1250$,

$1250 \times \frac{4}{3} = 1666$,

$1666 \div 0.7854 = 2121$,

finally, $\sqrt{2121} = 46$ very nearly.

C.

WEIGHTS AND MEASURES.

Name of material.	Weight per cubic foot.	
Air	0.077 lbs.	
Earth	112. "	
Water	62.5 "	
Ice	58.0 "	
Sand	132.0 "	
Clay	120.0 "	
Chalk	155.0 "	
Brick	110.0 "	See Chap. XI., masonry.
Brickwork	95.0 "	
Dry mortar	96.0 "	
Sandstone	140.0 "	
Limestone	142.0 "	Average 86 to 198.
Granite	175.0 "	
Coal, Bituminous	60 to 80.0 "	
Coal, Anthracite	85 to 95.0 "	
Coke	50 to 65.0 "	
Coal, Cannel	75 to 80.0 "	
Wrought Iron	480.0 "	
Cast-Iron	450.0 "	
Steel	487.0 "	

Hard Wood.

Green	62.0 lbs.
Air dried	46.0 "
Kiln dried	40.0 "

Soft Wood.

Green	53.0 lbs.
Air dried	30.0 "
Kiln dried	28.0 "

	Weight per bushel.
Wheat	60 lbs.
Corn on the cob	70 "

	Weight per bushel.	
Corn, shelled	56	lbs.
Rye	56	"
Oats . . .	35	"
Barley	47	"
Potatoes, Irish . . .	60	"
Potatoes, Sweet	55	"
Beans, White	60	"
Beans, Castor	46	"
Bran	20	"
Clover Seed	60	"
Timothy	45	"
Hemp	44	"
Flax	56	"
Buckwheat	52	
Peaches, Dried . . .	33	"
Apples, Dried	24	"
Onions	57	"
Salt, Coarse	50	"
Malt	38	"
Corn Meal	48	"
Salt, Fine	55	"

D.

VALUE OF THE BIRMINGHAM GAUGES.

Number.	Size in inches.
0	0.340
1	.300
2	.284
3	.259
4	.238
5	.220
6	.203
7	.180
8	.105
9	.148

Number.	Size in inches.
10	.134
11	.120
12	.100
13	.095
14	.083
15	.072
16	.065
17	.058
18	.049
19	.042
20	.035
21	.032
22	.028
23	.025
24	.022
25	.020
26	.018
27	.016
28	.014
29	.013
30	.012

E.

LOCOMOTIVE BOILERS.

If the ideas of Clark and Overman are correct, the value of *vertical flues* with the *water inside*, as compared with *horizontal flues* with *water outside*, is comparatively as follows: One half of the surface of the horizontal tube (the upper half) is available, but this half generates steam twice as fast as the same area of upright tube surface. Thus the amount of evaporation will be the same in either position, for the same absolute tube surface, not considering the increased diameter by applying the heat to the outside, or the advantage, so highly estimated by Overman, of applying the heat to the convex surface.

The following application of Montgomery's vertical flue boiler to the locomotive engine for heat generation and application, seems to satisfy nearly all requirements. Retaining the original furnace shell, produce it forwards so that it shall just clear the driving axle, let the sides drop to within two feet of the rail, and close up the bottom. Next, inside of this place a rectangular box which shall be a continuation of the inner box, the top being about nine inches above the diametric chord of the semicircular crown, leaving a water space of three or four inches between the sides and bottom of the two boxes. Fill the inner box with vertical tubes, the top and bottom being flue plates, the tubes being screwed in at one end and fitted with a screw thimble at the other, may be removed for cleaning at any time and will effectually stay the inner box against the enormous pressure upon the top and bottom. The pressure being inside of the tubes will tend to keep the end joints tight, where, in the common boiler, the reverse is the case.

That the burning gases may retain sufficient heat to burn until they are discharged, there should be less tube surface at the back than at the front end, a requirement which is easily satisfied by decreasing the number and increasing the size of tubes from the front to the back end. In the common boiler the ferrule area being less than the flue area, a stronger blast is used than is really necessary to draw the hot gases through the tubes, while in the vertical tube boiler the gas area may be equally large at all points.

Again, any amount of oxygen may be applied to the gases at any point of their passage from the furnace to the smoke box, by the admission of fresh air to any part of the barrel. Thus the advantage of a combustion chamber (if there is any) is obtained without the sacrifice of a single inch of heating surface, as we only require to admit air *between* the tubes and not *into* them; this may be done either by hollow stay bolts or by larger openings, to be open or shut at pleasure.

If the gases in passing through the boiler are left to themselves, we get, without an effort, the effect produced by Montgomery's third claim, namely, the application of the heat to the upper half of the tubes; and, however we wish to apply the passing heat to the flues, complete control over the motion of the gases may be had by the use of a venetian blind damper in the smoke box, in two parts; the upper and the lower parts moving independently, allow us to throw the heat upon any part of the length of the tubes. Of course, by heating most the upper part of the flues, we stand a better chance of getting circulation.

It might be objected that so much flat boiler surface would give a form more liable to explosion than the circular barrel. Experiments lately made by William Fairbairn, (England,) induced by the bursting of a locomotive fire box, show that the flat surfaces are the strongest forms of the boiler, or, to use his own words, "are conclusive as to the superior strength of flat surfaces as compared with the top, or even the cylindrical parts of the boiler." His experiments show that two plates one fourth and three eighths inch thick, connected by screw stay bolts four inches from centre to centre, will resist over one thousand lbs. per square inch.

By such a plan of engine we may always have any amount of heating surface with a moderate sized boiler, and a low centre of gravity.

The *excess* of cost of the engine, above described, over the common form would be about $500, the annual interest of which is $30, which must be saved by the new plan, (say ten cords of wood). Any saving beyond this is pure gain.

F.

EFFECT OF GRADES ON THE COST OF WORKING RAILROADS.

The cost of working a railroad will be increased by augmenting the steepness of grades. First, because of the mechanical effect of the inclines; second, on account of decreased capacity of the road. The cost of maintaining and working a road consists of items, a few of which are fractions of grades and many which are not. The chief items which are affected by grades are, fuel consumption, first cost of locomotives, and perhaps wear of rails, where grades are so steep as to require sand ascending, and application of brakes descending, the rails will be somewhat more worn. When not so steep as this the repair of superstructure will not be much increased. Steeper inclines involve the use of heavier engines, or more of them. Heavy engines generally have no more weight on one pair of wheels, and often not so much, as lighter ones; and though there is more abrasive power on increased total rolling weight, there is less deflection of rails, by means of less concentrated loads. It would seem, therefore, that the effect of grades upon the wear of superstructure was but little, if not inconsiderable. The first cost of engines may be increased from $1,000 to $2,500 to enable them to work steep grades. If the wheels are the same size in both engines, we should require greater steam pressure, consequently (see Chapter XIV.) more fuel; and if the steam power was the same, smaller wheels or larger cylinders, also requiring (Chapter XIV.) more fuel.

In doubling the work done by the engine we by no means double the amount of fuel consumed, (see Chapter XIV.,) but increase it by about ninety per cent.

The division of expenses upon five of the largest English railroads was for a certain time as follows: —

Salaries	$6.83
Way and works	15.76
Locomotives	35.15
Cars	38.14
Sundries	3.69
	$100.00
Percentage for engines	35.00

Upon the roads of Belgium,

Salaries	$5.47
Way and works	26.62
Locomotives	49.96
Cars	14.80
Sundries	3.15
	$100.00
Locomotive percentage	50.00

Upon the railroads of New York State (2,200 miles) (State Engineer's Report, 1854),

Salaries	$10.00
Way and works	15.00
Locomotives	40.00
Cars	20.00
Sundries	15.00
	$100.00
Locomotive percentage	40.00

Average percentage of all of the above charged to locomotives $41\frac{2}{3}$ of the whole locomotive expense; fuel absorbs $62\frac{1}{2}$ per cent.; and as a double amount of work requires ninety per cent. more fuel, we have, as the cost of working a grade causing a double resistance (say twenty-five feet per mile), $\frac{90}{100}$ of $\frac{62}{100}$ of $\frac{42}{100}$, or very nearly 22 per cent. of the cost of working the train; to which add $\frac{1}{10}$ more, interest on locomotive capital, and we have, as the bad effect of a twenty-five feet grade, when

$C =$ locomotive capital,
$D =$ annual cost of working,

$$\frac{1}{10} \text{ of } \frac{6}{100} C + \frac{22}{100} D.$$

Example.

Locomotive capital	$1,000,000	
Cost of working	200,000	
Annual expense of a level road (at six per cent.) .		$60,000
		+ 200,000
		$260,000
And upon a road with continuous 25 feet grades .		$60,000
		+ 6,000
		+ 200,000
+ 200,000 × $\frac{22}{100}$, or		44,000
Total		$310,000

or 120 per cent. of the cost of working the level road, the increase being twenty per cent., or allowing five per cent. for other contingencies, twenty-five per cent.; also the increase due to a fifty feet grade, fifty per cent.; and so on as long as only one engine is required to draw the full train, (its power being increased by varying its dimensions). When the train has to be broken and two or more engines are needed, the percentage will of course increase. The point at which the train ought to be broken may be found easily, either as depending upon the load or the grade, by a comparison of working expenses.

G.

SPECIFICATION FOR A PASSENGER LOCOMOTIVE ENGINE FOR THE A. AND B. RAILROAD.

Requirement.

Speed 20 miles per hour, including stops; fuel, wood; weight of train 150 tons; maximum grade 60 feet per mile; sharpest curve 3° or 1,910 feet radius; rail 60 lbs. per yard on ties 2 feet from centre to centre.

General Plan and Dimensions.

Outside connections; four five feet driving wheels with best Ames's tire, all tires being flanged; level cylinders 15 inches diameter of bore and 20 inch stroke. Centre-bearing truck, with inside and outside bearings, and Lightener boxes. Square wrought iron frame well braced, 4–30 inch Whitney and Sons' cast-iron truck wheels, spread 60 inches centre to centre. Lifting link motion working through rockers, valves described hereafter. Truck supplied with fore and aft safety chains, and safety beams beneath axles. Weight on drivers 30,000 lbs., on truck 10,000 lbs. Tender to be mounted on two trucks, each of 4–30 inch Whitney and Sons' wheels, spread 54 inches from centre to centre. To have square iron frames well braced with outside Lightener boxes; tank to hold 1,600 gallons.

Detailed Specifications.

Boiler. — Grate 38 inches wide, 54 inches long, surface 20″ above rail, grate bars cast solid for 6 inches of the front end, to be 4 inches deep, and $\frac{3}{4}$ inch thick, placed $\frac{3}{4}$ inch apart in the clear; lower edges chamfered on each side by a chamfer of $\frac{1}{2}$ inch deep and $\frac{1}{4}$ inch wide; centre of grate bars to be supported by a wrought iron bar 1 inch thick and 4 inches deep, attached as in drawing. *Fire-box.* — Outer sides of furnace shell 51 inches wide by 62 inches long; crown 8 feet above rail, to be made of $\frac{3}{8}$ inch iron plates with a 16 inch necking of angle iron to carry the rear dome; corners to be joined by flanges rounded to a 4 inch radius. The crown of the shell to be raised 9 inches above the barrel crown, the connection being made by a sloping offset 20 inches long on top. End plates lap jointed to sides and top; the seams joining the fire-box to the waist, to be double riveted. Furnace to be made of $\frac{1}{2}$ inch copper plates, $\frac{3}{4}$ inch at tubes, lap jointed, $42\frac{1}{4}$ inches wide, and $51\frac{1}{2}$ inches long inside; side water spaces to be 3 inches clear at the bottom, widening (by sloping inwards the sides of the furnace) to 4 inches at the top of inner box; front spaces 4 inches, rear spaces 4 inches at bottom and 5 inches at top. Doorway made with a wrought iron ring fastened with $\frac{5}{8}$ inch rivets, door of $\frac{3}{8}$ inch plate with $\frac{1}{4}$ inch shield. Furnace joined to shell with $\frac{7}{8}$ inch copper stay bolts, screwed and riveted at both ends, placed $4\frac{1}{2}$ inches from centre to centre. Eight roof-ribs laid widthwise of the crown of the furnace, being each 6 inches deep and $\frac{3}{4}$ inch thick, double welded at the ends and riveted at the centre, held down by T head bolts 5 inches between centres, bars to be raised above the crown sheet by $\frac{3}{8}$ inch thimbles. Dome opening, neckling to be made of angle iron which shall be connected with the roof-ribs by 4–$1\frac{1}{8}$ inch stays, connected and placed as in the drawing. The back and tube sheets of the furnace are flanged over on top; the crown is flanged downwards on the sides, but not on the back and front. One dome is placed on the crown of fire-box shell 26 inches diameter and 24 inches high; opening of dome into boiler 16 inches diameter. Lower part of dome of wrought, top of cast-iron, put on with a ground joint.

Furnace and shell to be connected at bottom by a wrought iron bar 3 inches wide, $2\frac{1}{2}$ inches deep. The whole boiler to be thoroughly caulked inside and out. Barrel of $\frac{1}{4}$ inch best Philadelphia stamped charcoal iron, 44 inches diameter outside of main crown next the fire-box, and 43 inches next the smoke box end, 10 feet long with 3 inch angle irons at ends. Front dome of $\frac{1}{2}$ inch plate worked in one piece, 23 inches diameter. End plates of boiler stayed with six 1 inch rods, cottered into blocks, riveted to plates; barrel plates riveted with $\frac{3}{4}$ inch rivets, and $1\frac{3}{4}$ inch pitch. *Smoke box*, 2′ 4″ long, same diameter as barrel, of $\frac{3}{16}$ inch plates well riveted, bolted to the angle iron so as to be easily removed for inside repairs; front tube sheet $\frac{5}{8}$ inch. *Tubes*, 140 two inch (outside) diameter No. 9 thickness at fire end, No. 14 at smoke end 10 feet long, placed $\frac{1}{2}$ inch apart. The smoke box end of tubes to be closed at pleasure by a venetian blind damper. Chimney of $\frac{1}{4}$ inch iron outside, diameter 16 inches, top 6′ 6″ above crown of barrel, fitted with proper stack, cone, and sparker. Ash pan of $\frac{1}{4}$ inch plate made with $1\frac{1}{2}$ inch angle iron, and band on upper edge, fitted with doors both before and behind, 7 inches deep and riding 6 inches clear of the rail. *Steam pipes*, 6 inch pipes of No. 10 copper running the whole length of the boiler, connected at the domes with 5 inch cast-iron stand pipes. Cast-iron branch pipes in smoke box leading to valve chests, 5 inches diameter. Throttle to be in a cast-iron chest in smoke box, as shown in drawing, having an area at least as large as the steam port. Changes of direction in pipes to be made by curves and not by angles. Exhaust pipe of No. 10 copper, 5 inches diameter at lower end, fitted with a variable blast orifice, ranging from eight to four square inches area, to be inclosed in a petticoat pipe.

Cylinders, 15 inches bore, and long enough for a 20 inch stroke, or $28\frac{3}{4}$ inches from outside to outside of ground faces, casting $\frac{7}{8}$ inch thick, covers $1\frac{1}{8}$ inch thick, placed level and firmly bolted to main frame and to horizontal truss brace, as shown in drawing; heads to go on with ground joint. Valve seat to have steam ports $14 \times 1\frac{3}{8}$ inches; exhaust port $14 \times 2\frac{1}{2}$ inches; outside lap of valve $\frac{5}{8}$ inch, inside nothing; $\frac{1}{16}$ inch lead on $4\frac{3}{4}$ inch throw of valve, gradually increasing as the throw is reduced, to scant $\frac{5}{16}$. Steam chests bolted to a level face, ground joint with $\frac{3}{4}$ inch bolts pitched 4 inches.

Valve motion. — Shifting link with lifting shaft, sector, lever, rocker, etc., of the most approved form; four solid eccentrics of $5\frac{1}{4}$ inches throw, fastened to axle by four square ended set screws pressing hardened steel dies, cut with sharp grooves on their ends, against the axle; the friction of the dies against the axle holding the eccentric in place. Eccentric straps of cast-iron, with oil caps cast on, and grooved out inside so as to shut over the eccentric and exclude dust. Link forged solid and case hardened, 17 inches by $2\frac{1}{4}$ inches inside the slot; thickness of iron all around the slot $1\frac{1}{2}$ inches, whole lateral thickness 2 inches. Eccentric rods of $\frac{7}{8}$ iron 3 inches deep, $5\frac{1}{2}$ feet between centres, fastened to link and to eccentric, as shown in the drawing. Link curved to a radius 6 inches less than the distance between the centre of driving axle and centre of link at mid gear. The links, boxes, stack, etc., to be of wrought iron, case hardened. *Pistons* with one outside composition ring and two circumferential grooves filled with Balbett metal, and one inside ring of wrought iron; outside ring cut obliquely at one place with a small wrought iron flap on each edge to prevent leakage of steam at the point of division. Glands of piston and valve rod stuff boxes of cast-iron with tight brass or composition bushings.

Frame forged from good scrap 4 × 2 inches, the main bar being straight from end to end with pedestals welded on; the rear end piece to be a heavy forged foot plate, the front end an oak beam 7 × 14 inches placed on the flat side. All the pedestals on one side having adjustable keys. Flat boiler braces averaging $4\frac{1}{2} \times \frac{7}{8}$ inches with broad palms riveted to the boiler; the attachment at the furnace to be made by the Rogers expansion brace, details of the frame as in the drawing; frame to be placed true wherever needed to receive the working parts of the engine.

Wheels, axles, and springs. — Four cast-iron driving wheels tired with best flanged Ames's tires 2 inches thick, diameter with tire five feet, tires to be turned to a true cone of .072 inches per wheel, wheels to be truly balanced. Best scrap or bloom axles, front 7 and rear 6 inches in diameter, bearings 8 inches long, collars of cast-iron held by set screws, axles to be cylindrical and not smaller at the centre than at the end. Four springs of seventeen steel plates, each $4 \times \frac{3}{8} \times 40$ inches; equalizing lever between springs. Inside bearing springs of truck hung from equalizer, which latter bears upon the axle boxes.

Slides, pumps, connecting rods, etc., etc. — Slides, flat wrought iron bars $3 \times 1\frac{1}{4}$ inches, case hardened. Cross head bearing of cast-iron 16 inches long and 2 inches thick. Pumps, full stroke brass pumps $\frac{5}{16}$ inch thick with $1\frac{7}{8}$ inch plungers, ram of wrought iron with an eye fixed on cross head and worked by it. Waterways in body 2 inches, in valves $1\frac{3}{4}$ inches. Three ball valves with $2\frac{1}{4}$ inch hollow balls, one for suction and two for delivery; pipes $\frac{1}{8}$ inch thick, 2 inches diameter, suction of iron, delivery of copper, cock of brass on delivery pipe worked by rod at cab. Air chamber on forcing side of pump equal to capacity of barrel; on suction side half the same. Flat connecting rods forged from solid piles without welds. Babbett lined boxes upon all stub ends. Straps held on each by two bolts, one key to each bearing. Safety-valves, one to be $3\frac{1}{2}$ inches diameter, placed on the rear dome, and one forward, 4 inches diameter, both to be well fitted and supplied with the proper beams and spring balances. Barrel to be covered with hair felting $\frac{1}{2}$ inch thick, to be furnished with a Russia iron jacket. Cylinders to be protected by an $\frac{1}{2}$ inch felt coat and cased in brass.

The engine to have all the usual fixtures, bell, whistle, gauges, heater, pet, blow-off, and other cocks, name plates, oil cups, sand-box, tools, oil cans, etc., etc. Pilot to be 5 feet long, of flat horizontal wooden bars $2\frac{1}{2} \times 4$ inches with a heavy centre piece, the whole to be well hung and firmly braced. Cab to be neatly built, with a projecting cornice, and windows, doors, etc., to be furnished in the best manner. The whole engine to be well painted and varnished. The draw bar to be strongly attached to the frame of the engine at 30 inches above the rail, and connected by a double elliptical spring to the centre beam of the tender.

Tender. — Tank to hold 1,600 gallons, top and side plates $\frac{1}{8}$ inch, and bottom plate $\frac{1}{4}$ inch well riveted and caulked inside and out. Brakes to apply from a single wheel to each side of all of the wheels, that is, at sixteen points; brake blocks hung with safety chains and springs to carry them away from the wheels. One spring 26 inches long, of ten levers $3 \times \frac{5}{16}$ inches over each wheel. Frame of seasoned oak 10×4 inches, centre beam 5×20 inches. The whole to be thoroughly painted and varnished.

General Provision.

All of the material, both of engine and tender, to be of the very best quality, and all of the construction done in the most thorough and workmanlike manner. The engine and tender being in every respect equal to the best that has heretofore been sent from the —— shops. For more detailed information, see plans accompanying.

H.

RELATIVE COST OF TRANSPORT BY RAILROAD AND BY STAGE.

Too great a reduction of the cost of travel was both expected of and given by railroad companies at the commencement of the system, as the following will show: —

Voted, "That the directors are hereby earnestly and urgently requested forthwith to increase the rates of transportation, both for passengers and freight, in all cases in which, in their opinion, they are now too low, and hereafter to decline all business that will not give to the corporation a full remuneration for expenses and a fair profit for its transportation."

Why the railroad rates should have been placed so low, it would be hard to show.

The cost of moving eight passengers by stage one hundred miles, would be somewhat as follows. Let a common road cost one thousand dollars per mile, and suppose the stage travel to use one tenth of the capital expended; the daily interest for one trip is

$$\frac{100 \times 1000 \times \frac{6}{100}}{365} \div 10 \text{ or} \quad . \quad \$1.64$$

Ten horses and one stage,

$$\frac{1500 + 500 \times \frac{6}{100}}{365} \text{ or} \quad . \quad . \quad 0.33$$

Daily salary of driver and stable hands, ... 5.00

Daily interest on stable cost, repairs, &c., &c., . . 1.03

Whole cost of moving 8 passengers 100 miles, . . . $8.00

Cost of moving one passenger one mile, ...01

Again. Let a railroad cost $25,000 per mile, one hundred miles cost $2,500,000, and if we run ten trains per day the daily interest, at six per cent., for one train is

$$\frac{2500000 \times \frac{6}{100}}{365} \div 10 = \quad . \quad \$41.10$$

A locomotive costs $10,000,

Two cars cost 4,000,

$$\text{and } \frac{14000 \times \frac{6}{100}}{365} \text{ is} \quad . \quad . \quad . \quad . \quad 2.30$$

And the daily cost of road and equipment, ... $43.40

divide by 100, for the cent per mile, . . . 0.43

The average number of passengers carried in one car, (see New York State Engineer's Report,) is 17; two cars, 34, whence $\frac{43}{34} =$ . . . . $1\frac{1}{3}$ cents

The daily cost per mile, per passenger, is then, for the use of the road and equipment, ... $1\frac{1}{3}$ "

The cost of maintaining and working is, per passenger, per mile, (see New York State Engineer's Report for 1854,) . . . . $1\frac{1}{4}$ "

Whence the whole cost of carrying one passenger one mile upon a railroad will be . . . . . $2\frac{7}{12}$ "

The relative cost of transport is, then, thus,

By stage, ... 1 cent

By railroad, ... $2\frac{7}{12}$ "

and the relative charge thus,

By stage, ... 5 cents
By railroad, ... 3 "

And the comparative profit as 5 less 1, or 4; to 3 less $2\frac{7}{12}$, or $\frac{5}{12}$; or as 1 to 9.6.

I.

FORM FOR RECORDING THE RESULTS OF EXPERIMENTAL TRIPS WITH LOCOMOTIVES.

In comparing the work done by different locomotives, we must know not only the relative amounts of material consumed, but also the exact nature of the work done, as depending upon speed, load, curves, and grades. The following blank, when filled, has been found to give complete information, for comparison.

Station, ... ———
Time of arriving, ... ———
Time of departing, ... ———
Time running, ... ———
Time standing, ... ———
Distance, ... ———
Rise, ... ———
Fall, ... ———
Degrees of curvature, ... ———
Equated distance, ... ———
Cars taken, ... ———
Cars left, ... ———
Load between stations, ... ———
Equated mileage of train, ... ———
Gauge pressure, ... ———
Notch of sector, ... ———
Fuel used, ... ———
Water used, ... ———
Lbs. of fuel per gallon of water, ... ———

Lbs. of fuel per equated mileage, per ton or per passenger, ———
Comparative effect, ... ———

K.

PROPER WEIGHT OF LOCOMOTIVES.

To move a given load the engine requires a certain amount of power; to exert such power there is needed load enough on the drivers to prevent slipping on the rail. This load varies from three times the tractive power, (in the best state of the rails,) to ten times the tractive power, and even more, (in the worst state). A fair working average (without sand), being one sixth, with much less. Sand must be used upon grades and upon bad rails. To find then the proper weight, we have only to estimate the tractive power upon the hardest point of the road, and multiply it by six.

Examples.

How heavy an engine is needed to draw two hundred tons (including engine and tender) at twenty miles per hour over sixty feet grades?

The resistance on a level is

$$200 \times \left(\frac{20 \times 20}{171} + 8\right) = \quad . \quad . \quad . \quad 2{,}060 \text{ pounds.}$$

The resistance due to the grade

$$200 \times \left(\frac{60}{5280} \times 2240\right) = \quad . \quad . \quad . \quad 5{,}200 \quad \text{"}$$

The resistance due to curves

$$200 \times 5 = \quad . \quad . \quad . \quad . \quad . \quad . \quad 1{,}000 \quad \text{"}$$

And the whole resistance, ... 8,260 "
Which multiplied by 6, is . . . . . 49,560 "

or 22.1 tons, to which add 5 tons as the necessary load upon the truck, and the whole weight is 27.1 tons, which is the necessary weight of an engine to draw 200 tons over 60 feet grades, at 20 miles per hour.

Or, generally,

Let $W=$ Weight of engine, tender, and train, in tons,
" $V=$ Speed in miles per hour,
" $\frac{a}{b}$ Fraction expressing the grade,
" c Resistance, in pounds per ton due to the sharpest curve, which, assume as 5 lbs., as we have no reliable data,

and we have, as the weight of the engine,

$$\frac{\left[W\left(\frac{V^2}{171}+8\right)+\frac{a}{b}\times 2240+5\right]6}{2240}=$$

weight of engine exclusive of weight on truck.

If we assume the adhesion as one fourth of the weight on the drivers, and load 150 tons, speed twenty miles per hour, and grade forty feet per mile, the above formula becomes,

$$\frac{\left[150\left(\frac{20\times 20}{171}+8\right)+\left(\frac{40}{5280}2240\right)+5\right]4}{2240}=$$

nine tons nearly.

To which add five tons, and we have as the whole weight, fourteen tons.

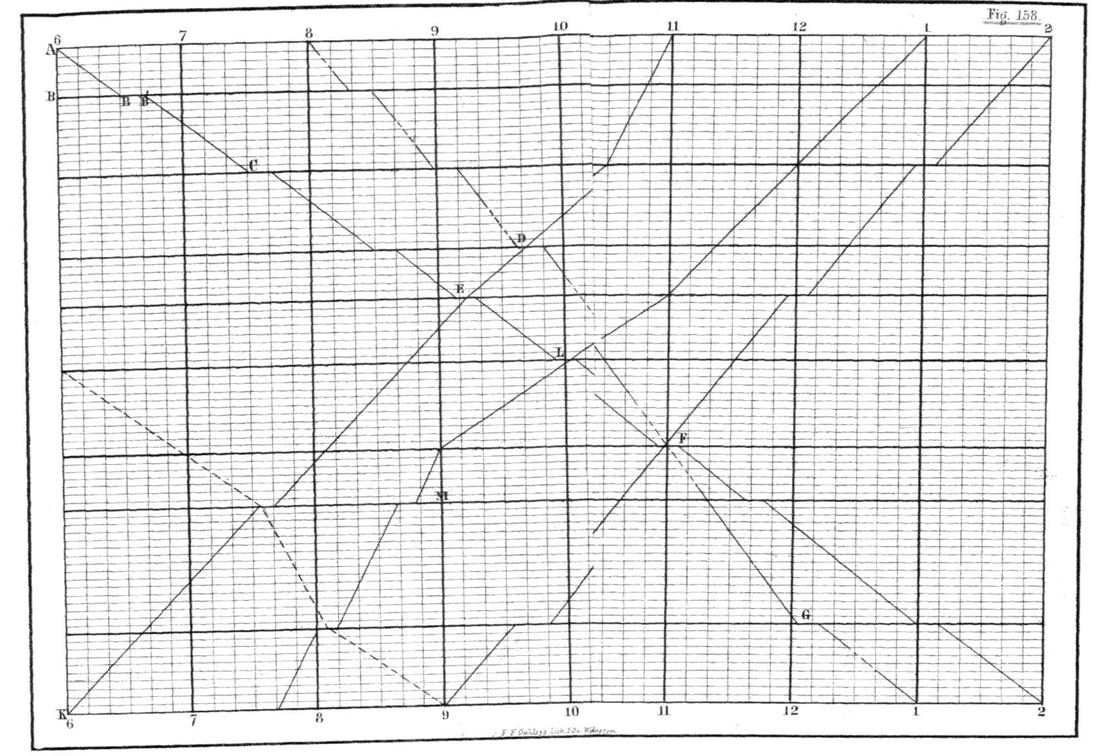
Fig. 158.
6
7
8
9
10
11
12
1
2
A
B
C
D
E
L
F
M
G
K

www.ingramcontent.com/pod-product-compliance
Lightning Source LLC
LaVergne TN
LVHW020912110826
845150LV00004B/657

9781425556440